POLITICS AND
THE STAGES OF GROWTH

POLITICS AND
THE STAGES OF GROWTH

W. W. ROSTOW

Professor of Economics and History
The University of Texas at Austin

CAMBRIDGE
AT THE UNIVERSITY PRESS 1971

Published by the Syndics of the Cambridge University Press
Bentley House, 200 Euston Road, London N.W.1
American Branch: 32 East 57th Street, New York, N.Y.10022

© Cambridge University Press 1971

Library of Congress Catalogue Card Number: 70–149440

ISBN: 0 521 08197 1 clothbound
      0 521 09653 7 paperback

Typeset in Great Britain
by William Clowes and Sons, Ltd., London, Beccles, and Colchester
Printed in the United States of America

To Elspeth

CONTENTS

TABLES

CHARTS

PREFACE

This book is the outcome of a course taught for three successive semesters at The University of Texas at Austin from February 1969 to May 1970. And my first acknowledgment is to the students who shared in elaborating this set of ideas.

They represent at least interim conclusions to a line of inquiry begun as an undergraduate at Yale in the mid-1930s. Two aspects of Marx' analysis interested me. First, his historical sequence from feudalism through capitalism and socialism to communism. *The Stages of Economic Growth* was, in part, an alternative to that sequence, done with the advantage of another century's knowledge of history. Second, there were Marx' propositions linking the economy and the technical relationships within it to politics. I found these challenging, while reacting against his underlying view that politics was essentially a super-structure to economic life.

The bulk of my subsequent professional work was in the field of economic history, more narrowly defined; but I continued to explore this relationship, assuming from the beginning that societies were interacting organisms and economic factors did not enjoy a peculiar priority. Later I introduced the additional dimension of war and its playback effects on economic, social, and political life.

At M.I.T., in the 1950s, studies on the Soviet Union, Communist China, and the United States forced me to explore more deeply the determinants of politics; and I concluded upon finishing *The Stages of Economic Growth* that I would next turn to formulate, in a systematic way, what I thought I had learned over the years about politics. I worked at this task in 1959–61, stimulated by the parallel efforts of my colleagues, notably, Daniel Lerner, Ithiel Pool, and Lucian Pye.

I then turned for a period to work as a public servant.

In the Policy Planning Council at the Department of State (1961–6) a number of my associates were equally interested in this range of problems. We exchanged views, kept in touch with those at work in the universities, and sought to crystallize for policy purposes our ideas on political development. Three of that group now hold distinguished positions in academic life: Robert Johnson, William Polk, and Howard Wriggins. I am in their debt and that of other government colleagues who were willing and able to draw back from the flow of day-to-day work and speculate on its shape and larger meaning.

I also had the privilege of sitting in on many meetings between chiefs of government – something like a hundred of them. Chiefs of government do their business together in a manner quite different from foreign ministers. The latter approach professionally, in a fine-grained way, the exact formulae which might resolve specific issues on their technical agenda. Chiefs of government – when meeting in relative privacy – usually expound to each other with candor their domestic political setting and problems; isolate, within those limits, how and where they can move together in military and foreign affairs; where they will have to live with differences of view; and how inevitable differences can best be kept from becoming enflamed.

I was coming by a longer academic route to the notion of politics as an eternal triangle of competing imperatives – the imperatives of security, welfare, and the constitutional order. But the succession of encounters I was privileged to observe – in fact, all I learned about the political process as a public servant – confirmed me in the judgment that this breakdown was useful and right.

Those experiences also confirmed the judgment that it was useful, in politics as in economics, to view the contemporary world as made up of nations at different stages of growth, whose problems bore a family relationship to those of nations at similar stages in the past as well as the present.

On several occasions while in government, I talked about aspects of politics and political development in terms similar to those used here; e.g. in Venezuela, on 'The Challenge of Democracy in Developing Nations' (Department of State *Bulletin*, 17 February 1964); in Argentina, 'The Chapter That Keynes Never Wrote' (Department of State *Bulletin*, 29 March 1965); in Bethlehem, Pennsylvania, on 'Sharing the Good Life' (Department of State *Bulletin*, 23 May 1966); in Leeds, England, on 'The Great Transition: Tasks of the First and Second Post-War Generations' (Leeds University Press, 1967).

It was while working in Washington that the basic structure which informs this book fell into place; and, on the morning of 20 January 1969, as I awaited in my office in the White House West Basement the departure of the President and the President-elect for the Capitol, I was outlining my first lecture for my seminar at Austin.

In writing this book, I acquired many debts.

Alan Kent and Gerald Sewell were first students, then teaching assistants – and friends. Their comments of substance – and pedagogical guidance in

Preface

teaching a new body of ideas stretching over time and the conventional disciplines in a somewhat unusual way – were exceedingly helpful.

A good many colleagues made important suggestions about aspects of this analysis or took valuable time to read and criticize drafts of the chapters. I am particularly grateful to George Arnakis, Henry Bullock, William Goetz-mann, Thomas Gould, Robert Johnson, William Jorden, Doris Kearns, Albert Kervyn, Frank Kierman, William Langer, William Livingston, Elliott Morss, Richard Musgrave, Ithiel Pool, Lucian Pye, E. V. Rostow, P. N. Rosenstein-Rodan, Howard Wriggins, and Whitney Young, Jr.

I benefited, also, from seminars on this approach to politics at M.I.T., Columbia, the University of Hong Kong, the University of Ottawa, The University of Oklahoma at Norman, the East Texas State University at Commerce, the North Texas State University at Denton, in the Government Department at The University of Texas at Austin, and at The School of Advanced International Studies, The Johns Hopkins University, at Washington, D.C.

Miss Lois Nivens, who shared with extraordinary devotion eight years of bureaucratic life in Washington, contributed greatly in many ways to this academic enterprise as well. Mrs Sheryl Patterson typed and retyped the text with good cheer. Mr Joseph Pluta helped develop the data which underlie table 40.

E. D. Yoes, and his crew of technicians at The University of Texas Communication Center, responded with memorable competence to the adventure of taping a graduate seminar, presenting a new set of ideas, warts and all, the first time round.

A grant from the Government Department at The University of Texas, financed by The Ford Foundation, permitted me to check directly certain hypotheses incorporated in this book, in some fourteen countries during the summer of 1969 – an exercise which enriched and strengthened it at many points.

My greatest debt is to my wife, Elspeth Davies Rostow. There is no aspect of this book which we have not discussed over the many years it has been germinating; and she read and criticized the text in draft. It is a vastly better book than it would have been without her insight and knowledge. My only regret is that she has not written a book of her own on the politics she has studied, taught, and observed.

I should, finally, acknowledge a debt owed my parents. Products of the pre-1914 social-democratic tradition, they encouraged their sons to find their own way and form their own judgments. But they impressed upon us one rule which every experience of politics – vicarious and direct – subse-quently confirmed: one cannot in politics separate ends and means; the

xii

results actually achieved are determined as much by the means used as by the objectives sought. As the reader will perceive, this assessment suffuses what follows from beginning to end.

W. W. ROSTOW

Austin, Texas
October 1970

INTRODUCTION

I

In the largest sense, politics helps determine the quality of the environment in which men live their lives. As Bernard Crick has said: 'Politics can not make men good, but they can make it easier or harder for us to be good.'

In the contemporary world this proposition has a particular meaning. On every continent, in almost every nation, men are caught up with unprecedented rates of change in their domestic lives. This is as true for rich countries as for poor; countries ruled by communist as well as non-communist governments, be they democratic or autocratic. And rapid change is hard for the political process to handle with grace.

It is equally true that the international environment is changing fast and changing in a particular way. The world is in transition from Cold War to something else.

It still contains ample explosive raw materials for chaos and even greater violence than we see every day in Southeast Asia and the Middle East. But it also contains the raw materials for substantial movement towards world order in the next generation. And whatever a man can do to tip that balance in the right direction, he ought to do.

This book contains quite a lot of historical analysis; and for this I do not apologize.

There is a kind of schizophrenia in the endless aphorisms about the usefulness – and lack of usefulness – of history to man. They are reflected in the two following examples, from Coleridge and Namier, respectively:

If men could learn from history, what lessons it might teach us! But passion and party blind our eyes, and the light which experience gives is a lantern on the stern, which shines only on the waves behind us!

A neurotic, according to Freud, is a man dominated by unconscious memories, fixated on the past, and incapable of overcoming it: the regular condition of human communities.

One asserts we ought to learn more from history than we will; the other, we remember the wrong things from history.

Introduction

I have tried to use history here in ways which isolate abiding aspects of the human condition in politics, from which we ought to learn something, from current and emerging problems which are special to our times and to the foreseeable future.

II

Since this is an essay in history and the social sciences as well as a tract for the times, I owe the reader a brief account of how I have proceeded.

In *The Stages of Economic Growth* I did not deeply explore the process by which nations made the broad collective decisions which determined the content of their national life at each stage of growth. My concern then was primarily with the pattern of growth itself – as common technologies were diffused to highly distinctive societies – and with certain consequences of those strategic decisions for the timing of industrialization, the allocation of resources, and war, as the stages of growth succeeded each other.

Immediately upon completion of *The Stages*, in 1959, I decided to turn the problem around in my hand and see what happened if politics, rather than growth, was made the focus of analysis. This book does explore the factors deep in history, culture, and the active political process which have shaped modern societies. But politics is clearly a different business than economics, intertwined as they are. And it took some time before I had constructed an intellectual framework with which I felt comfortable.

The essence of that framework is the linkage between a view of politics as the effort to balance and reconcile problems of security, welfare, and the constitutional order, with the stages of growth.

One element within the framework of the present book only fell into place in the course of teaching; that is, the linkage of the three abiding tasks of government to the tripartite Platonic-Freudian view of the human personality.

III

Once the central notion of connecting the three abiding tasks of government and the stages of economic growth was clear, I had to decide to what extent I would concentrate on the elaboration of a theoretical structure as opposed to applying it to history and the contemporary scene. I decided to lean heavily towards application for two reasons.

First, the inherent complexities of politics are such that pure theory can take us only a little way forward in our understanding. Given the roles of culture and ideas, of the accidents of history and human personalities, the unknowns are too many for the equations we can regard as reliable. On

2

balance, modern political scientists have been, I think, too anxious to emulate what they believe to be the formal elegance of economics, cybernetics, and other apparently more scientific fields. At best, political science can be only a kind of biological science and an art. It will be strengthened, not weakened, by an acceptance of that fact, which is fully compensated for by its importance and its human richness.

A second reason was more general. It has been my experience with economic and social as well as political theory that the meaning of abstractions – and their usefulness – can best be judged by observing how they applied to concrete bodies of fact. Here I felt it desirable, in presenting a general perspective on politics, to apply it, even if only in broad outline, to the sweep of history and the contemporary scene.

IV

Political development consists in the elaboration of new and more complex forms of politics and government as societies restructure themselves so as to absorb progressively the stock and flow of modern technology which is, essentially, uniform. The 'stages of growth' is addressed directly to the process whereby that absorption of common technologies occurs; and it poses automatically a good many of the issues thrown up for the political process to solve as that absorption proceeds, real income per capita rises, and government expands the proportion of the society's resources it mobilizes and allocates to public purposes. This linkage does not imply that politics is economically determined. The view here is that economic, social, and political forces fully interact. Indeed, the initial impulse to economic modernization is generally seen to arise from basically non-economic motives; that is, a reaction to one form of external intrusion or another, real or feared, by the more powerful on the less powerful.

V

In applying the view of politics developed here, I had, of course, to be selective. In general, chapters 2, 3, 4, and 5 were proportioned in such a way as to provide an historical perspective on the specific contemporary issues chosen for attention in chapters 6, 7, and 8. Because they relate to these later chapters, there is, for example, more attention to economic causes of political instability, multiple party systems, the causes of the outbreak of the First World War, and the doctrines of Mahan than in more conventional essays on the historical themes of the early chapters. I would hope that, in the end, the rationale for the emphasis given certain strands in history as opposed to others should become reasonably clear.

3

Introduction

In chapter 2 certain examples of pre-Newtonian political experience were chosen, many others put aside. The brief historical notes in chapters 3 and 4 cover only eight nations. They were selected because of their importance in modern history, the spread in time of their coming into take-off, and the range of their cultural and pre-industrial historical backgrounds. They are a device to recall and suggest certain historical sequences, not an effort to provide full historical documentation of the argument. Within the headings of constitutional change, growth and welfare, and security policy, many possibilities for illustration of the central propositions were set aside. My aim was to make clear the possibilities of this kind of analysis for those who found the general approach congenial. I could, evidently, not exhaust them in a book of this kind.

The sweep of American political history is presented in chapter 5 for three reasons: to illustrate the persistent elements of uniqueness as well as generality in the story of American politics; to show how the first experience of high mass-consumption flowed from the American experience; and to set the stage for the exploration of the politics of the search for quality in chapter 6.

I am conscious that each of the eight chapters, including those addressed to problems of the contemporary world, could easily have been elaborated into book length. They are each a compressed mapping of a complex terrain. The particular balance chosen between concept and empirical application is designed to make it easier for the reader to make his own assessment of the approach to politics developed here and its relevance to his own perspectives and concerns.

VI

In writing this book I had one thought in mind which should be made explicit.

As an economist I have been privileged over the past generation to share in helping create the remarkable consensus among economists concerning economic growth and economic development policy. There are, of course, debates among us, differences in emphasis and technique; but we have built a more or less common theoretical framework and a common vocabulary. This has permitted sustained international discourse on economic development policy; an exchange of good and bad national experiences; and a wide area of agreement on how to go about the business of economic growth. Economists and cabinet members can talk to each other with understanding and profit in almost every nation of the developing world. There is a powerful kind of freemasonry among those dedicated to the study and practice of economic growth.

4

There is no equivalent dialogue – no common language, no agreement, even, on how to pose the questions – among those concerned with the theory and practice of political devlopment.

Perhaps it can be brought about. For we know that there are ways in which men and nations can learn from each other in politics – and not merely from the Mother of Parliaments or the American Constitution or the French Revolution. From, say, the Japanese constitution of 1889 (which reflected much of Bismarck's Germany) to the Korean young officers' coup of 1961 (which was shaped, in part, by study of Atatürk), men have tried to learn and adapt from abroad in politics as in technology. But little effort has been made to take stock of our experiences of the past generation, and of history, in ways which might assist such adaptation of general political experiences to unique circumstances. For while every nation, like every individual, is unique, there are common problems and common types of solutions.

The 1970s ought to be the Decade of Political Development in something like the sense that the 1960s has been the Decade of Economic Development: something like the sense because political development is both a more difficult and more intimate experience than economic growth.

Despite the greater difficulty, three situations argue that the time has come to take a fresh look – backward, around us, and forward – at politics in general and democracy in particular.

First, the grave difficulties encountered in Asia, the Middle East, Africa and Latin America by those who have tried to make government by consent of the governed operate. We have seen in the postwar generation many earnest democratic efforts break down; and, where forms of democracy have taken hold, evidently they are precarious. Why? What lessons can be drawn from the many cases of failure and the fewer but significant cases of success? What accounts for the endemic political turbulence of the developing nations which yielded some sixty-seven irregular changes of government in the years 1961–8: Latin America, 16; Africa, 26; Near East and South Asia, 14; East Asia, 11?

Second, the searching political problems faced by democracy in richer nations of the world with deeply rooted habits and institutions of democracy. Why have we not learned to reconcile relatively full employment with price stability? What of the dangerous schisms in the United States, Canada, Belgium, Japan, and, indeed, the United Kingdom? Can they be managed within the democratic process? Clearly, high per capita income is no guarantee that democracy is secure: indeed, mass affluence itself is beginning to pose major problems for the democratic political order.

Third, what of the political future in the Soviet Union and in other nations gripped by Communist rule? Is there a road that can and will be found to more responsive forms of government, as levels of industrialization, education, and sophistication rise? Are these peoples doomed to the constraints of rule by a single party whose prime object of policy must be the perpetuation of its monopoly of power? Or is this what those thus ruled prefer to the strains and anxieties and strivings of democratic responsibility? The answers may effect the prospects for war and peace in the world.

VII

There is a further reason for stocktaking, especially with respect to democracy. In 1976 the United States of America will be two hundred years old. The United States was almost uniquely blessed – even in colonial times – with the possibility of experimenting with democratic political methods. The large meaning of the coming anniversary is that for two hundred years, despite many vicissitudes, including a bitter civil war, the democratic process has worked in continuity. It would seem a good occasion to take stock not merely of the American experience but the experience of others who have tried, with greater or lesser success, to make democracy an effective and stable form of government.

In the end, the glory of America has been not its relative material wealth but the sense of its transcendent political mission in reconciling liberty and order. However imperfectly fulfilled, that transcendent mission has been recognized, in the end, by Americans and by peoples in every part of the world. It would seem proper to carry forward that strand in the sentiment of the world community by examining critically and dispassionately and drawing lessons from two centuries of experiment with government of the people, by the people, for the people, in the United States and elsewhere.

If the 1970s is to be a Decade of Political Development, it will become so not because it is decreed by parliaments and congresses. The job will be done by the private effort of students, crystallizing what they have learned, finding their way into dialogue with the practitioners of politics. Such an enterprise will require many minds. In politics, for certain, each of us has hold of only a small piece of the elephant. Nevertheless, I would hope that this book might help stimulate such a convergence of reflection, stocktaking, and prescription in the decade ahead.

CHAPTER I

A WAY OF LOOKING AT POLITICS

Politics is here taken to be the exercise of power, within a defined territory, through government. This book examines the kind of power that goes with the concept of sovereignty – in particular, the power to deal with other sovereignties; to mobilize and expend resources for growth and welfare; and to dispense justice, on the one hand, enforce law and order, on the other.

Behind sovereignty is man himself whose nature is defined in three hypotheses which underlie the whole argument that follows.

THREE HYPOTHESES ABOUT MAN

Man: A Balancing, Not a Maximizing, Unit

The first hypothesis is that man is caught up in an effort to balance different and often conflicting impulses and aspirations, in the face of the environment he confronts. His actions represent a choice among the realistic alternatives he perceives to be available; and man must allocate his scarce time and energy, talent and physical resources among these perceived options. Or, in Freud's phrase: 'Happiness ... is a problem of the economics of the individual's libido' – a problem man solves mainly below the level of full consciousness.[1]

In dealing with consumers' demand, the economist has provided an elegant mechanism for reflecting and summing up the net choices unique human beings make as they set their priorities among the market alternatives before them, at given levels of real income. Only occasionally do economists probe beneath the process of choice by which the consumer equates relative marginal utility among his options.

In dealing with the entrepreneur the economist has provided an equally elegant formal mechanism for reflecting the producer's effort to maximize his profit in the face of given technologies, costs, and market possibilities. But even in the theory of production the simple, abstract market mechanism requires modification. As Keynes once said of investment: 'If human nature felt no temptation to take a chance, no satisfaction (profit apart) in constructing a factory, a railway, a mine or a farm, there might not be much investment merely as a result of cold calculation.'[2]

In the sovereignty it accords to individual tastes and relative valuations, economics provides for the complexity of human motivations without exploring them deeply. In the market-place of politics one must be more explicit; for the exercise of political power through government touches the individual, in fact or potentially, at many more points – and more sensitive points. It is not merely his income that may be at stake in the exercise of political sovereignty, but his life and property, his freedom and his status in the society; the underlying ideas and concepts which give shape and meaning to his round of life. Man brings relatively much more of himself into politics than into narrowly economic relations; although, again, man does not come into the market-place as pure economic man.

I am led to begin with this hypothesis about the individual because a good deal of sociological analysis, rooted in the concept of human 'roles' in society, has found its way into political analysis. Role analysis is, for certain purposes, useful and clarifying; but the human being, thus disintegrated for analytical convenience, is sometimes never reassembled again. One is reminded of Harold Lasswell's *bon mot*: 'Political science without biography is a form of taxidermy.'[3] What is at stake at this point is not biography, although the role in history of the unique individual is real and inescapable. What is at stake is a steady awareness that politics is ultimately shaped not by 'the masses' or 'elites' but by the interplay of complex but whole human beings, acting in different functional settings, but bringing to those particular settings the full, usually conflicting elements of their unique personalities.

The Tripartite Nature of Man

For the purposes of this exercise I am prepared to accept as a second hypothesis a powerful simplification of man as a balancing unit: the tradition that runs (or jumps) from Plato to Freud that man's nature can usefully be conceived as made up of three elements. Plato defined them in terms of the 'spirited' side of man, 'appetite', and 'reason'. Freud's id, ego, and superego can, for these purposes, be regarded as roughly analogous.[4]

Plato moved directly and systematically from his three parts of the soul – from the state within us – to politics and government. He did so by presenting a series of marginal cases, in his famous sequence of timocracy, oligarchy, democracy, and tyranny. Each is associated with the political triumph of one side of man's nature: timocracy, the dominance of the soldier's 'spirit', the others representing the successive dominance of various human 'appetites' – for money, freedom, and order. Plato's argument has helped stimulate in our time analyses of 'democratic' and 'totalitarian' personality types.

I would look at Plato's semi-satirical argument of Book 8 of *The Republic*

8

in a somewhat different way: as a sequence suggesting the relevance to politics of the economist's law of diminishing relative marginal utility. In Plato's politics man appears to place a low relative marginal utility on the value he enjoys in abundance and a high relative marginal utility on that which he judges to be scarce. Thus, surfeited with military adventure, political man turns to money-grubbing; bored with affluence, he turns to libertine democracy; in consequent disarray, he bows to a tyrannical restoration of order.

The 'insatiable' pursuit of one human object to the 'neglect of other things' yields these ideal types; and it yields also, through Plato's version of diminishing relative marginal utility, the sequence.[5]

One mechanism Plato evokes in moving through this sequence, in Book 8 of *The Republic*, is the reaction of the sons to the kind of constitutional system and environment of values built by the fathers.

This may or may not be a reading of Plato that would command universal agreement. The argument that follows, however, asserts in its own right that the political as well as private valuations of men are governed by the law of diminishing relative marginal utility. Men appear to try by, at best, a semi-rational process within them to bring their political life back towards a balance which is never quite achieved, the balance Plato thought could be created only by the philosopher king or by weaving together in power men of spirit and reason in ways that would balance the requirements of security and justice so that the people could prosper, pursuing their lesser appetites in moderation.[6]

At any particular moment, then, the citizen viewed collectively appears to want most of what he has least. In the face of invasion, man may seek security at the cost of welfare and even individual freedom. In the face of depression, he may pursue an improvement in welfare at the cost of other objectives, even national security. In the face of security and affluence, he may prize, above all, refinements in his degree of liberty. In the face of a decline in public order, he may elevate its reestablishment beyond any other dimension of the functions of government. These shifting relative evaluations are ultimately rooted in the balances struck by individuals within themselves. They appear to have affected the tides of politics and the performance of governments in both the short run and the long run. In the long run the changing priorities of successive generations have operated, as they formulated their objectives and raised their banners, often taking for granted the achievements of the previous generation, elevating objectives judged to have been relatively neglected or not successfully achieved in the past, or in the world around them.

Politics and the policies of government are seen here not, as in Plato, in terms of extreme marginal cases but in terms of ever-shifting intermediate balances determined by the problems thrown up to government for resolution, on the one hand, and, on the other, the evaluation of their environment made by those who could make their judgments felt under different constitutional systems.

Man: A Social Animal

The third basic assumption is that man is a social animal in the quite specific sense that ties to others are an inherent characteristic of his individuality, a proposition that runs from Aristotle to Freud. As Parkinson[7] explains it:

Human children must be taught (and therefore controlled) for so long that their subordination becomes habitual. And this obedience to those older and more skilled may survive after the child has become an adult. In the social group a certain authority is thus vested in the older members.

The authority of age merges into the parental authority. Although primitive people often fail to recognize paternity, developing communities have all come to see in it a heightening of the authority of age in the special relationship between father and child. It is this relationship which provides us with our basic notions of authority and discipline. Nearly all our common terms of respect are derived from it. We have thus the words 'Sir' (Sire), 'Monsieur', 'Little Father' (in Russian), 'Father' as addressed to a priest or 'Holy Father' as addressed to the Pope. Psychologists break up the idea of respect into the three elements of wonder, affection and fear. The child thus feels for his father some wonder at the ability of an older person to do what the child cannot; some affection for an older person whose intention is at least to ensure the child's survival; and some fear of an older person who may punish the child by smacking its head.

Here – in life with father – are the first rough essentials of the abiding tasks of government; although Parkinson omits the instinct to revolt against, as well as to accept, the values of parents and elders.

But the family provides more, even, than security, welfare, and a balance between order and justice. It provides a sense of fraternity – of ties to others – which, paradoxically, appears essential for human beings to establish a sense of identity. A great deal of political history is shaped by the manner in which men extended their loyalties out beyond the family: to tribe and region; religious and class groupings; to nation and humanity. It is, in part, to one dimension or another of this sense of fraternity that political leadership seeks to appeal: either to soften the harshness of conflicting interests within national societies, or to solidify a more limited constituency, even at the cost of sharpening the lines of conflict.

Sovereignty

Sovereignty has built into it an ultimate sanction over the lives and fortunes of citizens living under it; and sovereignty asserts the right, historically and with reserves, even, under the United Nations Charter, to destroy through war the lives and property of citizens of other sovereignties.

Men have accepted existence under the shadow and disciplines of sovereignty, for reasons that flow directly from our three basic assumptions. The valuations and operating objectives of individuals are bound to conflict in a social setting. They, therefore, require balancing, regulation, and arbitration if man, as a social animal, is to enjoy an environment of reliable order within the range of the sovereignty to which he belongs. In Freudian terms he must, therefore, narrow his pursuit of pleasure to avoid pain.[8]

Since man has lived in an environment of multiple sovereignties, this has required sovereign power to deal with other sovereignties; and this has meant chronic war. As Radcliffe-Brown has said:[9] '. . . at least a good half of the history of political development is in one way or another a history of wars.' Or, less abstractly, Kurt Vonnegut:[10] 'I think a lot of people teach savagery to their children to survive. They may need the savagery but it's bad for the neighbors.'

THE ETERNAL TRIANGLE: THE THREE ABIDING TASKS OF GOVERNMENT

Whether in an African tribe ruled by custom and the elders or a Greek city state, whether in Nixon's America or Mao's China, men look to government to find an acceptably balanced way to do these three things: protect them from others; provide acceptable standards of welfare; settle quarrels among themselves, peacefully, on terms judged equitable, holding the community together.

Whether in the American Constitution, or Sun Yat-sen's Three Principles, or the United Nations Charter, the three tasks emerge. And political debate centers on the appropriateness of a government's dispositions in these three directions: the balances it strikes in policy; the demands it makes of the people to carry forward that policy; and the way it distributes the limited resources available to it among the three tasks.

There is an eternal ring to this prescription for good government in Oriental lore: 'A ruler can have no power without soldiers, no soldiers without money, no money without the well-being of his subjects, and no popular well-being without justice.'[11]

In short, the impulse of men to live communally – under multiple sovereignties – poses immediately an array of tasks which are, essentially, universal. They can be described as follows under the headings of security; welfare and growth; and the constitutional order; and they are, in my view, capable of being broadly linked, respectively, to Plato's spirit and Freud's id; certain of Plato's appetites and certain aspects of Freud's ego; Plato's reason and Freud's super-ego.

1. *Security.* To protect the society's territorial integrity or, more generally, to secure or advance the nation's interests in the international arena of sovereign powers, as those interests are defined by those who wield effective power.

2. *Welfare and growth.* To provide for the general welfare (including, where relevant, growth) as welfare and the government's responsibility for welfare are defined within the society by those who wield effective power.

3. *The constitutional order.* To preserve the constitutional order or adjust it by the means the constitutional order prescribes; that is, to provide justice, maintain public order, orderly change, and legitimate succession by some enforceable balance between public constraint and individual freedom of action and expression of opinion. The constitutional order – explicitly or implicitly – also defines who shall wield effective power and how he shall do it.

In Montesquieu's terms the constitutional objective is stated as follows: 'The political liberty of the subject is a tranquillity of mind arising from the opinion each person has of his safety. In order to have this liberty, it is requisite the government be so constituted as one man need not be afraid of another.' [12]

In Freud's terms the constitutional outcome is similar: 'The end-result would be a state of law to which all – that is, all who are capable of uniting – have contributed by making some sacrifice of their own desires, and which leaves none – again with the same exception – at the mercy of brute force.' [13]

There is a double balancing built into this view of the art of politics. [14] It is not only likely that the imperatives of security, welfare, and constitutional order will clash among themselves, but each involves potential conflict and choice: war versus the possible costs of not fighting; welfare versus growth; justice (including individual freedom) versus order.

POLITICS AS WELFARE ECONOMICS WRIT LARGE

The Input–Output Approach and Its Limitations

The pursuit by government of these tasks raises immediately a kind of economic or, even, input–output problem. The execution of security, welfare, and constitutional tasks requires resources. Resources are inherently scarce and must be drawn away from private consumption and private investment. Once mobilized by government, resources must be allocated among uses that rarely converge and usually conflict. Lionel Robbins' classic definition of economics is relevant to a great deal of government and politics: 'Economics is the science which studies human behaviour as a relationship between ends and scarce means which have alternative uses.'[15]

In first approximation, the inputs are men, money, and obedience; the outputs are security, welfare, and the maintenance of the constitutional order. The inputs must be drawn away from what men would rather do with their lives, their resources, and their natural bent. The outputs must be allocated among the three tasks of government, usually in an environment of competition among them.

The view of politics as a kind of economics does not wholly apply for two major reasons.

First, because a nation's security policy, while partially reflected in the budget, involves fears, and sometimes hopes, so great as to make the economist's fine calculations at the margin misleading. One can deal in such quasi-economic terms with, say, the Anglo–German naval race before 1914 or, even, in relatively quiet times, the United States–Soviet missile race. The restraints of Bismarck's expansionist policy and that of the Japanese in the period 1895–1905 also permit a certain quasi-rational approach to limited war, parallel to that which governed some of the mercantilist exercises in limited violence during the eighteenth century. But in certain moments of crisis – for example, Europe in 1914, the Cuba confrontation of October 1962, or the Middle East in June 1967 – the discontinuities felt by the major actors are such that the elegance of welfare economics or game theory breaks down. One moves from fine calculations at the margin to grosser hopes and fears, and to grosser actions to achieve or to fend them off.

Second, a resource mobilization and allocation view of politics must take into account that persuasion – political leadership – as well as law enforcement, is an output of government. Those ultimately charged with setting the priorities and striking the balances must seek to make their decisions acceptable. Only in the marginal case of obsessive totalitarian rule is the resource primarily required to maintain an acceptable balance between justice and order physical; and, even with Hitler and Stalin persuasion and positive incentive played their part along with terror. Put another way, one critical instrument of government is normally the politician's effort to persuade men that their consent should be granted, by evoking some deep-rooted consensus, widely accepted ideas, the pull of shared memories, transcending the issues at conflict. And there is something in man, the social animal, to appeal to. There are positive values to be found for

some in commitment and, even, sacrifice in public, as in family, enterprises.[16]

This creative, almost artistic, dimension in the relation between ruler and
ruled does not easily fit a numerical input–output model.

But a political leader's capital in performing this task, as well as more
mundane tasks, is also limited and requires allocation among competing ends.
A recent analyst has put the point vividly in a particular context that I
would here make in general:[17]

> ... the political historian has a resource allocation problem to explain just as surely as
> does the economist. The resource over which Atatürk disposed was a capacity to persuade
> and to compel. This resource was deployed over many fields simultaneously, so he had a
> continuous problem of deciding upon proportions. To have leapt from one exclusive
> application of political resources to another would have been fatal. Or to have ignored the
> scarcity of political resources relative to the useful things that political action might have
> accomplished would have led to the Young Turk phenomenon of over-commitment. A
> major factor in Atatürk's success was that he was a better optimizer, in the economist's
> sense, than his forerunners.

One can go some distance, then, in framing the tasks of government as a
matter of mobilizing and allocating resources and viewing politics as welfare
economics writ large – extended to issues of national security, on the one
hand, and to the mobilization of consent by political leadership, on the
other.

Filling the Empty Boxes: The New Political Arithmetic

Apparently quite independent of the lively development of political science
over the past fifteen years, a new branch of public finance has emerged since
an article appeared in *The Manchester School*, September 1956, by Alison
M. Martin and W. Arthur Lewis, based on the comparative analysis of
government inputs and outputs under almost precisely the general headings
defined here: security; welfare and growth; and the constitutional order.[18]
For example, the accompanying table 1 shows how the British, German, and
American figures look for the seven decades after 1890.[19]

Efforts have also been made by a number of analysts to look at the outlays
of contemporary governments in cross-sectional terms, arraying the sums
mobilized, how they are mobilized, and their patterns of allocation in terms
of GNP per capita or other indexes of economic status.

The results of these analyses – the issues raised and the debates which go
on – need not concern us for the moment. (They are well summarized in
Richard Musgrave's *Fiscal Systems* and commented upon here briefly in the
Appendix.) The present point is, simply, that it is possible, to a degree
and after a fashion, to fill the empty boxes set up in this tripartite way of

TABLE I. *Government expenditures by functions as per cent of GNP (all levels of government): United States, United Kingdom, and Germany*

| | Total[a] | Defense | Civilian | | | |
			Law, order and adminis- tration	Economic and environmental services	Social services	Public debt
			United States			
1890	7.1	1.4	1.2	2.0	1.8	0.7
1902	7.9	1.5	1.1	2.1	1.9	0.5
1913	8.5	1.1	0.9	2.6	2.1	0.4
1922	12.6	1.9	0.9	3.6	3.5	1.9
1927	11.7	1.2	0.8	3.6	3.2	1.4
1932	21.3	2.8	1.6	6.0	6.3	2.3
1940	22.2	2.3	1.2	7.2	6.9	1.7
1948	23.0	8.4	0.9	3.4	6.2	2.0
1957	28.5	10.7	0.9	5.1	8.0	1.5
1962	33.2	10.6	1.0	6.3	11.0	1.7
			United Kingdom			
1890	8.9	2.4	1.7	1.3	1.9	1.6
1900	14.4	6.9	1.4	2.5	2.6	1.0
1913	12.4	3.7	1.6	2.2	4.1	0.8
1923	24.2	3.2	2.0	3.4	8.5	7.1
1929	23.9	2.7	1.7	3.4	9.5	6.6
1932	28.6	2.8	1.9	3.9	12.9	7.1
1938	30.0	8.9	1.9	3.9	11.3	4.0
1950	39.0	7.2	3.7	5.7	18.0	4.4
1955	36.6	9.6	2.3	4.3	16.3	4.2
1963	38.0	6.5	...	28.2[c]	...	3.3
			Germany			
1891	13.2	2.5[b]	...	9.9[c]	...	
1901	14.9	3.3[b]	...	11.5[c]	...	
1913	14.8	3.3	2.4	2.2	5.1	0.7
1925	25.0	3.6	4.3	2.7	14.3	0.2
1929	30.6	3.9	4.2	3.2	19.3	0.6
1932	36.6	2.7	5.6	3.3	24.8	1.2
1950	40.8	6.5	4.6	4.6	24.2	0.8
1958	44.1	5.2	4.0	6.1	27.9	0.9

[a] The total figures include certain minor items not listed separately. Therefore, certain of the totals exceed slightly the sum of the components in the present table.

[b] Includes public debt.

[c] All civilian outlays.

looking at government and politics; and the basis exists for fruitful cooperation among political scientists, historians, and experts in public finance which, I would hope, this book will encourage.

The Concept of Political Equilibrium and Disequilibrium

A concept of equilibrium flows directly from an input–output approach to government.

Political systems can be judged in equilibrium if the mobilization of resources roughly matches outlays; and if the pattern of outlays both solves the problems thrown up for political decision and generates pressures or discontents that are manageable within the framework of the existing constitutional structure. There are elements of circularity and ambiguity in such a definition: governments can be defined as in equilibrium until they are overthrown; and disequilibrium is one thing, for example, in a fully developed democracy, quite different in a one-party police state.

But within any given constitutional system, degrees of strain in the political process, as governments struggle to balance their books, are palpable enough to impart some common-sense meaning to the notion of equilibrium and departure from equilibrium – as every working politician knows and sensitive observers can detect. And the notion of political equilibrium and disequilibrium becomes vivid, indeed, if one looks again at how history has been shaped by the executive's problem of mobilizing inputs sufficient to match his commitments of policy: from the mortal budgetary crises of ancient empires to Prime Minister Wilson's departure East of Suez; from King John's concessions to the barons to President Johnson's struggle to gain from the Congress of 1968 a tax bill he could not have gotten as a candidate; from the cash shortages of George III and Louis XVI, laying the basis for the American and French Revolutions, to President de Gaulle's discomfiture after May 1968. The recurrent debates in Moscow over economic priorities and the debate on economic policy between Mao and his 'revisionist' opponents make clear that contemporary single-party dictatorships are not exempt from the strains of this calculus.

To anticipate a little some of the issues examined in chapter 7, a good many political crises in the contemporary developing world can be usefully viewed as resulting from misallocation of resources as between security and growth–welfare objectives (e.g. Sukarno, Nasser, and Mao); or a failure to generate from the society the tax resources and/or the political consent (that is, the inputs) to conduct a steady, non-inflationary development policy (e.g. Argentina under Illia, Peru under Belaunde, Chile under Frei).

16

THE LION IN THE PATH: THE PROBLEM OF DYNAMIC EQUILIBRIUM

Politics and Society

But to bring this way of looking at politics to bear on major problems of history and the contemporary scene, the model must be rendered dynamic. Change, and the causes of change, must be introduced within it; for, if there is one thing we know, it is that the problems of government and the issues of politics do not stay put for long; and, if there is another thing we know, it is that political problems have to be tracked back into the changing social and economic life of a nation and into the world outside.

The problems governments face arise from long-run forces, deep in culture and history, interacting with more immediate economic and social change within the society, with pressures and opportunities which derive from the world outside, and the playback effects of their own prior dispositions, at home and abroad. All this must be understood, as well as the role of ideas and unique personalities and accident, before mobilization and allocation decisions at a particular time and place make sense and before viable balances can be struck in making policy.

Politics is a limited arena of endless confrontation, where conflicting and everchanging interests and impulses, derived from the national society and the world society, press in for reconciliation and decision through changing rules and routes. The grand, unresolved problem of political science is how to relate politics in the narrow sense to the evolution of societies as a whole.

The Stages of Growth: A Way to Tame a Lion?

The problem still not satisfactorily resolved is to link the political process to the domestic and external forces which generate the major problems with which politics must cope, and which are, in turn, shaped by prior political decisions. I am not talking about abstract resolutions in the form of input–output and feedback flow charts: I am talking about linkages of substance that bring the raw materials of politics into the center of political science.

The device chosen here to make the linkage is the stages of economic growth. The decision to employ this device derived in turn from a long-held view of how the economic, social, and political sectors of society interact.[20]

Society is defined as a dynamic structure of three levels, each receiving and imparting impulses from and to the other levels.

Movements within the economic system, long-run in character, set the framework within which social life and its concepts evolve, pursuing, on the whole, a sluggish life of their own. The long-run impulses have their main impact on politics, having worked through the social structure, where they have been generalized, associated with non-economic aspirations, and crystallized into ideas and particular, often constitutional, objectives, involving changes in political structure. Similarly, the medium-run or trend impulses imparted from the economic system become associated with wider concepts and objectives before they make their full appearance in politics, often in the form of particular acts of legislation. The short-run economic forces tend to strengthen or weaken the relative forces making for or resisting political change; and they thus affect the timing and character of political events. The political level of society receives from the other levels this complex of impulses and by rules and conventions and ideas which are themselves partially the product of long-run economic and social influences, sorts them out, and seeks to resolve conflicts among them in a manner such as to avoid resort to settlement by trial of brute strength. In performing these functions the political level of society sets the basic terms of both social and economic relationships in society; and, in receiving and disbursing income, it actively engages in current economic activity of significance.

The stages of economic growth embraces this process of interaction in ways developed in the balance of this book. But a system of thought based on complex interactions of this kind does not yield neat Newtonian propositions. It yields patterns, where limited scientific generalizations can be achieved, as in biology, only by cross-comparison, and the isolation of rough uniformities in types or species of cases. The tendency in the modern study of political development to work in comparative history and by comparing cases in the contemporary world is, on this view, correct.

I would also underline that any such system for permitting systematic political cross-comparison must be partial.

It is the deep roots and staying power of culture and national style which render the stages of growth, or any other system, only a partial answer; for cultures are shaped by geography and climate; by cumulative habits and casts of mind arising from the way men organized their communal lives over thousands of years, within their special physical settings; by bloody and benign contacts with other peoples over the whole sweep of history and even pre-history; and by the shared memories that arise from all this. And, thus far, patterns of culture have demonstrated a high capacity to survive the fairly uniform exigencies of absorbing modern science and technology. Industrialized Britain is still recognizably linked to Britain of pre-Newtonian

18

times – as are contemporary Japan and Russia and Mexico and all the rest of us. And a good thing, too.

We must accept, then, irreducible elements of uniqueness, which persist throughout, with different political consequences at different times and occasions.

Dynamic Sectoral Analysis: Economic and Political

One technical characteristic of the stages of economic growth, relevant to political analysis, is that they are rooted in a dynamic sectoral analysis of the production process. They take their shape from the notion that new technology is introduced into an economy via particular sectors which, through linkages to others, provide dynamism to the economy over particular, definable periods of its history. But these sectors are inherently subject to deceleration and loss of capacity to lead. Regular growth, therefore, requires a succession of leading sectors (or linked sectoral complexes) with rapidly expanding new sectors carrying forward the overall process of growth as the older, retarding sectors lose their capacity to impart forward momentum.[21]

It follows from this notion of sectoral patterns that there is, in theory, an optimum balanced sectoral map which an economy would follow in dynamic equilibrium, and an optimum balanced pattern of investment.

But in real life economies do not work out their destinies by following neat balanced equilibrium paths.[22] These paths are distorted by imperfections in the private investment process, by the policies of governments, and by the impact of wars. They reflect business-cycles and trend-periods. Nevertheless, the economic history of growing societies takes a part of its rude shape from the effort of societies to approximate the optimum sectoral paths. The proposition here is that political life has also taken a part of its rude shape from the efforts of societies to approximate optimum sectoral paths. They seek an equilibrium never attained.

In politics, of course, the optimum sectoral paths are not the same as those for the economic structure. The issues thrown into the market-place of politics for decision may be related to, and may partially overlap, those with which the economy must deal. Political and economic modernization both reflect in the post-Newtonian era the contentious adjustment of men and institutions to the progressive introduction of new technologies of production and communication; and the coming in of new leading sectors brings with it new men, new interests, and new problems which project themselves into politics, whether those sectors are textiles or railroads, automobiles, or mass higher education. But political history is not simply a function of economic history.

Political Cycles Illustrated: America 1900–70

It may be worthwhile, therefore, to pause and, by way of illustration, make somewhat more concrete the notion of politics as movement about a theoretical equilibrium. Arthur Schlesinger, Sr., once put forward a trenchant proposition about the sweep of American history; namely, that Americans have experienced phases, even cycles, of passivity and activism in their national political life.[23] How could this sequence be formally explained?

Let us assume that the dynamics of American life in the twentieth century threw up a series of problems for which appropriate responses were, roughly, the elements contained in the legislative programs of Woodrow Wilson (plus the Sixteenth – income tax – Amendment to the Constitution); the New Deal legislation of the 1930s; and the Great Society legislation of the 1960s.

If these political actions are judged a legitimate part of the nation's dynamic political equilibrium path, the response of American political life would have been spaced out more evenly if its political system had responded sensitively and promptly to the problems forced upon it by its environment. That this did not happen – and that political initiative took place in three surges, over short periods of time – suggests that the political process in American democracy during the twentieth century may have been subject to a tendency to undershoot and overshoot optimum sectoral paths in much the way the growth of capitalist economies proceeded under a regime of business cycles.[24]

It follows, as in the economics of business cycles, that the American political system responded to its problems with a built-in lag; that is, the political process responded sluggishly to the emergence of problems which, in the end, required major legislation from the federal government. One could account for this lag in a number of ways but perhaps most simply by assuming that there is an element of inertia built into the constitutional process which requires a problem to assume a certain critical scale before the system, rooted in one-man one-vote, responds. Although great problems can be posed for the political system by such urgent and traumatic events as the Great Depression after 1929, many major domestic problems with which the three surges of legislation sought to deal, built up step by step, over considerable periods of time, from the dynamics of American society. When problems reached a scale such that a leader could build his political base on an active response to these accumulated problems, he was in a position to act dramatically and needed to act on a larger scale than if the problems had been dealt with incrementally.

Under these circumstances, political leadership may appear to over-react under the pressure of a constituency now authentically concerned or alarmed by the problems he addresses or the size of the gap that has accumulated. This appearance of over-reaction may, in turn, set in motion resistance in the rest of the society. The majority may come to regard the new efforts not as closing a previous gap but as launching a new trend whose projected implications they may not be willing to accept. This may yield, in a relatively short time, a political reaction which leads to a phase of consolidation, conservatism, and inactivity, until a new gap on a sufficient scale is opened up between the state of existing policy and the problems which have emerged out of the life of the society.

In fact, of course, the political life of the United States in the twentieth century with respect to domestic legislation, has interwoven with two world wars and a cold war. Nevertheless, the American political system can be viewed as responding, with a lag and convulsively, to problems whose solutions would, if achieved incrementally, represent a meaningful dynamic political equilibrium.

The sequence of American politics, from 1900 to 1968, is a not bad example of what is meant here by politics taking a part of its rude shape from the efforts of societies to approximate optimum sectoral paths. Such fluctuations in the tides of policy and political sentiment can be found in other democratic nations as well, and, indeed, in other cases, such as both Tsarist and Soviet Russia.

The general proposition, then, is that the 'stages of growth' analysis, based on the notion of economies seeking to approximate optimum sectoral paths in production, is a congenial mate to the kind of dynamic political equilibrium analysis explored in this book.

The Stages of Growth and the Substance of Politics

The general case for using the stages of economic growth is that they embrace within a dynamic political analysis many of the interconnections among the sectors of society which generate the sequence of substantive issues pressed into the political arena for decision. The proposition deserves some illustration here.

First, the process of growth placed on the political agenda a succession of welfare and constitutional issues. Something like the following sequence has been typical:

— the need, usually recognized relatively late in the preconditions for take-off, for government growth policies which would build or help build the minimum essential transport infrastructure, the foreign exchange earn-

21

ings, the educated men and the new institutions for mobilizing capital required for take-off;

— the thrust of the new urban leaders who generate (and are generated by) take-off for a central place in the political system, leading to constitutional change, peaceful or otherwise;

— the emergence of new issues of justice and equity as industrialization draws women and children, as well as men, into the factories and mines at a time when their bargaining position is weak and the conditions of work inhumane;

— the emergence of unions and strikes raises new issues of constitutional order;

— the changing skills required in the growing society raise major questions concerning the appropriate structure of the educational system and pose the question: who should have access to it on what terms?

— the demand for universal suffrage rises as the urban proportion of the population grows and asserts itself and rural life becomes modernized and more closely linked to the cities;

— as industrialization proceeds beyond take-off into the drive to technological maturity, a demand emerges that a higher proportion of the nation's income be diverted to social welfare purposes, and that the harshnesses of the industrial society be tempered by restraining law over a wide front.

In the contemporary developing world the problems of politics have been intensified because these demands for political participation, equity, status in the constitutional order, education, and social welfare – spaced out incrementally before 1914 in a stately, historical sequence – tend to come more nearly all at once, and at a time when still more basic issues of national political organization may not have been wholly solved.

Beyond the drive to technological maturity, the stage of high mass-consumption – of the automobile, durable consumers goods, and all their works – posed in the short-run relatively few problems for politics except to build the roads and manage the level of output and employment so as to keep the income elasticity of demand working to diffuse its ambiguous blessings.

But the deceleration of high mass-consumption in the United States in the mid-1950s opened a new stage – the search for quality. This stage lays a heavy set of demands on the political agenda: for increased outlays in education and health; for vast sums to ease, if not to remove, the pollutions and urban distortions of the automobile age; for programs to deal with pockets of poverty and areas of inequity which become more visible and less acceptable as the average level of income rises; and to deal with those who, surveying the life around them and the options before them, choose to protest or to opt out of the society in ways which break the law.

22

Second, security issues: war and conquest, their temptation and threat – issues which interweave erratically with the welfare and constitutional issues thrown up by the process of growth itself.

The differential timing of modernization, and the arrival of particular stages of growth, by raising the relative power of those who learned the tricks early rather than late, laid the framework within which wars have occurred over the past two centuries and their outcomes were determined.

War links to political development in several other ways:

— External intrusion, or its threat, is, in fact, the primary instrument by which modernization has been transmitted, destroying or weakening less advanced societies, evoking a reactive nationalism in response. And when the legitimacy of the old dispensation was attenuated or broken, new men rose within the existing system (or replaced it), moving their societies, soon or late, after greater or lesser travail, into early stages of political and social as well as economic modernization.

— The early stages of growth have been marked by a temptation to regional expansion by those who felt themselves now relatively more powerful than in the past. There is a family relation between the outward thrust, say, of Bismarck in the 1860s, the Japanese and the Russians in the 1890s, and the ambitious regional probings of Mao and Ho, Sukarno and Nasser.

— At technological maturity we have seen more grandiose efforts to seize the balance of power in Europe and Asia: the Germans, as they triggered their first-strike war plan in 1914; Hitler, Mussolini, and the Japanese, to exploit the disarray of Western power and confidence in the face of the Great Depression; Stalin, to exploit the vacuum in Japan and Germany, the hasty American demobilization, and the initial weakness of postwar Western Europe.

— And, of course, even for the winners wars play back on politics, requiring enlarged inputs of money and men, special skills and new sacrifices. Those who supplied them often exacted new privilege and status: from John's barons at Runnymede to the women's vote after World War I, to the full employment and welfare legislation of the West after World War II, to the forward thrust of the American Negro after the Korean War and during the war in Vietnam.

— For the losers, revolution and constitutional change have often been the result: the French in 1815 and 1870, 1940 and 1945; Russia in 1905 and 1917; Germany in 1918 and 1945; Japan in 1945; and the nations of Eastern Europe in the years immediately after World War II.

When the stages of growth are thus linked systematically to the eternal triangle of problems with which governments must deal, one does not get a closed, logical system in which all is neatly determined and the politics of all nations at all times and places fall into neat patterns. But one does have a dynamic framework within which those clamorous competitors – security, welfare and growth – can be related not merely to the resource mobilization and allocation process but also to pressures for change in the constitutional system and its balance. And suggestive patterns of human and societal experience do naturally emerge, without violating the inherent elements of uniqueness in the cases.

Like the economy, social life and structure, and international affairs, politics has a life and slow-changing inner continuity of its own, made up of men and institutions, traditions and ideas and ideologies. But one cannot get at the heart of it without some such linkages as those suggested here.

The stages of growth pose, then, for each phase of a society's development a package of problems and suggested linkages which may render somewhat more manageable the interconnections among the three dimensions of politics and provide a framework for the systematic comparative analysis of the political process, when it is viewed on a dynamic input–output basis. The stages may internalize, and make endogenous, a good many of Almond's 'dysfunctional inputs' and Easton's 'disturbances'; and they may provide a more detailed, flexible, and realistic sequence than statehood, nationhood, participation, and welfare. They may also permit a more sensitive reading and understanding of the statistical correlations now available which would relate the degree of economic and social modernization to forms of political life. And they may provide a somewhat wider setting for the intensive sociological analyses of the political process – including analyses focused on the elaboration of communications systems and the decision-making process – which have engaged so much of the talent now at work in political science.

But a method is as good as its results. It survives, and should survive, only if it meets the hard pragmatic test of usefulness to others: if it illuminates problems that deeply concern them. And that remains to be seen.

THE ROLE OF IDEAS IN POLITICS

A final word is necessary about the role of political ideas as they relate to political action.

First, I would underline that the use of the stages of economic growth as a framework does not imply an economic interpretation of politics. One of its central themes, in fact, is the primacy of reactive nationalism over other motives which have led nations to modernize their economies. And from the beginning to the end of the analyses of interaction that follow, there are only rare intervals when economic growth and welfare are not seen as ultimately subservient to the security or constitutional dimensions of politics.

Second, this argument underlines the staying power and influence of culture. If economic factors affect the contours of cultures, they do so not via stages of economic growth but through 'very long-run' economic factors. There is an irreducible element of mystery, in the present state of knowledge, about what precisely determines the contours of the unique cultural patterns which have emerged over long periods of time in various societies. These patterns include powerful ideas about good and evil, the proper relation between one man and another, man's relation to the Deity and to the state. These ideas must be accepted as given factors if for no other reason than that they continue to shape how different political systems deal with their problems.

But how do ideas change, including ideas which relate more directly and explicitly to political action?

The powerful simplifications which a culture transmits, alter only slowly; but they alter in such a way that they appear adequately to conform to the society's range of interests, and to match the phenomena which men confront daily in their lives. There is a hard long test of empiricism that societies, as opposed to individuals, apply to the large ideas they accept. Once accepted these ideas have an authority of their own and a great independent reality among the forces which move men to act. But they do alter in response to the changing settings in which men live.

If there is further observation to be made about ideas and political action, it would be Namier's:[25] 'A neurotic, according to Freud, is a man dominated by unconscious memories, fixated on the past, and incapable of overcoming it: the regular condition of human communities.' And, also, Solzhenitsyn's:[26] 'But the fabric of our soul, what we love and what we have grown accustomed to, is created in our youth, not afterward.'

If this view is correct, the struggle of governments and politicians to deal with the problems they confront – to generate the requisite inputs and allocate the limited resources available in ways which yield viable balance – is subject to a systematic lag between problems as they are and problems as they are likely to be perceived in the body politic. The central task of an effective political leader consists in narrowing the gap between the *status quo* and the theoretical optimum dynamic political equilibrium position, without destroying the leader's underlying basis of political support or the constitutional system itself, or, in Solzhenitsyn's terms, building on as much of what men love and have grown accustomed to as possible, while meeting the imperatives of change.

Failure to keep this gap within manageable proportions is the primary cause of constitutional crises and revolutions.

CHAPTER 2

POLITICS IN PRE-NEWTONIAN SOCIETIES

WHY NEWTON?

What distinguishes the world since the industrial revolution from the world before is the systematic, regular, and progressive application of science and technology to the production of goods and services. The resulting flow of innovation has been an additional factor of production which has the special characteristic that it is, so far as we know, indefinitely expansible. And the organized creativity of the human mind appears thus far to be of a productivity capable of compensating for limitations of land and natural resources. Thus, for two centuries have societies, which organized themselves to exploit the innovational stock and flow, fended off Ricardian diminishing returns to land and the Malthusian spectre. Only now have the rate of population increase and threats to the environment cast a shadow over the efficacy of the Newtonian revolution; although science and technology will surely play a part if man succeeds in coming to stable terms with his physical environment.

A number of conditions were required to achieve this transformation,[1] but the most basic change was psychological. It was the acceptance of the view that the physical world is capable of being understood and manipulated in terms of a relatively few stable rules which man could master. It is for that reason that Newton's concepts represent a watershed in history. As with Marx and Freud, it mattered little that few read and understood Newton. It mattered greatly, as with other great intellectual revolutionaries, that a new perspective could be vulgarized in the coffee houses and suffuse the life and work of many men.

Out of this atmosphere arose, in Ashton's good phrase, 'the impulse to contrive', which set men in the West to work, from country houses to grubby workshops, to break the bottlenecks which constrained the economic process: notably, in fuel supply for iron-making; in spinning; in the inefficiency of steam engines; and in the supply of cattle and grain. More than Newton, of course, was required to set substantial numbers of men on this path; for in some societies the link between modern scientific thought and economic innovation was weak or non-existent. But the Newtonian outlook was a necessary initial condition, and it remains so.

The pre-Newtonian world was not without inventors and contrivers; but men and societies lived within technological limits, because innovation was sporadic. The ceiling could be lifted – and was – by elements of innovation and technological advance; but it could not be lifted regularly. And, therefore, constraints operated: on the level of agricultural production; the level of output and employment in urban industry; the level of population that could be sustained; the level of taxable income; and the consequent capacity of governments to carry forward their security, welfare, and constitutional objectives.

The reason for beginning with such technologically inhibited societies is to observe the consequences of such constraints on the ability of governments to generate inputs and to sustain the allocations of governmental output to security and welfare consistent with constitutional equilibrium. This exercise should thereby illuminate the political meaning of the post-Newtonian environment which is the framework for the rest of this book.

We shall begin with a statement of two abstract situations and then look briefly at patterns of politics in some particular cases.

TWO PRE-NEWTONIAN MODELS

The world of pre-industrial revolution societies offers an enormous array of human and societal experience, reflecting political structures of different degrees of organizational complexity, operating against the background of a wide spectrum of technologies.[2]

For purposes of simplification, to dramatize the fundamental processes at work in traditional societies, it may be useful to consider two models, both inherently cyclical. First, a model of what might be called a small-scale traditional society; second, a model of a traditional empire.

The small-scale traditional society is one whose economic life is bounded quite rigorously by a relatively fixed area of arable or grazing land and by a narrow (or relatively stable) trading environment. It is mainly taken up with producing for local consumption. Its political and social organization is also tied intimately to the region and does not strain to enlarge the area of its political and economic power, although it may be drawn, from time to time, into offensive or defensive military activities. Production functions may change with chance discoveries or the occasional intrusion of knowledge from outside, such as knowledge of a new crop; but these are, essentially, once-over changes to which the society adjusts, moving to a new plateau.

The model, however, is not static: the small-scale traditional society does not ride smoothly along its plateaus. Within its existing production functions and acreage, population and income are likely to exhibit fluctuations of relatively short duration, determined by the interplay of the harvests, disease, and war. The pattern that Heckscher was able to present for eighteenth-century Sweden is likely to prove general for small-scale traditional societies; that is, of 'Nature auditing her accounts with a red pencil', with a rise in the death rate roughly, and fairly promptly, cancelling a population surge induced by intervals of peace, absence of epidemic, and good harvests.[3]

History also offers cases which suggest a somewhat different model, in which larger political and trading units are permitted, the possibility of substantial increase in acreage is envisaged, and the scale of allocations to military activities fluctuates over a much wider range than in the small-scale case, allowing for protracted intervals of peace and for wars yielding, directly and indirectly, greater economic damage and more profound political consequences than in the model of the small-scale traditional society. Here we are probing at the dynamics of the Asian empires and dynasties and those of the Mediterranean world and Western Europe.[4] Although history offers us no pure cases, not even the tempting case of the undulating sequence of Chinese dynasties, the most appropriate model appears to be a cycle of greater length than the relatively short compensatory adjustment of the small-scale model.

The abstract cycle of the traditional empire begins with the establishment of political order over a reasonably large area by strong purposeful administration which concentrates a high proportion of its energies and resources on the domestic scene. It comes to power at the trough of a previous cycle when war and epidemic have driven down the population, freed acreage, and disrupted trade. In this special sense, idle capacity exists.

Within the new framework of peace and order, agriculture revives; the routes for domestic (and sometimes international) trade are opened (or reopened) and kept open and reliable; and, where appropriate, the irrigation works are built or rebuilt and maintained. Agricultural output not only expands but shifts in its composition to exploit the possibility of trade with the cities in commodities of higher value than the basic grains. The taxes are collected with tolerable efficiency by the government; and the expanded outlays of a prosperous government, as well as those above the ranks of the peasantry, stimulate various forms of handicraft manufacture. Processing and handicraft manufacture – and, in general, higher degrees of specialization – are stimulated as well by an increase in interregional and, perhaps, international trade. And efforts may be made not only to repopulate the old acreage but to bring new lands under cultivation.

As time passes, however, three factors tend to set a limit on economic progress. First, the pressure of expanding population against good land; second, the built-in difficulty of maintaining over long periods of time efficient, honest, and purposeful administration; and, third, the likelihood that the state will become embroiled in wars whose cost outweighs their return either in expanded trade or in acquisitions of good land. At some stage these three factors yield a downturn in the cycle of the traditional empire, whose symptoms might take the form of some combination of grossly uneconomic military operations; excessive taxation; bad harvests arising from land pressed too hard; epidemics; peasants' revolts or other forms of civil strife; and the decay of central administration.

Proximately – operationally – the downturn is caused by a fiscal crisis: the empire cannot generate the inputs to government required to meet the security and welfare obligations that have accumulated; and its own efforts to deal with the situation may exacerbate an underlying constitutional crisis caused by the disequilibrium between resources and objectives.

After this upper turning point, economic, social, and political life retreats back to narrower limits, in which the society conducts its affairs on a less productive and a more self-sufficient basis, a process usually accompanied by a decline in population.[5]

The fundamental technical reason for the abortive character of these expansions (in both small-scale and imperial cases) lies, as suggested earlier, in the fact that economic invention and innovation in traditional societies were not regular features of their life. For reasons which reach deep into their cultures, their social values, and their view of the physical world, they did not regularly allocate a substantial proportion of their creative talent to the breaking of economic bottlenecks.

Nevertheless, the expansion phase of the traditional empire often contained all the preconditions for take-off except a flow of modern industrial, agricultural, and transport technology capable of fending off diminishing returns to land and coping with the Malthusian propensities of the people. And that phase also was marked by what would now be called a considerable degree of political modernization; that is, the emergence of specialized arms of government, professional bureaucracies, skilled military establishments, and professional standards of performance which can be associated roughly with 'secularization' – plus, of course, an increased mobilization of resources in the hands of the state.

Within limits set by the technological ceiling of traditional societies, the supply of good land, and the rate at which population responds to peace and prosperity, the central dynamic factor in the imperial model was the political process: the ability of the central administration to sustain, generation after generation, its integrity and purpose and to avoid military adventures whose economic cost outweighed their gain, leading to excessive taxation or other gross disruptions of the economy or the social balance in the society.

One can speculate as to whether a decline in administrative vigor and integrity was a built-in feature of traditional societies. Perhaps human and institutional frailty decreed, with the passage of time, that the Mandate of Heaven would be lost, as the court and administration were diverted by the blandishments of prosperity, the Buddenbrooks' Dynamics, or Parkinson's Law from their initial vigor, rectitude, and concern with the domestic scene. And, as contemporary life in more advanced societies is examined (chapter 6), with evidence that success as well as technological constraint can pose grave problems, one is not inclined wholly to dismiss such non-material theories of the decline of ancient empires and dynasties.

One can also speculate concerning the relation between pressure to acquire new fertile land and the military conflicts which sometimes marked the latter phases of expansion in traditional societies. Similarly, while subject to many possible exogenous circumstances, the timing and diffusion of epidemics were often determined by war. And certainly to a degree, peasant rebellions (or urban revolt) were often a response to both the economic pressures and the perception of waning power at the center which marked the process of downturn.

But it is clear that however competent and pacific the central rule, population increase, limitation on good land, and a technological ceiling created, when taken together, basic limitations on economic growth in traditional empires, gathering strains on the administrative apparatus and the political system as a whole; and a setting within which crisis and downturn might be initiated by a number of forces, within or from without the empire.

To understand the nature of modern post-Newtonian economic growth, and the politics that have accompanied and helped to shape it, we must, therefore, begin by accepting Postan's challenge: 'to lay bare the essential processes of a society held in by physical or, if the term is used in a broad sense, Malthusian checks'.[6] And, from what we know, his tentatively expressed insights have a meaning beyond the later Middle Ages: in the history of traditional empires, we can, indeed, 'find explanations of later decline in the conditions of previous growth'. It is not only in fourteenth-century Britain that 'the honeymoon of high yields was succeeded by long periods of reckoning when the marginal lands, no longer new, punished the men who tilled them with recurrent inundations, desiccations, and dust storms'.[7]

SOME AFRICAN TRIBES: THE MARGINAL CASE OF NO GOVERNMENT

We turn now to examine briefly what politics looks like under the most primitive and static circumstances we can observe. Examples are taken from the detailed descriptions in Fortes and Evans-Pritchard's *African Political Systems*.[8]

Fortes says of the Tallensi, about 1915:

> There was no one who had authority over all the Tallensi; no one who could exact tax, tribute or service from all. They never united for war or self-protection against a common enemy. They had, in short, no 'tribal' government or 'tribal' citizenship, no centralized State exercising legislative, administrative juridical and military functions in the interests of the whole society.

In short, none of the three abiding functions of government was exercised centrally; and, therefore, no resource inputs were centrally mobilized and allocated.[9]

Despite the lack in these tribes of central institutions to conduct war, distribute justice, or to collect central revenue, they were held together by concepts of community – and ceremonies – centered on religion and the exercise of magic.

They lived within a subtle and complex network of clans, with clan chieftains and men of magic maintaining the continuity of unifying religion and tradition on the basis of lineage and finding ways to settle disputes in conformity with custom. They lived close to the margin of subsistence. The fortunes of rainfall, yielding plenty, drought, or flood, were the central abiding short-run facts in their economic life and the focus for men of magic.

The security problem faced by these tribes arose directly from their economic situation. At the margins of their territory, war was endemic: to acquire new land and additional cattle, or to resist the efforts of others to do so. But war was a limited affair, engaging only a segment of the tribe and conducted with limited objectives. As Günter Wagner, writing of the Bantu Kavirondo, said:[10]

> ... a war expedition was never terminated by the annexation of a given area by the victorious side and a readjustment of the boundary line confirmed by the vanquished or any similar procedure. This would have required a much firmer military organization than existed and an organized protection of the borders, for which the political structure of the tribal groups was much too loose. The immediate result of a raid was rather to weaken and intimidate the neighboring tribe and to induce its members gradually to retreat, so that the uninhabited zone would widen and the grazing of stock and the cultivation of gardens could safely be carried on in what was formerly no-man's-land. The territory thus

31

gained by a very gradual process came under the control of the clan whose warriors had driven the enemy tribe into retreat and was shared out among them.

The lack of historical records does not permit us to say much about the dynamics, if any, of their apparently stable way of life. But there is some evidence in their traditional lore that they experienced cycles similar to those known elsewhere, in which phases of prosperity and population increase, as well as increase in the number of cattle, yielded erosion of the soil and pressure on the land available. This may have set in motion intensified tribal war and movements of migration. Epidemics and war may have brought them back to a balance consistent with their technology.[11]

What appears certain is that, although the scale of warfare was limited by technology and custom, still Kurt Vonnegut's old devil was in them: 'The attitude towards any neighboring tribe as a whole was chiefly characterized by a feeling of suspicion, to which was added either fear or contempt.'[12]

SOME OTHER AFRICAN TRIBES: CONQUEST AND PRIMITIVE GOVERNMENT

As Radcliffe-Brown's dictum on war and political development suggests, out of the further expression of such sentiments in wars of conquest comes the next stage of African political development.

There are African tribes which developed central governments of a highly recognizable kind; for example, the Zulu and Ankole kingdoms,[13] and the Zazzau.[14] In all three cases, the emergence of a central government is linked to conquest and its consolidation; and all lend some credence to Aristotle's dictum (*Politics*, Book VI, chapter 4) that a pastoral people is 'the best trained of any for war, robust in body and able to camp out' – the natural conquerors of those who would settle down to the routines of agriculture in a fixed area.

In the late eighteenth century the head of the Zulu tribe, primarily engaged in animal husbandry, organized sufficient military force to conquer a substantial region. On this basis, a political organization was created, centered in a standing army united by allegiance to the king who alone controlled the military regiments. In theory, the king was the sole executive, judicial, and legislative authority. But, in fact, a lively political life developed around him, within the royal family and among the tribal chiefs. Strong checks and balances were built into his exercise of power, assuring that he did not act without taking counsel. While alone retaining the right of life and death over his subjects and the right to go to war, the clan chieftain administered local justice, and a modest bureaucracy of agents and tax collectors emerged.

Of the people the king required military and labor service. Fines and war booty went to him, as well as a flow of gifts on customary occasions, which amounted to a kind of regular taxation of subordinates.

With these inputs, the king was required to protect the borders and maintain the unity of the Zulu kingdom; to help generously in times of famine; and to provide justice. These were his versions of the tasks of security, welfare, and constitutional order.

In short, the Zulu kingdom, in simple but recognizable form, had all the elements of government. But it did not engage, from this base, after its initial consolidation, in the pursuit of empire. It remained tolerably stable down to the time that white men came to Africa, with the British imposing decisive defeat in 1880.

The Ankole kingdom also arose from conquest: in this case, the permanent subjugation by the Bahima who tended their cattle in eastern Ankole, of the Bairu who tilled the soil in the west. Before this imperial act, legend had it that 'the Bahima had neither king nor chiefs, but important men in the clans settled the disputes'[15] – along the pattern of the simple tribal organizations we have just discussed. But with their victory

No longer were the Bahima cattle men free agents, united in extended families and loosely knit lineages and clans; they were now also members of a political group. If the Bahima were going to further their interests as Bahima, they had to organize and act together as Bahima. At bottom this new relationship was based on Bahimanship – upon race and cattle-ownership. But this special political bond had to be created, had to be consciously entered into. It involved leadership, co-operation, submission to authority. It gave rise to kingship and the dynastic principle, the organization of military forces and chieftainship. In short, it welded the Bahima into a State, the nucleus of the Banyankole kingdom.[16]

The king who emerged in the Banyankole state was called the Mugabe. Each cattle owner – a Muhima – had to enter into a client relationship with the king; swear to follow him in war and undertake to give the Mugabe a number of cattle periodically to keep this relationship alive. On the other hand, the Mugabe undertook to protect the client from cattle raiders and retaliate when his cattle suffered raids. He also helped enlarge the herds and the area for grazing. He maintained peace within the kingdom and administered justice. The defeated Bairu remained a lower order of serfdom, continuing to supply the beer and millet that in earlier times they had traded for the milk and butter supplied by the cattlemen.

This kingdom also generated a class of slaves mainly as a by-product of war; but the economics of their life did not make slavery on a large scale profitable.

The resources mobilized to maintain this system were much like those of the Zulu: military service could be called for; cattle acquired in private raids went to the king; and there were homage payments which financed the

33

royal treasury. Somewhat more than the Zulu, apparently, the Bahima engaged in some efforts to extend their area of control but did not generate a substantial empire beyond that which crystallized from the initial conquest of the Bairu.

As in all the African political systems examined here, the absolute powers of the Mugabe were hedged about by custom, by family influence, and by the role of the king's warriors and tribute collectors. The power of this surrounding structure was best revealed by the procedure of succession: always the critical moment and problem for societies which live politically by the principle of absolute monarchy. If the Mugabe was observed by his wives and followers to be weak, he was poisoned. The residual power establishment then launched an exceedingly complex and protracted competitive ritual to maximize the chance that a worthy successor would emerge, while military forces at the borders assured that other tribes would not exploit the period of disarray.

The Zazzau story, as detailed by M. G. Smith, is more complex than those of the Zulu and Ankole kingdoms. It includes:

— the historic, Islamic role in the northern region of Nigeria, reaching back to the fifteenth century and the element of holy war in the Fulani attack of 1804 on the Habe kingdom;

— the escape of the Habe king and survival of a truncated kingdom to the south;

— the rather sophisticated if pre-industrial economy of the Hausa, including institutionalized markets, currency, and long-distance cattle trade.

The Fulani consolidated their 1804 conquest into a system of government in which, under Islamic influence and as part of a larger Islamic sovereignty, they emerged 'as the guardians and teachers of the Faith on the one hand, and the Habe as the wards and pupils on the other'.[17]

For our limited purposes, however, the central point is that there emerged, on the basis of feudal links of clientage imposed by a conquering monarch, a system of taxation and of military and constitutional functions, centrally administered, which reflected all the abiding elements of government.

We can conclude, then, that minimally organized life could be maintained in certain tribes on the basis of custom and what might be described as extended family methods for maintaining justice, law, and order. This stability among the non-governmental cases depended on the lack of potential enemies with a capacity or will for conquest and on a reciprocal rejection of such ambitions. Equilibrium with the external tribes was maintained by what might be called limited private warfare. Such conflict might slowly shift the boundaries of the territory of the tribe but did not involve either substantial expansion or the threat of take-over. It also depended on a way of gaining livelihood so simple that no welfare functions developed requiring governmental action.

More recognizable government structures and administrations emerged when, from whatever motives or circumstances, some group developed the ability as well as the will to expand its territory. Then there emerged a political leader with a duty to provide food at times of thin harvests; to maintain or extend the boundaries of the enlarged territory; to maintain order as well as law. And to do these things he required a flow of resources and soldiers, as well as an at least rudimentary administrative system.

In Egypt and elsewhere the Africans showed a capacity to build extensive kingdoms; although they did not generate south of the Sahara a history quite so filled with imperial glory and tragedy as the peoples bordering the Mediterranean. They did, however, build habits in their relations to one another, both externally and within their political life, of checks and balances and accommodations which may, in the century ahead, serve them well in the peaceful organization of their continent. These habits and frames of mind may have stemmed simply from the unavailability of a technology which would have permitted efficient or large-scale warfare, rather than from special virtue or wisdom. But the tradition and habits may yet suffice to render African modern history less bloody than that of some of the other continents; although the Nigerian civil war, with its breakdown of intertribal diplomacy, and the tensions to be observed elsewhere between tribalism and the imperatives of modern politics, does not easily encourage the view that Africa can wholly escape the tribulations of its predecessors in political modernization.

ATHENS, FIFTH CENTURY B.C.: HYBRIS, OVER-EXTENSION, AND RAPID COLLAPSE

We move forward now in terms of economic and military technology, political and diplomatic complexity, but backward in time.

The agriculture of Athens of the fifth century was primitive. With only an iron plowshare and the slow beginnings of crop rotation, the Greeks mainly followed the old tradition of letting fields lie fallow in alternate years; although oil and wine had become important export crops. Given the limitation on productivity and the degree of urbanization, the basic food supply of the city had to come, in part, through imports; but this Athens could manage.

The largest factory of which we know at the close of the fifth century employed 120 slaves in making shields. Workers were massed in large numbers in the government silver mines; but production of textiles and household goods remained in the hands of artisans working in small shops, with extremely limited technology. The availability of young and healthy slaves, sometimes at half the cost of unskilled free labor, reduced what impulse there may have been for increases in productivity.[18]

On the other hand, commerce flourished: 'An Athenian citizen of the Periclean age might enjoy not only Attic olive-oil and wine but also the corn and the dried fish of the Black Sea, the dates of Phoenicia and the cheeses of Sicily; he might wear slippers from Persia and lie on a Milesian bed with his head resting on a Carthaginian pillow.'[19]

The 'leading sector' in this pre-industrial revolution economy was, clearly, trade by sea; and along with it came not only men of commerce but also shipbuilders and oarsmen, and a navy.

This lively society, mercantilist in spirit and policy, enjoyed a classic mercantilist asset in its silver mines. From the mines and other state properties, taxes on imports and exports, and a variety of minor levies, including court fees and fines, the state's revenues normally exceeded its expenditures in times of peace.

Athenian democracy had removed a tax proportionate to agricultural output, but accepted a property tax in time of war as an emergency measure. In addition, an important part in Athenian finance came to be played by the sums paid by members of the Delian League. But the state's expenditures were, in normal times, modest, and, even then, cushioned by the willingness of certain of the wealthier citizens to finance what were, in effect, public enterprises. The sums available sufficed in peaceful years to maintain the military and naval establishment; to build and repair public works; and, of course, to erect the great monuments. But, as Professor Tod has written: 'The supremely disturbing factor in state finance was war . . .'[20]

Politically, at the time of Pericles the full citizens of military age, numbering perhaps 30,000–40,000 (paid for their attendance), were the heart of political life – the Ecclesia. When not in session, the Ecclesia was represented by the Council of 500 which, through committees, operated on a functional basis: justice, war, finance, education, etc. One tenth of the Council (representing one of the ten Athenian tribes) was in charge of the presidency for one-tenth of the year. The Council members were chosen by lot by their tribes; and an Athenian citizen could serve twice in his lifetime. The courts of law were comprised of members of the Ecclesia, chosen by lot from a list of 6,000 jurors eligible for that year, sitting in numbers ranging from 101 to 1,001.

The citizens with full political rights were about one-tenth of the total population of over 320,000. No voting rights were accorded to women, minors, aliens, or slaves.

This, in briefest compass, was the political-economic system that had to make its dispositions after the Persian war.

For Athens there were two related questions to answer: What should the future be of the Delian Confederation? What of future relations with Sparta?

The answers unfolded, as they usually do in history, in a series of erratic particular circumstances. But the fundamental decision made by Athens was to hold on to its dominance of the sea, whatever the cost might be with respect to relations with those members of the old Confederation that joined with it against Persia, and whatever the cost to its relations with Sparta. Although this decision was executed at times with subtlety and moderation – at others with brutality and guile – it was a decision never revoked until the bitter end.

Behind this decision were certain economic and political facts that transcended the continuing threat represented by Persia. Athenian economic life and the public revenues had become dependent upon trade. And the maintenance of the trading system involved a navy in being, to battle where necessary to maintain or extend access to critical commercial centers.

Negatively, as Toynbee points out, withdrawal from a dominant naval role might have presented Athens with a formidable economic and political problem:[21]

One effect of the constitution of the confederacy of Delos, as it had operated in the course of thirty years, had been to make the earning of wages as oarsmen for the Athenian navy one of the main sources of livelihood for the landless urban majority of the population of Attica; and these wages had been paid out of the fund provided by the contributions of Athens' allies. There would be mass unemployment at Athens if the financial means could not continue to be found for providing the same wages for the same number of Athenian citizens in some alternative occupation to naval service. Could new work be found for which wages could be paid to the discharged Athenian naval crews? And, since Athens' own national budget would not run to bearing this formidable new charge permanently, would it be right to finance it out of contributions levied from the allies in peace-time?

In addition, the dominant force in the political life of Athens had become the new men brought forward by the dynamics of trade and the enlargement of the navy in the struggle against Persia.

It was this group that pressed simultaneously for a strong imperial policy abroad and a widening of the base of democracy in Athens. And these were the directions in which Pericles moved, despite the opposition of Cimon (down to 461) and others, like the 'old Oligarch', who took a dim view of democracy at home and incautious expansion abroad.

Cimon, a conservative with a firm grasp on the military realities which confronted Athens, advocated for a time a policy of peace; agreement with Sparta; and a conciliatory approach to the members of the confederation as they jointly faced the question of the future of their alliance and continued war with Persia.

After a judicious beginning with Aristides as the negotiator, Athenian policy moved by stages to a progressively harder stance: first, it negotiated, with certain members of the confederation, monetary payments in place of the ships and men which each had contributed in the struggle against Persia; and then came to insist that withdrawal from the arrangement was not permissible, applying diplomatic pressure to enforce the doctrine, and, finally, military force.

In effect, the Athenian navy was financed as a common instrument of military defense against Persia by the former allies. But the members accepted this arrangement, with the passage of time, only in the face of overwhelming Athenian naval power. The renegotiation of the terms of the Delian League became, in effect, negotiation of tribute to Athens as leader of a new empire. The arrangement brought, of course, mounting hostility to its leader, and opened the way to Persian financial support of Athens' enemies and the direct clash with Sparta.

In retrospect, as always, one can regard as inevitable the mortal conflict between Athens and Sparta. But, in fact, there were strong forces in Sparta, in the fifth century, prepared to live with a powerful Athenian empire, reaching out to Asia Minor and the islands, if it would not encroach on truly vital Spartan interests – on Sparta itself and its Peloponnesian bloc of old allies. Sparta had even acquiesced reluctantly in the rebuilding of the walls of Athens and Thucydides' construction of the Piraeus fortifications which gave Athens some kind of protection from superior Spartan ground forces.

The operational question to be answered is why, when Athenian commercial and imperial expansion brought it into conflict with other major Mediterranean trading centers – notably Megara, Corinth, Sicyon – was Sparta drawn into the struggle as an ally of the latter.

Rostovtzeff's answer is probably as good as we are likely to get. He argues that, if Athens achieved the virtual monopoly it sought in trade with the Western Mediterranean cities, the imports required for the north and west of the Peloponnese – Sparta's domain – would have to flow through Athens. Sparta, although not itself directly interested in this trade, was menaced and, therefore, inclined to listen to the complaints of Megara.[22] Thus Sparta decided that it had to contest the expansion of the Athenian empire; and the decisive phase of the Peloponnesian war was on (431 B.C.).

As Thucydides perceived, there was a convergent clash of power and ideology between centers with differing social and political structures. The rise of the Athenian empire could be seen in Sparta as a threat to its existence.[23] 'The Spartans voted that the treaty had been broken and that war should be declared not so much because they were influenced by the speeches of their allies as because they were afraid of the further growth of Athenian power, seeing, as they did, that already the greater part of Hellas was under the control of Athens.'

This is not the occasion to recall the whole tangled tale of battle, interspersed with devious diplomacy and sporadic intervals of peace. What is clear is that Athens became over-extended in pursuit of the Periclean policy and, in the end, in 404 B.C., Athens had to accept terms of peace as dictated by Sparta; her fortifications were levelled; and she was forced to join the Macedonian League in complete dependence upon a Sparta which was in no position to furnish the leadership required to unify the Greek states and let the interdependencies of commerce work themselves out in peace.

It was from Macedonia, in the fourth century B.C., that the next great Greek effort at unification came, with the commanding figures of Philip and Alexander.

What can be said of the famous tragedy of Athens in the special context of this book?

First, in terms of the approach developed in chapter 1 it can be viewed, in general, as a story of external over-extension and domestic-welfare neglect, yielding commitments to governmental outputs that could not be matched by inputs, bringing on constitutional change as well.

Second, there is a component that foreshadows later efforts at regional expansion by ideologically self-conscious powers. After their role in the struggle against the Persians, the Athenians were swept by pride not merely in their military prowess but in the vitality of their political ideology and institutions.

Indeed, certain of the Greek states, hitherto ruled by oligarchies, moved towards democracy in the first half of the fifth century B.C. in explicit imitation of Athens. E. M. Walker evokes an interesting analogy with French Revolutionary attitudes towards the external world:[24]

The policy pursued by Pericles . . . stands condemned not merely on account of the inadequacy of his resources. An Athenian empire on the mainland of Greece was a vain dream. It is to be remembered that at the time of the breach with Sparta democracy was, so to speak, a new thing in the experience of the Greeks. It was, at least, enough of a novelty to excuse the belief in those who were themselves convinced democrats that the population of every state in Greece would choose the 'government of the many', if once they got their chance. The leader of a popular party in all ages is apt to indulge in the illusion that 'the flowing tide is with him.' It was as natural for Pericles to imagine that the states in which oligarchies were established in power would declare for democracy as soon as Athens intervened, as it was for the Jacobins in France to persuade themselves that all Europe would embrace the principles of the Revolution when once the malign influence of priests and princes was removed.

39

Third, the strains created by Athens' diplomatic and military posture yielded vicious circles in both its relations with other city states and in its domestic political life. Abroad, the road from confederation to empire took the Athenians down the path Cleon memorably enunciated, when Athenians suddenly paused and debated (427 B.C.) before executing their decision to kill the male population of Mytilene and sell into slavery the women and children:[25]

> Let me sum the whole thing up. I say that, if you follow my advice, you will be doing the right thing as far as Mytilene is concerned and at the same time will be acting in your own interests; if you decide differently, you will not win them over, but you will be passing judgement on yourselves. For if they were justified in revolting, you must be wrong in holding power. If, however, whatever the rights or wrongs of it may be, you propose to hold power all the same, then your interest demands that these too, rightly or wrongly, must be punished. The only alternative is to surrender your empire, so that you can afford to go in for philanthropy. Make up your minds, therefore, to pay them back in their own coin, and do not make it look as though you who escaped their machinations are less quick to react than they who started them.

To which Diodotus responded:[26]

> If we are sensible people, we shall see that the question is not so much whether they are guilty as whether we are making the right decision for ourselves . . .
>
> If a city has revolted and realizes that the revolt cannot succeed, it will come to terms while it is still capable of paying an indemnity and continuing to pay tribute afterwards. But if Cleon's method is adopted, can you not see that every city will not only make much more careful preparations for revolt, but will also hold out against siege to the very end, since to surrender early or late means just the same thing? This is, unquestionably, against our interests – to spend money on a siege because of the impossibility of coming to terms, and, if we capture the place, to take over a city that is in ruins so that we lose the future revenue from it. And it is just on this revenue that our strength in war depends . . .
>
> But if you destroy the democratic party at Mytilene, who never took any hand in the revolt and who, as soon as they got arms, voluntarily gave the city up to you, you will first of all be guilty of killing those who have helped you, and, secondly, you will be doing exactly what the reactionary classes want most. For now, when they start a revolt, they will have the people on their side from the beginning . . .

The Athenian decision went narrowly with Diodotus; but this tactical victory for relative moderation did not break Athens out of the imperial web of struggle in which it was enmeshed; for at home the imperial process had led a generation earlier to a series of changes which constituted a strengthening of the new men with a vested interest in trade, the navy, and empire – changes democratic in form: a strengthening of the popular Assembly's role in the courts; the widening of access to higher office (the archonship); the payment of jurors by the state; and the (partially consequent) restriction of the franchise to those of citizen birth on both sides – a narrowing of the franchise by, perhaps, a quarter.

Of the restriction of the franchise, E. M. Walker notes:[27] 'It proclaimed that the Empire existed for the benefit of Athens.' And Professor Adcock concludes:[28] 'The more the democracy was organized to share the spoils of empire, the more natural it was to organize the Empire to produce them.'

But, as the imperial policy was pressed against increasing resistance abroad and straitened resources at home, the pressure on conservative men of wealth grew which, in the end, provided the motive and the leverage to overturn, for a period, Athenian democracy:[29]

The Athenian propertied classes were terribly shortened in their income by the Decelean War, through the ruin of their estates in Attica; the running away of their slaves (to the number eventually of over 20,000), with the consequent closing of mines and factories; the increased risks and diminishing returns of maritime trade; and the impossibility of attending to their business whatever it was. At the same time they were staggering under the fiscal burdens put upon them by the state ... Athens was rapidly becoming poor. The silver and gold amassed by the city and its inhabitants from the tribute and the mines and the profits of trade were being dissipated, in considerable part abroad, in payment for war-services and materials; and the profiteers were as often as not beyond the reach of the Athenian fiscus ... The more decisively finance came to dominate the conduct of the war, the more the classes financially important came to demand a larger voice in its decisions than they possessed under the existing democracy.

Behind these vicious circles was a deeply felt belief that life had to be conducted within resource limits that were finite, if not absolutely fixed – abroad and at home.

Abroad the Greeks viewed trade, in Charles Wilson's phrase, as a critical arena of both profit and power, an arena essentially fixed in extent where one sovereignty's gain had to be another sovereignty's loss. Speaking of mercantilist Europe, Wilson says, in a passage that evokes much of the Athenian dilemma:[30]

... in many countries [foreign trade was] an obsession with statesmen and the achievement of a favourable balance of trade a prime aim of policy. The explanation of the seeming paradox must lie in the close relationship between governments and strong groups with vested interests in foreign trade ... as well as in the fiscal interests of governments themselves. More than that, a trade stoppage might produce unemployment and danger to public order in particular areas, or even a threat to national security.

And at home, since no powerful new technological possibilities were available to expand agricultural yields, the struggle focused on an even more pervasive and classic question: who owned the relatively fixed amounts of land. Thus Rostovtzeff can say:[31]

Concurrently with the external wars there raged within the Greek cities, alike in Greece proper and in most of the islands, an unceasing class-warfare, which originated in the steady growth of a well-to-do *bourgeois* class and the corresponding impoverishment of the masses. This class-war made the growth and development of a sound capitalistic system very difficult. Indeed, it made a healthy economic life within the city-states almost impossible. The strife in the Greek cities assumed more and more the character of an almost purely social and economic struggle. The main aim of the struggle was, not the increase of production by the betterment of labour conditions and the improvement and regulation of the relations between labour and capital, but the redistribution of property, which was generally achieved by violent revolutionary means. The war-cry was the immemorial one of γῆς ἀναδασμὸς καὶ χρεῶν ἀποκοπή, redistribution of land and abolition of debts. This cry was so freely used as early as the end of the Peloponnesian war that the Athenians introduced into the oath of the Heliasts in 401 a clause which forbade the putting of such an issue to the vote . . .

The revolutions which aimed at such a redistribution of property were utterly disastrous for Greece.

In short, what we can observe in Athens of fifth century B.C. is a highly recognizable dynamic interplay of security, economic, and constitutional factors yielding dramatic collapse of an imperial venture. One historian has concluded:[32] '. . . the folly of the Athenians is explicable only on their own theory that those whom the Gods would destroy they first make mad.' But to Athenians, at the time they made their critical decisions, the case was straightforward as Thucydides reports the statement of a delegation from Athens replying to the Corinthians' plea for Spartan military support:[33]

We have done nothing extraordinary, nothing contrary to human nature in accepting an empire when it was offered to us and then in refusing to give it up. Three very powerful motives prevent us from doing so – security, honour, and self-interest. And we were not the first to act in this way. Far from it. It has always been a rule that the weak should be subject to the strong; and besides, we consider that we are worthy of our power.

But only in retrospect is the sequence inevitable; for Sparta of this period was relatively modest in its aspirations, and it is not difficult to envisage a less hard-handed Athenian manipulation of its naval and negotiating assets *vis-à-vis* the Delian League after 479 B.C., which would have avoided giving Persia the leverage to be paymaster to Athens' opponents in the Peloponnesian War.

The old story is worth study and re-study, since the margin between viability and disaster in national policies is often close, even where resources are more ample than those available to the Athenians. Politicians find little difficulty, in the face of the pressures they confront, absorbing all the inputs a politico-economic system can generate in the hands of government. Moderation abroad and a sensitive balancing of domestic and foreign objectives remain relevant lessons over the centuries. But, unless the Greeks had found their way to some solid political confederation – clearly, at this stage, beyond their capacity at a time of peace – their inherent competitiveness in an environment of continued external threat and technological limitation was likely to make transient their period of unique but contentious glory.

THE FALL OF THE ROMAN EMPIRE: CUMULATIVE EROSION AND COLLAPSE

The conclusion about Greece is reinforced by the fate of Imperial Rome which struggled forward over five centuries to consolidate successfully a great empire and, then, gradually found it impossible to sustain.

Like the Athenian imperial venture, that of Rome was in riposte to potentially mortal external struggle, of even greater brutality. As Toynbee says:[34]

Rome had been turned savage by her grim struggle for existence, and she had emerged from it in a vindictive mood. Her entry into the international arena had been inadvertent. She had been intent simply on making herself paramount in Italy, and her political horizon had not extended farther than that before she found herself at grips with Carthage and fighting, in the second round, on Italian soil for dear life. She had not wanted this alien world to close in on her in this frightful way, and, now that she had cut herself loose (so she thought) from the python's coils, she felt no responsibility for the world and wanted to hear no more of it. She had now made sure of her own security by eliminating every serious threat to this. She would leave the world to stew and would sit down to lick her own wounds. If she did give a thought to the world, it would be to plunder and exploit it.

The bitter but successful Roman struggle for survival that yielded Mediterranean hegemony had placed in the hands of the state and then in the hands of an upper class of senators and knights great tracts of land. These victories also yielded booty, taxes from conquered territories, and opportunities for trade from which generated wealth which could be converted into land ownership. And they yielded slaves for service and tending the estates.

The result was the conversion of a land-owning peasantry into farm workers; or, if they gave up their land, into an urban working class which met difficulty in finding employment.

They found their political advocates, of course, in the struggle of Tiberius Gracchus, and his brother, against a Senate committed to hold the wealth and privileges that had arisen out of the dynamics of the previous period of war.

The resolution of the civil struggle placed decisive power, however, not in the hands of the Senate but in the hands of an emperor who controlled the army and the imperial administration. It was Augustus, coming to power in the wake of the bitter civil war that followed the assassination of Julius Caesar, who rationalized the system that emerged and laid the basis for two centuries of peace – a period which, in its earlier phases, was also a period of prosperity and the flourishing of culture in many directions throughout the Mediterranean world.

There is a family resemblance between the dispositions of Augustus and

43

those of Pericles. Both achieved domestic political peace by a compromise that elevated new (but different) urban groups, but accompanied this with an imperial policy.

The question is this: Why was the Roman Empire incapable of maintaining itself in peace and prosperity for more than two centuries? What was it that brought on with the death of Marcus Aurelius, A.D. 180, a century of revolution which, while arrested under the hardhanded rule of Diocletian, essentially brought the downfall and fragmentation of the Roman Empire, leaving the Church in Rome as its major legatee in the West?

Few questions have more engaged Western thought over the centuries since a perspective on the whole drama of the Roman Empire could be attained.

Augustus started well with a political system which placed authority over the army and the administration of the empire firmly in his hands; with certain nominal concessions to the continuity of the power of the Senate; but, in fact, throwing the Empire's weight behind the nurture of the cities, the new commercial and industrial groups, and granting concessions to the poor urban population. At the frontiers the Roman Legions were locally recruited but granted citizenship. Provisional governors took over previously chaotic tax collection on an orderly basis, less capricious and autonomous than the publicans of the past.

In an environment of peace, trade and industry prospered.

The erosion of this system was marked by certain elements which are universally agreed:[35]

— the decline of agriculture and the continued flow of the population to the cities;

— the inability of the large land owners to increase output and, even, the inability of the state to induce by incentives all the available land to be worked;

— the growth of unemployment and partial unemployment in the cities where outlays to provide bread and circuses became an increasing burden on the state;

— the decline of industry and trade in response to the waning purchasing power in the countryside and the cities;

— a decline of the resources available to the emperor, leading to a situation where the army could not be paid in money, yielding, in the end, not a firmly controlled and loyal imperial guard at the frontiers, but a feeble militia;

— a rise in confidence, power and assertiveness of the provinces *vis-à-vis* Rome.

All of this laid the basis for the century of civil wars among the provincial rulers, increasing pressure on highly vulnerable frontiers, and rural struggle against the cities – a struggle which Diocletian (A.D. 284) was able to arrest only by imposing an absolutist rule which drained from Rome and the Romans such special status and privilege as they still enjoyed. Here is Toynbee's vivid picture of how the crisis came:[36]

The growing strain was widely spread. It was a strain on the peasantry to support the parasitic cities; it was a strain on the civil service to take over the decadent city-state governments' work in addition to its own; it was a strain on the taxpayer to support a growing civil service as well as a growing army. This multiple strain can be felt in the melancholy tone of the Stoic emperor Marcus Aurelius's private diary. The pressures were cumulative; and, within fifty-five years of Marcus's death in A.D. 180, they exploded in a general breakdown. The peasants in the countryside and soldiers on the frontiers revolted against their middle-class task-masters and pay-masters in the cities. The barbarians and the Persians broke through. In A.D. 251 one Roman emperor, Decius, was killed in battle with the Goths in Thrace; in A.D. 260 another, Valerian, was taken prisoner by the Persians in Syria . . . The currency depreciated to zero. The world-state broke up.

This process of decay was accompanied by a profound change in men's attitudes towards the empire itself, their lives and their culture: indeed, towards the meaning of their life on earth. The confidence and hope, the somewhat vulgarized but still aristocratic version of Hellenistic culture, generated and diffused from Rome, lost its capacity to serve as a viable framework for life. The rise of Christianity was both a result and an accelerating force in this process.

Here is Rostovtzeff's central observation on the phenomenon as a whole:[37]

From the intellectual and spiritual point of view the main phenomenon is the decline of ancient civilization, of the city civilization of the Greco-Roman world . . . there are two aspects of the evolution. The first is the exhaustion of the creative forces of Greek civilization in the domains where its great triumphs had been achieved, in the exact sciences, in technique, in literature and art. The decline began as early as the second century B.C. There followed a temporary revival of creative forces in the cities of Italy, and later in those of the Eastern and Western provinces of the Empire. The progressive movement stopped almost completely in the second century A.D. and, after a period of stagnation, a steady and rapid decline set in again. Parallel to it, we notice a progressive weakening of the assimilative forces of Greco-Roman civilization. The cities no longer absorb – that is to say, no longer hellenize or romanize – the masses of the country population. The reverse is the case. The barbarism of the country begins to engulf the city population. Only small islands of civilized life are left, the senatorial aristocracy of the late Empire and the clergy; but both, save for a section of the clergy, are gradually swallowed up by the advancing tide of barbarism.

In the face of a phenomenon which touches every aspect of a society's life, clearly no single cause can be isolated. We are in the face of an interacting process of great complexity, operating over a long period of time. Jones' summary and final dictum are apt:[38]

I have outlined what seem to me to be the principal causes of the empire's decline, and of its collapse in the West. It would be difficult, and probably profitless, to attempt to weigh

45

their relative importance, for they interacted upon one another so as to form a single complex. The strategic vulnerability of the west not only exposed it to severe military pressure, but diminished the economic resources on which its defence was based, while its economic disequilibrium reduced its military manpower. The decline of public spirit led to the growth of the bureaucracy, and the weight of bureaucratic control crushed public spirit, while the heavy financial burden it entailed doubtless contributed to the general apathy of the population. Other-worldliness weakened the economic and military resources of the empire, and the resulting distress and defeats made men turn away from this world and set their hopes on another. The decline and fall of the Roman empire was the result of a complex of interacting causes which the historian disentangles at his peril.

But operationally – at the core – was a simple fact: Marcus Aurelius, the last of the emperors in the two centuries of peace, could not pay his troops; the revenues available to the Empire could not be maintained; and they could not be maintained because there was no technology available capable of yielding a progressive increase in the productivity of agriculture and in engaging those who flowed to the cities in a rapidly expanding industrial process.

Although he flatly rejects an economic explanation of the decay of the ancient world, Rostovtzeff poses a haunting series of questions:[39] 'The problem remains. Why was the victorious advance of capitalism stopped? Why was machinery not invented? Why were the business systems not perfected? Why were the primal forces of primitive economy not overcome? They were gradually disappearing; why did they not disappear completely?'

And Toynbee, with his view of civilizations as a whole, suddenly throws out this proposition:[40]

The balance might perhaps have been redressed in civilization's favour by bringing civilization's technical resources into play ... Alexandria's toy turbine steam engine, applied to locomotion, could have solved the Roman army's logistical problems; and suggestions for eking out man-power by mechanization were presented in a Latin treatise on military questions written, by an author unknown, in the fourth century of the Christian Era. But the practical application of scientific discoveries never appealed to the Hellenic imagination. So the strain on the imperial frontier defence force increased with the passage of time; and this strain was transmitted from the frontier to the interior in the form of rising costs to the taxpayer for less efficient military protection.

In short, like Athens, Rome generated the power and resources to create an empire; but it could not generate over a long period of time the resources to maintain the peace and prosperity which were its universal appeal when Augustus came to power and made his first dispositions.

For our narrow purposes, what can we conclude?

First, buffeting in the then international arena of power set the terms for domestic politics in the Italian Peninsula, while war and the imperial necessity forced the elaboration of a complex system of law, administration, taxation, and military organization.

Second, more specifically, the resolution of the domestic struggle over land-

46

holding, interacting with requirements of imperial administration and defense, defeated the forces of wide-based republicanism, weakened, even, the Senate, and left rule by emperor and an elaborate bureaucracy as the only realistic alternative.

Third, the political base for imperial policy was initially found, in part, with new urban groups, associated with trade and supply to the military forces.[41] But, as with the supporters of Pericles, they did not command the technological means to increase agricultural productivity or supply industrial jobs to those who flocked to the cities.

Fourth, as the system labored under burdens it could not sustain, the struggle for the extra margin of input to government became more desperate, yielding, with Diocletian, an absolutist rule which violated definitively the privileges and status which the Roman elite had sought and gained – and had then seen attenuated – as Rome moved from city-state to nation to empire, gripped by an environment of conflicting sovereignties that never permitted stable equilibrium among the imperatives of security, welfare, and the constitutional order.

But, of course, this reasonably clear mechanism of interaction is incomplete without a recognition of the loss of faith and morale in the imperial enterprise as a whole, the suffusion of weariness and fatalism, and the rise of Christianity, with all its consequences.[42]

CHINA: CYCLES WITH CONTINUITY OF CULTURE

The Athenian and Roman empires were overwhelmed, fragmented, and, ultimately, suppressed. In China, a nation was built and unified. It maintained, for very long periods, its essential contours, and, along with it, the continuity of a great culture.

To be sure, from time to time China was subject to fragmentation and periods of regional conflict when there was little or no effective central rule. At times it pressed its borders out to include other peoples. And there was a continuing problem of maintaining the borders against others, with engagements of varying intensity, complex interaction between cultures, and phases of conquest – or limited conquest – by outer barbarians who were only partially absorbed by those over whom they exercised power.

Nevertheless, in China one studies primarily cycles in domestic organization and politics over the centuries, within a continuous civilization, rather than the rise and fall of civilizations which are transient, despite the long shadows they cast on the minds of those who followed.

This may have been due, in part, to China's size and population relative to its neighbors. The take-over of all of China was always a formidable undertaking.

And, as Karl Wittfogel has so strongly pressed upon us, it may also be because to organize the water supply, especially in the Yangtze Valley, sturdy imperial institutions and powers were required to maintain the public works and permit the crops to be grown. Although responsibility for this welfare function helped shape Chinese government and the bureaucracy, including the claim for large supplies of corvée labor, 'every dynasty was founded on military strength or by the transference of military power'.[43]

But the heart of Chinese history is the tale of some nine domestic dynastic cycles from the legendary Yü and Shang dynasties more than a millenium B.C. to the fall of the Manchus and the coming of the Republic in 1912. It is a tale to be taken seriously if only because it has been the way Chinese have tended to view their experience; although some modern scholars have come to feel that the dynastic cycle obscures important progressive changes in Chinese political life.[44]

The Chinese cyclical theory, in terms of human and institutional strength and frailty, has been well paraphrased by Mary Wright:[45]

In brief, the theory was this: A new dynasty at first experiences a period of great energy, and vigorous and able new officials put in order the civil and military affairs of the Empire. In the course of generations the new period of vigor is followed by a golden age. Territories acquired earlier are held, but no new territories are conquered. Learning and the arts flourish in an atmosphere of elegance. Agricultural production and the people's welfare are supported by the maintenance of peace, attention to public works, and limitations of taxes. This golden age, however, carries within it the seeds of its own decay. The governing class loses first the will and then the ability to meet the high standards of Confucian government. Its increasing luxury places a strain on the exchequer. Funds intended for irrigation, flood control, maintenance of public grain reserves, communications, and payment of the army are diverted by graft to private pockets. As morale is undermined, corruption becomes flagrant.

This process of decline may be retarded by the vigorous training of officials and people in the Confucian social philosophy, but the basic direction of events cannot be altered. Sooner or later, the governing class, blind to those reforms which alone can save it, taxes the peasants beyond endurance and fails to attend to the public welfare. Sporadic local rebellions result, necessitating additional taxes and the recruiting of troops from an increasingly disaffected population. Their stake in the existing order gone, the people express their disaffection in a great rebellion. If the rebellion is successful, the 'swarming bandits' become in the eyes of history the 'righteous forces'.

The great rebellion is usually successful. One of its leaders slowly consolidates his power by securing (1) military superiority; (2) support from the literati, to whom he offers a revived Confucian state that they will administer; and (3) support, at least tacit, from the peasantry, to whom he offers peace, land, reduced taxes, and a program of public works to protect the agricultural economy. The new dynasty thus begins where its predecessor began, and its destiny will follow the same pattern.

Are we to take this doctrine as conclusive? Are we to take as the kernel of truth over the centuries the initial legend of Yü and Shang that their dynasties failed as 'the result of the wickedness of a final representative who gave himself to debauchery and misgovernment'?[46] Or are there more material bases for this cyclical experience?

The body of material on movements in Chinese population assembled and analyzed by Ping-ti Ho is impressive, although the data are inherently fragmentary.[47] They reveal fluctuations over the centuries which tend to support the theory and conclusion of Malthus' Chinese predecessor Hung Liang-chi (1746–1809):[48]

1. The increase in the means of subsistence and the increase of population are not in direct proportion. The population within a hundred years or so can increase from five-fold to twenty-fold, while the means of subsistence, due to the limitation of the land-area, can increase only from three to five times.
2. Natural checks like flood, famine and epidemic, cannot diminish the surplus population.
3. There are more people depending on others for their living than are engaged in productive occupations.
4. The larger the population, the smaller will be the income *pro rata*; but expenditure and the power of consumption will be greater. This is because there will be more people than goods.
5. The larger the population, the cheaper labor will be, but the higher will be the prices of goods. This is because of the over-supply of labor and over-demand for goods.
6. The larger the population, the harder it will be for the people to secure a livelihood. As expenditure and power of consumption become greater than the total wealth of the community, the number of unemployed will be increased.
7. There is unequal distribution of wealth among the people.
8. Those who are without wealth and employment will be the first to suffer and die from hunger and cold, and from natural calamities like famine, flood and epidemics. Some may ask: 'Do Heaven and Earth have remedies?' The answer is that their remedies are in the form of flood, drought, sicknesses and epidemics. But those unfortunate people who die from natural calamities do not amount to more than 10 to 20 per cent of the population. Some may ask: 'Does the government have remedies?' The answer is that its methods are to exhort the people to develop new land, to practice more intensive farming, to transfer people from congested areas to virgin soils, to reduce the fiscal burden, to prohibit extravagant living and the consumption of luxuries, to check the growth of landlordism, and to open all public granaries for relief when natural calamities strike . . . In short, during a long reign of peace Heaven and Earth could not but propagate the human race, yet their resources that can be used to the support of mankind are limited. During a long reign of peace the government could not prevent the people from multiplying themselves, yet its remedies are few.

It would be wrong to rule out the hypothesis that sustained periods of rule could lead to the weakening of the fiber of the administrators and the institutions they managed; or that the succession of emperors might yield periods of weak executive leadership. But there is much in the ebb and flow of Chinese history to suggest that the expansion in population in a period of peace and order might have set in motion pressures in the society which ultimately sapped the prosperity of the empire and the capacity of the emperor to mobilize the resources necessary to maintain both the military forces at the frontiers and the great public works of irrigation and transport upon which the welfare of China depended.

Although the role of population pressure in the whole sequence of Chinese dynastic history cannot be documented with confidence, its part in the downfall of the Manchu dynasty is reasonably firm. Ho concludes his studies on population:[49]

> ... it may be guessed that China's population, which was probably at least 65,000,000 around 1400, slightly more than doubled by 1600, when it was probably about 150,000,000. During the second quarter of the seventeenth century the nation suffered severe losses in population, the exact extent of which cannot be determined. It would appear that the second half of the seventeenth century was a period of slow recovery, although the tempo of population growth was increased between 1683 and 1700. The seventeenth century as a whole probably failed to register any net gain in population. Owing to the combination of favorable economic conditions and kindly government, China's population increased from about 150,000,000 around 1700 to perhaps 313,000,000 in 1794, more than doubling in one century. Because of later growth and the lack of further economic opportunites, the population reached about 430,000,000 in 1850 and the nation became increasingly impoverished.

What that impoverishment meant to Chinese rural families is suggested by C. C. Chang's estimate of per capita acreage (measured in mou):[50]

1685	5.43	1766	4.07
1724	4.83	1812	2.85
1753	4.43	1872	2.49

Thus, the Manchu dynasty faced the intrusion of the West in mid-nineteenth century at a time of inherent vulnerability and trouble, as the Taiping Rebellion revealed.

It is tempting to introduce into the model of the cycle the notion that the military conflicts, which tended to mark its latter phase, were the result of pressure for land induced by population increase. But there is no firm evidence that the Chinese were caught up, like imperial Athens, in a compulsion to extend their territory or their trade to maintain the financial basis of the state. One general theory of China's relations with the people on its frontiers is, of course, Naitō's cycles in cultural extension and external pressure, cited earlier (p. 48, n44). The more general view is one of complex interaction, in which '"barbarian" vigor helped to regenerate the political process by setting the dynastic cycle in motion at times when the empire under Chinese rulers had fallen into chaos or decay'.[51] It is decay at the center rather than either internal imperial pressure or the wickedness of the outer barbarians which is generally held accountable for the success of the nomads with their horses.[52]

SOME CONCLUSIONS

The cycle emerges as the natural pattern of pre-Newtonian societies.

There are cases of relatively static equilibrium at low levels of technology and of violence among competing sovereignties; and this capacity to persist holds even, perhaps, for cases of tribes which developed the essentials of central government to consolidate conquest of other peoples, when they did not press excessively towards further expansion. But our knowledge of tribal history over the sweep of centuries is imperfect; and from what we do know, there is also some suggestion, at least, of a Malthusian cycle.

In the upswing of cycles in the more complex cases, what we would now call modernization takes place over a wide front: economic and political. One can, in effect, observe many of the preconditions for take-off:

— an improvement of communications and an enhanced sense of nationhood;

— an expansion in agriculture, of transport and irrigation works, and intensified exchanges with the cities;

— an enlargement of external, as well as internal, commerce;

— an expansion in manufactures within the limits of existing industrial technology;

— a rise in the number, confidence and political influence of men of commerce and industry, of bureaucrats, and of technical and professional groups associated with modern urban activities;

— an emergence of governmental structures with important degrees of specialization and even some sub-group autonomy within the framework of imperial rule;

— and a spreading through the society, during the phase of prosperity, of secular standards for judging the performance of men and the pursuit of secular objectives by the people. To a degree, and up to a point, military requirements accelerate modernization. But the costs of war, in all its dimensions, outweigh its stimulus; and, soon or late, depending on the intensity of conflict, the system is sent into a self-reinforcing decline.

As Eisenstadt perceives, the mechanism of decline is the struggle of the rulers for inputs of resources to meet demands beyond the capacity of the system to supply. He sees the decline of the bureaucratic empires as

characterized by a shrinking supply of the free economic and manpower resources available. This was manifested by the depletion of mobile manpower; by the decreasing importance of exchange and of monetary means; by the growing political apathy of many groups; and by the lack of adequate personnel to perform the major bureaucratic and administrative tasks. This diminution of free resources was usually initiated by the excessive demands of the rulers and by the conflicts between the more flexible and the aristocratic groups, and created a vicious circle in the political and social processes of these societies.[53]

Although we know less than we would wish to know about population movements in the ancient empires, the mechanism of technological constraint appears to be more complex than a simple shortage of food in the face of an expanding population: the devastation of war and the attractions of the city pull men off the land; the limits of agricultural technology prevent an adequate increase in production; the limits of industrial technology prevent full and productive employment in the cities, throwing welfare burdens on the state which become increasingly burdensome in the face of simultaneous and enlarging claims of security policy; the struggle for Eisenstadt's 'free economic resources' leads to levels of taxation so high that they accelerate rather than stem the decay.

Custom and the elders rule in the simplest cases examined; but conflict and conquest lead to kingdoms and empires. The requirements for expanded inputs lead, on the upswing, to improvements in administration and, even, to a widening of the ruler's political base. In the downswing, his methods harden in the face of an increasingly desperate struggle. Where experiments emerge in democratic and republican governments, war, again, is ultimately their enemy. Empire requires centralized bureaucratic management whose imperatives erode the freedoms, as well as the resources, at the center.

With few exceptions the story of pre-Newtonian politics is suffused with a sense that land is scarce and finite, and so is trade: what one class or sovereignty gains, another must lose. Although technological limits vary, there is no pervading awareness that innovation could be an extra factor of production available to soften the clash within nations or among them.

And, in fact, it is not until the industrial revolution comes, and demonstrates its productivity, that this underlying harshness is at least partially lifted from men's affairs. And the industrial revolution came none too soon. Eighteenth century Britain moved forward in agriculture, trade, and manufactures, notably after mid-century. But population and urbanization proceeded more briskly; and an ominous shift to wheat imports occurred. Imports were required in two years during the 1750s; twice also, but on a larger scale, in the 1760s; in five years of the 1770s; four times in the 1780s; and in eight years of the 1790s.[54]

Ashton's conclusion is relevant to the centuries before as well as those which followed.[55]

The central problem of the age was how to feed and clothe and employ generations of children outnumbering by far those of any earlier time. Ireland was faced by the same problem. Failing to solve it, she lost in the 'forties about a fifth of her people by emigration or starvation and disease. If England had remained a nation of cultivators and craftsmen, she could hardly have escaped the same fate, and, at best, the weight of a growing population must have pressed down the spring of her spirit. She was delivered, not by her rulers, but by those who, seeking no doubt their own narrow ends, had the wit and resource to devise new intruments of production and new methods of administering industry.

The British take-off – and its diffusion – broke, at last, the cyclical pattern under which men had lived for all of previous recorded history.

CHAPTER 3

THE POLITICS OF THE PRECONDITIONS FOR TAKE-OFF

A GENERAL FRAMEWORK

Introduction

We consider here a period in the evolution of a society dated by an end-point; that is, by the beginning of its first sustained phase of industrialization, the take-off. And we examine how interactions within the political system of security factors, economic forces, and constitutional changes related to the moment when the society began to absorb as a more or less regular matter the stock and flow of modern technology hitherto not applied systematically to its round of life.

This is, in effect, the period during which a traditional society becomes sufficiently modernized in all its dimensions to undertake the first serious, even if limited, phase of the enterprise which, more than any other, is the hallmark of modernity; that is, industrialization, including, of course, regular innovation in agriculture, transport, communication, and other services. We are considering, therefore, a complex as well as critical transitional process. It is, in effect, mainly this process to which the bulk of contemporary literature on the politics and sociology of non-Western societies has been addressed, as well as the 'early modern' history of Europe.

The Dating of the Preconditions: Short and Long Views

If the initiation of take-off is taken as the end-point, where do we begin?

There are two options. The first is to define the preconditions as a relatively short period of usually active public and/or private preparation, before industrialization first takes hold. The second option is to reach much further back, taking into account earlier indecisive reactions to the impact of modernizing influences and political and economic movements in the direction of modernity, which, while not definitive, sometimes abortive – and even negative (e.g. Japan, 1640) – had long-run significance.

To set dates for the beginning of the preconditions period is inherently an arbitrary and impressionistic business; for there are no dramatic surges of production in particular sectors which serve to date later growth stages. The task is particularly difficult for the longer sweep, where each of the dates could be legitimately pushed backward in time to catch earlier experiences of greater or lesser relevance to later times. The dates given in table 2 for selected nations suggest, at least, the kind of intervals involved.[1]

TABLE 2. *Preconditions for take-off: some dates for nine countries*

Country	Initial date: long sweep (say)	Initial date: short period (say)	Take-off begins
England (UK)	1688 (Glorious Revolution)	1750	1780s
United States	1763 (end of Seven Years' War)	1788	1840s[a]
France	1660 (Colbert)	1789	1830s
Germany (Prussia)	1713 (Frederick William I)	1815	1850s
Russia	1696 (Peter the Great)	1861	1890s
Japan	1853 (Commodore Perry arrived in Tokyo Bay)	1868	1880s
China	1842 (Opium Wars)	1895[b]	1950s[c]
Turkey	1789 (Selim III)	1908	1930s
Mexico	1877 (Porfirio Díaz)	1920	1940s

[a] New England began a regional take-off in the 1820s.
[b] Because it opened up a vigorous stage of railway building, mine exploitation, and limited industrialization, the Treaty of Shimonoseki is taken as the starting point for the Chinese preconditions period in the narrower sense.
[c] Take-off aborts, 1958–68.

When we come later in this chapter to illustrate briefly this way of looking at politics, we shall take the longer view of the preconditions. This is because our focus here is politics rather than economics; and the political performance of nations during the later preconditions and take-off cannot be well understood without reference to earlier experiences with modernization.

But even this longer look at the preconditions period cannot explain how the political life of nations has responded to modernization. Over the centuries, cultures have gradually been formed out of the interplay of men and their environment. Climate and geography certainly played a part; contacts with others in the process of making a nation, including phases of domination by men of different cultures or more benign external contacts; and other factors we, perhaps, do not even understand. Important aspects of political behavior flow from these abiding patterns of national cultures, yielding distinctive national styles; that is, typical ways of acting and dealing with problems.[2]

Technical Conditions for the Transition to Modernity

It was the central theme of chapter 2 that pre-Newtonian politics is to be distinguished from that of later times by the constraints imposed by technological ceilings which existed in the absence of attitudes of mind and of systematic action which would have provided innovation as a more or less regular flow. Ultimately, these constraints, operating in complex ways, were judged the cause of the cyclical patterns typical of the history of traditional societies. They limited the inputs available to governments relative to the outputs required to sustain them either at their existing level of welfare or to fulfill commitments to military activities to which they were committed by themselves or by others around them.

It was also asserted that the acceptance of a Newtonian perspective on the possibilities of understanding and manipulating the physical world was a necessary but not sufficient condition for the transition to modernity.

What were the technical conditions for sufficiency?

The most basic condition for sufficiency was the existence not only of a corps of inventors but also of a new kind of entrepreneur (private, public or both) willing to engage capital in enterprise whose risks differed substantially from those of traditional agriculture, commerce, and banking. In industry, the relative illiquidity of agriculture is combined with the more mercurial market risks of commerce and banking, and with that special risk (and psychological inhibition) that the installation of new techniques occasions. The extent of the innovator's risk has, however, a compensation: if successful, his profits are great. And if he is loyal to his initial commitment (and the price elasticity of demand for his product permits), expansion can take place rapidly from the ploughback of profits. Thus, initially small commitments of capital to industry can often suffice to set in motion an ongoing process, whereas a higher threshold has to be overcome before significant volumes of social overhead capital can be accumulated.

But the existence of a minimum stock of social overhead capital is also a condition for sufficiency.

While the fabricating or processing sectors are the hard core of industrialization, the society cannot progressively modernize unless certain non-industrial sectors expand in the early stage of development – to a degree before industrialization, but also as industrialization proceeds. Industrialization can be slowed down or aborted by a lack of agricultural output, foreign exchange, sources of power, or by a lack of sufficient trained men of minimum competence.

Agricultural output must expand to feed the enlarging and increasingly

56

urban population, at least until industrialization has so progressed that foreign exchange can be earned economically and massively to finance food imports.

Increased imports of industrial equipment or industrial raw materials must be provided for by enlarged exports, based on expanded (and usually improved) exploitation of natural resources and/or by foreign exchange economies permitted by the development of import-substitution industries.

Above all, the society must mobilize from its own resources (and, where possible, from capital imports) the materials, labor, and skills required for a massive buildup of social overhead capital, notably to provide education, transport, and energy. The proportion of total investment in industry itself is always relatively modest in an ongoing industrial system. It is, of course, particularly so in the early stages of industrialization.

Technically, it is the requirement of expansion in these three nonindustrial sectors which makes the role of the political process in the preconditions for take-off so important; for, with few exceptions, the buildup of an initial minimum quantum of social overhead capital (including the role of education), the bringing about of expansion in agriculture, and the generation of a supply of imports adequate for modernization have required important interventions and leadership by national governments.

Once begun, industry, in an environment of adequate social overhead capital (including men of modern training and orientation), can be infectious: backward, laterally, and forward. Modern industrial activity sets up behind it a demand for inputs of raw materials and machinery which require, in turn, an extension of the contriving attitudes and methods. Laterally, modern industrial activity surrounds itself with men, services, and institutions whose existence strengthens the foundations for industrialization as an ongoing process: a disciplined working force organized around the hierarchies decreed by technique; professional men to handle the problems of law and relations to the various markets for input and products; urban overhead capital; banking and commercial services. Forward, modern industrial activities may be induced, either by cutting the cost of an input to another industry or by creating a bottleneck whose removal would evidently be profitable and, therefore, attract inventive talent and entrepreneurship.

This many-sided process can yield postponement not merely of Ricardian diminishing returns but of Malthusian population pressure. The rise in real income it grants, altering the old fatalistic expectations about the level of welfare, may induce a new calculus with respect to family size in which the joys of the new baby in the household are foresworn in favor of a better life for those who remain; and this shift is likely to be strengthened by the greater net cost of children in urban than in rural life.

Taken all together, these appear to be the linked elements which, along with the inventor, define the central technical difference between a traditional and a modern economy.

When introduced into the two models of traditional societies presented at the opening of chapter 2, they remove the ceiling and open the way to self-sustained growth.

The Underlying Process of Modernization

But how little they really tell us about the travail and the complexity of the process through which traditional societies must pass before industrial growth becomes their normal condition!

Embedded within this somewhat antiseptic characterization of the conditions for sustained industrialization is, in fact, a profound set of changes which touch every dimension of the society. The introduction into a traditional society of the Newtonian view of the physical world, and a corps of innovators and effective industrial entrepreneurs; the changes in both social structure and in politics required before the preconditions for industrial growth are achieved in the key non-industrial sectors; the development of an institutional, social, and psychological setting such that the society reacts positively to the potential spreading effects of modern industrial activity – all of this is a way of stating that a profound revolution has occurred.

Leaving aside, for a moment, the economics of the transition to modernization, how are these revolutions detonated and how may they be described in an orderly way?

The general answer is, of course, that traditional societies were fractured – losing their unity, cohesion, prestige, and self-respect – by contact with more advanced societies. The impact of more advanced societies has taken three distinguishable forms: physical intrusion, including both colonial rule and military intrusion short of colonialism;[3] economic example or pressure; and the communication of ideas and skills.[4]

These intrusions violated, or threatened to violate, the security of traditional societies and pushed them into a transitional process, often a lengthy and turbulent process; for it is one thing to intrude on a traditional society, introduce within it certain modern elements and new dynamic trends; but it is quite a different matter to achieve a working system sufficiently modernized to mount a take-off. Before a society sufficiently modernized for take-off can be achieved – before the modern elements within it can become dominant and effective even over a limited economic range – a profound and positive series of changes must take place at every level.

Psychologically, men must transform or adapt the old culture in ways

58

which make it compatible with modern activities and institutions. The face-to-face relations and warm, powerful family ties of a traditional society must give way, in degree, to new, more impersonal systems of evaluation in which men are judged by the way they perform specialized functions in the society. In their links to the nation, to their professional colleagues, to their political parties, to their labor unions, men must find a partial alternative for the powerful, long-tested ties and symbols of the traditional life, centered on family, clan, and region. And new hierarchies, based on function, must come to replace those rooted in land ownership and tradition.

The balance of social and political power must thus shift, in degree, from the village to the city, from the tasks and virtues of agricultural life to those of commerce, industry, and modern administration. The people must come to accept new forms for the organization and for the transfer of political power. They must begin, in a process with many difficult stages, to judge politics and politicians in terms of policies rather than merely inherited status or even personality; and, if they are to emerge as democracies, they must develop forms for granting and transferring power by registering consent.

To achieve these conditions requires the passage of time: time for the social structure to be altered; time for new political attitudes and institutions to be created and consolidated; time for the skills and habits and institutions on which capital formation depends to be built. Above all, time must pass for new generations to succeed one another, each finding the environment, techniques, and goals of modernization a bit more familiar and acceptable.

At every step of the way, moreover, the forces making for modernization confront elements of resistance and of distraction which slow the process of modernization – if, indeed, they do not altogether frustrate it for a time.[5] There is nothing which decrees that the forces of modernization will win prompt or automatic victory. It is, in fact, of the nature of the transitional process that the impulses making for modernization live in active contention with powerful forces tending to retard and to frustrate the transformation of the traditional society to full modernity. The struggle takes place not only as between groups with different interests and aspirations; but it takes place also within the minds of men torn between the attractions of what modernization appears to promise and attachments to values and institutions of the traditional life.

It is against this broad background, touching every dimension of society's life, that politics, in the narrow sense, proceeded.

In colonial societies, after a certain point in the revolution induced by the metropolitan power, the energies of those who had acquired some modern skills tended to focus around the security goal of independence; and this objective helped to unify men who, in fact, might take quite different views

59

of the modernization process and who might bring to public life quite different motives, interests, and objectives.

Where the colonial problem did not exist, the transitional process was moved forward, in different degrees in each case, by a sense of military inferiority and national danger; by the pressure of the educated elite for a chance to exercise their new skills; by the spreading perception that higher standards of welfare were attainable; and by enlarged possibilities for profit.

But it was also moved forward by a negative fact. The fracture of the traditional society opened the way for men of political ambition – men who enjoyed the exercise of power – to contend for the vacated or weakened places of traditional authority. Transitional societies which did not experience colonial rule – or newly independent ex-colonial states – generally underwent a period of unstable rule in which various individuals and groups sought to seize and consolidate power. These struggles for power were often merely just that: the contention of men for positions of prestige and authority, quite unrelated to movements towards or away from modernization. But, over substantial periods of time, these struggles for power reflected and became suffused with the views and objectives of various specific groups in the society who wished to achieve – or forestall – various aspects of the modernization process. The raw struggle for power in succession to the traditional leaders or the colonial power, or both in combination, thus became in itself an active element in the transitional process.

A Way of Analyzing the Transition

What kind of intellectual order can we establish in this process of contention, where economic, psychological, social, and political factors interact in a unique cultural setting determined by previous centuries of pre-modern history?

As a first approximation, it is possible to discern certain key characteristics in the process of interaction.

First, it should be noted that, once the traditional society is fractured, certain forces operate more or less steadily to move the society towards modernization: widened contact and communication with more modern societies; the rise of trade and of cities; and the emergence of new generations less committed than their elders to the old ways, born into a world where modern activity is increasingly a fact of life rather than a perceived break with the past. Taken together, these mutually reinforcing factors decree that there will be a gradual shift in the society, yielding an increasing proportion of persons knowledgeable in modern skills; tending to accept, in part, modern ideas and attitudes; basing their lives increasingly on the cities and on urban points of view. There is, to a degree, then, a kind of automatic slide in the direction of modernization set up by the nature of the forces which have fractured the traditional society.

But the second major feature of the transition is that there are limits to the pace of this slide towards modernization. The rate of training of modern men is dependent on the scale of travel and education abroad and on the creation of modern educational institutions within the society; the rate of increase of trade and the growth of cities have built-in limitations, as well as the possibility of wide variation, depending on the particular economic setting in which the transition occurs, notably the degree of population pressure; and the rhythm of human life itself sets limits to the sequence of generations and their perspectives.

And beyond these technical damping factors there is the possibility of wide variation in the extent to which different inherited traditional cultures and social structures, and the national operating styles they yield, prove amenable to modernization or resistant to its requirements.

Within, as it were, the floor and the ceiling set by the force of the modernizing elements, on the one hand, and the power of the constraints, on the other, certain particular problems with profound dynamic significance tend to emerge as central at different stages of the modernization sequence. How each of these problems is resolved helps determine the pace and the contours of modernization.

The first of these modernizing problems centers on the nature of the intrusion of more advanced societies and the character of the reaction to them by the traditional society. The early phase of the transitional process is likely to be taken up with this essentially international relationship, and it is likely to yield a coalition, united by resentment of the foreign presence or threat, whose goal is national independence or increased power. The security dimension of this first phase of modernization has helped determine that soldiers often emerged as the first new men in the transitional period.

In the next phase, the focus of modernization is likely to shift to the domestic scene – and to politics. Some version of a struggle is likely to occur between traditional and modernizing elements and, even, among contending modern elements; e.g. France in the 1790s; Germany, 1848–66; Mexico, 1911–20; China, 1927–49; Indo-China, 1954–. The struggle normally focused around these questions: Who shall control power in the society newly independent or freshly committed to modern goals? On what principles shall modernization be based?

If this struggle results in clear-cut victory for a group seriously committed to modernization, a third phase is likely to occur in which alternative directions of policy are explored, including this key question: To what extent should the emerging but limited modernizing energies be turned to redress old wrongs and humiliations as opposed to concentrating those energies on further modernization at home? Or, put another way, should dignity be sought primarily in modernization itself or in some form of compensating assertiveness on the world scene?

How that question is answered helps determine when the technical conditions for take-off are achieved. But it is policy and the allocation of scarce resources, rather than independence or merely the new locus of power, which come to the center of the stage of politics.

This perspective on the modernization process has a particular meaning for its economic dimension. Economic progress must be regarded as both a result of movement towards modernization in other dimensions and as a force making for further change. Economic progress needs, for example, a minimum group of modern men in the society before a take-off can begin; but the expansion of modern economic activities itself trains more such essential men. Similarly, economic progress usually needs a certain degree of central direction before it can get well under way; for example, with respect to the buildup of social overhead capital. But a central government gains in efficiency, authority, and stability by the very act of taking effective leadership in economic development.

In terms of social groups and their outlook, economic progress needs effective elements in the elite to accept growth as a goal before growth can get well under way. But economic progress itself creates new kinds of professionals, new urban technicians, new attitudes in the working force, which help shift social authority away from traditional attitudes and vested interests.

The politics of the preconditions period is, then, unlike that of pre-Newtonian life. It is not inherently cyclical. It moves – against resistances, irregularly, fitfully, often with setbacks – but it moves in an interacting, self-reinforcing process towards the norms of modernity, until the take-off occurs.

The transition is, on this view, initiated by some form of intrusion from abroad; and it is first necessary to examine the character of the intrusion and the reaction or reactions to it. That nationalistic reaction is likely in time to merge with the interests and motives of others who, for reasons of profit, domestic power or status – or whatever – are prepared to act or press for the modernization of the economy. It is also likely to interact with the assertiveness of those who have felt repressed or unjustly treated in the traditional society and who exploit the uncertain character of transitional politics to make their grievances felt and to press for remedy. These convergent pressures are likely to develop strong impetus, in turn, to alter the political system. Whether formal constitutional changes occur under the pressure of revolution or otherwise – and when they occur – depends on the particular historical situation of each country. It depends, in particular, on how the old system adjusted to new imperatives and new men; and on whether new men could find consensus among themselves.

But whether revolutionary political changes occurred along the way or not, a temptation might arise to external adventure, whether to right old wrongs or otherwise.[6] In those cases, security and welfare factors might conflict and the preconditions process could be complicated and prolonged, depending on the character of the military adventure, its scale, and outcome.

If this view of the politics of the preconditions period is valid, its principal characteristics should be revealed by posing and answering these three complex questions:

— Did intrusion by a more advanced power play a part in the preconditions period? If so did a mood of reactive nationalism contribute not only to modernization but also to military or diplomatic effort to expand abroad?

— Were there major constitutional changes during the preconditions period and to what extent were they related to intrusion from abroad or economic and social change within the society?

— Did public policy play an active role in preconditioning the economy for take-off?

Taken together, they are designed to permit us to explore in reasonable order certain critical security, welfare, and constitutional dimensions of the politics of the preconditions period.

HISTORICAL NOTES ON THREE KEY ISSUES OF THE POLITICS OF THE PRECONDITIONS

Prefatory note. The analytical notes on historical cases which follow are designed for two purposes: to suggest the reality of the three key facets of the politics of the preconditions period developed above; and, equally, to suggest the variety of the patterns they assumed in the light of unique national histories and relationships to external intrusion.

The Role of External Intrusion and External Adventure

Britain

If a sense of vulnerability in the face of more advanced powers is taken to be the primary instrument for the transmission of modernization, this initial case deserves special attention. In theory, all one requires for the diffusion of modernization in an inter-connected world is a single case of modernization, if one assumes that the relative military and economic advantages of prior take-off will lead more advanced nation states to press against the less developed and evoke a compensatory response.

The question arises, therefore: Did external intrusion – or its threat – play any role in the British case or was it *sui generis*?

Looking back as well as forward from 1688, I would still hold a view expressed some time ago.[7]

The British experience of freeing itself from the Church in Rome, and from the Spanish power that backed it in the sixteenth century; the phase of relatively spacious Elizabethan nationalism; the painfully achieved national consensus of the seventeenth century, brought about by 1688, accompanied by an obsessive effort to break Britain free of what was regarded as the quasi-colonial relationship to the Dutch; the eighteenth-century struggles with the larger and apparently more powerful French . . . all of this is a not wholly unfamiliar story of reactive nationalism, creating a setting in which modernization – in its post-1688 context – was a widely sanctioned, and even encouraged, goal.

It is possible, then, that British nationalism, transcending caste loyalties, created by a series of intrusions and challenges to a lesser island off a dominant mainland, may have been a major force in creating a relatively flexible social matrix within which the process of building the preconditions for take-off was hastened in Britain; and in that limited sense the first take-off takes its place, despite many unique features, with the others.

In particular, the hard-won political consensus and domestic reconciliation represented by 1688[8] created a setting for the non-conformists of reduced – but still real – deprivation, but also a setting of open educational and economic opportunity. And the non-conformists were foremost in linking the world of Newtonian attitudes to the gadgets and new enterprises which ultimately set in motion the industrial revolution. As Crouzet concludes:[9]

England experienced a real outburst of inventiveness, which in France was almost completely lacking, and this decisive British superiority in ingenuity and willingness to innovate is the basic fact which has accentuated the structural discrepancy between the two economies during the second part of the eighteenth century . . .

The political reconciliation of 1688 also created a base of national stability and confidence from which the British, having surpassed and come to terms with the Dutch, could contest a France containing more than three times its population.

The struggle with France dominated the period preceding the British take-off; and it was costly. The arena of commerce was widening out in earnest, from India to the West Indies; and the two nations clashed at many points. Despite the prevailing tradition of limited war for limited objectives, the chronic conflict imposed a heavy burden on the finances of both countries, although the six million British were better organized to carry the load than the nineteen million French.[10]

But the continued mercantile struggle had two effects which advanced the preconditions process. First, it tightened the social and political link between those more traditional groups concerned with the nation's security and the newer men interested in profit.[11] Second, the British contact with India confirmed the place of Indian cotton goods as a factor in the British domestic market. The interplay between those imports and the rise of the British cotton industry is thus related to the mercantilist struggle.[12]

The balance sheet of Britain's eighteenth-century conflicts is difficult to cast; but Nef's central theme is relevant: Whatever the cost of the eighteenth-century wars, they were sufficiently restrained, as opposed to those ultimately unleashed by the industrial revolution, so as to be bearable without national disaster.[13]

In general, then, while Britain was never invaded, threat from abroad played a role in the preconditioning process: indirectly in helping find, after much travail, a national identity and a limited domestic religious reconciliation which freed and channelled the talents of the nonconformists; more directly through the mercantile and colonial struggle with eighteenth-century France which, in the end, provided both an expanding framework for trade and a national consensus that economic modernization was an appropriate objective of public policy. These political, social, and economic conditions formed part of the backdrop for the take-off in the 1780s; although it was only the differential economic development of Britain and France during the Revolutionary and Napoleonic Wars that consolidated the relative primacy of Britain – a primacy palpable by 1815.

France

The role of external intrusion and external adventure in French modernization must be understood against a background quite different from that of Britain.

The story of France is that of a larger nation which, to the east, faced not a protective body of water but an open land frontier, always latent with temptation or threat. It achieved an unstable primacy in the continental dynastic struggles of the seventeenth century and it staked out, but could not effectively hold, an impressive colonial position. Eighteenth-century French political life took its formal shape from the past, not the future: from a time of maximum *grandeur* achieved under absolutist monarchy in the face of the problems posed by the emergence of national states out of feudalism in a highly competitive and contentious continental setting.

From the remarkable but financially inadequate base created by Louis XIV at his peak, French absolutism suffered progressive erosion under the pressure of modernizing changes of social structure, attitude, and political purpose taking place within its society as well as from the cost of adventures without. Its fundamental constitutional crisis takes place a full century after that in Britain. The effort of Colbert and his successors to generate in support of the *ancien régime* the inputs required to match its requirements failed not because the resources were not technically available, but because they could not be mobilized under the constitutional terms set by the *ancien régime*. The privileges granted the nobility to assure their impotence and docility in relation to the King proved exceedingly costly to the sequence of distinguished finance ministers who struggled to keep the French monarchy viable.

But, in the end, intrusion from abroad does play a part in the French preconditions period: first, in the counter-revolutionary movements of the early 1790s; and, then, in the gathering sense, after 1815, that France was lagging behind Britain and others in industrialization. But the relative slowness of France in its modernization may have been related to a deep inner conviction, reaching back at least to Louis XIV, that it was, in some sense, naturally the leading power of Europe. Its reaction to the dangers and opportunities of the world of modern technology may have been, in part, a product of this inner historic complacency, reinforced by values from the past which regarded commerce and industry as second-order business.

But one phase of France's relation to the external world is not an exception but a rather dramatic illustration of a recurrent pattern; that is, the interplay of revolution, foreign reaction to the revolution, and then France's outward thrust.

From the beginning the Girondists looked abroad, as well as at home, to install their republican ideas – notably to Belgium and Alsace. They were challenged by the émigrés gathered in Coblenz, the priests who refused to accept the revolution, and, above all, by the Austrian Archduke at once concerned for the revolutionary precedent and his sister Marie Antoinette. War came when his young successor refused to respond to the Girondin ultimatum that the armed émigrés at Coblenz be dismissed from the territory of the Elector of Trèves. And so, in April 1792 Europe was plunged into twenty-three years of virtually continuous war.

It brought on the worst excesses of the Terror; bound French nationalism to the Revolution; evoked a new kind of popular army; yielded power to Napoleon and, through him, the legal and administrative structure of the modern French state. It diffused republican ideas throughout Europe; evoked, in turn, a new reactive nationalism from Madrid to Moscow; and laid the basis for the partial restoration of 1815.

In short, it was a critical phase in the political modernization of the European continent during its period of preconditions.

Like other massive external projections of revolution and reactive nationalism, the Revolutionary and Napoleonic wars, on balance, diverted France from its economic modernization.[14] But the statesmanship of the ultimate victors – that is, their concern for the stability of the restored French monarchy – left France without a revanchist grievance. France moved forward, after 1815, with disparate memories of a great revolution and a great external adventure endlessly to debate; but with no solid consensus on the meaning of its experience or on the substance of its national agenda. And there was neither the pressure of acute economic crisis nor the attractive force of great deposits of coal and iron to induce such a concentration of attention and energy.

Nevertheless, the gap between Britain and France in 1815 – indeed, the gap between Britain and continental Western Europe as a whole – set in motion forces which ultimately (by, say, 1873) brought the region much closer to uniformity in terms of level of economic modernization.[15] In part, the engine of French and continental transformation was public policy:[16]

For the state, British progress was a direct, unavoidable challenge. The governments of Europe had long come to look upon economic development as the key to a favourable balance of trade – hence wealth; to large tax revenues – hence power; and to stable employment – hence public order. They had traditionally encouraged enterprise as best they knew, cherishing especially those trades that furnish the means of war. Now they found the entire balance of economic forces upset. Industrialization was, from the start, a political imperative.

Britain's relative head-start was, in short, a kind of intrusion, in terms of power, which evoked a response in France and elsewhere – sluggish or purposeful – even if Britain did not, in fact, invade the continent.

But British manufactured goods did intrude; and, on the whole, benignly. And so did British capital, entrepreneurship, and technology, evoking mixed reactions not unlike those to be observed on the continent with respect to the United States in the 1950s and 1960s. Many on the European continent developed a frame of mind like Friedrich Harkort:[17]

A feeling of nationalism was also present in Harkort. An admirer of English political institutions, he resented the commercial and industrial monopoly of contemporary England. While he could start his own industries only with the help of English engineers and foremen, he longed for the day when German industries would be fully independent of English industries.

The preconditions for take-off after 1815 were, in a sense, the continent's reaction to *Le Défi Brittanique*.

Germany

The story of Prussia and the emergence of modern Germany involves a more straightforward role for military factors than that of France. As H. A. L.

Fisher wrote: 'Prussia was manufactured'; and it was manufactured by the Hohenzollerns out of a contentious military environment, for military purposes – to survive and to expand.

One can begin earlier, but it is with Frederick William I that Prussia's distinctive character becomes clear. As his son, Frederick the Great, summed up the evolution of affairs from 1688 to 1740:[18]

Under Frederick the First . . . Berlin had been the Athens of the North. Under Frederick William the First it became its Sparta. Its entire government was militarized. The capital became the stronghold of Mars. All the industries which serve the needs of armies prospered. In Berlin were established powder mills and cannon factories, rifle factories, etc. Frederick William the First strove less to create new industries than to abolish useless expenditures. Formerly, mourning had been ruinously expensive. Funerals were accompanied by extremely costly festivities. These abuses were abolished. Horses and carriages were no longer allowed to be draped in black, nor were black liveries given to servants. Henceforth people died cheaply. The military character of the government affected both customs and fashions. Society took a military turn. No one used more than three ells of cloth for a coat. The age of gallantry passed away. Ladies fled the society of men and the latter compensated themselves with carousals, tobacco, and buffoonery.

It was in this time of peace that a central administration was consolidated, taxes collected and the treasury filled, a good school system established, and a large army trained.

It was on these foundations that Frederick II seized Silesia and fought the desperate war which wracked Europe, and beyond, for the seven years down to 1763. Aside from consolidating his position in Silesia, the bloody struggle demonstrated the important negative fact that Prussia could survive in conflict against the great empires of Russia and Austria: 'Forged in such a flame of adversity, the Prussian will took on the hardness of steel, and by the gentler courts of Germany, where the arts flourished, was regarded as something minatory and barbaric.'[19]

But the Prussian state, erected in the eighteenth century, underwent a traumatic shock in the face of Napoleon's armies, his diplomacy, and French revolutionary ideas. Frederick William III was defeated at Auerstädt and Jena, 14 October 1806. Napoleon's subsequent settlement with his transient Russian ally on the raft on the Niemen River, was largely at Prussia's expense. Napoleon's exploitation of anti-Prussian as well as anti-Austrian sentiment among the lesser German states, and the diffusion to Germany of French revolutionary ideas and sentiments yielded, after 1815, a clear modernizing reaction. And Prussia remained the center of that German reaction in the wake of Napoleon's defeat, in part, because the Prussian rulers drew from their earlier humiliation significant political as well as military lessons. Politically and psychologically – as well as in the field – semi-modernized Prussia, built over the previous century, was judged by Prussian leaders incapable of dealing with a rampant post-revolutionary France. And steps were taken. Prussian towns were granted a measure of self-government and the plight of the peasantry was eased.[20]

Equally important, Prussia, and other German states, began to look to the other form of power which had generated to the West; namely, the British industrial revolution. New men of enterprise emerged, some out of the old nobility, some new to social status, in East Prussia and Upper Silesia, Hamburg, Bremen, and the Rhineland.[21] But the military and power implications of industrialization were never far from the surface of Prussian thought in these years after 1815. A sense of German backwardness *vis-à-vis* Britain, but also of potentiality for unity and of enlarged power in Europe, became the framework of struggle, in 1848 and after, for the organization and destiny of modern Germany.

It was natural that doctrines appropriate to the status and policy of less developed nations confronted with a more advanced power should crystallize at this time, notably those of List who combined the outlook of Hamiltonian America with that of post-1815 Germany.

Russia

The Russia which Peter the Great dramatically began to open to the west had been shaped over the five previous centuries by a struggle for independence and identity against intrusive forces generated from the East and the West. Its culture, politics, and obsessions were rooted, on the one hand, in the two centuries of rule by the Golden Horde which fastened itself on Russia, after the Mongols were turned back at the gates of Vienna in 1241;[22] and then by the struggle against Swede and Pole which yielded finally in 1613 the accession of the first Romanov.[23]

In fact, the Russia of Ivan the Great (1462–1505) and Ivan the Terrible (1533–84) already owed something to architects and engineers from Western Europe; but the purposeful policy of Peter is an authentic benchmark in Russian modernization.

He wanted for Russia more than the accretion of power which the technology and administrative skill of Western Europe might supply. He responded to and wished to transmit to his nation something of the civilized amenities and quality of life he had experienced in his travels. And, even now, Leningrad is a monument to that aspiration. But, above all, he wanted the guns and ships and skills of administration necessary to fight his wars against Persian, Turk, and Swede. His reforms were incomplete; his victories, indecisive. But he set Russia on a new course.[24] For good or ill, he brought Russia once and for all into the equation of the balance of power of Europe; and the streams of Western ideas and technology never thereafter ceased to flow, erratic as the flow has sometimes been.

It is, of course, out of the interplay between Russia and the other participants in the endless European balance of power struggle of the eighteenth and nineteenth centuries that arose the intrusions and responses most immediately relevant to the preconditions for take-off.

There were three events of particular importance.

First, Napoleon's invasion. Unlike the perceptive response of Prussia to its humiliation at Jena and afterward, Russian policy turned reactionary rather than progressive. But beneath the surface, the experience of the invasion and, especially, Russia's enlarged role in Europe after 1815 brought an infusion of liberal thought and aspiration for a more modern Russia in military as well as intellectual circles, reflected by the ill-fated Decembrists of 1825, and beyond.

Second, there was the shock of the Crimean War. This time Russia did respond in something like the spirit of post-Jena Prussia. Alexander II's freeing of the serfs, reform of the judicial system, introduction of local government, and widening of the limits of press and academic freedom were major steps, despite their incompleteness and, in some cases, fragility. But the Czar, reforming from the top for reasons of state, could not engage the minds, the loyalties, or the assistance of the growing group of reforming intellectuals who speculated, theorized, or simply threw themselves into destructive enterprises against their nation's archaic rule and way of life. But the connection between the humiliation in war of a traditionalist regime by more modern adversaries and subsequent reforms is clear.

Third was the frustration of the Congress of Berlin in 1878. One aspect of Russia's post-1815 role in Europe was the evolution of the Pan-Slavic idea. As Russia lumbered towards modernization and the Turkish empire felt the weight of multiple and growing strains from within and without, the Russians began to posture as protector to their racial brothers. The Turkish repression of spreading revolts in Bosnia-Herzegovina, Montenegro, Serbia, and Bulgaria led to the Russian declaration of war in 1877 and to its victory in March 1878. But the other powers insisted, in the shadow of ultimatum, that the terms of the Russo-Turkish Treaty of San Stefano had to be renegotiated. In diplomatic isolation and from an inadequate military base, the Russians disgorged a good deal of what they had won.

The diplomatic lesson of German and Austrian unreliability as allies led Moscow to begin to look to Paris; but the experience as a whole strengthened the impulse, already gathering strength, to turn to industrialization.[25]

Historical notes on three key issues of the politics of the preconditions

Japan

The role of external intrusion and the reaction to it, in the case of Britain, France, Germany, and Russia, are complicated because they emerged into modernization out of the recurrent interactions among nation-states caught up in a competitive dynastic and colonial arena of conflict, within which wars, great and small, were endemic. The case of Japan, more isolated, is, in that sense, simpler and more straightforward.

The story begins with the negative decision of 1640 excluding all foreign trade and foreign contacts except for the few Dutchmen and Chinese permitted to operate at Nagasaki under rigid supervision. The Tokugawa, reflecting on the implications of foreign contacts which had been growing up in the previous century, decided that it was wise and possible to insulate the feudal empire in which they had come to power.

In a classic pattern of the Malthusian cycle, peace and prosperity, under conditions of limited technology, induced from, roughly, the middle of the eighteenth century a set of disruptive forces which weakened the economic, social, and political fabric of Tokugawa rule. The population surge begun in the mid-seventeenth century was arrested; but, as Lockwood notes, the slow population increase of the mid-nineteenth century reflected a 'precarious equilibrium . . . maintained only by famine, disease, abortion, infanticide, i.e., by operation of all the Malthusian checks save war'.[26] Commodore Perry confronted a Japan in 1853 already undergoing domestic strain, suffused for other reasons by the sense of a failing dynasty.

It was also a Japan whose leaders were conscious that retreat from modernity had already been tested and found wanting.

In fifteen years the forces gathered, under the leadership of the samurai, and a consensus was reached which took form in the Charter Oath of the reinstated emperor: 'Intellect and learning would be sought for throughout the world, in order to establish the foundations of Empire.'

In short, the beginnings of Japanese modernization are as clearcut a case of positive reaction to external intrusion as the inherently tangled patterns of history are likely to yield; but the promptness and clarity of the Japanese decision in dealing with the intrusions of the 1850s and 1860s must be understood, in part, against the background of a dynasty rendered highly vulnerable by the dynamics of the pre-Newtonian cycle and of a prior effort to fend off modernity, which had failed.

As Landes notes, it was the inescapable and potentially mortal nature of the challenge faced by Japan after 1853 which explains its subsequent pursuit of modernization with greater single-mindedness than post-1815 continental Europe:[27]

... how, with this limited recourse to the usual remedies for backwardness, did this latecomer accomplish these gains so quickly?

The answer, it seems to me, lies paradoxically in the severity of the challenge that confronted Japan in the middle of the last century. The steady aggrandizement of Western commercial and political power in the Far East threatened nothing less than the dissolution of the Japanese policy and the reduction of the society to colonial status. All efforts, therefore, had to be applied to enhancing the country's national power, so that Japan could treat with the 'barbarians' on equal terms; and this required the adoption of modern military technology and the establishment of a centralized government that could effectively promote and focus the strength of the nation.

The Japanese external projection of nationalist ambitions, as in the case of Germany, begins during the period of take-off.

China

The case of Chinese modernization is equally a reaction to external intrusion. Moreover, like Japan, China was confronted with the challenge of intrusion at a time of dynastic weakness brought about by the prior economic pressures of an excessively expanding population on the political and social life of the nation. But Chinese history, culture, and social structure failed to yield the relatively united and single-minded drive to modernization which marked Japan.

The early phase of China's reaction to external intrusion interwove with the period of domestic unrest, centered in the Taiping Rebellion. Western thought and religion contributed obliquely to the banners and concepts of that Rebellion; Western power, joined with the Manchu dynasty and elements of the Chinese gentry, helped suppress it.

Mrs Wright has analyzed in detail the subsequent failure of the negotiation with the British which might, conceivably, have established a livable equilibrium within which China might have found its way slowly forward to modernization in dignity.[28] It is her theme that this effort failed in part because the British merchants in China did not accept the Alcock Convention. That failure and the so-called Tientsin Massacre of 1870 set the stage for a period of progressive internal Chinese disintegration and increasingly hardhanded intrusions. In 1895 Japan, in the midst of take-off, defeated the Chinese decisively, acquiring control over Korea; and the Boxer Rebellion occurred in 1900.

The Chinese, under these pressures, cast about in many directions for a formula to restore unity, self-respect, and dignity. After 1868 they looked to the Japanese model among others. There was in 1898 the hundred days of reform during which a monumental series of edicts was issued; but there was no effective means, as in Japan, to implement those reforms – no samurai to serve as a purposeful modernizing group; no effective central government.

Power fell back, as often when dynasties were failing, into the hands of regional warlords. The effort of Sun Yat-sen's revived China society, begun in 1894, led to the overthrow of the Manchu dynasty in 1911 and the formation of the National People's Party in 1912. Its principles were nationalism – that is, the reassertion of China's dignity; democracy; and the people's livelihood. Those were his definitions of security, constitutional, and welfare objectives. But Sun Yat-sen could not organize effective government in the face of the warlords; and in the decade after 1911 such reform and innovation as took place occurred piecemeal and regionally. The First World War initially gave China a chance to breathe, since the western states were preoccupied elsewhere; and there was some significant industrial development. The Japanese, however, were able to press their expansion into China, in an effort to supplant German extraterritorial status, evoking strong, widespread nationalist reactions, symbolized by the 1917 demonstrations and the boycott of Japanese imports.

With the Russian Revolution of 1917 the Chinese reformers turned to a new model. They were impressed not by communism as a whole but by the success of the Leninist party structure in bringing effective unity to Russia after the First World War. In effect, they saw that national dignity could not be achieved and economic progress could not take place until China was unified. That became the key constitutional question.

The two major contenders for power, the Kuomintang and the Chinese Communist Party, were both built on the Leninist party model. They worked in uneasy collaboration in the early 1920s and then Chiang Kai-shek, from a southern base, moved out to unify China under his leadership in 1927. With victory in the KMT grasp, the left and right wings within the KMT split; and the possibility of effective consolidation of unitary rule was lost. The KMT won out temporarily over the Communists; but China faced twenty years of civil war combined, after 1931, with Japanese aggression against it. The Communists were never crushed; the difficulties with the warlords persisted; and only between 1929 and 1931 did China enjoy external peace. During the Second World War the Chinese Nationalist government, driven back into the interior at Chunking, lost its cohesion and vitality; and, although Chiang Kai-shek came back in 1945 with great prestige, he failed in his military and political struggle with the Chinese Communists who took over in 1949.

The Chinese Communists hold a peculiar place in the sequence of revolution in modern China. We can place Sun Yat-sen as among the first generation of modern Chinese revolutionaries. Born in 1866, he had ties and memories that went back directly to the aftermath of the Taiping Rebellion of 1848–64. Sun's generation defined China's revolutionary problem, experimented with reform, but never solved the primary problem of establishing a foundation of national authority capable of achieving its purposes. It was a generation more concerned with ends than means.

In these terms, the men who came to power on the mainland, and also those who came in defeat to Taiwan in 1949, belonged to a second generation who were initially technicians in the problem of power, concerned primarily with the means for controlling societies rather than with the ends a modern China should pursue. Over the past generation they, and those they brought within the framework of power, have had to make dispositions of substance – dispositions still unresolved and in conflict on the mainland, but which yielded remarkable economic and social progress on Taiwan.

Turkey

The interaction between external intrusion and the modernization of Turkey has been so thoroughly told in terms similar to those employed in this chapter that brief reference will suffice.[29]

The process was longer and more painful than in the case of Japan; and it has in common with that of China that the Turks had to form for themselves, in the end, a new vision of who they were and what their destiny should be – an escape to conventional secular nationhood from the role of imperial masters of a large and complex domain, linked to a religious mission.

The story of modern Turkey unfolds in counterpoint to a series of military problems; the role of the soldiery is central throughout the critical period of transition; and various non-military dimensions of modernization emerge in reflex to straightforward military and security considerations.

The rule of Selim III (1789–1807) is taken here – as conventionally – to mark the opening of the Turkish preconditions period, after a prolonged period of military setbacks at the hands of the Hungarians and Russians. As in other cases, this 'first' modernizer had predecessors. He himself pointed out that his ancestors had permitted Muslims to use the enemy's tricks to overcome them.[30]

Selim's reforms involved both the imposition of new taxes and a shift in power among groups within the imperial structure. It was followed by a conservative reaction – setting a pattern of tension between modernizing and conservative forces that was to persist down to the nationalist revolution of 1919–23 and the final emergence of a nationalist and modernizing Turkey from the hard-fought war with Greece, with lucid boundaries and strictly limited objectives in its regional arena of power.

From Selim III down to the peace treaty of Lusanne in 1923 it was the recurrent demonstration that Turkish modernization was not moving fast enough to cope with the rise of military power around it which was the engine of modernization; and the Turkish soldier was its principal instrument. Starting with the need for greater military strength, the scope of modernization spread, step by step, into the society's administration and public institutions, attitudes and aspirations. As in a number of other cases (France, Russia, China, Mexico), economic modernization emerged as a prime objective of policy relatively late in the process.

Delay in modernization arose not only from the reluctant surrender of empire – diverting, as it did, energy, talent, and resources – but also from the hold over the people of conservative religious institutions, including the schools. As Rustow sums up:[31]

In a political sense, her inherited form of organization was dynastic-imperial and her empire was steadily disintegrating under both internal and external pressures. Some new and more stable form of political organization had to be found. In terms of boundaries and peoples to be included, a variety of solutions to this problem were possible. The normal tendency was to define the new form in the most expansive and inclusive terms thought to be militarily defensible. Consequently, it took a long time and much experimentation with other and more grandiose schemes, including Pan-Islam and Pan-Turkism, before the Turks became desperate enough to settle for the boundaries of their present state. This point was not finally reached until the War of Independence. As a consequence, Turkey did not really face or resolve the basic territorial aspect of her crisis of identity until at least 1919 or even 1922. Between 1912 and 1923, the secession of non-Turkish Muslims such as the Albanians and Arabs, the decimation of the Armenians, the defeat of the empire itself, and the population exchange with Greece had reduced the nationality problem to manageable dimensions. Nonetheless, the Kurdish minority remained as a challenge to national unity into the 1930s. And there still remained the massive problem of superseding parochial village loyalties with national identifications in the minds and hearts of the Turkish people. This attempt continues in the present.

Mexico

Latin America, taken as a whole, has been less buffeted about by more advanced nations in moving towards modernization than the major regions of Eurasia.

Mexico, however, caught up in the westward drive of the United States and, later, in heavily unbalanced economic ties with the United States, had to find its way to nationhood and modernization in a more conventional bloody and hard-pressed sequence, well summarized by Daniel James: a sequence with reactive nationalism at its center.[32]

The history of modern Mexico is essentially the history of Mexican nationalism, and both fall into three neat compartments marked by three great national movements extending over a century: The Independence of 1810, the Reform of 1857, and the Revolution of 1910. Each of these movements, which commenced on the dates given and lasted for years, had important social objectives, to be sure; but, in the last analysis, each represented a new stage in the evolution of Mexico as a nation and thus of Mexican nationalism. If the last of the three movements, the Revolution of 1910, boasted more profound social objectives than the others, it also marked the floodtide of Mexican nationalism. Each movement turned out to be, in the end, more a response to an external challenge rather than an internal one (with the result that Mexican nationalism early acquired a distinctly antiforeign cast), for uppermost in all three cases was a foreign threat, whether military, political, or economic, to the right of the Mexicans to rule themselves. The three movements, that is to say, had this overriding common attribute: They were struggles to win or maintain the independence of Mexico from foreign domination of any kind.

Although the Mexicans early committed themselves to republican rule, they suffered in the first quarter-century of independence all the classic post-colonial problems of democratic government: 'freedom was mistaken for license, independence for anarchy, government for corruption, and nationalism for factionalism.'[33]

As in many other more contemporary examples, the consequence was a conservative movement towards dictatorial rule – but a rule which never fully consolidated the territories inherited from colonialism, thus leaving Mexico vulnerable to manifest destiny as conceived to the north.

And so Texas was lost – and much more out to the Pacific – between 1836 and the Treaty of Guadalupe Hidalgo of 1848. The memory of Scott's army in Mexico City was never erased.

Mexico within itself struggled for stable rule and reform; that is, a shifting of power from the Church, the military, the large landholders, and from the pure European *criollo* to the majority of mixed blood. And this unresolved civil conflict left Mexico vulnerable to external intrusion. In December 1861, with the United States also in civil war, Spanish, French, and British forces were emplaced on Mexican soil. And in April 1864 Napoleon III, in pursuit of gold and grandeur, was able to install the hapless Maximilian.

Through the war years Lincoln and Juárez maintained attitudes of mutual respect for each other's domestic aspirations and, of course, a common hostility to the French position in Mexico.[34] Juárez – his stature, objectives, and determination in the battle for independence – caught the imagination of Americans as no other Mexican had. After Appomattox there was, then, both a sentimental and national interest in helping Juárez defeat Maximilian, a task accomplished by early 1867.

The heritage of nationhood left by Juárez was taken over in 1877 by Porfirio Díaz who ruled, in effect, down to the revolution of 1910. In his time, Mexico moved forward in building some of the technical preconditions for take-off, but did so under conditions of domestic rule and external economic intrusion which laid the basis for a decade of revolutionary bloodletting, which ended in 1920.

The extraordinary, obsessive interventions of Ambassador Henry Lane Wilson in Mexican political affairs under President Taft left a deep heritage of distrust. President Wilson's subsequent intrusions, ideological, diplomatic and military, were well meant, if that concept has relevance in the relations between nations; but they yielded the traumatic occupation of Vera Cruz in 1914 and Pershing's unsuccessful pursuit of Pancho Villa in 1916–17. The anti-American cast of Mexican nationalism was strengthened, although Mexico decided that its problems with the colossus to the north did not justify the risks of association with America's enemies during the First World War.

The limit of Mexican riposte was the nationalization in 1938 of United States oil and mining firms. From roughly that time forward, Mexico has found in its own sustained modernization the basis for the dignity and inner equilibrium for which it had struggled for a hundred and thirty years.

Constitutional Change

Prefatory note. The brief evocation of the role of external intrusion in the preconditions period of the eight countries selected for illustrative analysis suggests the complex counterpoint between external and internal pressures in the process of modernization.

In all cases, of course, political life and its institutions altered under these converging pressures. In a few cases the old system adjusted towards modernity without formal constitutional change in the system itself. But in most cases the formal structure of rule was transformed before a political system consistent with take-off was achieved.

This section briefly summarizes the constitutional changes – or absence of them – during the transitional period.

Britain

The system of 1688 sufficed as a constitutional framework for Britain, unless one is to interpret the American Revolution, as many colonists did, as an essentially British constitutional crisis. Behind that concept, of course, was not merely the vocabulary in which the debate evolved across the Atlantic between 1763 and 1776, but also complaints in London against George III's management of affairs within the loose and evolving conventions of the British constitution. But Namier is almost certainly correct in his assessment of George III not as a 'man arrogating power to himself, the ambitious schemer out to dominate' but rather of a man caught in a gap between an idealized version of his mission and duties and a reality which he could never effectively grip.[35] Whatever the cause, the British constitutional system proved too inflexible to contain the American colonies on the terms they demanded and ultimately, with the help of Britain's continental enemies, enforced.

But at home the British system survived not only the vicissitudes of George III in his phase of personal rule but also evolved a cabinet system which, while rooted in a parliament without a stable party structure, still permitted responsible government to rule, while providing the framework for the take-off and the energy and resources to survive successfully the Revolutionary and Napoleonic Wars.

France

If one dates the French take-off from the 1830s, one must account, of course, for a series of constitutional crises and changes in the previous two generations. So far as French modernization is concerned, however, Napoleon's crystallization of the revolutionary heritage in the period 1799–1804 cast the longest shadow: confirmation that feudalism was at an end; centralized control over the prefects and sub-prefects; the rationalization of the French financial structure and the creation of the Bank of France; the Concordat with Pope Pius VII, balancing successfully the claims of Rome, French nationalism, and the faithful; the legal codes; a modernized school system; and an extensive program of public works. The formal constitutional structure of French politics underwent, and was to undergo, several subsequent changes; but these were abiding heritages of the great upheaval for a century and more.

Louis XVIII accepted with some grace his task of presiding over a society profoundly altered by the Revolution, but with its constitutional balance not yet resolved. Royalist and clerical forces revived in confidence and assertiveness but, especially in Paris, the Revolution still lived. And when his successor Charles X overplayed his hand, Paris exploded. The upshot was Louis Philippe who managed for eighteen years to hold in tolerable balance the revolutionary and monarchical traditions, while the French turned, at a modest pace, to their first protracted phase of industrialization.

Germany

The critical constitutional crisis of Germany came on the eve of take-off; and it came in the form of the change which did not occur – the failure of the Frankfurt parliament and its proposed constitution for a liberal German empire. Those gathered at the Paulskirche sought a democratic resolution to the problem of German unity; but to overcome the Princes they needed the assent and leadership of Prussia and its king. Frederick William IV received the offer from Frankfurt to become the German Emperor after revolt had been crushed in Prussia. He was not in a mood to accept the legitimacy of a constitution rooted in universal suffrage and the secret ballot from a body which had set aside the Princes. And Frankfurt's resolution of the Austrian problem – an exclusion voted by a majority of only four – posed a potential issue of war and peace Prussia was not then ready to confront.

And so Prussian autocracy turned its back on Frankfurt and held its ground until Bismarck could rescue it from the liberal parliamentarianism which dogged the Prussian rulers until September 1862 when Bismarck took over and installed, in succession to the old absolutism, a modern Hegelian state.

But by then the German take-off was under way.

Russia

Less modernized than France and Germany, better insulated from the currents of liberalism that flowed through the Atlantic world and Western Europe, Russia was able to maintain Romanov rule down to the take-off and beyond. But its leaders came to appreciate the costs in military capacity of certain elements of its backwardness; and, on this basis, significant changes in legal and social structures were launched, most notably the formal freeing of the serfs in 1861 – in effect, a major constitutional event altering – even if only gradually – the social and economic status of nobility and peasant.

Japan

The restoration of the Emperor in 1868, under the aegis of the samurai leaders, was, of course, the fundamental constitutional change of the preconditions period in Japan; although the release of the daimyo from enforced residence at Edo in the early 1860s was a quasiconstitutional adjustment, reflecting the gathering economic and political pressures on Tokugawa rule, foreshadowing its bankruptcy.

The story of the Japanese constitution of 1889 belongs, strictly speaking, with the period of the take-off; but its authoritarian and (literally) Prussian character reflected the uneasy, turbulent, and experimental period between 1868 and the political and economic consolidation of Meiji rule in the 1880s. The most basic change was, of course, the ending of feudalism, including the great land-reform scheme. There was also the Satruma Rebellion, repressed in 1877; the emergence of a modern press; the groping for a modern system of law; and the pressures for representative government yielding, in 1881, the commitment to promulgate a constitution before the end of the decade.

Meanwhile, under the aegis of the Emperor, the Meiji leaders evolved through a council of state the beginnings of a modern governmental structure which kept effective power in their hands, while permitting functional branches of administration to evolve capable of executing their purposeful policies of modernization.

Scalapino summarizes this period of pragmatic experimentation in these terms:[36]

The early Meiji experience was like that of the Southeast Asian societies after World War II: the attempt to borrow Western political institutions issued first in failure, then in reexamination and the quest for suitable adaptations. In Japan, a period of retreat began as early as 1872 and became pronounced in the 1880s. The final Meiji Constitution was not a hastily conceived or naively imitative document; but might be said to have prescribed guided democracy, Japanese style.

China

The constitutional vicissitudes of China between the 1840s and the effort to initiate take-off in the 1950s, interwoven as they were with the role of external intrusion, are already familiar:

— the various defensive efforts to modernize within the framework of the Manchu dynasty, from the 1860s to the Revolution of 1911;

— the prompt subsequent triumph of regionalism and the warlords over the central rule of the Chinese Republic;

— Sun Yat-sen's reorganization of the Kuomintang, announced in January 1923, following the structure of the Russian Communist Party, embracing the Chinese Communist Party as a faction, under the explicit tutelage of the Soviet Ambassador Adolph Joffe;

— the elimination of the Chinese Communists from the KMT in 1927, and the subsequent failure wholly to suppress them;

— the apparent unification of China in 1928, under the KMT;

— the considerable, if limited, progress made in consolidating Nationalist rule in the period down to 1937, despite the loss of Manchuria in 1931;

— then the sequence of war and civil war yielding the Chinese Communist takeover of 1949.

This troubled passage was marked by erratic movements towards modernization: military, initially via the Whampoa Military Academy and, then, the endemic struggles in the field; in education, at home as well as abroad; in central and regional administration; and in the public and private sectors of the economy, including the Japanese modernization of Manchuria.

As a society, the mainland China that Mao took over and consolidated in 1949 was a quite different and more modern China than that which had overthrown the Manchu dynasty thirty-eight years earlier; but the domestic struggle for the inheritance, compounded and, indeed, made possible by the Japanese assault, determined that the politics of China's preconditions period would be the most difficult of all.

Turkey

Although there is formal continuity within the Turkish Empire down to November 1922, when the end of the sultanate was proclaimed, there were important constitutional developments – under the impact of gradual and cumulative pressure and contact with the West – which can be summarized as follows:

— the reforms of Selim III and the sharp reaction against them;

— the destruction by Mahmud II (1800–39) of the Janissaries and the supplanting of the Ottoman bureaucracy with civil and military figures loyal to him;

— the Tanzimat reforms culminating in the Constitution of 1876: an effort to accommodate western notions of law, parliamentary government, and administration (including at least formal status of equality for the minorities) with continuity for basic Islamic institutions, notably in the traditional countryside – an accommodation less of substance than designed to appease external pressures on the Empire: the Constitution of 1876, for example, was proclaimed in the face of the prospect of a conference of great powers on Turkish affairs, and it went into long abeyance shortly thereafter;[37]

— the Young Turk Revolution of 1908, in the wake of the consolidating autocracy of Abdul Hamed, launching the phase of uninhibited modernization that culminated – after the vicissitudes of war, defeat, and the successful struggle against the Greeks – in the emergence of the Turkish republic;

— the Turkish Republic under Atatürk, down to 1938: the consolidation of political and social modernization and development of the preconditions for take-off. Between 1922 and 1928 the sultanate was declared defunct, the republic proclaimed, the caliphate abolished, a representative constitution enacted, and the law, the calendar, and dress westernized. This phase proceeded under Atatürk's personal rule, through a virtually monopolistic Republican People's Party.

As Davison notes, the Turkish sequence, taken as a whole, is a vivid and prolonged exercise in the interplay between external and internal pressures for change:[38]

... there was no period of concentrated political reform which did not begin with one or more specific stimuli from without. This is true of 1833, 1839, 1854–6, 1876, 1908 1919–22, and 1945. Though in no case was the external stimulus a sufficient explanation or cause for the reforms which ensued, it presented at least an opportunity which could be seized and a warning to conservatives that change was necessary.

Nor is there serious doubt as to who the new men were who seized the opportunities offered by the recurrent demonstration of the traditional Empire's weakness: Turkish modernization was led by successive generations of soldiers and, then, civil servants who perceived that only by westernization could their people reacquire and retain dignity in a world relentlessly pressing in on their rapidly obsolescing empire; and that the surrender of the Empire itself and of traditional Muslem institutions was, in the end, justified to achieve that end.

Mexico

The story of Mexico from September 1810, when Hidalgo called upon Mexicans to act for their independence, and the accession of Camacho to the presidency in December 1940, launching the stable administration which mounted the Mexican take-off, ranks with that of China as one of the most complex, troubled, and bloody passages in modern political history.

Behind some twenty formal constitutional documents, chronic civil and international strife, the rise and fall of a gallery of picturesque and passionate leaders, was a Spanish colony, split three ways on racial lines, finding its way to nationhood and modernity by solving a sequence of basic problems: the appropriate degree of centralization for republican government; the relative status of the *mestizos* versus the *criollos* in the structure of political power; the role of the church; the system of land ownership; the role of the labor unions; the place of foreign capital in the economy; a viable, nationalist stance towards the United States; and an appropriate ideology for an industrializing modern Mexico.

The issues unfolded in the following rough sequence, once formal independence was attained by the victory of the *criollos* over the 80,000 or so European born *gachupines* who had dominated Mexican colonial life:

— the 1824 Constitution which settled the question of monarchy versus republicanism, but provided for a federal structure of diffuse power, unrealistic in the disorganized condition of Mexican state governments; it represented a transient victory of liberal *mestizo* forces over the more conservative *criollo*-dominated party;

— the 1836 Constitution, sanctioning central and more conservative rule;

— the Juárez Constitution of 1857, formally restricting the power of the army and the Church as landowners; seeking to establish a secular nation-state, with all under civil law, land for the peasant, and the *mestizo* majority dominant;

— the modernizing dictatorship of Porfirio Díaz (1877–1910) who came to power on the battle cry 'No Re-election and Effective Suffrage' to rule for thirty-four years, carrying Mexico through an important phase of building the preconditions for take-off but at cost of converging discontents (centered on the *hacienda* system, excessive foreign ownership, and the limitation of democratic political rights) which produced the explosion of 1910–20;

— the Constitution of 1917, with its resting of ownership of land and other natural resources in the nation, laying the basis for both agrarian reform and, later, oil expropriation and including a chapter specifying in detail the rights of labor;

— the emergence of the National Revolutionary Party (1928–9) embracing left, right, and center groups within the broad ambiguous consensus represented by the Mexican Revolution;

— the Cardenas–Toledano flirtation with international communism of the 1930s, constrained at critical moments by a profound Mexican nationalism; the setting of limits on the power of the labor unions; the oil expropriation of March 1938;

— the coming to power of the quiet, pragmatic Camacho in December 1940, launching a period of national unity and industrialization.

In terms of the three dimensions of government, this stormy tale is a protracted struggle for national security (independence) and for justice in all its dimensions: for the political rights of the *mestizo* majority; the right of the peasant to own land; the right of the worker to social justice. But Mexico had to find ways to reconcile these objectives with other security, constitutional, and welfare objectives: a rational relationship to the United States and the external world; national unity and order; and economic modernization. The ultimate political instrument for reconciling these conflicting objectives proved to be a large but not quite monopolistic national party, embracing virtually all interests and factions; controlling a dominating central government, headed by a one-term President with large powers, concentrating after 1940 on the tasks of progressive industrialization which alone could provide the resources necessary to make good its commitments to justice and welfare; building a consensus on loyalty to the long Mexican cultural past as well as the Revolution of 1910–20; finding in its success an equilibrium of dignity with the United States and the rest of the world.

Public Policy and the Technical Preconditions for Take-off

Britain

British policy of the second half of the eighteenth century is taken generally to represent a classic exercise in *laissez-faire*, permitting private initiative its

83

head and thereby yielding the triumph of initiating what was to prove a global industrial revolution. The flexible and relatively permissive political and social framework which developed after 1688 was certainly the most important contribution of public policy to the British take-off, through its linkage to the inventors and innovators.[39]

Nevertheless, three more direct functions of government were significant in creating the environment for the emergence of modern cotton textiles as a leading sector in the 1780s:

— first, the international trading environment created and permitted by the Royal Navy and the colonial structure, not excluding an independent United States with which post-1783 commerce flourished;[40]

— second, the granting by Parliament of acts of enclosure and of canal and turnpike bills, which permitted private enterprise to proceed with important improvements in agricultural production as well as the building of critically important infrastructures with Parliament sometimes actively sustaining the latter type of enterprise;[41]

— third, the patent laws (and occasional public as well as private awards) which managed a reasonable balance between incentive for the inventor and the avoidance of the dead hand of monopoly.[42]

France

The story of the French preconditions for take-off includes three distinct periods: mercantilism from (say) Colbert to 1789; the years of revolution and war; post-1815 progress yielding, at last, a radical move towards industrialization with the building of the French railway system and the full emergence of heavy industry (coal, metals, and machinery) as a leading sector.[43]

The first period is colored by apparently conflicting images: on the one hand, of a France moving forward irregularly through the eighteenth century at a pace not radically different from that of Britain, responding in its own way to possibilities for expansion in trade, industry, and agriculture;[44] on the other hand, of a France so hobbled by an archaic social system, and the fiscal system related to it, that the King had, in effect, to declare himself bankrupt before the Notables in 1787. There is truth in both images; and, indeed, starting with Colbert (if not Sully) and ending with Colonne, the struggles of the King's men of finance to generate the resource base to support his court and French external adventures helped goad on the French economy and thereby helped produce by the end of the 1780s a social structure no longer prepared to acquiesce in the absolutist dispensation. The role of French mercantilist policy in encouraging trade, developing artisan factories, protecting industry, and building ships is substantial. But the Revocation of the Edict of Nantes (1685) (so close in time to the British reconciliation of 1688) helped dissipate the corps of men who might have performed the acts of invention and innovation which, in the end, most distinguished the British from the French industrial position when war came. It is Crouzet's judgment that, in effect, the English capital structure was deepened in the latter part of the eighteenth century, whereas French expansion simply involved a widening of the capital structure:[45]

The fundamental difference between the two economies . . . is in the technological field. The relatively fast expansion of French industry during the eighteenth century took place within a framework which was still, as regards organization and methods, largely the traditional one . . . On the eve of the Revolution, the French economy was not basically different from what it had been under Louis XIV; it was merely producing much more. In England, on the other hand, where growth during the first half of the century was of the 'French' type, that is, within the traditional framework, after 1760 some revolutionary changes appeared and [the] economic structures were modified in depth by a series of technical inventions which heralded a general revolution.

The balance sheet of revolution and war was heavily unfavorable to France in the short run. It did, however, yield a political and social structure and a system of law and institutions consistent with postwar movement towards industrialization. And among the innovations was the Patent Law of 1791.

Clapham concluded: 'If legislative and administrative action could industrialize a country, France would have moved more quickly. The Revolution had removed all obstacles to free enterprise.'[46]

The building of the preconditions for take-off after 1815, down to the French railway legislation of 1842, was mainly in private hands, except for a tariff policy, on balance strongly protectionist, although constrained by a steady liberal opposition.[47]

It was the French private entrepreneur, stimulated by British (and then Belgian) contacts and example, constrained by British predominance in textile markets abroad and by limitations in France's raw material base, who laid the technical foundation for the mid-century railway boom which was to overcome, in part at least, the relative lag of 1815.

Germany

Germany was not fully unified until 1870 when its take-off had occurred. The role of public policy in the creation of the preconditions for take-off varied, therefore, among the German states.

That role is tersely summarized by Wolfram Fischer, under headings which constitute a useful general check list for contemporary as well as historical cases:[48]

    (i) Governments acting as legislator:
        (*a*) patent law
        (*b*) trade law
        (*c*) customs law
    (ii) Governments acting as administrator:
        (*a*) fiscal policy
        (*b*) general economic policy and in particular industrial promotion
        (*c*) infrastructure
   (iii) Governments acting as entrepreneurs:
        (*a*) landed property, including forests
        (*b*) mines and industries
        (*c*) banking, insurance and other institutions for capital formation

German public authorities, most notably in Prussia, assumed initiatives under each of these broad headings, in purposeful pursuit of the new technologies and a framework for trade which would encourage industrialization. Aside from the Zollverein of 1834 and the role of German governments in fostering and helping build the railways, the Gewerbeinstitut in Berlin, founded in 1821, and similar institutions elsewhere may have been the most effective means for accelerating German industrialization; although the direct industrial and commercial operations of such state-owned financial institutions as the Prussian Seehandlung also played a significant catalytic role.

In the end, however, industry grew within this benign framework, led by an able group of private entrepreneurs, mainly self-financed, in coal mining, iron, and machine production. The proportion of private financing of the German railways was also high: 92 per cent in 1840, falling to 57 per cent in 1870; although these figures somewhat underestimate the government role.[49]

In railways Germany stole a march of perhaps a decade on France due to the enthusiasm of King Ludwig of Bavaria and the Prussian Crown Prince, on the one hand, and French procrastination over the railway law.[50] The Prussian railway legislation was promulgated by November 1838. And Treitschke could conclude:[51] 'It was the railways which first dragged the nation from its economic stagnation; they ended what the Zollverein had only begun; with such power did they break in upon all the old habits of life, that already in the forties the aspect of Germany was completely changed.'

As with France, then, Germany created between 1815 and 1840 the industrial and technical foundations for the railroadization which took both nations into sustained growth. Its initially lower level of economic life was more than compensated for by better national resources for heavy industry and greater public purposefulness. By the end of take-off Germany was already moving rapidly ahead of France.

Russia

By all accounts, the Russian take-off is to be dated from the 1890s and the period when public policy turned purposefully towards modernization, from the setback in the Crimean War.

Although the question of land and the serfs was central in the 1850s and 1860s, railroadization was begun seriously in the latter decade.[52] Sensitive to the international cyclical pattern, the Russian economy felt the depressions of the late seventies and mid-eighties; but in the 1890s the full cumulative stimulus to trade, raw material exploitation, and, above all, heavy industry stemming from the railways, was felt. The early railways were built over-whelmingly from imported products:[53] by the 1890s Russian industry could increasingly do the job. But industrial progress in the pre-1890 decades was not trivial, as the accompanying estimates of workers employed in large Russian private enterprises suggest (in thousands).[54]

Years	In factory industry	In mining industry	On railroads	Total
1865	509	165	32	706
1890	840	340	253	1,433

Although foreign capital directly invested in Russia by 1900 was three times the figure for 1890, the latter amounted to 580 million roubles.[55]

The critical directing role of the Russian government during the 1890s, under Count Witte, is familiar. But it was important, as well, in the less dramatic developments of the previous thirty years, quite aside from the decision to begin, at least, the ending of serfdom in 1861.

Specifically, the Russian state:

— built up its gold reserves as the basis for a stable currency and international credit-worthiness, and generated budget surpluses for direct investment and industrial subsidy;

— encouraged and undertook foreign borrowing;

— directly stimulated industry through orders to meet government requirements;

— shifted gradually, beginning in 1877, from a liberal to a protectionist tariff policy, climaxed by the high duties of 1891;

— purposefully generated foreign exchange by forced grain exports;

— encouraged industry through the policy of the state-owned banks;

— provided direct government financing of the railways: about evenly divided in the 1890s between private and public, quite aside from important indirect government support.

Lyashchenko's judgment is well-founded that the policy of the 1890s had been thoroughly prepared by 'Witte's predecessors since 1870, men like Bunge and Vyshnegradsky'.[56]

In the end, although the role of the state in creating the technical preconditions for the Russian take-off was more substantial than in Germany or France – let alone than in England – heavy reliance was placed on an existing and emerging class of private entrepreneurs, arising from commerce and industry with a long Russian tradition.

Japan

The leading sector of the Japanese take-off, which began in the mid-1880s, was textiles: cotton and, to a degree, silk which not only earned foreign exchange but spread widely the habits and disciplines of quality control for an export market. Japan could move forward with less industrial preparation than, say, France, Germany, and Russia where heavy industry underpinnings were required to mount and enjoy the spreading effects of a railway boom during take-off. But wide-ranging government policies were needed – and provided – after 1868 to set the stage for the accelerated industrial expansion of the 1880s:[57]

— a land reform scheme which gave the former owners national bonds, the peasants strong incentives, and the government a vital flow of revenue available for infrastructure and industrial investment over the period until a wider tax base emerged from growth itself;

— creation by the state of a technical school, banks, insurance companies, railways, steamshipping, postal and telegraph services, and factories, many linked to the military establishment;

— creation of the Kobu Sho (Department of Industrial Matters) which, in the critical preconditions years 1870–85, 'served as an indispensable midwife of almost all the industrial projects including the task of rounding out social overhead capital';[58]

— a remarkable financial and currency stabilization in the early 1880s, ending inflation and providing an adequate monetary base for the take-off.

The preconditions process was aided (as in England) by the relatively low requirements for transport expenditure in a small island nation, with coastal shipping available, and by the fact that housing outlays in the expanding cities were modest. A relatively low proportion of GNP invested could, therefore, produce striking industrial results.

Social, institutional, and structural changes marked the pre-take-off period in Japan, as well as civil conflict, inflation, and its rigorous taming by Matsukata. Statistical data before the 1880s are sparse. They exhibit some erratic expansion of investment, notably government construction and production of durable equipment.[59] Ohkawa's national income and sectoral data, beginning with 1878–82 averages, can only tell us that there was some momentum prior to the rapid and steady expansion which is clearly marked across the board from the mid-1880s.[60]

The pragmatism that marked these initial two decades of modern Japan led the government to sell to a rapidly emerging private enterprise some of its inefficient factories and to leave the new dynamic textile industry in private hands.

The broad headings of Japanese public policy in the preconditions period are familiar; although their context, like that of other nations, had particular features. Policy towards popular education, however, was unique among the Eurasian cases of the nineteenth century.

The preamble to the new school regulations of 1872 read: 'Henceforth, throughout the land, without distinctions of class and sex, in no village shall there be a house without learning, in no house an ignorant individual.' Although Japanese educational policies and institutions did not evolve smoothly in this Jeffersonian – almost Emersonian – spirit, the initial dispositions of the Meiji period yielded by 1910 a situation where 98 per cent of the total population aged 6–13 was registered in primary schools, while technical and advanced education flourished.[61]

China

The economy of the Chinese mainland, taken over by the Communists in 1949, was, in its general proportions, similar to that of other underdeveloped nations on the eve of take-off: some 75 per cent of the population was in agriculture, contributing about 40 per cent to national product; an additional 10 per cent lived in rural areas, engaged in non-farm tasks, producing about 20 per cent of national product; and 15 per cent lived in cities, producing about 40 per cent of national product.[62]

Amidst all its vicissitudes, from the 1840s China moved forward piecemeal in economic modernization, yielding a century later an economy made up of three sectors: a vast, largely self-sufficient, labor-intensive agriculture; a modern sector, located in the coastal cities, largely devoted to the management of a normally substantial foreign trade as well as the manufacture of modern textiles and other light industrial products; a heavy industry sector in Manchuria, built mainly under Japanese occupation after 1931 and not linked to the rest of the Chinese economy until after 1949.

This structure had evolved in, roughly, the following sequence:

— 1840–95: trade expansion, largely under foreign pressure and auspices, with little industrialization except the building of government arsenals and armament works in the 1860s and 1870s;

— 1895–1914: first phase of industrialization launched by rights granted in treaty ports to foreigners under the Treaty of Shimonoseki, as well as foreign development of railroads and mines; also a first phase of import-substitution consumer goods industries, including modern textiles;

— 1914–31: rapid expansion of light industry in coastal cities in the face of import shortages during the First World War, continued thereafter under protectionist policies, with a shift from Western to Japanese and Chinese entrepreneurship and ownership;

— 1931–45: rapid development of Manchurian heavy industry capacity by the Japanese.

Table 3 combines 1943 Japanese-controlled output in Manchuria and 1936 figures for the rest of China.[63]

TABLE 3. *Estimated pre-1949 peak production of selected industrial products in Mainland China*

Product	Unit	China proper	Manchuria
Pig iron	Metric tons	290,640	1,700,000
Crude steel	Metric tons	50,000	843,000
Rolled steel	Metric tons	Negligible	485,700
Coal	Metric tons	33,000,000	25,630,000
Crude oil	Metric tons	n.a.	214,300
Cement	Metric tons	608,000	1,532,000
Paper	Metric tons	n.a.	76,000
Flour	Metric tons	1,800,000	650,000
Sugar	Metric tons	392,000	17,600
Cotton yarn	Bales	2,100,000	n.a.
Cotton cloth	Bolts	30,000,000	n.a.
Cigarettes	Billions of sticks	57	25
Electric power:			
Capacity	Thousands of kw	893	1,786
Output	Millions of kw-hr	2,425	4,475

As this industrial structure emerged, manufactured and semi-manufactured consumer goods, which dominated total import figures at the turn of the century, gave way slowly but steadily to industrial equipment and raw materials. On the other hand, the rise in urban population, combined with a lag in agricultural productivity and in internal transport development, led to an increasing food import requirement.

The Chinese Communist regime, with the mainland at last unified effectively, was able to achieve by 1952 production figures close to previous peak years.[64]

TABLE 4. *Estimated production of selected commodities in Mainland China, 1949–52*

Product	Unit	Peak	1949	1950	1952
Pig iron	000 metric tons	2,000	210	827	1,589
Crude steel	000 metric tons	900	144	551	1,215
Rolled steel	000 metric tons	500	90	259	740
Coal	000 metric tons	59,000	26,000	35,000	53,000
Crude oil	000 metric tons	330	125	207	389
Cement	000 metric tons	2,140	663	1,412	2,311
Paper	000 metric tons	120	108	101	264
Flour	000 metric tons	2,450	1,911	1,200	3,087
Sugar	000 metric tons	410	164	198	328
Cotton yarn	000 bales	2,400	1,728	2,040	2,784
Cotton cloth	000 bolts	41,000	29,930	3,230	56,580
Cigarettes	000,000 sticks	82,000	47,000	54,520	102,500
Electric power	000,000 kw-hr	6,900	3,600	3,800	5,700
Rice	000 metric tons	48,600	..	46,900	55,890
Wheat	000 metric tons	24,000	..	19,300	22,800
Soybeans	000 metric tons	10,000	..	5,890	8,900
Cotton	000 metric tons	1,115	..	..	1,290

On this basis the Five Year Plan was launched in 1953, seeking to bring China into sustained industrialization on a national basis.

As for the role of the Chinese government in creating the technical preconditions for take-off, one can conclude that at no time, down to 1949, did external pressures and internal struggles over the control of China's modern destiny leave the government as free to concentrate on the tasks of economic modernization as, for example, post-1815 France and Germany; Russia from 1861 to 1914; or post-1868 Japan. Nevertheless, a mixture of foreign and Chinese enterprise, private and public, yielded an economy in 1949 which contained many of the preconditions for take-off: a minimal transport infrastructure; a potential heavy-industry as well as light-industry base at last under firm national control; an agriculture capable of moving forward if the right inputs and incentives were supplied; a bureaucratic structure which had accumulated, under all manner of vicissitudes, considerable practical experience, including experience in data collection and the techniques of national economic planning; a generation of modern men, trained abroad as well as at home, sufficiently substantial to manage a take-off if organized around a viable strategy.[65]

Turkey

Economic modernization in Turkey begins, in a sense, with the Capitulations granting to foreign governments quasi-autonomous rights within the Empire. They have a long history reaching back to 1740 at least. Coupled with the power to grant letters of protection (the *berats*), the Capitulations permitted a certain minimum of modern commercial activity to be conducted by foreigners and minority groups within the Turkish Empire.

In the 1860s, the Turkish economic environment began to shift in important respects.

The financial requirements of the Empire, in the face of an archaic and inadequate tax system, led to the acceptance of substantial foreign loans; and the pressure for enlarged revenues also yielded the transfer to the state of feudal and church land-holdings, and to an increase in tariffs on imports.

It was in the 1860s also that modern infrastructure was expanded. Starting in 1866, foreign companies began to construct railway lines and public utilities, as well as to expand ports. And this kind of activity persisted in subsequent decades.

But it was not until the Young Turks that a group emerged in authority which took the view that economic modernization was not only acceptable but an essential component of Turkish survival in a modern world. They passed in 1909 a Law for the Encouragement of Industry; and by the time the law was revised in 1915, during the wartime boom in import substitution, some 282 industrial establishments existed, employing about 14,000 workers. In this period, the concepts and institutions of national planning and government control were first developed. But the external and domestic struggles of the period 1908–23 diverted energy, talent, and resources in other directions.

With the final emergence of Kemal Atatürk and the Turkish Republic after thirteen years of war, the first sustained effort at Turkish industrialization began. Before 1929, steps were taken in land reform; the banking system was geared to encourage industrial expansion; and railway lines were extended.

The depression hit hard this modest set of developments and Turkey turned to the relatively stable Soviet Union for assistance and, to a degree, as a model. It launched a five-year plan in 1933 with the state itself as principal entrepreneur. Backed by two large government banks, the government controlled the chemical, ceramics, iron and steel, paper and cellulose, sulphur and copper mining, cotton, woolen, hemp and sponge industries, as well as the classic state monopolies (salt, tobacco, alcoholic products, matches and explosives). But Atatürk quite consciously avoided locking the nation into a rigid system of permanent state ownership and management of industry, leaving the way open to a later expansion of private enterprise, along lines which recall the Japanese sequence.

Lifted by the worldwide recovery from the depth of depression and by the plan itself, Turkey was encouraged to design a second plan in 1936, which went into effect in 1938. Table 5 roughly measures progress down to the outbreak of World War II.[66]

TABLE 5. *Changes in total and per capita national income, Turkey, 1927–39*

Year	National income (in TL. millions, at 1938 prices)	Population (in millions)	Income per capita (in TL.)
1927	1,000	13.6	73
1929	1,147	14.2	80
1935	1,315	16.2	82
1938	1,589	17.2	92
1939	1,652	17.5	95

It sought to move beyond textiles and the building of infrastructure towards the processing of agricultural products and raw materials.[67]

The inevitable foreign trade and other distortions of the war years slowed overall growth but proved consistent with some continued net increase in industrial output. And after an initial postwar adjustment, Turkey moved, in the 1950s, to complete what is here regarded as its take-off.

Turkey's economic development in the 1930s and during the difficult wartime years was marked by inadequate attention to agriculture. Moreover, the state's limited entrepreneurial capacity was over-burdened, yielding many inefficient plants. But the foundations for a thoroughgoing modernization of Turkish economic life were laid in these years.

Mexico

The building of the technical preconditions for the Mexican take-off (say, 1940–60) clearly began under the long dictatorship of Porfirio Díaz. One of his harshest critics concludes:[68]

The dictator's record was not entirely black, however. When Limantour became Finance Minister in 1893, the country verged on bankruptcy; after a year in office, he showed a balanced budget for the first time in Mexican history, and within another year or so he began to produce an annual series of surpluses that gave Mexico a high credit rating in world markets. National income under Díaz rose from about $20 million to $100 million. Exports quintupled, and imports went up eightfold; gold and silver production, among the biggest sources of revenue, increased in value from $25 million to $160 million. A steel industry was begun, rail mileage was expanded, and port facilities were improved.

With Mexico opened to foreign capital, in a peculiarly uninhibited way[69] (including large tracts of land), railways and electric power plants were built, oil resources and mines developed, a commercial banking system established, and the first generation of light industries inaugurated; for example, textiles, shoes, beer, tobacco, soap, sugar refining, and flour milling.[70]

There was a reason for the disproportionate role of foreign capital and entrepreneurship in the Mexican economy before 1910, as a nationalist historian of the electric power industry has underlined:[71]

The inability of Mexican capital to create a truly national electric power industry is explained by the same reasons which allowed the country's principal economic resources to fall into foreign hands in the nineteenth century. The history of the metal smelting and refining industry, to name just one, developed in a fashion very similar to that of the electrical industry. In both instances a small group of Mexican capitalists launched and tenaciously developed an economic activity at whose head they could remain only as long as they did not have to face up to the problems of large-scale production. Modern and costly machinery were not within the reach of the scant resources of Mexican capital which was sorely harried by the land-tenure pattern, commercial anemia, monetary instability, and low purchasing power of the working masses. It would have been impossible by all odds to find Mexican capital to supply electricity for a city of 750,000 inhabitants, or undertake to stretch lines for more than 300 kilometers through the craggy mountain ranges encircling the central plateau.

But, in the end, the constitutional dispensation of the Porfirian years, the sense of violated independence and endangered security, and the welfare inequities proved too much. Ideological, nationalist, and rural dissatisfactions with Díaz' dictatorial economic revolution from above converged. They yielded not a prompt movement into take-off but thirty years of revolution and reorganization of national life until Mexico could find a viable and stable political and social balance, consistent with sustained industrialization.

Briefly the period unfolded as follows:
— a modest recovery from the period of revolution, from 1920 to 1929, marked by an increase of GNP by perhaps 20 per cent and of manufacturing output by perhaps one third;[72]
— 1929–33, depression years, severely felt in Mexico as elsewhere;
— 1934–40, a concentration of public enterprise in land reform, agricultural improvement, highway construction, irrigation projects, electrifica-

tion, and school construction. Important in its own right and a symbol of this period was the founding in 1934 of the *Nacional Financiera*, which, along with three other major institutions (the Bank of Mexico, the National Bank for Agricultural Credit, and the National Bank for Urban Mortgages and Public Works), provided Mexico for the first time with strong centralized credit institutions, sensitive to government policy. Mexican recovery from the bottom of the depression proceeded strongly in tolerable order; and with a final dramatic expression of Mexican nationalism, in the oil nationalization of 1938, the country was ready for a new political and economic phase of development.

In chapter 4 (p. 139) we shall present some statistical data which suggest the character and pace of economic and social progress in these transitional years as compared with the phase of sustained growth that followed.

With the coming of the Second World War and the healing advent of Camacho, Mexico had assembled all the preconditions for take-off and proceeded to a phase of rapid industrialization rooted in a protectionist encouragement of consumer goods production – sectors which carried Mexican growth forward rapidly until their inevitable deceleration, which occurred in the late 1950s.

Conclusions

A quick review of the political experience of these eight nations in their pre-take-off periods underlines the significant sense in which each case is unique. The thrust and counter-thrust of their experiences with foreign intrusion; the changes they underwent in the structure and balance of their domestic rule, and in the doctrines which informed it; the functions carried out by the state in the decades preceding take-off – these passages of history represent a wide spectrum. No simple, uniform pattern emerges under the headings of security, of constitutional change, or policy towards welfare and growth.

Nonetheless, certain generalizations are possible.

— In all cases, reaction to foreign intrusion, actual or threatened, is relevant to the domestic thrust towards modernization. Intrusion appears in many forms, military, political, and economic, as does one kind or another of nationalist, modernizing response.

— Where external pressure is sufficient to underline the importance for security of modernization but does not intrude excessively on the conservative transitional regimes, they exhibit a considerable capacity to modernize incrementally, moving with the march of progressively more modern generations towards reform of agrarian arrangements, the modernization of the bureaucracy, the expansion and re-orientation of education, the development of a corps of private entrepreneurs and bankers, the reduction of the role of religious institutions, and, finally, the building of the technical preconditions for take-off. Where foreign intrusion, in effect, humiliates before its own people the conservative transitional regime, more violent and palpably revolutionary change occurs; for example, in China, Turkey, and Mexico.

— In terms of degree of democratic practice within the political system, and commitment to democratic goals, the cases represent a wide spectrum: from parliamentary government with a narrow electoral base in eighteenth-century Britain to nineteenth-century Russian czarist rule; from the Meiji oligarchs to post-1920 Mexican politics dominated by the party of revolutionary consensus; from the limited monarchies of post-1815 France and Germany to the strong personal rule of Atatürk to the KMT and Chinese Communists, both rooted in the conviction that only a single party dictatorship, derived from Lenin's model, could achieve effective unity in China. The inherently troubled and contentious nature of the transition from a traditional society to one capable of sustained industrialization did not lend itself easily to stable democratic rule.

— The technical preconditions for take-off were built in various combinations by foreign enterprise, local private enterprise, and out of government initiative. They tended to embrace, however, very similar basic elements: an expansion of commerce, of transport facilities, and, latterly, of an electric power base; the development of modern banking institutions; an increase in the number of those exposed to modern education; change, or the beginning of change, in land tenure arrangements, and the emergence of modern bureaucracy.

— The groups which assumed responsibility for purposeful policies looking to industrialization were, in differing combinations, soldiers, modern bureaucrats, and men drawn from pre-modern commercial or industrial life. They were, in short, the new men thrown up by the limited but real modernizing process of the preconditions period itself. Soldiers often emerge as major actors in the drama of the preconditions for multiple reasons: they are evoked or come forward to deal with external intrusion or civil war; they are among the first to become acquainted with modern technology through weaponry and modern concepts of administration, through training abroad or foreign advisers; they move by profession more easily than other groups towards loyalty to nation and sentiments of nationhood; and, in inherently turbulent times, when the legitimacy of traditional rule is shaken, they have access to raw power.

— The proportioning of power among the new men – and the relative role

of private and public sectors – can, in each case, only be explained in terms of each nation's:
— structure of political rule;
— military experience and problems;
— the extent to which private modern commercial and even limited industrial sectors developed during the sweep of the preconditions period, yielding a potential group of modern industrial entrepreneurs;
— and the scale of social overhead requirements, notably with respect to transport outlays which, in particular, tended to draw the state into an active role.

CHAPTER 4

THE POLITICS OF THE TAKE-OFF AND THE DRIVE TO TECHNOLOGICAL MATURITY

INTRODUCTION

The Unfolding of Industrialization

This chapter deals with politics during the first two stages of sustained industrialization itself. Here the primary engine of change becomes internal rather than external. We are dealing with interactions among the economic, social, and political dimensions of society mainly initiated from within, rather than by intrusion, pressure, or humiliation from without.

We examine how industrialization, beginning on a narrow front, proceeds unevenly – but proceeds. As it does so, it sets in motion forces and poses choices and dilemmas whose resolution constitutes a good deal of the political agenda. But now, unlike the situation during the preconditions period, growth itself provides an environment of rising real incomes and increased inputs to government which can be allocated to ease the new pressures generated by the industrializing society. Specifically, we shall try to suggest how certain major policy issues of constitutional equity and justice, of growth itself and welfare, and of national security were thrown up for decision and dealt with as societies began systematically to absorb the backlog and current flow of modern science and technology believed relevant to their economic situation. We shall look at the same illustrative cases as those covered by the historical notes in chapter 3.

The two stages are here dealt with in the same chapter. In economics, sectoral analysis permits the two stages to be quite sharply distinguished. But the rhythms of political life have a timing of their own. They render unrealistic excessively refined linking in time of economic stages and specific political events.

The Take-off[1]

The take-off is a phenomenon limited to relatively few sectors and, often, to limited regions within a nation. During the take-off, modern industrialization begins and expands rapidly. There are spreading effects from the key sectors of the take-off; e.g. modern cotton textiles and other light consumers goods manufactured in substitution for imports induce an expansion in the production of machinery and sources of power; railways lead to an expansion in coal, iron and engineering production, as well as an expansion in the size and efficiency of the market. The cities and all that go with them grow disproportionately. The society becomes increasingly caught up in the international economy and subject to cycles, trends, and other disturbances which play back on its economic and political life. The industrial worker comes on the scene as an increasingly important and assertive member of the society, as does the manufacturer and those who supply him credit and provide services to his plants.

But much of the society remains still caught in an older matrix, moving towards modernization at a slower pace, if at all. Some of the most difficult political problems of the take-off and drive to technological maturity thus lie in agriculture and rural life, modernizing to some degree but generally lagging behind the dynamic cities while still retaining great political leverage.

The take-off brings forward new urban men and groups of men who assert a claim on power and policy, putting pressure on the constitutional system. And it yields new problems of policy, equity, and, even, public order, usually centered around the organization of labor, human conditions in the factories, strikes and other forms of collective action. But it does so in a political setting where the old groups and problems still have heavy weight.

The surge of national confidence and ambition that accompanied this first phase of industrialization – as well as the increment of relative industrial capacity and military potential it generated – led certain nations to undertake limited adventures of external expansion in the competitive arena of power which persisted out of the mercantilist world, but widened with the extension of the international market and the increased efficiency of transport.

Industrialization lifted the restraints on income and income per capita built into the dynamics of the pre-Newtonian world. But it did not expand the globe's extent. Tempted by control over land, resources, and peoples beyond their borders, the stronger pushed outwards. They thereby set in motion fears and reactions which brought wars, small and great, as the differential timing of industrialization shifted the real or apparent balances of power.

Historically, this first sectoral surge of industrialization took about a generation to work itself out – until the natural forces of deceleration gradually slowed the rate of growth in the key sectors and reduced their capacity to impart momentum to the economy as a whole. A structural crisis can generally be observed towards the end of take-off, brief or protracted, as the economy relatively levelled off for an interval, until the underlying impulses for growth asserted themselves in the form of a new group of leading sectors. These intervals of transition have also had their effects on politics, as the setting in which long-gathering forces for change asserted themselves.

A view of economic growth in its early stages – as the process of diffusing new technologies to particular sectors of the economy which are subject to deceleration – poses the question: How sustained is self-sustained growth? To what extent is growth truly automatic after the take-off?

In one sense, it follows directly from the fact of sectoral deceleration that growth is not automatic. If a society is to sustain a high average rate of growth it must engage in an endless struggle against deceleration. The flow of modern science and technology may offer the potentiality of fending off Ricardian diminishing returns indefinitely. But a society which wishes to exploit this potentiality must repeat the creative pain of actually introducing new production functions as the old leading sectors decelerate; and it must demonstrate the capacity to exploit with vigor their potential spreading effects. In this sense sustained growth requires the repetition of the take-off process. It requires the organization around new technology of new and vigorous management; new types of workers; new types of financing and marketing arrangements.

There is, then, nothing automatic and easy about the inner mechanics – the logistics, as it were – of sustained growth.

In a larger sense, however, the experience of take-off appears, on present evidence, to be a definitive transition, like the loss of innocence. The reason for this judgment is that behind the whole industrial process lies the acceptance of the Newtonian outlook, the acceptance of the world of modern science and technology. Phases of difficulty and even relative stagnation after the take-off may, of course, occur; and they may be protracted. Men in societies must continue to struggle to keep growth moving forward. But it appears to be the case that the larger psychological, social, technological, and institutional changes required for a take-off are such as to make it unlikely that there will be a true lapsing back. The deeper fundamentals required for an effective take-off appear sufficiently powerful to make growth an ongoing process, on long term; and, in the ruthless arena of world power, a slackening of effort, stagnation, or a drawing back have brought danger from those abroad who persisted and moved relatively ahead.

The Drive to Technological Maturity

In the cases examined in this chapter, excepting mainland China, the post-take-off structural adjustment was achieved, with greater or lesser difficulty; and the drive to technological maturity took place – or is now taking place.

The drive to technological maturity is a longer period than the take-off. During this stage economies proceed to absorb and apply more or less fully what the unfolding stream of science and technology can provide. Historically – and on the contemporary scene as well – this is the time when steel, engineering and metal fabrication, chemicals, and the electric industry take the lead; although the expanding flow of invention altered the technological content of these broad industrial categories. Agriculture, with its working force steadily declining, becomes modernized – in a broad sense, industrialized. In most cases the cities come to dominate social and political life; although agriculture contends stubbornly to hold political prerogatives granted at an earlier time. The educational system is reorganized to meet the imperatives of progressive industrialization; although, given the inherent conservatism of educational institutions, there may be significant time lags. The bureaucracy expands, takes on new functions related to economic and social modernization, and becomes more professionalized.

It is in the drive to technological maturity, also, that efficient communications become truly national, with important effects on the proportion of the population linked both to commercial markets and to the national political process. In societies committed to democratic principles, the electorate generally expands; in autocratic societies, the problem of rendering docile, apathetic, or content large, better educated urban populations requires new methods of appeasement, persuasion, and control.

Progressive industrialization tends to be accepted as the central task of the society in this period; and those who manage it, in the public and/or private sectors, are substantially given their head. But as the process moves forward, a reaction develops, in one form or another, against the harshnesses and inequities that mass industrialization may bring. Pressures develop for tempering social reforms, for more equitable income distribution, and for one form or another of political control over concentrated industrial power. Men demand that some part of the enlarged potential inputs to government, provided by industrialization, be mobilized politically and applied to social welfare purposes rather than ploughed back in investment or diffused for private consumption.

Conscious of their emerging industrial stature, nations may also be tempted to translate their unfolding technical and economic capacities into enlarged power on the world scene at the expense of less advanced societies; thus, for example, the expansion of colonialism in the late nineteenth century.

In modern history, also, three nations weighed the weaknesses in the environment of military and political power around them and launched great enterprises of expansion designed to gain control not of limited areas close to their borders, as during take-off, but control over the balance of power in Europe, Asia, or both; that is, Germany in 1914 and 1939; Japan in 1931; and the Soviet Union in 1946.

This is the general background against which we turn to examine certain elements of uniformity and uniqueness in the evolution of politics in societies experiencing these first two stages of modern industrial growth.

Method of Analysis

In reviewing the politics of nations from the beginning of take-off through post-take-off adjustments down through the longer sweep of the drive to technological maturity, we are arraying some of the most thoroughly studied passages of modern history. Evidently, the purpose here must be limited. It is to establish if the view of politics represented by this book can contribute a useful perspective to these familiar stories. The political issues chosen to illustrate the unfolding of modern political life will, of course, be selective.

As in chapter 3, we shall summarize analytically the history of selected countries under the three headings into which political life is here divided; but because the primary engine of change is, for this period, taken to be domestic industrialization rather than external intrusion, we shall proceed with the following sequence of questions:

— What constitutional problems of justice and order arose including within the former enlarged participation in the political process?
— What policies were adopted towards growth and welfare?
— How did security policies alter during the sweep of industrialization, particularly in the two classic times of temptation to expansion: during the take-off and towards the end of the drive to technological maturity? The time periods examined are indicated in each historical case.

HISTORICAL NOTES ON THE POLITICS OF THE TAKE-OFF AND DRIVE TO TECHNOLOGICAL MATURITY

CONSTITUTIONAL CHANGE

Britain

The economic framework

The time period we consider in this stylized way for Britain is 1783–1914. Two factors in British history extend the time period to be treated under the headings of take-off and drive to technological maturity. First, there were the French and Napoleonic Wars and their immediate aftermath. The period 1803–19 – from resumption of war after the Peace of Amiens to the trough of the first postwar business cycle – can be regarded as so distorting

British economic development as to constitute a hiatus in the take-off. With export markets opened, cotton textiles moved forward rapidly after the war; and expansion was on a broad front to 1825, including an acceleration in coal and iron production;[2] but Britain then experienced seven uneasy years until the boom of the 1830s launched in a substantial way the railway age. This difficult interval, which was the political and social setting for the first Reform Bill, can be regarded as a period of readjustment between the take-off and drive to technological maturity.

Whether British attainment of technological maturity is dated by, say, the Crystal Palace Exhibition of 1851 or whether Britain is placed in the category of Germany, France, and the United States, achieving maturity in the period before the First World War, can be argued either way.[3] The view taken here is that Britain, after Crystal Palace, moved onward in growth at a modest pace. It used its capital and entrepreneurship substantially to help acquire resources through imports with which it was not sufficiently endowed; and it thus helped build the preconditions and assist the take-offs of other societies. It suffered along the way some of the costs of having led in the process of industrialization, to enter the new century with most of its initial lead gone. Put another way, the achievement of maturity by Western Europe and the United States early in the twentieth century, at the then existing level of technology, found Britain in a roughly equivalent position: while the newer nations had moved from take-off to maturity in the sixty years or so before the First World War, Britain had moved, in terms of income levels, from being a relatively poor mature society to being a relatively rich mature society.

The British economy, in its relations to Western Europe and the United States over these years, is to be understood, in part, as analogous to regions within developing nations that first moved into industrialization; for example New England, Milan-Turin, São Paulo. Britain continued to advance, but supplied along the way capital and technology to other regions at similar levels of cultural, social, and political development, which, relatively, caught up with the passage of time. British capital exports expanded both the sources for British imports and British export markets; they earned interest and repayments; but they also, on balance, probably yielded a slower rate of domestic expansion than might otherwise have taken place. Moreover, Britain exploited earlier than those who followed the lift in output that accompanies the shift in working force from agriculture to industry and other urban pursuits.

As Professor Kuznets' calculations indicate, real product per capita increased about twice as fast among the late comers of the Atlantic world as it did in Britain.[4]

TABLE 6. *Rates of economic growth in the five decades*
ending in 1913

Country	Period	Percentage change in real product per capita per decade
United Kingdom	1860–9 to 1905–14	12.5
Germany	1860–9 to 1905–14	21.6
Canada	1870–9 to 1905–14	24.7
Sweden	1861–8 to 1904–13	26.2
United States	1869–78 to 1904–13	27.5
Japan	1878–87 to 1903–12	33.7

Over this century and a quarter, excepting the years of the war with France, the British economy evolved mainly on the basis of private enterprise. There was hardly a year when one or another issue of economic or welfare policy was not before Parliament; but public interventions were limited to releasing or imposing constraints on a functioning market economy which was also at the center of the international economy.

The international economy, however, was subject, in turn, to business cycles and trend movements which were thrust into the arena of British politics.[5] The trend periods affected price levels and the relative prices of agricultural products; interest rates and profit margins; the terms of trade and the course of real wages. They can be roughly dated: 1790–1815; 1815–48; 1848–73; 1873–96; 1896–1914.

Over the whole span, British industrial production moved forward at an average annual rate of about 2.6 per cent; real national product at 2.8 per cent; population at about 1 per cent[6] – a more modest rate of progress, under less pressure from the side of population, than we find in contemporary nations which have moved into sustained growth. The accompanying table 7 indicates movements over shorter periods.

The electorate

The impact on politics of business cycles, harvests, and long-run economic forces interwove, in Britain as elsewhere. For example, the three most famous demands at Peterloo in 1819 were: 'A fair day's wages for a fair day's work', reflecting cyclical depression; 'No Corn Laws', reflecting high food prices; 'Equal Representation or Death', reflecting the anomalies of the old electoral system in an age of industrialization and urbanization.

TABLE 7. Basic data: pre-1914 British economy

Decades	Total national product	Total national product per capita	Agriculture, forestry, fishing	Manufactures, mining, building	Trade and transport
	(Compound percentage growth rates per annum for decade averages measured over 30-year periods[a])				
1801/11–1831/41	2.9	1.5	1.2	4.7	3.0
1811/21–1841/51	2.9	1.4	1.5	3.7	2.5
1821/31–1851/61	2.3	0.9	1.8	2.3	2.8
1831/41–1861/71	2.2	0.9	1.3	3.0	2.8
1841/51–1871/81	2.5	1.4	0.7	2.7	3.2
1851/61–1881/91	3.2	2.0	0.5	3.5	3.7
1861/71–1891/1901	3.3	2.2	0.7	3.5	3.6

Agriculture, forestry, fishing as proportion of total national income[b] (%)	Urban proportion of total population[c] (%)	Total government expenditure as proportion of GNP[d] (%)
1801 32.5		1792 11
1811 35.7		1800 24
1821 26.1		1814 29
1831 23.4	1831 25	1822 19
1841 22.1		1831 16
1851 20.3	1851 50	1841 11
1861 17.8	1861 55	1850 12
1871 14.2	1871 57	1860 11
1881 10.4	1881 60	1870 9
1891 8.6		1880 10
1901 6.4	1901 77	1890 9
		1900 15
		1910 13

[a] Phyllis Deane and W. A. Cole, British Economic Growth, 1688–1959, Cambridge, 1969, pp. 170 and 172 (where sources are indicated).

[b] Ibid., pp. 166–7, where sources are indicated.

[c] General Reports of the Census of England and Wales.

[d] A. T. Peacock and J. Wiseman, assisted by J. Veverka, The Growth of Public Expenditure in the United Kingdom, London, 1967, pp. 37 and 42. The 1910 figure is calculated by the authors in terms of 1900 prices (p. 42).

The decisive role of Parliament in English politics was, of course, settled in pre-industrial times; and, on the land, the feudal structure had long since been superseded by a commercialized agriculture, carried forward in the eighteenth century by the process of enclosures sanctioned by a Parliament heavily weighted with agriculture interests. The most important constitutional issue faced over this span in Britain was, therefore, the widening of the electorate, bringing in, successively, the new urban middle class, the industrial worker, and the agricultural worker (and miner).

The reform movement was, in fact, gaining ground in the early 1790s; but the excesses of the French Revolution and the moods of war yielded a conservative reaction which postponed decision until 1832. Even then the limited expansion of the electorate and reform of the rotten boroughs yielded a major crisis in Parliament which might not have been successfully resolved if the confidence of the older political leadership was not shaken by an environment of widespread unrest, due to cyclical depression, high food prices, and revolutionary events on the continent.

But the volatility of the urban worker in 1832 – and the fears he generated – was not sufficient to win him the vote. In Britain at that time, only a quarter of the population lived in towns of over 20,000 inhabitants.[7] But the balance shifted rapidly in the railway age that was gathering momentum in the 1830s. By 1870 the urban proportion was about 57 per cent.

The Reform Bill of 1867 reflected the expanding numbers and assertiveness of the urban worker, but also Disraeli's doctrine that the worker could be drawn away from middle class Liberal leadership.

The Reform Bill of 1884, which brought Britain close to universal male suffrage,[8] had as an immediate objective the strengthening of the left wing of the Liberal Party; but by that time the concept of universal suffrage had gathered much strength, and the stability of British politics after the Reform Bill of 1867 was sufficient to reduce anxiety about unpropertied voters.

The period closes with Lloyd George's great struggle over the veto powers of the House of Lords. The substance of the issue falls within the scope of welfare problems: social insurance and its financing. But the constitutional battle had to be won if the state was to play the role universal suffrage would decree for it in the twentieth century.

The status of organized labor

A second constitutional strand can be tracked over this span of British history – the role of organized labor under the law: the status and legitimacy of trade unions and strikes, raising fundamental questions of both justice and public order; and the role of unions in politics.

In an environment of rising food prices and expanding demand for labor, England experienced a series of strikes in 1799, mounted by the expanding friendly societies of workers. Dealing with a new phenomenon out of an old tradition, the Combination Acts of 1799 and 1800 made illegal all collective working class activity except the old guild functions. The Combination Acts were repealed in 1824, in the liberal and *laissez-faire* mood of Parliament. Alarmed by a wave of strikes which followed, in a year of high food prices and full employment, the repeal was considerably hedged in the Act of 1825.

The unions gathered strength as the British economy moved to industrial maturity; and the precise rights of and restrictions on collective action became the subject of public policy from time to time. In February 1867, for example, the unions felt endangered by the setting up of a Royal Commission which enquired into the use of violence by unionists; and their financial integrity was endangered in the same year by a court ruling that unions could not sue for the recovery of funds appropriated by dishonest officials. But the Reform Bill of 1867 gave an underlying strength to the political position of the working class, reflected in clarifying legislation of 1871 and 1875.

The unions carried forward with their right to strike protected until 1901. The House of Lords then upheld the right of the Taff Vale Company to sue for damages incurred in a strike triggered by a group of railwaymen acting without approval of their union; and the matter became an issue in the election of 1906. The Liberal victory yielded a reversal by Parliament.

A further constitutional issue was raised in 1909 when the House of Lords upheld a court judgment that it was unlawful for a union to expend funds for political purposes – a ruling supplanted by Parliament in 1913.

In short, labor's power at the polls, acquired in 1867, and its *de facto* acceptance of the society's basic structure, ultimately resolved in its favor the contentious issues within the constitutional system.

France

The economic framework

The period of French political history considered here is 1830–1914.

As the accompanying table 8 indicates, French politics unfolded against a background in which French industrial production expanded at about an average annual rate of 2.5 per cent; gross domestic product, in constant prices, at about 1.2 per cent; population at a rate as low as 0.5 per cent.[9]

The urban population rose from about 24 per cent (1846) to only 44 per cent (1911).

TABLE 8. *Basic data: pre-1914 French economy*

	Nineteenth-century rates of growth in real product[a] (gross domestic product at constant (1905–13) market prices)				Agriculture as proportion of gross domestic product[a]		Central government expenditure as proportion of gross physical product[b]		Urban proportion of total population[c]	
	gross domestic product	gross domestic product per capita	agriculture	industry and crafts						
	(%)	(%)	(%)	(%)		(%)		(%)		(%)
1799–1839	—	—	0.92	2.78	1788	50	1788–90	15		
1839–52	1.11	0.67	1.01	2.36	1852	45	1825–74	15	1846	24.4
1852–80	1.15	0.98	0.38	2.66	1880	39	1875–84	21	1866	30.5
1880–92	1.11	0.92	0.20	2.49	1892	32	1885–1913	20	1876	32.4
1892–1902/3	2.00	1.87	1.11	2.69	1902/3	30			1886	35.9
1902/3–12	1.67	1.41	1.01	2.38	1912	27			1896	39.1
									1906	42.1
									1911	44.1

[a] J. Marczewski, 'The Take-off Hypothesis and French Experience', in *The Economics of Take-off into Sustained Growth* (ed. W. W. Rostow) New York, 1963, p. 136. Marczewski's calculations of physical product at constant prices covering shorter periods (p. 135) exhibit more clearly the expansion in growth rate in what I take to be the French take-off period, 1830–60.

[b] J. Marczewski, 'Some Aspects of the Economic Growth of France, 1660–1958', in *Economic Development and Cultural Change*, April 1961, p. 372.

[c] J. H. Clapham, *The Economic Development of France and Germany, 1815–1914*, Cambridge, 1928, p. 159. See, also, C. P. Kindleberger, *Economic Growth in France and Britain, 1851–1950*, Cambridge, Mass., 1954, p. 253, for certain intermediate dates and the rate of growth of Paris.

By 1914 France had partially caught up with British industrialization, but Britain had at last surpassed France in population (approximately 42 versus 40 million on the eve of 1914, as against 21 versus 30 million in 1820). France remained still a country with a high proportion of its people in the countryside.

The electorate and its government

Politically, the French take-off occurred under the auspices of the quasi-constitutional monarchs Louis Philippe and Louis Napoleon, the latter elected in 1852 with the kind of nationalist popular appeal represented later in Europe by Disraeli and Bismarck.[10]

The underlying problems of French politics in this period were, of course, the unresolved divisions left by the outcome of the Revolution and Napoleon's adventures, symbolized by the tension between Paris and the rest of the country, in which progress came only after Paris went too far; the nation as a whole asserted itself; and uneasy compromise solutions emerged from the bitter counterpoint.

From 1815 to 1871 France straddled the issues of monarchy versus republicanism, catholicism versus anti-clericalism. The rise of industry and the cities gradually shifted the balance towards the republican and secular resolution of the 1870s; but that unstable resolution, like the restoration of monarchy in 1815, was brought about only after defeat in war. Struggles over the size of the electorate and the locus of power in the government reflect this underlying lack of a national political consensus in France.

The July Revolution of 1830 was brought about proximately by the publication of three reactionary ordinances, one of which would have restricted the electorate to about 25,000 persons, mainly landed proprietors. The electorate was widened after 1830 to include some of the new manufacturers, numbering perhaps 200,000 on the eve of the Revolution of 1848. Electoral reform remained a central focus for French discontents, although industrialization also brought socialist ideas into French political life of the 1840s.

Against this background, high food prices and unemployment detonated the Revolution of 1848 and yielded an expansion of the electorate from 200,000 to some 9,000,000, as all Frenchmen over twenty-one were granted the vote. The resultant conservative parliament and the failure of the provisional government to provide jobs for the unemployed brought on the violence in Paris of June, leaving another traumatic scar on French political life.[11]

The new constitution of November 1848 retained the principle of universal suffrage for both parliamentary and presidential elections, but left the relative powers of the legislative and executive branches in a state of ambiguity. Louis Napoleon was elected president in December 1848. In three years he felt sufficiently strong to sweep away the constitution of 1852. A much weakened parliament was to be elected every six years, which could sit for only three months a year under severe restrictions.

Like the powers of parliament, the degree of freedom of the press in France oscillated over these years, as it had since 1789.

The rapid growth and prosperity of the 1850s appear to have sufficed to maintain political calm in France; but liberal pressures against imperial rule gathered in the 1860s. The growing urban electorate became restive at the lack of representative government; and this uneasiness was compounded by French failure in Mexico and the swift rise of Prussia. There was movement toward parliamentary government, with the Ollivier ministry forming in January 1870 the first government of the Second Empire responsible to Parliament. And in other ways the 1860s was a period of piecemeal liberal progress within the framework of the monarchy.

Then came defeat in the Franco-Prussian war, with the humiliation of Napoleon's capture and the bitter failure of the Paris Commune. The Royalists were the initial residual legatees. The National Assembly elected in February 1871 was composed of almost 400 Royalists of one stamp or another, 200 assorted Republicans, and some 30 Bonapartists. But, in the end, the events of the 1870s confirmed the Third Republic, with legislative power anchored firmly in the National Assembly and the principle of universal male suffrage reaffirmed. The Royalists could not agree on a king; their parliamentary strength proved transient; and by 1875 France had stumbled its way to a constitution which reflected something like a national consensus.

This dispensation persisted through ninety-nine governments in seventy years, rooted in a fragmented multi-party system. This instability was balanced by the strength and continuity of the French civil service which, from Colbert to Jean Monnet and beyond, plays a critical entrepreneurial role in French modernization. Nevertheless, the French Parliament had, at last, won the initiative; and it held on through the crises of Boulanger and Dreyfus, of militarism, clericalism, and imperialism that marked the relatively successful and vigorous march of French industrialism down to 1914.

The Third Republic must be accounted a formidable political achievement, given the tensions of nineteenth-century French political life. The marks of its birth in the protracted struggle over the legitimacy of the Revolution, however, and the haunting confrontation of Republicans and Reactionaries after 1848 and of their counterparts twenty-three years later, fragmented and distorted French political life thereafter.

A political system of one-man one-vote yielded less strength for urban interests and the working man in France than Britain. And this fact is reflected not only in the recurrent bloody contrapuntal tension between Paris and the countryside but also in the constitutional evolution of the French trade unions.

The status of organized labor

The years of revolution and war had resulted, as in England, in an initial denial of the French workers' right to organize and to strike. Legislation of 1791 had declared all associations of either masters or men illegal. It was reinforced by articles under the Civil Code which made the master's word decisive in the courts; prohibited association of more than twenty persons; defined as a criminal offense concerted striking or picketing. These provisions were reinforced by a law of 1834 which forbade associations of even twenty persons if they were part of some larger whole. This measure responded to a certain amount of secret labor organization and illegal activity.

As in Britain, however, labor organizations devoted to mutual help were tolerated in the old guild tradition. Labor's banners in Paris during the Revolution of 1848 reflected both the dreams of the early Socialist thinkers and urgent problems, such as unemployment and the length of the working day. The brief flowering of these hopes and proposals ended in Louis Napoleon's takeover of 1851 and the exiling of many Republican and Socialist leaders. The shorter working day, briefly granted by the Republic, was denied. The effort to revise the laws of 1791 was frustrated by the law of November 1849 under which combinations remained illegal.

Nevertheless, as with parliamentary government, the 1860s saw some significant *de facto* liberalization. In 1864 the clause of the Penal Code which made concerted action a crime was abolished. And four years later the ruling that the master's word would be decisive in the courts as against the worker's was removed from the books.

As in 1848, violence and tragedy cut across these ameliorative developments, destroying for a time labor's capacity to make its interests felt. The Commune united briefly passionate dreams of a new social order – and protest against real discontents – with a surge of national pride and desperate courage. Both were set back in 1871. Survivors were transported. Amnesty to leaders of the Commune was not offered for eight years; and the Third Republic waited until 1884 until complete freedom of association was formally granted to the wage-earners of France.

In the previous decade, however, the unions in Paris grew. More than 130 were in existence by 1875 and the first French Labor Congress took place in

1876. By the eve of the First World War there were just over one million unionists in France, as opposed to three times that number in Britain. The French worker, like others throughout the more advanced part of the industrial world, felt in the prewar decade the pressure on real wages of rising prices; although the pressure was less than in Britain, Germany, and the United States. The direction of response in France was similar to that in Britain. Clemenceau's radical program of 1906 included provisions for old-age pensions, income tax, workmen's compensation, an eight-hour working day, and governmental control of labor contracts and the mines. But the parliamentary balance converged with the erratic syndicalist performance of the unions to yield only a modest result. The party ideologies of France, arrayed on lines that reached back to 1789, did not encourage either stable labor alliances with the Radicals (like British labor's early association with the Liberals). By doctrine, experience and perhaps temperament, the French worker was led to think in terms of the general strike and great moments at the barricade – providing, along with the limited funds the C.G.T. could mobilize, a reason for French labor's pre-1914 incapacity.[12]

Germany

The economic framework

We consider here the period from 1840 to 1914 in Germany. Constitutional change unfolded against the background of growth indicated in the accompanying table 9. The German population increased at about 1 per cent per annum over this period, output at 2.6 per cent. It was the high rate of industrial growth (3.8 per cent) which permitted Germany to close the gap on Britain and France. In 1914 Germany was more urbanized (at 60 per cent) than France (44 per cent); less urbanized still than Britain (77 per cent).

The electorate and its government

Even the Frankfurt Parliament, dominated by German liberals, could not agree on a lucid constitutional form for the liberal German state. Its proposal of 27 March 1849 left final executive power in the hands of the emperor, balanced in an ambiguous way by the principle of universal suffrage.

With the refusal of Frankfurt's offer by Frederick William, the constitutional issue came to focus in Prussia itself. Under the Constitution of 1850 two-thirds of the votes were held by citizens paying taxes in the two highest brackets; one-third were allocated to the poorer majority. The Diet springing from this limited electorate nevertheless confronted the new

TABLE 9. *Basic data: pre-1914 German economy*

	Nineteenth-century rates of growth (1913 prices)[a]			Industry and handicrafts as proportion of net domestic product (1913 prices)	Agriculture, forestry, fisheries as proportion of net domestic product (1913 prices)	Urban proportion of total population[b]		Government expenditure as proportion of GNP[c]	
	net domestic product	agriculture, forestry fisheries	Industry and handicrafts						
	(%)	(%)	(%)	(%)	(%)		(%)		(%)
1850–54	..	..	..	20.4	45.2	1816	26.5 (Prussia)		
1855–59	..	..	..	21.5	44.3	1852	28.5 (Prussia)		
1860–64	..	..	..	22.5	44.9	1861	30.7 (Prussia)		
1865–69	..	..	..	25.1	42.4				
1870–74	4.6	..	..	29.7	37.9	1871	36.1	1872	7.2
1875–79	0.4	..	..	30.7	36.7				
1880–84	2.3	..	..	29.8	36.2	1880	41.4	1881	8.8
1885–89	2.8	..	..	31.3	35.3				
1890–94	2.9	..	..	34.0	32.2	1890	42.5	1891	11.1
1895–99	3.8	..	..	35.6	30.8				
1900–04	2.8	..	..	36.6	29.0	1900	54.4	1901	16.2
1905–09	2.7	..	..	38.4	26.0			1907	14.4
1910–13	4.0	..	..	40.9	23.4	1910	60.0	1913	15.3
1850–1913	2.6	1.6	3.8						

[a] W. G. Hoffman, *Das Wachstum der Deutschen Wirtschaft Seit der Mitte des 19. Jahrhunderts*, Berlin, Heidelberg, New York, 1965, pp. 13, 26, 33, 37, 63. For a breakdown of German national product by industry and agriculture under somewhat different definitions, see S. Kuznets, 'Quantitative Aspects of the Economic Growth of Nations', II. Industrial Distribution of National Product and Labor Force', *Economic Development and Cultural Change*, July 1957, p. 69.

[b] J. H. Clapham, *The Economic Development of France and Germany, 1815–1914*, Cambridge, 1928, p. 278.

[c] S. Andic and J. Veverka, 'The Growth of Government Expenditure in Germany since the Unification', *Finanzarchiv*, January 1964, p. 183.

emperor William I twelve years later on the classic issue of parliamentary power, the military budget.

Bismarck, called as the Emperor wavered, ruled for four years as minister-president without a formal budget.[13] Those four years saw his triumphs in Schleswig-Holstein and over Austria. The elections held on the day of the battle of Sadowa (3 July 1866) yielded a parliament no longer prepared to struggle in the spirit of 1862. The Progressive Party, whose formation in 1861 signalled the opening of the acute phase of the constitutional crisis, split. Bismarck's success in moving towards unity, his proposal for a parliament elected by universal suffrage, his acknowledgment of the illegality of tax collection since 1862 through a proposed act of indemnity were sufficient for an overwhelming majority to accept on 3 September 1866 a government in which the power over the purse lay ultimately with the executive.

This decision was formalized by the Constitutions of 1867 and of 1870, in which the Reichstag, elected by direct universal manhood suffrage, could not deny the government its flow of revenue and thus could not make and unmake the ministries.

The German Reichstag was, however, more than an instrument of popular protest. German chancellors became sensitive to its shifts in mood and composition. Bismarck himself was rendered vulnerable by the defeat of his Coalition of Conservatives and National Liberals in 1890. But at critical moments the Reichstag could be ignored, as Bethmann ignored the vote of censure in 1913.

Its relative impotence stemmed not merely from a formal lack of vital parliamentary powers but also from the fragmentation of the German parties.[14] In the eight major elections from 1884 to 1912, the number of parties ranged from seven to nine. The rise of the Social Democrats in the early years of the century, for example, brought it in 1912 only about 30 per cent of the votes. The parties tended to look on themselves as instruments to deflect in favorable directions a national policy made by others rather than as instruments to make a responsible national policy.

The tendency was strengthened by the acceptance of Prussian leadership as the realistic condition for national unity. The overriding priority Germans had accorded unity since 1848 lay behind Kaiser William II's remark after the outbreak of war in 1914: 'There are no more parties; I see only Germans.' The mood had been, in fact, foreshadowed in the previous year by Social Democratic support for the large finance bill to expand the German armed forces.

What part does the constitutional structure of Imperial Germany play in the outbreak of the First World War? There is, of course, no answer that can be given with confidence. What was required to maximize the chance that war could be avoided was a firm coalition in the Reichstag that might have strengthened the hand of those in the executive who did not wish to pursue grandeur at the cost of war. The elements for such a majority coalition were there in the Social Democrats, Center, and Progressive People's Party. But the habits of special interest, protest politics and of emotional attachment to half-meant ideological formulations kept such a majority from crystallizing. And to this outcome the lack of true parliamentary responsibility may have contributed.

But it is by no means sure such a coalition would have stiffened Bethmann's back as he confronted Moltke, imprisoned, in turn, by Schlieffen's rigid plan, or strengthened the Kaiser's last minute impulse to pull back from war. Nor, indeed, is it sure that the parliamentary leaders could have withstood the temptation that plan represented for a quick, decisive movement of Germany to European hegemony. German nationalism was on the rise; and the surgical Franco-Prussian War was the memory and the model most men in central and western Europe tended to carry in their heads. Few in responsibility could conceive of the bloody stalemate which trenches and barbed wire, machine guns and artillery, backed by massive steel and engineering industries, could contrive; although a sense of impending tragedy was present among some, as the flags were broken out and mobilization begun.

Reflecting on the political roots of the tragedy, Holborn looks not to the fragmented parties as a possible staying hand but to those closest to the emperor:[15]

The emperor might have proved pliable, if a strong *Fronde* among the nobility or a powerful opposition among the bourgeoisie had arisen. As a matter of fact, among his advisors and friends there were quite a few who knew his frightful shortcomings and entertained grave doubts about the general course of German policy. But they remained voices in the wilderness, since the Prussian *Junker* class saw in an authoritarian monarchy the indispensable shield of their class privileges and since the German upper bourgeoisie was equally convinced that its interests were best protected by such a strong monarchy. The national idea, which half a century earlier this bourgeoisie had championed as a means for the realization of freedom, had become largely, and for some exclusively, the lever for higher rank among the nations of the world. William II's colonial and naval policies were most heartily supported by the German bourgeoisie. In their general direction the German policies of this period expressed the sentiments of the ruling classes, which, blinded by Germany's rapidly rising economic strength, were unaware of the harsh realities of political life that strong as well as weak powers must meet responsibly.

The status of organized labor

The paternalistic absorption under Prussian nationalist leadership of assertive new strands arising from industrial and urban life which marked German constitutional history down to 1914, characterized also the handling of organized labor.

The shock of the French Revolution and Napoleonic rule weakened the control of the guilds over German labor in the early years of the century. It widened in degree the working man's freedom of movement from one trade to another. Guild attitudes, institutions, and control were, nevertheless still powerful in 1848.

At that time the journeymen began to assert a program independent of the master craftsmen which was similar to the worker's agenda in other nations in the earliest phase of industrialization:[16]

They wanted freedom of migration throughout Germany, a minimum wage, and a twelve hours' day. They wanted representative trades councils and a responsible Labour Minister for all Germany. They wanted to abolish the absolute legal compulsion to belong to a gild, if you were even to practice a trade, which was still quite common outside Prussia, where it was only the taking of apprentices in specified trades that was confined to qualified masters. And they wanted factory owners to be free to hire gild trained journeymen if they liked – such freedom was often denied – because factories might pay better than the qualified masters. On the whole, what they asked for was an easing of the old shoes where they pinched, not a new pair. They were not thinking of general principles or planning a new society.

Nevertheless, the Prussian law of 1849 reasserted the system of government and guild control over entry and standards of competence in some seventy trades. It was not until the 1860s that the momentum of industrialization swept away the old quasi-feudal structure. In 1869 the law of the North German Confederation opened access to all but medical trades and navigation.

Along with this pragmatic recognition of the needs of a modern labor market, the dynamics of the swift German take-off yielded almost simultaneously the emergence of a German Socialist party with a heavy commitment to Marxist doctrine. The struggle for parliamentary status – and, from 1878, the struggle against Bismarck's repressive legislation – occupied the Socialist leadership down to 1881. They then turned part of their energy to union organization which was then permitted; although the unions continued to be harassed by police commissioners.

Union membership rose slowly, amounting to only about a quarter million in the mid-1890s. The trend rise in German prices and cost of living down to 1914 put a new premium on collective efforts to redress the pressures on real wages imposed by the cast of developments in the world economy. By 1909 there were three million union members in Germany, since 1880 mainly voting Socialist at elections, but primarily concerned with wage levels and hours of work. Collective bargaining took hold quickly in the first decade of the new century. By 1914 collective bargaining governed the wages and hours of some two million members of the work force; and the workers' pragmatism gradually suffused the Socialist movement, diluting its doctrinal character while leaving its rhetoric largely intact.

Russia

The economic framework

For Russia the take-off and drive to technological maturity embrace phases under both tsarist and Communist rule: from 1890 to, say, 1962, with the drive to technological maturity beginning in the years of recovery just before the First World War. For reasons suggested below, the Cuba missile crisis is taken as an arbitrary end of this phase of Russian history.

The definition of the period – and its analysis – is complicated by three factors: the heavy impact on Russia of two major wars; the total reorganization of Russian society after 1917; the commitment made by Stalin in the early postwar days to pursue Soviet power short of war with the United States rather than to base Soviet security on major power accord within and outside the United Nations. The resultant protracted Cold War affected the allocation of resources within the Soviet economy. There were, roughly, two waves of Soviet expansionist enterprise: Stalin's from 1946 to 1951; Khrushchev's from 1958 to 1962.[17] A defensive phase for the Soviet Union (excepting the Middle East) began with the outcome of the Cuba missile crisis and the exacerbation of Sino–Soviet relations at that time. This turn of events coincided with a period of marked deceleration in the heavy industry sectors which had dominated the Russian drive to technological maturity in the 1930s and the 1950s. The upshot was a decline in the rate of growth of the Soviet economy as a whole. The 1960s also saw slow movement towards the automobile and durable goods sectoral complex on which the next surge in Soviet growth would most naturally be based, given the level of income per capita attained in the 1960s and what we know of Soviet consumer tastes. Although there is no assurance that the Cold War will, in fact, wane, it is, *ad interim*, not inappropriate to regard the Soviets as caught up in the 1960s in a version of a structural crisis between two stages of growth: a drive to technological maturity, extended by a phase of effort at external expansion; and the age of high mass-consumption.

The broad sweep of Russian development over this period is suggested in the accompanying table 10.

Industrialization and constitutional change: two regimes

The emancipation of the Russian serfs in 1861 set in motion social and economic processes which altered the locus of power under a constitutional system which maintained an essential continuity down to 1905. The transfer of land from an increasingly hardpressed nobility continued: by 1877 they had sold 13 per cent of their holdings; by 1916, 59 per cent. Industrialization, at first slow but gathering real momentum after 1890, drew former serfs into a factory working force of over two million by 1913, when industry, mining,

TABLE 10. *Basic data: Russia and U.S.S.R., 1850–1969*

Annual rate of growth: total population	Annual rate of growth: total output		Annual rate of growth: industrial output[b]		Urban proportion of total population[c]		National income per capita 1900 prices (rubles)[d]	
(%)	(%)		(%)		(%)			
					1850	5.5		
			1860–80	4.2	1870	12.3	1870	50.0
	[a]1860–							
[a]1860–1916 1.5	early 1880s	c. 2.25	1880–1900	7.9	1890	12.7	1885	53.5
	early 1880s–							
	1913	c. 2.75	1900–13	4.1	1900	12.8	1900	66.5
			1870–1913	5.4	1910	14.3	1913	76.5
[e]1913–28 0.6			1913–28	0.1	1920	16.7		
1928–37 1.0	[f]1928–40	4.2	1928–40	9.9	1930	19.9	1928	74.5
1937–40 6.4								
1940–50 −0.9	1940–50	1.9	1940–55	4.6	1940	31.6		
1950–5 1.7	1950–58	6.8	(1950–5	9.6)	1950	38.4	1954	166.9
	1960–69 (say)	5.0	1913–55	4.4	1960	48.8		

[a] R. W. Goldsmith, 'The Economic Growth of Tsarist Russia 1860–1913', *Essays on the Quantitative Study of Economic Growth*, presented to Simon Kuznets on the occasion of his Sixtieth Birthday, 30 April 1961, *Economic Development and Cultural Change*, April 1961, pp. 441–43.

[b] G. W. Nutter, *Growth of Industrial Production in the Soviet Union*, Princeton, 1962, pp. 164–5. Nutter's estimate is based on an index of industrial materials production. The pre-1914 estimates are, as in other cases of rapid growth from an initially narrow industrial base, sensitive to weighting. For other estimates see A. Gerschenkron, 'The Rate of Industrial Growth in Tsarist Russia since 1885', *The Tasks of Economic History*, 1940; and Goldsmith, *op. cit.*, especially p. 465. For Soviet period, see A. Bergson and S. Kuznets (eds.), *Economic Trends in the Soviet Union*, Cambridge, Mass., 1963, p. 155.

[c] Bergson and Kuznets, *op. cit.* pp. 72–3.

[d] S. Kuznets, *Quantitative Aspects of the Economic Growth of Nations*, 'I. Levels and Variability of Rates of Growth', *Economic Development and Cultural Change*, October 1956, p. 81. The figures for 1870 to 1913 are for European Russia; 1954 for interwar territory of the U.S.S.R. Basic calculations are from R. W. Goldsmith.

[e] Nutter, *op. cit.* p. 288. The figure for 1937–40 includes territorial acquisition. The figure for 1940–50 reflects severe war losses.

[f] Bergson and Kuznets, *op. cit.* p. 6. The rough estimate for 1960–9 is the author's, from various sources.

and communications employed almost five million workers. The zemstvos introduced an element of local self-government. There were significant reforms in the courts and in the recruiting of the army. And new groups of modern administrators and industrialists emerged. The Soviet historian Peter Lyashchenko thus summarizes the critical take-off decade of the 1890s:[18]

During the last decade of the nineteenth century, industrial capital, displacing small-scale production, routine technology, and backward social relationships, was rapidly advancing Russian industry. To be sure, by volume of production in specific industries Russian industry still lagged far behind the advanced nations of the period. In the course of one decade, however, it had none the less progressed substantially, reaching a degree of industrial concentration much higher than the most advanced capitalist countries. With respect to its tempo of development during these years, Russian industry outstripped nearly all countries. The smelting of pig iron during this ten-year period, for example, increased in England by 18 per cent, in Germany by 72, in the United States by 50, and in Russia by 190, as a result of which Russia became the seventh ranking power in 1880, sixth in 1890, fifth in 1895, and fourth in 1900. The production of iron during this period increased in England by 8 per cent, in Germany by 78, in the United States by 63, and in Russia by 116. The coal industry of Great Britain expanded by 22 per cent, that of Germany by 52, of the United States by 61, and that of Russia by 131. Finally, in number of spindles operating in the cotton industry, England made a gain of 3.8 per cent in the course of the same decade, the United States, 25.6, the European continent, 33, and Russia, 76. By virtue of this number of spindles, Russia in 1890 owned 4 per cent of the world's total number of spindles and 14 per cent of the total spindles in use on the European continent, while by 1899 it accounted for 6 per cent of the world total and 18 per cent of the European total number of spindles.

... the 1890s definitely brought the national economy of Russia into the world system of capitalist economy as a major national–capitalist entity with vast natural possibilities for development and with capitalist institutions penetrating deeply into the nation's economy.

But while the content of Russian life changed, the autocratic basis of government and politics was strongly reaffirmed:[19]

I know that recently in some of the gatherings of the zemstvos voices of persons were heard who were carried away with senseless dreams on the participation of the representatives of the zemstvos in the matters of internal government. Let all know that I, while devoting all my powers to the good of the people, will maintain the basis of autocracy with the same firmness and steadfastness as did my unforgettable late father.

The growing forces pressing for constitutional change found their opportunity in the converging discontents of the period 1900–5: the railway boom lost its momentum as the take-off came to an end; Russia felt the weight of international cyclical depression; and the war against Japan was lost.

These forces brought together, into a critical mass, discontents long present but not hitherto explosive:

— rigid, increasingly outmoded autocratic rule;

— a massive, unpopular bureaucracy incapable of moving fast enough to keep up with the inherent pace of economic and social change;

— an articulate but politically ineffective and fragmented intellectual opposition;

— deeply resistant non-Russian nationality groups within the Empire;

— an urban working force seeking, essentially, ameliorative improvements in real wages, working conditions, etc.;

— a long-smouldering peasantry, increasingly restless at the substantial remnants of serfdom, despite progress since 1861.[20]

The circumstances of Russia in 1905 evoke elements from both the British position in 1832 and the French position after the defeat in the Franco-Prussian War. The structural transition from one phase of growth to another, cyclical stagnation and unemployment (as in Britain, 1832), and the loss of legitimacy that accompanied defeat (as in France, 1871), created an environment in which the new modern men, emerging with the take-off, forced a change in the constitutional system. In the Russian case this occurred through widespread strikes and violence in which workers, peasants, and students participated.

Perhaps a thousand workers were killed during a demonstration in front of the Winter Palace in St Petersburg on Bloody Sunday in January 1905.[21] This set in motion a chain of events leading to a general strike and the Manifesto of October formally altering Russia from an absolutist to a constitutional monarchy.

In the next two years the scope of the electorate and the powers of the Duma were progressively reduced by Nicholas II, frightened by the depth of the discontents revealed among workers, peasants, and the non-Russian nationality groups. Nevertheless, under Stolypin, Russia had from 1907 forward a prime minister and a ministerial council; a parliament which could serve as a forum for protest; political parties; a relatively free press; and trade unions could exist, without the right to strike. Like France and Germany, however, Russian political life was bedevilled by the fragmentation of the political parties, of which ten or more were represented in the pre-1914 Dumas.

As in France after 1830, 1848, and 1871, the revolution of 1905 yielded movement forward, far short of the objectives of those who carried the burden of revolt. Nevertheless, the new dispensation served as the political framework for economic and social progress on a wide front down to 1914. Stolypin's gamble on the more enterprising peasant led to a sharp increase in agricultural production (see table 11), including rapid expansion in farm machinery and chemical fertilizer application.[22]

Although the rate of increase in industrial production slowed down, there was about a 50 per cent increase in the years from the cyclical peak around the turn of the century to 1913, as opposed to a doubling in the 1890s.[23] In this phase the railway boom decelerated, but (excepting oil) industry moved forward on a more diversified basis. The Russian standard of living – still low relative to Western Europe – was rising. With its political structure in transition from autocracy to constitutional monarchy, with the Emancipation of 1861 at last fully implemented, Russia moved beyond take-off into the early phase of the drive to technological maturity.

Perhaps the most remarkable development of these years was the expansion of education at all levels, including the acceptance in 1908 of a policy of universal primary education. Zemstvo outlays in primary education rose from 25 million rubles in 1905 to 105 million rubles in 1914, representing an

TABLE 11. *Index numbers of crop production in 72 provinces of the Russian Empire, 1895–1913*

(1896–1900 = 100)

Year	Grains	Potatoes	Industrial crops	All crops
1895	97.8	98.0	102.0	98.3
1905	117.6	117.8	100.4	115.8
1913	169.1	146.5	134.0	162.9

increase from 20 per cent to 31 per cent of total zemstvo expenditures. At the national level the Ministry of Education spent 44 million rubles in 1906 (2.1 per cent of the budget), 143 million rubles in 1913 (4.6 per cent of the budget). By 1915 more than half the school-age population (8.1 million) was enrolled in elementary schools.[24]

The strains of protracted major war proved more than this massive complex society, working its way out of a backward traditional past, could surmount in continuity. Lenin had sensed in 1902 that the majority of Russian workers would follow the pragmatic choice of the workers of Western Europe, opting for gradual improvement in their lot rather than violent revolution. He looked to the seizure of power by a disciplined conspiratorial minority rather than the building of majority support for the Bolshevik faction of the Social Democrats. And he found his time in November 1917 to seize 'the commanding heights' of Russian society against a moderate revolutionary regime hobbled by inexperience and a commitment to continue to fight with its allies against the Central Powers.

Lenin permitted the election for the Constituent Assembly, that Kerensky's government had scheduled for the end of November, to take place. It occurred with the Bolsheviks already in power and considerable capacity to influence the result. They earned only 168 of 703 seats, about 24 per cent. A clear majority was held by the more moderate Russian and Ukrainian Social Revolutionaries. On 18 January 1918 the Constituent Assembly rejected by 237 votes to 136 the superiority of the soviets as constitutional organs; the Bolsheviks and their supporters walked out; and the Constituent Assembly was disbanded, leaving latent in Russian history a challenge to the legitimacy of Communist rule.

Once power was seized, the Bolsheviks had to fill the gap left by Marxist theory with respect to the actual handling and administration of power. This they did, step by step, by extending, from the practice of conspiracy to the practice of government, the notion of a highly disciplined elite corps whose leadership and legitimacy were justified in terms of their knowledge of Marxist theory and the correctness of the decisions they would make in terms of the course of history. It followed directly that the first and overriding priority of the Soviet government was the perpetuation in power of the Communist Party.

Having survived the civil war, the Soviet Union was preoccupied in the 1920s with economic recovery, including a reversion to private incentives in agriculture under the N.E.P. It took some five years of political manoeuvering after Lenin's death for Stalin to emerge in 1929 as his unambiguous successor.

Stalin then faced a situation marked by three key facts:

— The success of N.E.P. was strengthening the hand of the independent peasantry and even small businessmen, and was producing a political, social, and economic situation which threatened the power of the Communist Party over the country.

— Russia's industrial advance from the Revolution to 1928 had been slow, representing merely a recovery back to 1913 levels. Russia as an industrial and military power was still weak.

— By 1928 Stalin fully controlled the instruments of power within the Soviet state: the Party organization, secret police, army, and state administration, all of which were much strengthened since the days of decision in 1921–2.

In this setting, Stalin inaugurated in 1929 the second phase of the Russian drive to technological maturity with his program of accelerated collectivization and industrialization. At enormous human cost and a disastrous reorganization of agriculture, a high rate of industrial growth was achieved in the 1930s, centered on heavy industry.

This high growth rate reflected, in part, the long-term result of the basic restructuring of the society after 1921, including increased literacy and technical training, improved management, and other factors difficult to measure. The Soviet regime in these years had to reorganize or create afresh, within the framework of the new structure, elements which had been generated between (say) 1861 and 1917, but which war, and especially revolution, had damaged, e.g. a class of industrial managers (now state rather than private), a substantial group of technicians, an industrial working force.

TABLE 12. *Average annual growth rates of industrial production, by industrial group: Soviet Union, 1928–40*[25]

	(%)
ALL PRODUCTS	9.9
All civilian products	8.5
Intermediate products	11.9
ferrous metals	12.8
nonferrous metals	19.8
fuel and electricity	15.5
chemicals	11.9
construction materials	6.6
Civilian machinery and equipment	18.9
transportation equipment	27.7
agricultural machinery	−0.1
Consumer goods	4.8
food and allied products	5.3
textiles and allied products	3.7
consumer durables	25.0

The high growth rates after 1928 also reflect a rapid rate of growth in population. They were achieved against this background of favorable influences, however, only by a sharp increase in the volume of resources currently devoted to investment. The collectivization of agriculture was designed, in part, to contribute to this result. Collectivization was reinforced by programs of state finance which succeeded in diverting resources away from urban consumption (by taxation and inflation) and away from agricultural income. Soviet Russia moved from a position in the 1920s where perhaps 15 per cent of the national income was invested to one where investment input has steadily taken about 25 per cent of current resources, except in periods of very high armament outlays.

The major constitutional event of the 1930s was, in effect, the Great Purge. In a unique, insane historical passage virtually a generation of men was removed from key posts, destroyed or exiled, carrying with it millions of minor figures who fell within categories judged *prima facie* suspicious by Stalin.

The ability of the Soviet structure to survive this period hinged not only on Stalin's ruthless will but also on the fact that a new second generation of men was emerging toward the end of the 1930s. Unencumbered with memories of the Revolution and of Lenin and trained in the Soviet system, these men were prepared to take over the posts in the bureaucracy (including the Party) vacated by the victims of the Purge.[26] In effect, the young engineer took over from the old revolutionary as the key figure in the Soviet structure of power.

With allied help and a surge of nationalist sentiment deeply rooted in the Russian past, the Soviet system recovered from Stalin's grotesque miscalculation of Hitler's intentions and survived the German invasion. It recovered quickly, and proceeded forward on the basis of a continued concentration of investment in heavy industry and high military outlays. The inevitable deceleration of the heavy industry sectors was predicted by Soviet planners in the late 1950s and took place in the 1960s.[27] As the planners looked ahead to 1970, that deceleration would continue; and the lift would have to come from vehicles, durable consumers goods, and the modernization of agriculture (see table 13).

TABLE 13. *Selected output targets of Soviet industry,*
1958–70

	1958	1965	1970
Electric power (billion kWh)	235	507	830–50
Oil (million tons)	113	243	345–55
Gas (billion m³)	29.9	129	225–40
Coal (million tons)	493	578	665–75
Steel (million tons)	54.9	91.0	124–9
Passenger-cars and trucks (thousands)	511	616	1,360–1,510
Tractors (thousands)	220	355	600–25
Mineral fertilizers (in conventional units, million tons)	12.4	31.3	62–5
Textile fabrics (billion m²)	5.8	7.5	9.5–9.8
Leather footwear (million pairs)	356	486	610–30
Granulated sugar (million tons)	5.2	8.9	9.8–10
Radio receivers (millions)	3.9	5.2	7.5–8.0
Television sets (millions)	1.0	3.7	7.5–7.7
Refrigerators (millions)	0.4	1.7	5.3–5.6

SOURCE: Directives of the 23rd Congress of the CPSU for the Five-year Economic Development Plan of the Soviet Union for 1966–70 and Mr Kosygin's introductory statement.

In a sense, these movements bring to an end the drive to technological maturity launched after the Revolution of 1905.

Under Soviet rule Russian society continued to move forward in economic and social modernization, on a wide front. Illiteracy was brought low; the educational system geared to the requirements of advanced industrialization; social services made available to the population as a whole; increased consumers goods erratically provided as income per capita rose.

Technically, agriculture has remained relatively inefficient under collectivization, requiring an abnormally high proportion of the working force as compared to other nations at similar levels of per capita income.

The major constitutional event of the postwar years was change in the system of managing the Soviet secret police. The secret police had become, under Stalin, a personal instrument for control not only of the population as a whole but over his immediate subordinates, the bureaucracy, and the Communist Party itself. As Khrushchev told his colleagues on 24 February 1956 the Soviet leadership under Stalin lived in a state of terror, like the population as a whole. His successors first killed Beria, who initially inherited this ultimate instrument of power, and then placed the secret police under collective committee control. This led to a higher degree of legal order in Soviet life; and it was accompanied by a reduction in the population of forced labor camps and political prisons. The secret police has been less capriciously used since Stalin's death; but it remains in being and active when the present collective leadership can agree on the appropriate direction of its use.

Politically, the Soviet system remained a single-party dictatorship, based on the co-option of talent, with major debates confined to its own organs and only sporadically reflected in the press. Within the Communist Party, the Central Committee, when controlled by Khrushchev, was used as a constitutional organ to install him in power in 1957; and the Presidium was used to remove him in 1964. There is no evidence that stable constitutional arrangements have evolved governing the inner political life of the Russian Communist Party.

Unions were converted, during the 1920s, to instruments of state and party control over the working force. The right to strike was denied; but significant allocations were made to welfare and social security, as outlined below (pp. 148–9).

What we see in Russia, then, is the industrialization of a society under two quite different political regimes. As of 1914 forces were clearly at work moving towards a constitutional monarchy based substantially on private ownership of land and industrial property within which economic expansion, increasing equality of social opportunity, increasing individual freedom, a widened electorate, enlarged power for the Duma were predictable trends. At an early point in the drive to technological maturity this system – broken by the strains of war – was seized and converted into a single-party dictatorship in which government ownership was pervasive. The continued unity of the Russian Communist Party – or, better, its capacity to contain its quarrels short of disintegrating struggle – has permitted more than a half century of Communist rule, under modern conditions of popular control.

The problems faced as Russia modernized were similar to those confronted by other societies proceeding through and beyond the drive to technological maturity. The balance of incentives and controls by which the continuity of Communist rule has been maintained has proved consistent with the development of men and institutions capable of absorbing the bulk of relevant modern science and technology into Russian life. It is still to be demonstrated that the system can be efficiently converted to high mass-consumption. The difficulties are great but do not appear insuperable.

The pattern of development that Russia might have pursued, if the continuity of its evolution had not been broken by war and the Leninist takeover, cannot, of course, be predicted. If consumer sovereignty had worked in the markets and voter sovereignty increasingly at the polls, the rate of investment might have been somewhat lower; the allocations to military purposes somewhat lower after 1945; allocations to agriculture, housing, and consumer goods somewhat higher. Recovery after the First World War might have been brisker, as in Western Europe. And with these differences in balance, there is no reason to believe Russian economic and social life – taken overall – would be less modernized than at present. It seems most unlikely, for example, that so high a proportion of the working force would still be tied up in agriculture.

Politically, the central questions posed by the Soviet experiences are: why has the impulse observable elsewhere – including pre-1917 Russia – for government by the consent of the governed not asserted itself? Will it assert itself in the future?

Is the *de facto* passivity of the Soviet citizen a result of his perceiving no realistic and viable alternative, in the setting of controls and threats he confronts? Do the institutions of controlled participation in Soviet society, and the rewards for performance that society offers, provide an alternative to conventional democratic politics which the Soviet citizen would choose if the option became realistic?

We do know that the secret police and the forced labor camps are hated and feared; and that the humane values of pre-1917 Russian culture survive in Soviet life. We also perceive, in such testimony as Solzhenitsyn's, that the dialogue among the damaged and dissident includes, in its moving assertions of human integrity, no clear vision of a path to an alternative political system, despite frustration, or worse, in the setting in which they find themselves.

In a remarkable essay Andrei Amalrik, a Soviet citizen, has recently addressed himself to the sub-structure of political sentiment in contemporary Russia. He describes a small intellectual 'Democratic Movement', split three ways: towards a Marxism-Leninism, purged of deviations attributed to the present Soviet system; a Pan-Slav Christianity; and Western liberalism. This group, as a whole, he regards as relatively impotent.

Second, he identifies a substantial bureaucratic middle class aware of the system's inadequacies but committed by sentiment, habit, and interest to the *status quo*.

Third, the bulk of the population, which he describes in these terms:[28]

As I see it, popular views can best be described by the words 'passive discontent.' The discontent is directed not against the regime as such – the majority do not think about it, or they feel that there is no alternative – but rather against particular aspects of the regime, aspects which are, nevertheless, essential to its existence.

The workers, for example, are bitter over having no rights vis-à-vis the factory management. The collective farmers are resentful about their total dependence on the kolkhoz chairman, who, in turn, depends entirely on the district administration. Everybody is angered by the great inequalities in wealth, the low wages, the austere housing conditions, the lack of essential consumer goods, compulsory registration at their places of residence and work and so forth.

This discontent is now becoming louder, and some people are beginning to wonder who is actually to blame. The gradual though slow improvement in the standard of living, due largely to intensive housing construction, does not diminish the anger though it does somewhat neutralize it. It is clear, however, that a sharp slowdown, a halt or even a reversal in the improvement of the standard of living would arouse such explosions of anger, mixed with violence, as were never before thought possible.

Inasmuch as the regime, because of its ossification, will find it increasingly more difficult to raise industrial output, it is obvious that the standard of living in many sectors of our society may be threatened. What forms will the people's discontent take then? Legitimate democratic resistance or an extreme form of individual or mass acts of violence?

He sees these groups as incapable of initiating change except in the environment he predicts for the period 1975–80: a protracted war with China whose strains unleash forces in the Soviet Empire with which neither bureaucrats nor soldiers can cope. Under circumstances of such disarray, Amalrik believes pent-up desires for constitutional change and improved welfare would find expression. On his assessment, nationalism in Eastern Europe and within the Soviet nationality groups would break the bonds with Moscow.

In effect, Amalrik evokes the mechanism of breakdown of the traditional pre-Newtonian empires and Russia of 1905 – a linkage of which he is clearly aware.

We do not have analyses of the Soviet Union parallel to those of Almond and Verba on the United States, Britain, Germany, Italy, and Mexico, measuring the citizen's assessment of his capacity to influence the course of political events and his degree of apathy and withdrawal.[29] Such a study would, presumably, show a low degree of confidence in the Soviet citizen's ability to affect his political environment and a high degree of apathy. Clearly, the Soviet system is geared to encourage these moods and assessments; and it has been skillful as well as purposeful in neutralizing political activists outside the formal machinery of the system.

What has been demonstrated clearly is that a single party can seize the powers of state and hold them for a long time in the world of modern methods for control, if it maintains its unity of purpose; and that a well-educated population can be induced to live and perform with reasonable efficiency in this setting. The Soviet leadership has thus far lived successfully by Plato's dictum:[30] 'Is it not a simple fact that in any form of government revolution always starts from the outbreak of internal dissension in the ruling class? The constitution cannot be upset so long as that class is of one mind, however small it may be.'

Japan

The economic framework

The period considered here for Japan runs from the beginning of take-off in the 1880s to postwar recovery in, say, 1952. The technically mature Japanese economy is then rounded out and turned with extraordinary exuberance to the purposes of high mass-consumption.

The broad contours of Japanese economy over these years are suggested in the accompanying table.[31]

The electorate and its government

As the take-off began, the Meiji oligarchs were committed, by the Imperial Rescript of 1881, to constitutional government by 1890. The constitution presented to the people in 1889 was explicitly modeled on that of Bismarck's of 1867. Two Germans, Roessler and Morse, played a significant role in its design. As in Germany, the Cabinet was the instrument of the Emperor, not the Parliament; and parliamentary powers were limited. The bicameral Diet could supervise expenditures but not deny the executive the right to collect taxes and carry forward the tasks of government. The government was authorized to carry on with the previous year's budget should a finance bill be rejected by the Diet.

TABLE 14. *Basic data: Japan 1878–1942*

Period	Annual rate of growth: total population[a] (%)	Urban proportion of total population[b] (%)	Proportion occupied population in primary industry[c] (%)	(period)	Annual rate of growth: real national income[d] (%)	Annual rate of growth: industrial production[e] (%)	(period)	Consolidated government expenditures as proportion of GNP[f] (%)
1878–82	..	..	82.3	1878/87–1883/92	4.3	8.6	1879–83	10
1883–7	0.8	..	79.2				1884–95	15
1888–92	0.9	..	76.1	1883/92–1888/97	4.9	7.4		
1893–7	1.0	..	73.1					
1898–1902	1.1	..	69.9	1888/97–1893/1902	5.5	8.4	1896–1904	20
1903–7	1.2	..	66.5	1893/1912–1898/1907	3.0	3.9		
1908–12	1.3	..	63.0	1898/1907–1903/12	2.9	2.9	1905–12	25
1913–7	1.2		59.2	1903/12–1908/17	3.6	6.5		
1918–22	1.2	1920 51	54.9	1908/17–1913/22	4.0	5.6		
1923–7	1.4	1925 56	52.0	1913/22–1918/27	5.2	4.3		
1928–32	1.5	1930 60	50.5	1918/27–1923/32	5.6	6.6		
1933–7	1.4	1935 64	47.7	1923/32–1928/37	4.8	7.5		
1938–42	..	1940 68	44.6	1928/37–1933/42	4.3	7.8		

a K. Ohkawa, *The Growth Rate of the Japanese Economy Since 1878*, Tokyo, 1957, p. 19. See, also, estimates for phases of Japanese growth roughly parallel to the stages of growth used in the present volume, K. Ohkawa and H. Rosovsky, 'A Century of Japanese Economic Growth,' in W. W. Lockwood (ed.), *The State and Economic Enterprise in Japan*, Princeton, 1965, pp. 89–92.
b Census data.
c Ohkawa, *op. cit.* p. 28.
d *Ibid.* p. 21.
e *Idem.*
f Harry T. Oshima, 'Meiji Fiscal Policy and Agricultural Progress', in Lockwood, *op. cit.* p. 366.

In wider terms this constitution consolidated in practical form the political organization of modernizing Japan which had emerged from the swirling currents of thought and policy which flowed from 1868. It left power centered in the group of samurai which had overthrown the Tokugawa in the name of national dignity; but it accepted a degree of parliamentary authority and political freedom as an authentic sign of modernity.

The drive for parliamentary government was conducted from 1874 by Liberals through an organization called the Liberty and Popular Rights Movement. And concessions were, in fact, made to their demands.[32]

Three political parties emerged out of the constitutional debates of the early 1880s: a hard-driving Liberal Party; a more cautious Progressive Party; and a narrower but still influential Imperial Party, conservative in outlook but also committed to a constitutional process. In the difficult years of deflation and rural unrest (1881–5), the parties were curbed. In effect, they disappeared to re-emerge with the approach of the election of 1890, the Liberals and Progressives in relative continuity.

The initial electorate was exceedingly narrow: some 450,000 in a population of about 40 million. Only men over twenty-five and with a prior record of paying national taxes of 15 yen or more per year, could vote.

The House of Representatives, which met at the end of November 1890, was made up as follows:

Liberals	130
Progressive	40
National Liberals	5
Pro-Government	80
Independents	45
Total	300

A breakdown by occupation in the table below (p. 131) indicates the relative dominance of the propertied village gentry.[33]
Mason concludes:[34]

... the politics of 1890 are of a piece with the politics of the next half century ...

... the essential argument in the political arena [was] between the Government bureaucrats and the upholders of popular rights. The former wanted statism with an element of Liberalism; the latter combined an underlying commitment to the State with a Liberal programme for its organization and government. The argument persisted, and with it the process of achieving constitutionalism through interaction. In many ways, it was a mistrustful and badly geared process; but it worked, has gone on working, and has accomplished much ...

The counterpoint between entrenched bureaucracy and elected politicians continued as the backbone of Japanese political life. But, as in Germany, the limit on parliamentary power did not prevent the Diet from becoming something more than an instrument of protest and debate. An experiment in party government was conducted as early as 1898. Without formal change in the constitution, more or less responsible cabinet government had emerged in the late 1920s.

This trend was strengthened by the progressive expansion of the electorate, with the reduction in property qualification. By 1912, the electorate was three times the 1890 figure, at 1.5 million; 3 million voted in 1920; and after universal manhood suffrage was granted in 1925, over 12 million voted in 1928.[35]

Occupation	No. of members
Senior officials (in office or recently retired)	18
Junior officials (i.e. Kuchō and Gunchō in office or recently retired)	22
Agriculture	125
Trade and industry	33
Law	22
Journalism	16
Medicine	3
Others	61

Neither party structures nor the constitutional system as a whole could weather the strains and temptations of the Great Depression and the disruption of the power equilibrium it caused in the world. With respect to the parties, Ike observes:[36]

Although by the 1920s political parties had become strong enough to form cabinets occasionally, they had not become a wholly integral part of the political structure. It will be recalled that the concept of a party was something borrowed from the West. During their formative years, the parties had to work within an alien and even hostile setting. Even after decades of existence they were exercising no very immediate power. They were unable, therefore, to exhibit or even to develop a lively sense of political responsibility. More often than not, they appeared to the public as symbols of factional strife and corruption.

The parties, perhaps undercut by the military exploitation of the association of reservists, were unable to resist the military take-over of the 1930s and were dissolved.

Behind the institutional failure was the constitutional provision which centered in the Emperor ultimate control over both the military and civil arms of government. The civilian politicians as a body were not prepared to advise the Emperor to resist the military thrust for power.

In turn, this diffidence in confronting the issue of military–civil authority stemmed from the convergence, in the 1930s, of problems of welfare (the depression), constitutional order (conservative fears stemming from universal suffrage), and security (the apparent opportunity for Japan to achieve hegemony in Asia).[37]

The Japanese political equilibrium which had evolved since 1868 collapsed, to be reconstructed only after military defeat which, as in France, Germany, and Russia, proved a powerful instrument of constitutional change. The Constitution of 1947 shifted authority unambiguously to the Diet and to the leaders of the majority party which has proved to be the Liberal Democrats. Women acquired the vote. With military expenditures virtually ruled out, Japan concentrated its energies and its technically mature industrial establishment on tasks of growth and welfare, enjoying a generation of progress unique in its history – or anyone else's.

The status of organized labor

Freedom of labor to organize and to strike came only slowly and late to Japan. The ricksha men protested the introduction of the trolley car as early as 1883; and this initiative was treated as a criminal act, a general view incorporated in Police Regulations of 1900.

In the years after the First World War, as Japan joined the I.L.O., trade unions were permitted. The labor market did not provide a setting in which unions could easily flourish. There were ample reserves of rural workers flowing from the countryside. And there was a dual industrial system containing small-scale, scattered labor-intensive production as well as modern capital-intensive plants. Peak union membership in the 1930s was only 420,000 of a working force of perhaps 3 million in industry, mining, and modern transport.

It was only after 1945 that modern unions emerged, with constitutional rights approximating those in other more advanced industrial nations.

China

The economic framework

Since 1952 there has been considerable expansion in the Chinese economy; although statistical data, aside from foreign trade, are not firm. Steel production may have increased from under two million tons to something over ten million. Electric power expansion and new oil development have greatly increased the energy base. A substantial chemical industry has been built underpinning an otherwise dangerously weak agricultural position. Major progress has been made in engineering and electronic industries. But this progress was mainly achieved in the 1950s. Important setbacks occurred after the Great Leap Forward and the Cultural Revolution. The economy of China in 1970, taken overall, had not advanced greatly beyond the position ten years earlier, despite its nuclear weapons, missiles, aircraft, submarines, and a satellite in orbit.

Foreign trade data confirm the image projected by such production data as are available. They show a doubling of the volume of imports between 1952 and 1960, to a level of about $2 billion; a decline to $1.5 billion in 1961; a recovery to the 1960 level in 1966; a more limited setback in the wake of the Cultural Revolution, about retrieved by 1969. The weakness of agriculture decreed, however, higher expenditures of foreign exchange for food and fertilizer in the 1960s than in the previous decade, a lesser level of capital goods imports.

The central constitutional fact about Communist China since the effort to launch sustained industrialization in 1952 is, then, that the take-off effort aborted at the end of the 1950s; and in the 1960s the mainland was thrown into a rolling unresolved crisis touching every dimension of political life: military and foreign policy; policy towards welfare and growth; the locus of power within the single party system clamped on the nation in 1949.

The failure of the take-off stemmed from a classic distortion of policy. In urgent pursuit of security objectives abroad and a romantic revolutionary vision at home, Mao designed an unworkable policy towards growth. The welfare demands and aspiration of the Chinese people could be contained by the control system; but the control system could not substitute for the lack of incentives and investment in agriculture. The system failed to generate inputs to government consistent with its objectives.

A constitutional crisis under Communism

From their own perspective, the Chinese Communist leaders faced five major and urgent tasks as they came to full power on the mainland in 1949:

1. To create and install a new national government structure under effective total Communist domination.

2. To bring the Chinese population immediately under full control.

3. To exploit promptly and to the limit compatible with avoiding major war the perceived potentialities for external expansion.

4. To alter permanently the balance of social power in rural and urban areas (by eliminating or weakening the landlords, rich peasants, and urban middle class), and to bring the newly elevated classes (poorer peasants, urban workers, youth, and women) under full Communist leadership and control.

5. To meet the requirements of government finance, to end inflation, and to reconstruct the economy in such a way as to provide a foundation for sustained and state-controlled economic growth.

The constitutional evolution of the system interweaves with Mao's effort to generate from an unyielding peasant agriculture the inputs necessary to fulfill a military and foreign policy beyond China's grasp at this period in its history. The most fundamental question faced by Mao was the organization of rural life where perhaps 80 per cent of the Chinese population lived. He moved progressively from a bloody land redistribution at the expense of the larger landholders; to forced grain collections at government-determined prices; to collectivization. The basic decision to move to collectivized agriculture appears to have been made towards the end of 1953. It was announced in January 1954 in the form of a scheduled rate of movement of peasants into producers' cooperatives. The institutions of collectivization, the intensity of pressure on the peasant, the efficacy of local administration, and the role of private plots have oscillated over the sixteen years that followed. There were, for example, the grandiose communes of the Great Leap Forward of 1958 and their failure. But Mao never wavered in a policy of virtually eliminating private ownership of the land and substituting for it organization and central power, projected down to the village level. Like Stalin's reversal of the N.E.P., Mao reversed the Communist insurrectional appeal to the peasant that revolution would provide him land and the fruits of his labor. Like Stalin, he wished both to assure total political control over the rural population and to acquire agricultural output on favorable terms for the cities, industry, and export. The result of damping private incentives has been sluggishness in output and patient, stubborn peasant evasiveness. These have helped frustrate Mao's ambitions and limited Chinese modernization over the whole first generation of Communist rule.

It was against this background of endemic frustration that Mao's two great ventures were undertaken to substitute political, spiritual, and revolutionary energy for conventional material incentives: the Great Leap Forward of 1958 and the Cultural Revolution of 1966. The first aimed to yield a surge in agricultural and industrial resources available to the state by labor-intensive methods. The second aimed to produce a social and political base in China which would supplant the rising tide of bureaucratic pragmatism and perpetuate Mao's revolutionary principles beyond the span of his life.

Both efforts failed. They yielded a *de facto* constitutional structure within the continuing framework of Communist rule in which:

— the military is the least damaged and most powerful of the administrative systems;

— the Communist Party is weakened and riven as a bureacratic apparatus;

— the remarkable unity of the Long March veterans is broken;

— the youth and students have been stimulated, then split and frustrated by the outcome, including the virtual shut-down for two years of the educational system.

The organization of power and policy in post-Mao China cannot be confidently predicted. But the underlying tendencies, beneath the two waves of romantic intervention by Mao, have been towards meeting in degree the peasant and worker's requirements for material incentives, and providing agriculture with the chemical fertilizers which are necessary if productivity is to rise in a system where the possibilities of water control and double-cropping were well exploited before 1949.

In effect, Mao used his immense power and prestige to pursue policies inappropriate to the modernization of China. He thereby postponed that process for a decade at least and exhausted the revolutionary zeal of his supporters. He may have opened the way for a second generation to get on with the job in a more conventional way if a stable social and political balance can be found among them.

He also granted to the rest of Asia a decade to find its feet and begin to fashion a framework of progress and cooperation which might balance in the long run the power and influence of the modernized China which, in time, would surely emerge.

In short, Mao failed, where Stalin succeeded, in finding under Communist dictatorship a formula by which his nation could move forward, after a fashion, in the process of industrialization. Mao's failure of the 1950s lay in his desire to emulate Stalin of the 1930s at a time when China's tasks were more nearly those of Russia in the 1890s – an agenda of take-off. He lacked the insight or patience to accept the fact that China of the 1950s was not yet sufficiently modernized to serve as the vehicle for his external ambitions.

Turkey

The economic framework

The constitutional evolution of Turkey in the thirty-five years since its take-off began, occurred against the background of the broad pattern of economic development indicated in the accompanying table 15 (p. 136).

The judgment here is that the first surge of industrialization occurred in the late 1930s; the war years; and the postwar surge to the mid-1950s. After an awkward period of readjustment in the late 1950s, the economy moved forward in the 1960s, on a more diversified basis, in the early phase of the drive to technological maturity.

TABLE 15. Basic data: Turkey, 1927–1967

Annual rate of growth: total population[a] (%)		Urban proportion of total population[b] (%)		Annual rate of growth: real national product[c] (%)		Annual rate of growth: real product per capita[c] (%)	Annual rate of growth: industry[d] (%)		Proportion of gross domestic product originating in manufactures, mining, construction, transport and communications[e] (%)	
1927–35	3.4	1927	24	1927–37	4.1	2.0			1939	23
1935–40	2.0			1937–47	2.0	0.4			1948	19
1940–5	1.1								1955	26
1945–50	2.2	1960	32	1945–57	5.8	3.1	1950–60	5.9	1960	29
1950–60	2.9								1965	32
1960–5	2.5			1957–67	6.3	3.6	1960–5	7.4		

[a] Z. Y. Hershlag, *Turkey, The Challenge of Growth*, Leiden, 1968, p. 299.
[b] *Ibid.* pp. 297 and 299.
[c] Lester Pearson, *Partners in Development*, New York, 1969, p. 318.
[d] Z. Y. Hershlag, *op. cit.* p. 342.
[e] *Ibid.* p. 340.

From dictatorship to democracy

Turkish politics has been shaped by the movement from a single-party to multi-party rule. Atatürk organized early the Republican People's Party whose unity under his leadership provided him a base for his rule. It also permitted him to dominate a parliament which, while constitutionally feeble, still reflected conservative and other opposition elements. Atatürk twice experimented with the toleration of a second competitive party. In each case disruptive results led to its abolition or withdrawal.

Atatürk died in 1938. His successor, Inonu, moved promptly, after the end of the war in Europe, to open the way to the building of an opposition party. The Democratic Party was founded in January 1946. It came to power with Menderes as Prime Minister in 1950, in Turkey's first free, modern competitive general election.

Caught up in the structural crisis of the late 1950s, Menderes used military forces and other measures against the opposition, judged inappropriate by many Turks. His response to an acute problem of growth led directly to a constitutional crisis, and he was overthrown in a military coup of May 1960.[38] For a year and a half Turkey was ruled by a National Unity Committee of military men.

Popular pressure for a return to civil constitutional rule was palpable. The People's Party accepted that prolonged military rule would undermine its popular strength. Its friends on the junta accelerated the writing of a new constitution and the calling of elections.

The new constitution of the Second Turkish Republic set narrower limits on executive power and provided for a bicameral legislature. A proportional rather than majority system was installed for parliamentary elections. In this period the Democratic Party was banned.

As the electoral process was resumed, two new parties competed for the voters who had supported the Democratic Party: the Justice Party and the new Turkey Party. This fragmentation yielded three fragile coalition governments and two abortive military coups until Demirel won a 53 per cent popular majority for the Justice Party in 1965. In the election of October 1969, eight parties ran candidates under the system of proportional representation.

As Turkey emerged from its structural crisis, towards the end of take-off, and moved in the 1960s into a more diversified stage of growth, the old alignment of reformers versus conservatives gave way to a new emphasis on growth itself, with the degree of freedom in the private sector in some contention. Demirel, reflecting an emerging, well-trained younger generation of public and private administrators, but with strong ties also to an increasingly modernized countryside, was able to hold a majority as the nation enjoyed an annual growth rate of about 6.5 per cent. The rhythm of economic and social change decreed that Demirel would deliver in his first five years something of what Menderes promised but could not fulfill.

Although in many ways a successor to Menderes, Demirel mended his fences with the military whose role was reduced with the rise of other modern elements in Turkish society, but still remained powerful.

Basically, Turkey found in the 1960s at least transient reconciliation between a policy consonant with rapid movement towards industrial maturity and a competitive democratic political system, with a mercurial and activist youth the major dynamic element on the scene, as in many other parts of the world, as well as an expanding trade union movement, granted the right to strike and organize on a modern basis in 1963. It remains an open question whether the constitution of 1961 will provide a basis for stable democracy.

Mexico

Progress and continuity

Mexico moved forward in straightforward constitutional continuity during the thirty years after 1940, against a background of steady economic expansion suggested in the accompanying table 16.

Growth decelerated briefly towards the end of the 1950s and in the early 1960s; but then strongly resumed as the drive to technological maturity, with its diversified pattern of industrialization, took hold. In this setting the PRI – and the presidential system which evolved with it – has been able to maintain its unity with little fragmentation or defection.

The quasi-monopolistic position of the PRI and the extraordinary powers granted to a Mexican president for a single six-year term have posed the question: How democratic a political system does Mexico enjoy?

Assessing the situation in the early 1960s, a thoughtful commentator could conclude:[39]

Lopez Mateos allowed opposition into the House of Representatives, for the banner of revolutionary democracy had worn unbelievably thin. In fact the only people who have found democracy in Mexico in recent years have been naïve foreign commentators who have given up assessing political democracy and turned to analysing 'social democracy.' The Mexicans themselves have not been misled, however, and the lack of political democracy has been continually criticized, especially by the intellectuals. Still, the people are philosophic about the Revolutionary Family, for they have always been governed by one elite group or another. If the official party continues to sponsor national growth and cedes to the demands or desires of pressure groups, complaints will be neither loud nor effective.

A similar conclusion is expressed by Brandenburg who places more emphasis on the role of the President and the Mexican security agencies, less on the PRI as an institution.[40]

Mexico enjoyed a path of remarkably regular economic and social progress by the stop-and-go standards of other major Latin American nations.

TABLE 16. *Basic data: Mexico, 1895–1964*

Annual rate of growth: total population[a]	Urban proportion of total population[b]		Annual rate of growth: gross national product[c]	Annual rate of growth: manufacturing[d]	Federal government expenditure as proportion of GNP[e]	
(%)	(%)		(%)	(%)	(%)	
			1895–1910 2.9	5.0		
	1910	28.7				
			1910–21 0.7	− 0.8		
	1920	31.0				
			1921–9 1.7	4.8		
					1925	6.3
			1929–34 2.6	0.0		
	1930	33.5			1930	6.4
1931–40 1.7						
	1940	35.1			1940	8.6
			1934–45 6.1	9.4		
					1946	6.6
1941–50 2.8						
	1950	42.6				
					1952	10.8
1952–60 3.1	1960	50.7	1945–64 6.1	7.5	1958	11.1
					1961	13.7

[a] *Mexico's Recent Economic Growth, The Mexican View*, ed. and intr. by Tom E. Davis, Austin and London, 1967, p. 175, Victor L. Urquidi.
[b] J. W. Wilkie, *The Mexican Revolution: Federal Expenditure and Social Change since 1910*, Berkeley and Los Angeles, 1967, p. 218.
[c] T. E. Davis, *op. cit.* p. 26 (Enrique Pérez López).
[d] *Idem.*
[e] J. W. Wilkie, *op. cit.* p. 7.

Mexico has also enjoyed, as Brandenburg notes, important degrees of freedom of speech, press, religion, and assembly. And opposition parties exist, although they are frail.

The Almond and Verba analysis reveals that in most tests of democratic attitudes – notably of the individual's capacity to influence his political environment – Mexico rates higher than Italy, close to Germany, but below Britain and the United States. Tables 17 and 18 suggest the character of their findings.[41]

In comparing Germany and Mexico, at very different stages of growth and income per capita, they conclude:[42]

Mexico lacks the developed educational system that produces the high levels of cognitive political skills in Germany, but it has what Germany lacks to produce a high level of system affect. Mexico has had a symbolic, unifying event: the Mexican Revolution. This revolution, as we have argued, is the crucial event in the development of the Mexican political culture, for it created a sense of national identity and a commitment to the political system that permeates all strata of the society.

TABLE 17. *Percentages who say the ordinary man should be active in his local community, by nation and sex: five countries*

Nation	Total (%)	(No.)[a]	Male (%)	(No.)	Female (%)	(No.)
United States	51	(970)	52	(455)	50	(515)
Great Britain	39	(963)	43	(460)	36	(503)
Germany	22	(955)	31	(449)	16	(506)
Italy	10	(995)	14	(471)	6	(524)
Mexico	26	(1,007)	31	(355)	34	(652)

[a] Numbers in parentheses refer to the bases upon which percentages are calculated.

TABLE 18. *Levels of subjective civic competence: five countries*

Percent who report:	U.S. (%)	U.K. (%)	Germany (%)	Italy (%)	Mexico (%)
national and local competence	67	57	33	25	33
national competence only	8	5	4	2	5
local competence only	10	21	29	26	19
neither national nor local competence	15	19	34	47	43
Total per cent	100	100	100	100	100
Total number of cases	970	963	955	955	1,007

Mexico's citizens and observers of the scene assess in different ways the constitutional balance struck between liberty and order out of its long contentious struggle for independence and modernization. It has clearly produced a considerable sense of identification between people and government, as well as continuity in progress and political stability, despite a high degree of autocracy in its political system.

The critical issues of the future lie in the capacity of the system to adjust to the coming of new generations, better educated and more urban. They are likely to take for granted the achievements of the Revolution and look to a more conventionally competitive political life. In particular, the ability of the PRI to recruit able younger men and keep within its orbit the major groups which emerge from an increasingly sophisticated industrial society may prove the critical factor.

POLICY TOWARDS GROWTH AND WELFARE

Britain

During the British take-off two issues of welfare arose: the hunger of the poor in the face of the rise of food prices, in the early war years; and the first humanitarian response to the conditions of work in the new and spreading factory system. Each initiated areas of debate and legislation that were to persist to 1914 and beyond.

The sharp rise in the cost of living in 1794–5 was met by the Speenhamland system of wage subsidy, out of local rates. Although rooted in older Poor Law precedents, it represented a quick response to the danger of substantial starvation in an anxious environment of war against a revolutionary state.

Wage supplements under the Poor Laws rose to a figure close to £7 million in 1830–1; and in 1834, Parliament, yielding to Malthusian argument, formally ended outdoor relief to able-bodied men. The line was, for the time, sharply drawn between the labor market and the poor house.

The Factory Act of 1802 is mainly remembered as the opening of a long series of conflicts centered on the extent to which Parliament should intervene in the labor market to protect women and children and, ultimately, men as well. The Act of 1802 was limited to the pauper apprentices being drawn from all over the country to do minor tasks in the factories, covering perhaps 20,000 children at the time. A twelve-hour day and certain minimum conditions for work and education were specified. Enforcement, left in the hands of magistrates or parsons, was slack until government factory inspectors were introduced in 1833.

In the postwar years the movement gathered strength, with Factory Acts in 1819, 1833, 1842, and 1847. It was supported not merely by an authentic humanitarian impulse but by the debating posture of agriculturalists trying to fend off pressure for Corn Law Repeal and by the desire of labor to restrict the labor supply in slack depression years. A ten-hour bill was, for example, defeated in 1844 in a period of prosperity, but quietly passed in 1847 when the mills were working short time. Although addressed to women and children in the factories, it installed, in effect, a limit on the work day for men as well.

As often in the take-off and drive to technological maturity, agricultural policy was at the center of politics.

Agriculture, having expanded dramatically to feed Britain during the war years, was able to exact in 1815 a limit on imports of corn should the price fall below 80 shillings. The road from 1815 to Corn Law repeal in 1846 reflects a counterpoint between the steadily rising pressure of urban Britain for cheap food, on the one hand, and, on the other hand, the luck of the harvests as they affected the relation between agricultural and other prices. The latter were generally responsive to the ebb and flow of business cycles. The Corn Laws of 1822, 1828, 1842, and 1846, for example, all came at moments when the relative movements of agricultural prices were unfavorable to the consumer. These oscillations were climaxed, of course, by the traumatic effects of the Irish famine.[43]

The Free Trade victory came under challenge in the days of declining prices and profits and intensified international competition, between 1873 and 1896. But by the time the Conservatives put the issue to the test, in the General Election of 1906, British exports were expanding on the basis of large investments abroad. Prices and profits were rising. The critical issue lay elsewhere, in the downward pressure of real wages on an increasingly well organized and assertive working class.

The Poor Law Commission, appointed earlier under the Conservatives, reported in 1909 that the arrangements of 1834 were obsolete, and the issue of a successor scheme was joined.

Lloyd George's response, as Chancellor of the Exchequer, was to bring in the National Insurance Bill, modelled on the German laws of the 1880s. It provided for individual, employer, and state contributions to insure against sickness and, to a degree, against unemployment. Unlike the German scheme, administration was placed in the hands of 'approved societies', the trade unions and the friendly societies, already working in the field. A modest tax on land values was to provide additional resources for the state's contribution. The House of Lords in 1908 had accepted a non-contributory scheme for Old Age Pensions. In the face of Lloyd George's challenging rhetoric and the long-term implications of the Land Tax, it dug in, to be defeated only in 1911.

The Insurance Bill, the new taxes, and the constitutional crisis were part of a surge of converging sentiment and political effort to balance the harshnesses of advanced industrialization. It had many other manifestations: Balfour's Education Act which greatly strengthened elementary and secondary education (1902); a trade disputes bill (1906) which directly exempted unions from all legal actions of tort, and undid the Taff Vale decision; the provision of meals to needy children (1906); medical inspection of school children (1907); regulation of employment of children outside school hours (1908); a nominally eight-hour day for the miners (1908); the setting up of labor exchanges and a legal minimum wage for women in sweat shops (1909); a new housing and town planning act.

Behind this wave of legislation lay years of gathering moral revolt and active discontent with some of the social and human consequences and costs of mature industrialization; the studies of the Fabians and others; the rise of the Labour Party; and the political weight of virtually universal manhood suffrage in an urbanizing age. These long-term forces converged with the reversal of the favorable trend of real wages from about 1900, as prices tended to rise more rapidly than money wages in the more advanced industrial countries. The worker turned from the economic to the political market for redress.

The rise in outlays for social services as a per cent of GNP was real: from 1.9 per cent in 1890 to 4.1 per cent in 1913; there was also a rise in economic and environmental services from 1.3 per cent to 2.2 per cent of GNP.[44] These acts of legislation and reallocation of national resources served to hold British society together at a moment of potentially explosive strain; and they laid the foundations, in concept, precedent, and administration, for later more massive measures of welfare and intervention. But they did not wholly compensate for pressures on real wages that marked the trend period down to 1914. Wages and salaries as a proportion of national income, which had risen since the 1870s, fell from 49.8 per cent in 1890–9 to 47.2 per cent in 1905–14, while profits, interest and mixed income rose from 38.8 per cent to 42.0 per cent.[45]

France

Something of Napoleon's Continental System continued to suffuse French tariff policy from 1815 to 1848. Protectionist tariffs were promulgated in 1816, 1820, 1822, 1826, 1836, and 1841, as cotton, coal, and iron interests sought to shield the French market from Britain's post-1815 onslaught. Agricultural interests used their weight in the Parliament for increased protection for corn, wool, and flax.

Under Napoleon III the trend was reversed in a series of executive moves leading up to the Cobden Treaty of 1860, an executive *tour de force*, since the balance of sentiment in French politics remained heavily protectionist.

Nevertheless, it took more than twenty years after the end of the Second Empire for the protectionist interests to undo the liberal treaties. The position of export industries weakened in the global cyclical depression of the 1870s. The international price of wheat fell, as American grain moved to

Europe at a time of declining freight rates. But the French government used its treaty-making powers and played off agricultural against industrial interests. It held the free trade line in the tariff of 1881. But a decade later the Méline Tariff brought protectionism back to agriculture as well as industry.

With respect to welfare policy, French politics exhibits the same impulses that yielded a substantial reallocation of national resources in Britain and Germany, but the results were modest, due to a fiscal system which tended to transfer resources without income redistribution, relying heavily on excise rather than progressive income taxation and workers' contributions to welfare schemes.[46]

In 1884 the legality of unionism was confirmed and a new phase of effort on behalf of French labor opened. It was hampered by the split between those who wished to work with the institutions of French government and parliamentary life and those who clung to the tradition of direct action.

Neither group was markedly successful down to 1914; although some steps were taken to improve the position of labor in the society. Like Napoleon III in the face of a protectionist parliament, the French government moved by decree to bypass, in this case, a conservative Senate. Millerand's decrees of 10 August 1899 defined the terms on which state contracts with labor should be based: a day of rest; a reduced working day; a minimum wage for each category of workers; limitation on the number of foreign workers employed. Administration was to be carried out through collective contracts entered into by employers and workers' syndicates, working with the Labor Councils set up in the early years of the century. And there were other administrative and organizational arrangements which brought organized labor into the process of government as a partner, improved factory inspection, and mediation procedures.

Building on the precedents of free medical assistance for the poor (1893) and an old age and invalid scheme for miners (1894), a protracted debate was launched in 1901 on a pension scheme that would have embraced some 9 million workers. But, relatively, the results were meager.

Summing up the pre-1914 French experience, Lorwin concludes:[47]

The response of government in terms of social legislation was not impressive. It enacted an employers' liability law for work accidents in 1898; a women's and children's ten-hour-day law in 1900; an eight-hour-day law for underground miners in 1905; and a one-day's-rest-in-seven law in 1906. A weak first attempt at old age pensions (1910) was stillborn because of CGT opposition. French social insurance and labor legislation could not compare with those of Lloyd George's England – or Bismarck's Reich . . .

Pioneer in political democracy and in socialist thinking, France failed to move toward social democracy. A broad social legislation program did not come until the Popular Front in 1936.

Germany

Germany was unified in the 1850s in an era when free trade ideas were accepted as a mark of modernity. Prussia imposed on the Zollverein and the new Empire an initially liberal trading policy.

But Bismarck, unlike the French government, did not resist as the international environment changed. The cyclical recession of the 1870s and falling grain prices set the stage for the German protectionist tariff of 1879. These influences converged with Bismarck's shift away from parliamentary reliance on the Free Trade Liberals. He also wanted customs revenues to free his finances from direct taxes and the negotiations involved in exacting them from the German states.

The departure of Bismarck and the reversal of world agricultural prices (and trends in cost of living) in the 1890s created a new setting. It turned an increasingly industrialized and urban Germany, becoming, like Britain, dependent on expanding exports, back towards liberalism. Its trade agreements moved irregularly towards lower tariff levels down to 1914; although the international trading environment remained substantially protectionist. As Clapham noted,[48] in 1904 'the average *ad valorem* equivalent of the import duties levied by Germany, on the principal manufactures exported by the United Kingdom, was 25 per cent. The corresponding figure for Italy was 27; for France 34; for Austria 35; for the United States 73; and for Russia 131.'

For Germany we have available a full analysis of the budget from 1872 forward in terms of the three major tasks of government.[49] They show an overall expansion down to 1913 in the proportion of public outlays to GNP. Andic and Veverka explain this movement as follows:[50]

The growth during that period was mainly the result of three factors: *social reform*, *imperialism* and *urbanization*. The order indicates their relative quantitative importance. Out of the additional 81 DM spent per head by public authorities between 1872 and 1913, these factors accounted respectively for 28, 18 and 13 DM, i.e. for almost three quarters of the additional expenditure. The great importance of social services at this early period is partly due to the introduction of an obligatory social insurance. This altered the balance of taxation of the Reich which consisted until the First World War of indirect taxes only. The expenditure on social insurance was mainly financed from contributions which represent direct taxes. Quantitatively even more important than social insurance had been the provision of *education*. Education expenditure, which was negligible in 1872, accounted for almost as much of the additional expenditure as the more spectacular military effort of the Reich, adding 16 DM per head as against 18 DM of increased *military expenditure*. It comes as a surprise that the military effort of Imperial Germany, which had so profound an influence on the subsequent history, was based on a slender material foundation. It claimed no more than 5% of additional output.

Germany's most significant move in the realm of economic policy was,

TABLE 19. *German government expenditure by level of government, per head of population, at constant (1900) prices, selected years, 1872–1913.*

Year	All levels		Central government						State government		Local government		As percentage of total expenditure				
			Total		Other than social insurance		Social insurance						Central			State	Local
													Total	Other than social insurance	Social insurance		
	DM	Index	DM	Index	DM	Index	DM	Index	DM	Index	DM	Index					
1872	21.6	28	6.3	21	6.3	28	..	..	..	..	..	..	29	29	..	..	..
1881	36.8	48	12.4	41	12.4	55	..	..	14.6	61	9.8	43	33	33	..	40	27
1891	53.0	69	21.3	71	18.1	80	3.2	42	17.5	73	14.2	62	40	34	6	33	27
1901	77.1	100	30.1	100	22.5	100	7.6	100	24.1	100	22.9	100	39	29	10	30	30
1907	90.0	117	36.0	120	26.1	116	9.9	130	23.8	99	30.2	132	40	29	11	26	34
1913	103.1	134	42.0	140	29.8	132	12.2	160	26.3	109	34.8	152	41	29	12	26	34

of course, Bismarck's pioneering initiatives in social insurance: against accidents (1871 and 1884); sickness (1883); old age and invalidity (1888). By the time these measures were codified (1913), they extended to domestic servants, agricultural workers, casual workers, and salaried persons.

In 1891 legislation provided a maximum working day of eleven hours for women, ten hours for children; prohibited night work for both; and debarred employment of children under fourteen from most categories.

The emergence of social insurance as a significant component in German governmental expenditures before 1914 is suggested in table 19.[51]

Musgraves' calculations for 1913 would indicate that social service expenditures as a whole (including also health, housing, and education) had reached the level of 5.1 per cent of GNP,[52] social insurance itself, about 1.8 per cent.[53]

Russia

From the relatively liberal tariff policy of 1868, Russia moved to a strongly protectionist system as its take-off began in the 1890s (see table 20).[54]

TABLE 20. *Russian tariffs: 1868, 1891*

	1868	*1891*
Coal	Duty free	2 to 3
Iron ore	Duty free	10.5
Pig iron, raw	5	45 to 52.5
Pig-iron products	50 to 250	112.5 to 255
Iron	20 to 50	90 to 150
Forge and boiler products	100	255
Rails	20	90
Machines, industrial, other than copper	30	250
Locomotives	75	300
Locomobiles	30	170
Machines, agricultural	Duty free	70 to 140
Cotton, raw	Duty free	120 to 135
Cotton yarn, bleached	325	420 to 540
Cotton manufactures	28 to 110	35 to 135

As noted earlier (pp. 87–8 above), the role of government policy between 1870 and 1914 was more positive than in equivalent periods of development in Western Europe. Budget, railway, banking, and agricultural policy, as well as the leverage provided by government contracts, were all used to foster the development of transport, raw material resources, and industry.

Perhaps the most striking difference, however, lay in the acceptance of a much larger flow of foreign capital, including direct investment. As table 21 indicates, the relative role of foreign capital began to decline in the years before 1914.[55]

Labor legislation in Russia, as elsewhere, began with efforts to cushion the impact of factory work on women and children and to limit hours of work. In 1882 a decree restricted work which could be done by minors and set up a factory inspection system. Night work for women and children was

TABLE 21. *Russian and foreign corporations formed: 1899–1913*

Years	All corporations		Russian companies		Foreign companies	
	Number	Basic capital (million rubles)	Number	Basic capital (million rubles)	Number	Basic capital (million rubles)
1899	325	363.7	256	256.2	69	107.5
1900	202	250.7	162	201.2	40	49.5
1904	94	119.2	81	92.5	13	26.7
1909	131	108.8	116	95.9	15	12.9
1910	198	224.3	181	190.5	17	33.8
1911	262	320.9	222	240.9	40	80.0
1912	342	401.5	322	371.2	20	30.3
1913	372	545.2	343	501.1	29	44.1

outlawed in unhealthy occupations in 1885. In 1886 a law was promulgated outlawing payments in kind and regulating periods in which wages had to be paid in cash by employers. In 1897 the work day was limited to eleven and one-half hours and provided Sunday and holidays for rest. And, in 1903, workingmen's compensation in case of accidents was provided for.

These steps were symptomatic of the direction public policy was taking; but welfare legislation did not advance far in either scope or administrative effectiveness before 1914.

Under Soviet rule an elaborate system of social services evolved covering health and education, working hours and holidays.[56]

Immediately after the Russian Revolution the eight-hour day and a two- to four-week paid vacation were promulgated in the Soviet Union and, except for the war years, the work week was further reduced with the passage of time, perhaps as an inducement for wives to enter the working force. The revolutionary promise of social security was consolidated in the Labor Code of 1922. Despite adjustments to discourage labor turn-over, it has provided more generously than in most nations at comparable levels of income per capita. Similarly, a relatively disproportionate effort has been made in the field of education.

On the other hand, Soviet allocations for housing and consumers goods generally have been disproportionately low.

TABLE 22. *Public expenditures in Socialist and Western economies (includes all levels of government; purchases and transfers) as per cent of GNP*

	U.S.S.R. 1962	U.S. 1961	Federal Republic of Germany 1961	U.K. 1961	Sweden 1961
Current expenditures					
Education	4.5	3.7	1.9	4.5	2.5
Public health	2.8	1.3	3.9	3.4	0.8
Social security	5.7	5.0	12.2	6.4	5.6
Defense	6.2	5.0	3.5	6.7	4.3
Other (including interest)	4.3	9.2	14.5	10.1	6.8
Total, current	23.5	24.2	36.0	31.1	20.0
Capital expenditures					
Total, capital	26.1	6.0	3.2	3.4	3.9
Total expenditures	49.6	30.2	39.2	34.5	23.9

By 1962 public expenditures in the Soviet Union in the major welfare sectors approximated, relative to GNP, those in more advanced Western societies; although the comparison is, in degree, misleading, due to the role of private outlays for education and health in non-Communist societies.[57]

Japan

Down to 1899 Japan was burdened and blessed (by treaty agreements of 1858 and 1866) with an externally imposed tariff limit of 5 per cent. She had to enter world markets on a competitive basis and managed to expand exports rapidly in this framework, using various forms of subsidy. After recapturing increased freedom of action, tariffs moved up only modestly until 1911. Japanese tariff policy thereafter – notably in the revisions of 1926 – sought to protect the new, more sophisticated industries that evolved in the drive to technological maturity, some finding their feet in the period of opportunity offered by the First World War; e.g. iron and steel, chemicals, machinery, rayon, etc. In agriculture, policy balanced the protectionist thrust of the farmer with some compensating attention to consumers' interests. The Great Depression after 1929 drove Japan into still deeper protectionism, heightened by the objective of military self-sufficiency. In its protectionist phase, Japanese policy also sought to limit access to foreign luxury consumers goods.

With respect to labor legislation, the protection of women and children in the factories first stirred the public conscience in Japan, as elsewhere, and was first reflected in public policy. Japanese policy evolved in the following major steps:[58]

— Factory law introduced into the Diet in 1898. Not acted upon.

— First legislation: Mining Act of 1905 and Factory Act of 1911. Not enforced until 1916.

— under the influence of Japanese membership in the I.L.O. and gradual gathering of public opinion, substantial progress was made in decade after 1921: Bureau of Social Affairs was set up in Home Ministry; Act of 1921 laid basis for a national system of employment exchanges; 1924 ordinance curbed some of the abuses in the recruitment of contract labor; Health Insurance Act of 1922 provided benefits after 1927 to all factory and mining workers in the event of sickness, accident, maternity, or death.

Lockwood concludes:[59]

Had the progress of 1921–36 been maintained for another five years, her position would have invited comparison with that of any other industrial nation facing similar economic handicaps. Unfortunately, a rapid retreat set in after 1937 from the gains of the previous decade. The political reaction brought about by the resurgence of the military, and the exigencies of the war which followed, ended by sweeping away most of the structure of labor protection. After the war it had to be built anew.

Harry T. Oshima has provided us with some valuable interim calculations on the changing scale and composition of Japanese central and local government expenditures, from the 1870s to 1960.[60] Unfortunately, they do not permit linkage with national income data beyond 1910.

Tables 23 and 24 adapt Oshima's calculations to the security, constitutional, welfare, and growth categories used here.

The following are particularly to be noted:

— The sharp relative rise in military expenditures from the mid-1890s to the period of the Russo-Japanese war and after, as well as their relative decline in the 1920s and drastic deflation, post-1945.

— The modest rise in relative social expenditures in the 1920s, the sharp rise after 1945. (Educational expenditures rise from 4 per cent of total public outlays in 1873–7 to 7 per cent in 1880, reach and remain at about 10 per cent from 1900. They dominate social expenditures until the post-

TABLE 23. *Total central and local expenditures, by functions, as proportions of national income: Japan, selected years, 1878–1912*

National income[a] at current prices (Oshima estimate) Million yen		Total central[b] and local expenditures		Security (military and foreign affairs)		Law, order, and administration		Social services		Economic growth		Other	
		Million yen	Proportion of national income	Million yen	Proportion of national income	Million yen	Proportion of national income	Million yen	Proportion of national income	Million yen	Proportion of national income	Million yen	Proportion of national income
			%		%		%		%		%		%
1878–82	1880	667	92	14	13	2	52	8	11	2	14	2	2	. .
1888–92	1890	809	127	15	27	3	57	7	13	2	26	3	2	. .
1898–1902	1900	1,978	425	21	143	7	100	5	60	3	104	5	19	1
1908–12	1910	3,366	834	25	373	11	142	4	114	4	135	4	70	2

[a] K. Ohkawa, *The Growth of the Japanese Economy Since 1878*, Tokyo, 1957, p. 7.

[b] Harry T. Oshima, 'Meiji Fiscal Policy and Economic Progress', in W. W. Lockwood (ed.), *The State and Economic Enterprise in Japan*, Princeton, 1965, p. 370. For these purposes I have separated security from other 'State Services' in Oshima's table. Oshima adjusts Ohkawa's estimates of national income produced for James Nakamura's higher figures for agricultural production, an adjustment not judged necessary for present rough purposes. This adjustment presumably explains, in part, his lower figure (10%) of public expenditures to national income for 1879–83 (p. 366). For a discussion of Oshima's view that Ohkawa's national income estimates in the early period are too low (and Meiji growth rates, therefore, too high), see pp. 354–6. Oshima argues that excessive military expenditures yielded a lower rate of growth than is often attributed to the period after 1880.

151

1945 years, when conventional health, welfare and security expenditures for the working force emerge on a substantial scale, at 11 per cent of total outlays for 1955 and 1960.)

— The substantial outlays of the Japanese government on behalf of economic growth are evident throughout, enlarging with the passage of time and the sophistication of the Japanese economy.

The figures, with all their limitations and imperfections (which Oshima underlines), suggest what is involved in the generation of additional inputs

TABLE 24. *Proportioning of total central and local expenditures, by functions: Japan, selected years, 1880–1960*[a]

	Security (military and foreign affairs)	Law, order, and administration	Social services	Economic growth	Other
	(%)	(%)	(%)	(%)	(%)
1880	14	57	12	15	3
1890	21	46	11	20	2
1900	34	23	14	24	4
1910	45	17	14	16	8
1920	24	28	12	23	13
1925	11	31	18	26	15
1955	4	16	25	33	22
1960	2	10	23	44	21

[a] Adapted from Harry T. Oshima, 'Meiji Fiscal Policy and Economic Progress' in W. W. Lockwood (ed.), *The State and Economic Enterprise in Japan*, Princeton, 1965, pp. 370–1. Because of rounding, totals for 1880 and 1925 come to 101 per cent; 1900, to 99 per cent. For the composition of 'Other' expenditures, see pp. 388–9.

and allocation to new outputs as a traditional society (where non-military state expenditures dominate) moves through the preconditions for take-off (allocating more to education, transport, communication, and primary industries); into take-off, where economic outlays (especially in direct support of secondary industry) expand; down to the drive to technological maturity (when public outlays to tertiary industry expand and social expenditures increase somewhat); to the welfare state and high mass-consumption. In the Japanese case the figures take on a dramatic character due to the extraordinarily high relative military outlays associated with the Sino-Japanese and Russo-Japanese wars, at an early stage of growth, and the virtual suppression of security outlays after 1945, with consequent radical expansion of expenditures in support of welfare and growth.

China

The abortion of the take-off on the Chinese mainland since the failure of the Great Leap Forward, and the turbulent and chaotic state of affairs during and after the Cultural Revolution, leaves policy towards growth and welfare unresolved at the end of the 1960s, but at the center of the debate on China's future.

Turkey

The role of government in the economic development of Turkey since 1924 is briefly outlined in chapter 3. Turkey has moved since the period of intense state administration of the economy in the 1930s and the war years to a more conventional mixed economy. As industrial production expanded and diversified, a new corps of private entrepreneurs emerged from Turkish society.

Turkish rights to protective tariffs were limited for the five years after the Treaty of Lausanne (1924) came into effect. In 1929 powerful protectionist tariffs were introduced in addition to other measures to reduce the level of imports and to encourage industrialization. These hardened under the impact of depression and war. Until the postwar period foreign trade remained under tight direct control.

The evolution of the position of industrial labor reflects the fact that the early stages of Turkish industrialization occurred under strong state controls, in an international environment quite different from that of the nineteenth century. Turkish law governing labor had to be made in a world where labor had already acquired, in the more advanced countries, considerable political power and legal status. Standards for protection of the rights of labor were institutionalized in the I.L.O. and in the ethos of international politics.

On the other hand, the capacity of the Turkish economy to enforce labor regulations and to provide the resources for welfare schemes was extremely limited. The bargaining leverage of labor in the face of the flow to the cities from the rural areas was weak. The imperatives of labor peace and, even, of long hours of work were real.

The counterpoint between aspiration and the realities of under-development can be read in a succession of labor codes and regulations. The right to strike, for example, was only granted to Turkish labor unions in 1963.

But, from the first days of the Turkish Republic, the cast of the nation's modern revolutionary ideology required some recognition and respect for labor problems and rights. As early as September 1921 a special act was issued, designed to improve the lot of coal miners. In 1923 some of its regulations covering working hours, welfare and relief funds, social conditions, and medical services were put into effect. An eight-hour working day was recognized in principle, but regulations allowed, in fact, for a sixty-hour working week. In the end, the plan was abandoned. In 1932 a liberal labor law was drafted but then rejected by the Grand National Assembly. The labor code of 1936 prohibited strikes and lockouts but made collective bargaining obligatory. Employers became responsible for labor accidents; maternity benefits were assured; a forty-eight hour week was accepted with some considerable upward flexibility, requiring, however, higher wage rates for overtime. Women and youths under eighteen were forbidden in underground, underwater or night work.

The code of 1936, in its content and main headings, belongs in the family of labor legislation during take-off in other societies. It is more indicative of the direction of political thought and sentiment than of enforceable policy.

After the Second World War social welfare policy was elaborated, including accident insurance, maternity benefits, and minimum wages to be set by special committees. In the first competitive party election of 1950, the Democratic Party advocated the right to strike. Upon achieving power, however, the older prohibitions were retained. Nevertheless, in the 1950s labor union organization expanded, and the 1936 code was amended in various ways, generally to strengthen labor's rights. Labor's political bargaining power increased somewhat as the Menderes government sought both labor votes and labor compliance with policy.

After the revolution of 1960, labor began to assert itself, including some limited strikes, against which the law was not applied. A new Labor Code of 1963, responding to these pressures, finally granted the right to strike, automatic dues checkoff, and the principle of collective bargaining. Union membership is on the rise. The modernization of union activities has been stimulated by the substantial flow of Turkish labor to Western Europe and the lessons learned there, as well as by the growth and increased sophistication of the industrial sector. There has been a parallel strengthening of the Workers' Insurance Scheme which, by the end of 1966, covered almost a million workers.

A recent study, from which table 25 is drawn, illuminates how Turkey has allocated its resources between growth and welfare purposes, on the one hand, and security purposes, on the other, over the period 1948–62.[61] In the 1950s, social security outlays (included under development in the accompanying table) were of the order of 1.3 per cent of national income;[62] but allocation for education, health, and welfare may have doubled, as a proportion of GNP, over the past generation, reaching a figure of about 4.5 per cent in the mid-1960s.[63]

TABLE 25. *Turkey: total resources and their disposal, expressed in ratios, 1948–62* (Percentages of GNP)

Calendar years	Gross national product (1)	Import surplus (2)	Total resources (3)	Expenditures			Index of real GNP 1948 = 100 (7)
				Military (4)	Development (5)	Consumption (6)	
1948	100	4.3	104.3	7.3	13.8	83.2	100
1949	100	3.4	103.4	7.7	16.1	79.6	89
1950	100	2.3	102.3	7.0	15.2	80.0	103
1951	100	3.2	103.2	6.7	15.2	81.3	119
1952	100	6.4	106.4	7.9	17.6	80.9	129
1953	100	5.2	105.2	7.8	17.1	80.2	144
1954	100	6.2	106.2	9.1	19.5	77.7	131
1955	100	4.0	104.0	7.3	19.4	77.2	141
1956	100	2.3	102.3	6.7	18.8	76.7	150
1957	100	3.0	103.0	6.8	18.0	78.2	160
1958	100	6.8	106.8	9.7	17.7	79.3	179
1959	100	4.6	104.6	6.9	19.0	78.7	187
1960	100	3.6	103.6	6.3	19.7	77.6	191
1961	100	3.5	103.5	6.5	19.5	77.5	189
1962	100	5.8	105.8	7.2	19.5	79.1	201
Average, 15 years	100	4.4	104.4	7.3	18.6	78.6	
(Percentages of total resources)							
Average, 15 years	95.7	4.3	100	7.0	17.8	75.3	

Mexico

Mexico's movement through the take-off into the early stages of the drive to technological maturity was marked by a rise in the proportion of gross investment to gross national product from just over five per cent in 1939 to the well over ten per cent, where it remains, although subject to some fluctuation (see table 26).[64]

Government policy played a large role in producing this result through direct and indirect interventions. Direct public investment approximated 40 per cent of the total over these years.[65] In the decade 1950–9, public investment (including social, administrative, and military outlays) was distributed as indicated in table 27 (p. 157).[66]

Through a number of government agencies – perhaps most significantly the Bank of Mexico – the pattern of private investment outlays, domestic and foreign, was geared to the sectors judged appropriate to the desired pattern of Mexican growth. As Vernon notes:[67]

The Mexican government has gradually worked itself into a position of key importance in the continued economic development of Mexico. It governs the distribution of land,

TABLE 26. *Mexico: gross national product and gross domestic investment, 1939–64* (millions of pesos at 1950 prices)

Year	Gross product		Gross invest-ment[a]	Ratio of investment to product (%)	Marginal capital–output ratio[b]
	Total	Increase			
1939	22,339	..	1,169	5.2	..
1940	22,588	249	1,600	7.1	..
1941	24,751	2,163	2,006	8.1	1.25
1942	26,291	1,540	1,728	6.6	1.14
1943	27,471	1,180	1,730	6.3	1.22
1944	29,676	2,205	2,206	7.4	1.47
1945	30,494	818	3,191	10.5	2.33
1946	32,319	1,825	4,391	13.6	3.00
1947	33,496	1,177	5,034	15.0	3.40
1948	34,987	1,491	4,712	13.5	3.07
1949	37,108	2,121	4,240	11.4	2.05
1950	40,577	3,469	4,828	11.9	1.66
1951	43,621	3,044	6,242	14.3	2.18
1952	45,366	1,745	6,483	14.3	4.52
1953	45,618	252	6,243	13.7	4.46
1954	50,391	4,773	6,509	12.9	2.02
1955	54,767	4,376	7,288	13.3	1.77
1956	58,214	3,447	8,605	14.8	2.13
1957	62,708	4,494	9,116	14.5	2.23
1958	66,177	3,469	8,652	13.1	2.72
1959	68,119	1,942	8,699	12.8	2.88
1960	73,482	5,363	10,008	13.6	2.55
1961	76,038	2,556	10,141	13.3	2.90
1962	79,691	3,653	10,044	12.6	2.84
1963	84,700	5,009	11,056	13.0	2.13
1964	93,200	8,500	13,631	14.6	..

[a] Preliminary data estimated by Bank of Mexico.
[b] Adjusted by means of moving averages.

water, and loans to agriculture; it mobilizes foreign credits and rations the supply of domestic credit; it imposes price ceilings, grants tax exemptions, supports private security issues, and engages in scores of other activities that directly and immediately affect the private sector. Governmental policies, therefore, are critical – critical to a degree which is not matched in many other developing economies based on a private enterprise system.

TABLE 27. *Mexico: functional breakdown of public investment*
(thousands of pesos)

Type of investment	Annual average during 1950–9 decade	Proportion of total (%)
Total	4,401,370	100
Basic development	3,633,840	82
Agriculture and livestock	638,040	14
Manufacturing	1,334,400	30
Transport and communications	1,661,400	38
Land	1,517,450	35
Maritime	124,440	3
Other	19,510	..
Social	609,680	14
Administration and defense	157,850	4

In particular, the leading sectors shifted from consumers goods to the chemical, paper, iron and steel, and transport equipment industries. The scale and timing of this shift is suggested by the accompanying index numbers for the production of steel and certain chemicals.[68]

	Steel (1940 = 100)	Caustic soda (1950 = 100)	Fertilizers (1950 = 100)
1940	100	—	—
1950	265	100	100
1960	1,048	825	581
1967	2,096	1,482	2,301

Welfare policy has been determined by a balancing of social commitments arising from the Mexican Revolution, and the imperatives of orderly industrial growth. This balance was achieved by a succession of presidents reacting to and assessing the pressures felt within the spacious confines of the PRI, with the results reflected in changing contours of the federal budget.

The process and the outcome have been traced in a study by James W. Wilkie whose approach closely approximates that pursued here. Wilkie traces and measures the shifting balances in public outlays among objectives of social welfare and economic growth, as well as the course of administrative expenditures designed to create 'an orderly atmosphere in which development can take place'.[69]

The politics of the take-off and the drive to technological maturity

On the basis of the accompanying tables (28 and 29) showing percentages and real allocations to economic, social, and administrative purposes, he characterizes modern Mexican political history as follows:[70]

In sum, ideological periods of political revolution (emphasizing administrative forms of change), social revolution, economic revolution, and balanced revolution may be quantitatively seen to encompass four respective time spans: 1910–1930, 1930–1940, 1940–1959, 1959–1963.

TABLE 28. *Mexico: average per cent of federal budgetary expenditure by type of emphasis and presidential term*
(Actual expenditure)

Years	President	No. of years in average	Total	Economic	Social	Administration
1869–70	Juárez	(1)	100.0	5.0	1.6	93.4
1900–11	Díaz	(2)[a]	100.0	16.0	6.6	77.4
1911–12	Madero	(1)	100.0	17.6	9.9	72.5
1912–13	Huerta	(1)	100.0	15.2	8.9	75.9
1917–19	Carranza	(3)	100.0	16.3	2.0	81.7
1920	De la Huerta	(1)	100.0	17.2	2.3	80.5
1921–4	Obregón	(4)	100.0	17.9	9.7	72.4
1925–8	Calles	(4)	100.0	24.8	10.1	65.1
1929	Portes Gil	(1)	100.0	23.2	12.9	63.9
1930–2	Ortiz Rubio	(3)	100.0	28.1	15.8	56.1
1933–4	Rodríguez	(2)	100.0	21.7	15.4	62.9
1935–40	Cárdenas	(6)	100.0	37.6	18.3	44.1
1941–6	Avila Camacho	(6)	100.0	39.2	16.5	44.3
1947–52	Alemán	(6)	100.0	51.9	13.3	34.8
1953–8	Ruiz Cortines	(6)	100.0	52.7	14.4	32.9
1959–63	López Mateos	(5)[b]	100.0	39.0	19.2	41.8

[a] 1900–1 and 1910–11.
[b] Data for 1964 not available.

The outlays of the Mexican federal government, as a whole, as a per cent of gross national product were relatively constant from 1925 to 1946, fluctuating between 6 and 8 per cent; but subsequently rose to about 14 per cent by 1961.[71]

What is clear, in general, is that until the Mexican economy moved into take-off after 1940, the real resources available for allocation to social purposes were severely constrained. On the basis of rapid and regular growth, allocations to social purposes rose even during the 'economic' period, still more swiftly during the phase of 'balanced revolution' in the 1960s.

Wilkie traces out the components of government investment and social

TABLE 29. *Mexico: average amount of budgetary expenditure by type of emphasis and presidential term*
(Actual expenditure)

| Years | President | No. of years in average | 1950 pesos per capita | | | |
			Total	Economic	Social	Administration
1900–11	Díaz	(2)[a]	31.9	5.1	2.1	24.7
1911–12	Madero	(1)	33.4	5.9	3.3	24.2
1912–13	Huerta	(1)	38.6	5.9	3.4	29.3
1917–19	Carranza	(3)	15.1	2.5	0.3	12.3
1920	De la Huerta	(1)	25.3	4.3	0.6	20.4
1921–4	Obregón	(4)	55.8	10.0	5.4	40.4
1925–8	Calles	(4)	67.9	16.8	6.9	44.2
1929	Portes Gil	(1)	61.5	14.3	7.9	39.3
1930–2	Ortiz Rubio	(3)	56.4	15.9	8.9	31.6
1933–4	Rodríguez	(2)	59.6	12.9	9.2	37.5
1935–40	Cárdenas	(6)	82.2	30.9	15.0	36.3
1941–6	Avila Camacho	(6)	103.0	40.4	17.0	45.6
1947–52	Alemán	(6)	146.7	76.1	19.5	51.1
1953–8	Ruiz Cortines	(6)	180.8	95.3	26.0	59.5
1959–63	López Mateos	(5)[b]	245.4	95.2	47.0	103.2

[a] 1900–1 and 1910–11.
[b] Data for 1964 not available.

welfare policy, and relative allocations to them. Measured in 1950 pesos per capita, for the year 1963, they array as follows:

Economic
Agriculture and irrigation 18.7
Agricultural credit 5.1
Communications and public works 20.8
Investments 22.7
Subsidies, etc. 26.0

Social
Education 33.2
Public health, welfare, and assistance 7.7
Potable water and sewage disposal
systems 0.9
Allocations to Mexican Social
Security Institute 7.7

Among the economic outlays, the heavy role of subsidies, some designed to keep prices of essentials low in urban areas, has been a major feature of the Mexican scene.

Among the social outlays, the heavy allocation to education stands out.

In an interesting innovation, Wilkie calculates a poverty index based on census data, with equal weight given to those who were: illiterate; spoke only Indian language; lived in community with less than 2,500 persons; went barefoot; wore sandals; regularly ate tortillas instead of wheat bread; without sewage disposal.

The pace of progress thus measured by the decline of poverty emerges as follows, with 1940 = 100:[72]

1910	124	1940	100
1921	115	1950	86
1930	109	1960	72

The acceleration during take-off is marked – a rough doubling in the decline of poverty. But progress still to be made is suggested, for example, by the fact that in 1960 illiteracy was still 38 per cent; 49 per cent of the population lived in communities of under 2,500 population; 71.5 per cent lacked indoor sewage disposal.

But levels of welfare at the stage of growth at which Mexico had arrived in the 1960s are always uneven, if one starts from where Mexico did at the beginning of take-off.

SECURITY POLICY

Britain

British security policy during the take-off focused, of course, on the struggle against Revolutionary and Napoleonic France.

It was the French take-over of the Low Countries in 1792 which initially brought Britain into the anti-French coalition on the continent; although the French challenge was ideological, commercial, and colonial as well as direct. The direct threat ended when Napoleon broke up his invasion encampment at Boulogne (built during 1803–4) and Nelson triumphed at Trafalgar in October 1805, leaving Britain in full control of the seas.

But, equally, by 1806 Napoleon was master of the continent. He launched from Berlin in November his mercantilist blockade designed to drain away Britain's trade surplus which was the basis for its substantial assistance to Napoleon's adversaries. Britain's Order in Council, forbidding neutral trade with France, joined the issue. The opening up of Brazil and other Latin American markets bought time for the British balance of payments in 1808–10. Even on the continent the flexibility of sea power and the potentialities of bribery and smuggling tipped the contest to British advantage, but not without some awkward moments in the period down to 22 December 1812, when Napoleon informed his Minister of Commerce that he needed some additional 150 million francs in customs revenues: 'Undoubtedly it is necessary to harm our foes, but above all we must live.'[73]

British loans and subsidies, based on profits from the re-export trade and expanding cotton exports, combined with control of the seas and judicious engagement of British forces alongside those willing to fight the French, permitted Napoleon's defeat. Its terms allowed Britain to retain an empire expanded to include Malta, the Cape of Good Hope, Mauritius, and Ceylon, as well as an initial, almost monopolistic foothold in trade with the liberated portions of Latin America.

Like other ambitious expansionist efforts of modern history, the French failed because they encountered three forces: other people's nationalism; the power (in this case, British) of those who did not wish to see the balance of power upset; and a relative deterioration in their economic position *vis-à-vis* others, due to their military exertions.

The security policy pursued by Britain from 1815 to 1914 was rooted in essentially the same principles that governed policy towards Napoleon: opposition via coalition to any power that threatened control over the European continent; the use of naval power to maintain command of the seas and the major routes of strategy and commerce. The latter largely determined British policy towards Russia and the fragmenting Ottoman Empire. To these abiding strands of policy were added the opening up of China in the 1840s and the expansion of imperial holdings in Africa later in the century.

The imperial advantages gained by eighteenth-century victories over the French, confirmed and enlarged in 1815, and, above all, strengthened by the relative industrial and commercial advantage that went with mounting the first take-off, left Britain, down to 1870, a relatively satisfied, if still acquisitive, power.

To that point there was something of potential substance in the Liberal vision of a free trade world in which the colonies would drop from the imperial tree like ripe apples.

But the environment in which British policy was pursued was treacherous in two respects. First, the spread of nationalism and liberalism through southern and eastern Europe and the eastern Mediterranean basin eroded the Ottoman Empire at one point after another, opening up areas for contention among the major powers. The Ottoman weaknesses, as the region experienced the early phases of the transition to modernization, created temptations and fears the world was to experience on an even larger canvas in the generation after 1945. The inherently turbulent regions mattered in terms of the relative power positions of the more advanced and more stable nations.

Second, in counterpoint, the German Empire emerged. From 1871 it became the central new element in the equation of power.

For a century Britain, France, Germany, Austria, and Russia managed to keep this precarious competitive system in balance, short of major war, by incessant negotiation setting limits on the ambitions and fears of the parties. The cement of anti-republicanism disintegrated soon after 1815, definitively after 1848. The habit of consultation and concert, nevertheless, persisted. Along the way the system weathered, among others, major crises over Spain and Latin America (1823); the emergence of Greece (1827–30); the emergence of Italy down to 1870; the Russian–Turkish crisis of 1878; the Bulgarian crisis (1885–6); the Algeciras crisis (1906); the Balkan wars of 1912 and 1913. A kind of security council of the major powers operated to pull back from a brink that was often approached. What is, in retrospect, remarkable about the efforts of the major powers to avoid conflagration between 1815 and 1914 is that the system survived extraordinary constitutional and ideological changes within the principal nations concerned.

The Ottoman Empire could be dismantled, step by step, without producing a convulsion. But Vienna's ties to Berlin, in the environment created by Wilhelm's insensitivity to the precarious pre-1914 structure of power, ultimately made the problems of the Austro-Hungarian Empire mortal. As Germany came forward, France, Russia, and Britain moved, against many resistant memories, into alliance. The Russian defeat by the Japanese in 1905 revealed to London how deep its implicit reliance had been on the balancing weight of the French and Russians against Germany. The Kaiser promptly underlined the point by going to Tangier. But in the face of the Triple Entente, the Kaiser, too, became governed by fear as well as ambition, and became implicitly more dependent on an ally in Vienna.

In one sense, the First World War was caused by the weakness of two partially modernized but insecure powers, whose ambitions came into conflict: Russia and the Austro-Hungarian Empire. A struggle for the balance of power in Europe, as a whole, was triggered by the clash of regional interests between two empires at a much earlier stage of modernization than the three principals: Germany, France, and Britain.

Taken as a whole, the Austro-Hungarian Empire was modernizing quite rapidly between, say, 1871 and 1914. Its most vital centers, however, lagged somewhat behind the economies of Western Europe. It contained large, virtually traditional agricultural regions. It lacked the raw material base available to Russia. But it was in a quite different situation than the Ottoman Empire before 1908: in economic, social, and political terms it was moving forward, not backward.

Its problem lay in its scale and diversity, combined with the strength of nationalist feelings generated by modernization itself, notably among the Slavic minorities – the Poles of Galicia, the Slovenes, the Serbs, and the Czechs in Bohemia.[74] The effort to keep these groups minimally satisfied within the Empire, along with the Austrians and Hungarians, was conducted in the late nineteenth century with considerable imagination. Substantial elements of de-centralized administration and local autonomy were balanced by the bureaucracy and military on whom the Empire relied for its ultimate unity, like many empires of the past.

Committed by geography and history to manage the area from Tyrol to Transylvania, from Prague to Bosnia (after 1878), policymakers in Vienna were led instinctively to seek consolidation of their rule in the face of the inherent forces of fragmentation at work. In particular, to protect positions on the Adriatic, they were led into confrontation with the ambitious Serbs over the disposition of Bosnia and Herzegovina, which the Berlin Congress had passed to Vienna's rather than Belgrade's administration. A plan of 1871 to make Bohemia an independent kingdom broke down in the face of German and, especially, Magyar opposition. The latter feared the precedent in racially complex Hungary. In 1903 a similar concept emerged for the creation of a Yugoslav state within the Empire. It foundered on similar opposition, combined with a change of dynasty in Belgrade that altered relations with Vienna for the worse.

In 1908 the famous meeting between Izvolsky and Aehrenthal occurred. The two men agreed to support each other in the Russian purpose of opening the Bosphorus and Dardanelles to Russian warships and the Austrian purpose of annexing firmly Bosnia and Herzegovina to frustrate Serb ambitions. It was occasioned by the emergence of the vigorous Young Turks, still committed to galvanizing the Empire. Its second focus was another emerging, ardent group of nationalists in Belgrade. Contrary to their understanding, Vienna moved unilaterally to announce its action. The reaction in Russia and elsewhere to the Austrian initiative made it impossible for St Petersburg to acquiesce as Izvolsky had promised. Russia turned to apply its Pan-Slav policy to Serbia.

From this tangled struggle of two harassed empires, in the early stages of modernization, over the remnants of a third, somewhat behind, but galvanized by the Young Turks, came the central, initial inflammatory elements in the equation of July 1914: the Belgrade–Vienna confrontation; and St Petersburg's view of the Serbs as blood brothers.

Two Balkan wars intervened as the newly assertive independent nations of the area joined Russia and Austria in the struggle for the spoils of the Ottoman disintegration, which the Young Turks could not prevent. Anglo-German restraint succeeded in containing the conflict in 1912 and 1913; but it was not done a third time.

The frictions over competitive imperial expansion in the second half of the nineteenth century were clearly less vital to the outcome than the struggle over the Ottoman corpse. The downward trend in prices and profits after 1873 brought a protectionist mood to Britain and protectionism elsewhere. Africa was divided up, with Britain acquiring domination over Egypt and colonies in West and East Africa. But the French swallowed their pride over the Suez Canal and Fashoda; and the tensions over the Boer War subsided.

Moreover, imperialism yielded unpleasantness as well as pride for most and profit for some. The Boer War was profoundly divisive in Britain; earlier (1896) the Italians were slaughtered at Adowa; a little later the Russians ran into the Japanese; and, one can add, the Americans were quickly sobered after 1898 by guerrilla war in the Philippines, which continued painfully until 1902.

Perhaps more important, the trends in prices and profits turned up after the mid-1890s. The post-1873 neo-mercantilist vision of constricted markets lifted, with the opening up of Canada, Argentina, and the industrialization of Russia. Not only was imperialism proving more costly and bloody than it initially looked but less necessary as a basis for national economic progress. The peak of the imperialist wave had passed in the decade before 1914. It was not Joseph Chamberlain but the Liberals who dominated British politics as Fisher carried forward the modernization of the British fleet, Haldane evolved the general staff, and the quiet staff talks with the French were undertaken.

In short, Britain in the preconditions and take-off periods expanded its power greatly. As it came to industrial maturity, its control of the seas permitted further imperial expansion in Africa, the Middle East, and Asia, along with others; but the coming to industrial maturity of strategically-located Germany, with which France and Russia alone could not cope, brought Britain back to its classic defensive security problem – how to deal with a power with a potential capability for dominating the Continent, including the Channel ports. And the plans of the German General Staff provided a quick circuit that translated the rivalry between Teuton and Slav in Eastern Europe into a thrust through Belgium. In the face of those plans and the still critical role of Russia in dealing with them, there was neither the strength nor will in London to deflect St Petersburg from its Pan-Slav course in the crisis over Serbia in 1914. And it is by no means sure London's influence would have sufficed.

France

Defeated in its great adventure of the preconditions period, but treated sensitively by the victors to make the restoration more viable, France remained passive for only a short time. By 1818 the indemnity was paid and foreign troops evacuated French soil; and by 1823 French troops were in Madrid, in support of Ferdinand VII, against Canning's wishes, to suppress a Spanish revolution. But French external enterprise was mainly geared not to enforcing the conservative dispensation of 1815 but to gaining its share of power in areas hitherto left to their traditional devices or opened up to exploitation by the decay of the Ottoman empire.

By 1827 the French Consul at Algiers had felt the bey's famous fly whisk; and after some twenty years of intermittent campaigning, Algeria was organized in 1848 as three French departments.

In 1840 an attempted independent French role in the conflict between the Ottoman Empire and the assertive Mohammed Ali in Alexandria failed; and, in the face of possible war, Louis Philippe accepted Thier's resignation.

The larger French adventures, however, belong to the time of Napoleon III and the generation when French industrialization was moving strongly ahead and a tolerable but transient political equilibrium had been established in French domestic political life.

The French played a leading role in the Crimean War and were the chosen instrument of the powers in suppressing the Moslem–Christian conflict in Syria (1860–1). France was a major actor in the movement towards a unified Italy, although its defeat in 1870 was the occasion for its completion. In the tradition of Napoleon's Egyptian victory and the ties to the Egyptian modernizer Mohammad Ali, de Lesseps fulfilled Colbert's dream in 1869 with the Suez Canal. The French connection and military operations in Southeast Asia yielded by 1862 French control over the three provinces of Cochin China. Meanwhile, French positions in West and East Africa were created – in Senegal, Somaliland, and Madagascar.

But this phase of external adventure yielded also the humiliation of Maximilian's execution at Queretaro in 1867. The outcome of the American Civil War, the strength of Mexican nationalism, and the power required to keep an Austrian ruler in Mexico City were miscalculated. Bismarck almost simultaneously consolidated his victory over Austria with restraint (August

1866). The stage was set and the outcome foreshadowed of the Franco-Prussian War. Few more dramatic reversals in relative position have occurred than that from Napoleon III's condescending interview with Bismarck in 1862 to his capture in 1870.

As the Third Republic found its feet, and industrialization accelerated in the generation before 1914, France persisted in rounding out and developing its colonial footholds. By 1893 French Indo-China had extended to include protectorate status in Cambodia and Laos. Grave tensions with Italy and Germany were accepted to complete the empire in North Africa by 1912. And France pressed along in negotiations with Britain and Germany, to consolidate its holdings south of the Sahara. It accepted after Fashoda a junior role in the Suez Canal and Sudan, although the Egyptian problem kept Britain and France at arms length from 1882 to 1904.

In the wake of Bismarck's departure – and the end of his careful nursing of German–Russian relations – the French tie to Russia was consolidated. It committed France to mount a force of 1,300,000 men against Germany in case of war, Russia, 7,800,000. In the wake of Russia's defeat by the Japanese and virtual German ultimatum to France over Morocco, Britain and France slid quietly into secret staff talks based on the half explicit assumption Britain would fight on the continent if the Germans violated Belgian neutrality. They began after preliminary contacts in December, on 10 January 1906, six days before the Algeciras Conference opened.

As in London, the obsession in Paris with maintaining a Russia within the Entente, willing to mount an offensive from the east if Germany attacked France to the west, stayed the hand of French diplomacy in the Austrian–Russian confrontation over Serbia in 1914.

Germany

Against the background of a remarkable surge of growth and railway building in the 1860s, Bismarck conducted his three wars to round out the German Empire. He then managed German diplomacy for nineteen years with extraordinary sensitivity to the need to keep a revanchist France from building a coalition that might embrace Britain and Russia against him. He avoided a naval and colonial challenge to Britain. He shielded his relations with Russia from the implications of the 1879 alliance with Austria through the Alliance of the Three Emperors (1881) and the Russian–German Treaty of 1887.

The interplay of German policy with that of others to yield the confrontation of the two alliances in 1914 is complex – crosscut by efforts to keep Russian–Austrian, British–German, German–French, and German–Russian tensions within manageable limits.[75] Nevertheless, Vienna's determination to eliminate Serbia had behind it knowledge that the German General Staff wanted war sooner rather than later. Still, at the highest level, men paused for a moment in the face of catastrophe. The feverish inner debates and diplomacy of the days between 28 June, when Francis Ferdinand was assassinated, and 4 August, when England declared war on Germany after the violation of Belgium, cannot be examined without a sense that war was not the sole conceivable outcome of the forces at work. Restraint in Vienna, as it became clear that the assassination could not be proved the work of the Serbian government; restraint in St Petersburg, in the face of the plight of Slavic brothers; above all, a firm determination in Berlin to lean against Vienna, and, if necessary, to revise the rigid plans of the German General Staff – these, at least, could have surmounted the crisis. For a century, confrontations heavily laden with national honor and pride had been dealt with by restraining muddy compromises. These had avoided major war while respecting the shifting balances of power, as processes of economic and political modernization had their differential impact on the regions of Western Eurasia. As in successful domestic politics, diplomacy had reduced to complex balances and incremental adjustments conflicts which, in their essence and emotional content, were capable also of yielding unrestrained violence.

There was no way to avoid the break-up of the Ottoman Empire or prevent the emergence of the Young Turks. There was no way to avoid the assertive nationalist and racial pressures within the Austro-Hungarian Empire, or the rise of German power relative to Britain, France, and Russia. There was no way to avoid the latent ambitions of Germany for a larger place on the world scene; Russia for effective control over the Bosphorus and Dardanelles; France for a return to Alsace-Lorraine; Britain to retain its naval primacy. Every Foreign Office – even the most modest – had its unfulfilled ambitions, behind which powerful national sentiments and pride could be mobilized. But these did not make war inevitable.

The essence of the problem lay in the convergence of Vienna's felt weakness, translated into an overbearing insistence on the humiliation of Serbia, and Germany's sense of both gathering strength and the limits of that strength in the face of the triple entente. That sense of limitation had been reflected in Bismarck's policy of diplomatic restraint, tragically abandoned; but it was reflected also in the convulsive character of the Schlieffen Plan, which appeared to promise both a solution to Germany's two-front dilemma and a fulfillment of its maximum ambitions. German political leadership in 1914 proved incapable of refusing the risk of testing the plan and of accepting the possible cost of restraining Vienna once again, as in 1912 and 1913. Only a 'first strike' military plan could promise Germany European hegemony. Otherwise, a continuation of Bismarckian restraint was required of Berlin; and of this Wilhelm was temperamentally incapable. He did not seek war; but he did not pursue a diplomacy or insist on military planning consistent with an alternative. In the ultimate crisis he let the General Staff press the button, a staff led by a Hamletian figure who appalled his assistants by quoting from time to time the German adage: 'Many dogs are the hare's death.'[76]

As one re-reads the tale, it is as if in one man after another – one nation after another – a restraining spring, long eroding, finally snapped. The self-disciplines which had somehow held in check for a century the raw ambitions and fears of this dynamic and bitterly competitive system of power were broken – first in Vienna, then in St Petersburg; but the surrender to madness, still capable of limitation, spread to Berlin. In all three capitals, political power lay ultimately in the hands of weak or second-rate men. A very high order of strength and statesmanship in one of the three capitals was required to keep the genie still in the bottle in 1914. At their best (in Theodore Roosevelt's characterization of Bethmann) those who acted or failed to act meant well feebly.

The outbreak of the First World War deserves continuing study and attention. If the terrible strains which still exist in the world arena of power yield major war, they are likely to do so not out of the bilateral tensions of the U.S.–Soviet arms race or other aspects of direct competition. The greatest danger of major war remains the interweaving of the stature of the great powers with the rivalries and struggles of lesser powers, at earlier stages of growth. The interdependence of the strong and the weak – and the desperation with which the weak can sometimes act – requires of the strong balanced self-discipline if the human community is to make its way safely through the process, described in chapter 8, to something approximating stable peace. The coming of the First World War is the major and most relevant morality tale we have to underline the importance of that balanced self-discipline between the major powers.

Russia

Despite the burden of great domestic problems, the coming of the industrial revolution to Russia led, as in other cases, to a sense of increasing relative military potential and to policies which would apply that potential against those both accessible and relatively weaker.

Russian policy towards the Ottoman Empire and the Slavs of Eastern Europe is reflected in notes on the diplomacy of others. But Russia pursued interests to the East as well as the West.

In the wake of the Crimean War, in counterpoint to Alexander II's reforms, Russia moved in Asia on the basis of still earlier probes. Vladivostok was founded in 1860. Russia joined the other powers in imposing on China and Japan (Sakhalin Island) imperial conditions and depredations.

It also pressed south to the Caspian and southeast to Bokhara.

Thus, the stage was set for the Trans-Siberian railway and all that followed. The railway was begun in 1891. In 1895 the Russians intervened along with the French and Germans to limit Japanese gains from the defeated Chinese. They then proceeded to exact, in return, the right to run a spur line through Harbin to the Liaotung Peninsula, denied the Japanese, and to manœuver to a position of sustained influence in Manchuria, given substance by troop movements into Manchuria in the wake of the Boxer Rebellion (1900).

The Japanese joined in the ineffective clamor to effect a Russian withdrawal. They then planned and bided their time to strike the Russian fleet at Port Arthur on the night of 8 February 1904.

Despite the tempering restraints on Japan of the other powers at Portsmouth, Manchuria was evacuated by the Russians, and the Japanese acquired positions in Port Arthur, Korea, and the Liaotung Peninsula.

After the setback of 1854, Russia turned to the East for redress of pride and power. It turned West after the rebuff of 1905. At home it pursued a policy of Russification, temporarily lifted in degree for Poland and Finland after the revolution of 1905. Abroad, Pan-Slavism came to rest in the dour feud with Vienna, after Izvolsky's deal with Aehrenthal fell through in 1908.

When the crisis of 1914 came, there was in St Petersburg an attempt to draw back. Even as Russian partial mobilization began, on 29 July, Nicholas II appealed to his cousin in Berlin 'to do what you can to stop your allies from going too far'. There was just enough hope in the exchange between kaiser and tsar for Nicholas briefly to cancel an order for general Russian mobilization. But Berlin would not restrain Vienna, and on the evening of the 30th the general mobilization order was signed. In the end, war was accepted by the leaders in St Petersburg with a kind of classic Russian fatalism.

The price of an independent peace with Germany after the November Revolution and civil war came high for the Soviet Union: Finland, Estonia, Latvia, Lithuania, Poland, Bessarabia, and – almost – the Ukraine. But the

Revolution was saved. Moscow's policy of the 1920s and 1930s came to focus obsessively on preserving communist control over the Soviet Union, when that objective clashed with ideological or other objectives.

Soviet policy after the Second World War is considered in chapter 8. The limited point to be made here is that a moment of critical decision for Moscow arrived in 1945–6 with the allied victory over the Axis. Through Russian eyes and memories, the moment was incredible: all the powers that had restrained Russia over the centuries were prostrate or weak: Germany and Japan; the smaller nations of Eastern Europe; France and Britain. At Potsdam Averell Harriman greeted Stalin by suggesting that he must be gratified to be in Berlin after all his country and people had experienced at German hands. Recalling the outcome of the Napoleonic Wars, Stalin replied: 'Tsar Alexander got to Paris'.[77]

The question mark was the United States, for no other power of significance lay in Moscow's path.

Stalin, through the exertions of the Russian peoples and their allies, was in a position to retrieve directly in Asia all and more that was lost in 1905; much that was lost in Europe after 1917; and, in addition, to move through the Control Councils in Berlin and Vienna, as well as the Security Council of the United Nations, to a position of powerful indirect influence in Western domains – and beyond – where the Russian voice had not been relevant, except briefly, after 1815. The price would have been a relatively independent (but militarily controlled) Eastern Europe and a unified (but de-militarized) Germany, whose political fate would be left to truly free elections. In his speech of 9 February 1946 Stalin rejected, in effect, the advantages of such wide, legitimatized dilute influence. He pursued a course with more concrete objectives: first, to consolidate via satellites Soviet power to the Elbe, excepting Berlin; second, to probe beyond, via the French and Italian Communist parties, exploiting also the vacuum of power in Germany and the disarray of Western Europe in general. He judged it not impossible to emulate Tsar Alexander I.

American strength and will were obviously critical to how far Russia's power could be extended; for Stalin wanted no war with the United States. He therefore tested the ground with some caution. At the opening session of Yalta, Roosevelt had given him grounds for great hope. He said that while the United States would take all reasonable steps to preserve peace, it would not keep a large army in Europe, and its occupation of Germany could be envisaged for only two years.

In Eastern Europe Stalin had given pledges to Polish political freedom of the most explicit kind, and more general commitments for the others. But he gradually established that he was not seriously obstructed in moving to consolidate his control over the Eastern European satellites from 1945 to 1948.[78] But from the spring of 1947 Truman moved to stem the rot in Western Europe along the Elbe; and Berlin was held against the blockade in 1948–9.

Stalin, frustrated to the West, turned in classic Russian style to Eastern adventures in 1947. And these came also to a point of at least interim frustration in June 1951, with the beginning of the Korean truce talks. Then, after a pause, Khrushchev engaged in a second major wave of expansionist enterprise, beginning with Sputnik in October 1957, ending five years later with the Cuba missile crisis.

For present purposes, it is sufficient to note:

— Russia, as modernization began in the nineteenth century, was behind the other major powers. Its initial efforts to extract major advantage from the break-up of the Ottoman Empire, during the preconditions period, were frustrated by the economically more advanced nations, despite the superior weight it could bring bilaterally against Turkey.

— The frustrations of 1854 and 1878 led Russia to accelerate industrialization as a national policy.

— During take-off, it moved vigorously in the Far East but there, again, met superior local power in the form of Japan, also at the end of its take-off.

— In the wake of its 1905 defeat, Russia turned back to the West and to a Pan-Slav policy which helped detonate the First World War.

— Up to this point Russia pursued limited objectives of expansion against a basically defensive strategic position created by the rise of Germany.

— War and revolution led to major setbacks.

— The course of the Second World War and its aftermath, including the Chinese Communist victory in China in 1949, opened up a vista for Stalin of achieving primacy at both ends of Eurasia which was frustrated in the West in 1949, in the East in 1951; but strategic missiles, relative U.S.–Soviet growth rates in the 1950s, and the state of the developing regions opened up to Khrushchev a vision of even larger if more dilute global primacy, which he pursued from 1958 to 1962.

In short, the Soviet Union from 1945 to 1962, on the basis of the technological maturity it had achieved, sought the kind of large objectives which in the past had only been attempted through major war; but it sought them by means short of direct military engagement of the Soviet Union. It was frustrated in the oft-repeated formula, by the nationalism of others; the exertions of those unwilling to see the balance of power shifted; and by rising claims at home for resources, as the heavy-industry–military cast of its economy decreed deceleration of growth in the 1960s.

Japan

Japan's external adventures, as it moved forward in modernization, are less complex than the intertwined affairs of Western Eurasia.

In 1895 internal unrest in Korea led to Sino-Japanese intervention. The partners fell out; Japan thrashed the Chinese on land and sea. Faced with a direct threat to Peking, the Chinese surrendered Formosa and the Pescadores, the Liaotung Peninsula, and its claim on Korea, which passed under Japanese control. In addition, China paid Japan a substantial indemnity.

As noted above, Russia's take-off thrust into this area, as the Siberian railway pushed to the Pacific, was turned back, setting up shock waves in Europe that hardened the confrontation between the Triple Alliance and the Triple Entente.

Just as the Axis defeat in 1945 opened up to Stalin vistas he could not resist, the depression after 1929 did the same for the Japanese military. The almost total disarray of the West weakened the prestige of Japanese democratic forces at home and led Tokyo to seek a grandiose hegemony in Asia. The failure of effective Western reaction to the takeover of Manchuria and to the Italian and German thrusts and probes of the 1930s, combined with an apparently confirmed American isolationism, led Japan deeper into China.

With the coming of the war in Europe, Japan moved beyond China towards Southeast Asia; and American diplomacy began to react:

— on 17 April 1940 Hull warned the Japanese against changing the *status quo* in Indonesia by force;

— on 4 September 1940 Hull warned that aggressive moves against Indo-China would have an unfortunate effect on public opinion in the United States;

— on 26 September 1940 the Japanese move into Indo-China led to the American embargo on shipments to Japan of iron and steel scrap after 15 October;

— on 26 July 1941, Japanese credits in the United States were frozen.

A good part of the substance of the Japanese–United States diplomatic exchanges down to the attack on Pearl Harbor concerned Japanese intentions in Indo-China and Indonesia. It was in Southeast Asia that Roosevelt drew a line on the limits to which the Japanese extension of power could proceed without United States military reaction. In the face of that threat, Tokyo decided to proceed and to seek a neutralization of United States power in the Pacific by the attack on Pearl Harbor and the invasion of the Philippines.

Behind the Japanese and American decisions was Berlin's pressure on Tokyo to weaken and distract Britain to the maximum and London's pressure on Washington to limit Japanese capacity to interfere with trade and shipping routes to the Far East, notably to Australia and New Zealand.

With Pearl Harbor (or, perhaps, Midway), the great adventure of Japan's period of technological maturity reached its apogee. The full American weight was brought gradually into the struggle for the balance of power at both ends of Eurasia; for Hitler eased Roosevelt's and Churchill's task by declaring war on the United States in the wake of Pearl Harbor.

China

The security policy of Communist China in the wake of its consolidation of the mainland in 1949 is a mixture of grand aspirations, which might have marked its arrival – or near arrival – at technological maturity, combined with more limited and cautious efforts to extend its power within its own region, typical of an ambitious young power during take-off.

Its economic policy was geared initially to the slogan: heavy industry and modernization of the armed forces – the two phrases hardly ever separated in official pronouncements of the 1950s. Mao believed the nearest relevant analogy was Russia in 1931. But this was a nuclear age, and he moved directly to mobilize his talents and resources to acquire nuclear weapons as well as missiles, tanks, jet aircraft, and submarines.

This vision of China's power in a future not far distant colored the challenge to Moscow's leadership within the world Communist movement in the late 1950s; Mao's willingness to go it alone when the crunch came on Russian aid, in 1960; and his overt effort to seize the leadership of communism in the developing regions after the debacle of the Cuba missile crisis and his simultaneous adventure in Tibet.

On the other hand, Mao was cautious in engaging his own forces and moved them only shallowly across his *de facto* frontiers. He entered the Korean War under strategically defensive circumstances to keep American forces off his borders. Undoubtedly in the spring of 1951 he hoped to throw the Eighth Army into the sea; but he accepted the line at the 38th parallel as sufficient for Chinese purposes, after the terrible Chinese communist losses in the battles of April and May. He probed at Quemoy and Matsu in 1958; but drew back when challenged and the Soviet Union refused him support. He confined his determined refusal to accept the legitimacy of the Nationalists on Formosa to politics and diplomacy, notably, the bilateral conversations with the United States.

Heartened by Sputnik, he encouraged Ho, among others, to adventurous versions of wars of national liberation; but he kept his own support well within limits which might have resulted in direct Chinese military engagement with the United States.

A similar mixture of frontier adventure and caution characterized Chinese Communist posturing during the Indo–Pak war of 1965.

Through a process not wholly clear, on present evidence, the hostility between Peking and Moscow built up during the inner-party debates of the 1950s, eased briefly in the wake of the first Sputnik (October 1957) and became overt with the Soviet withdrawal of aid in 1960. It seems likely that the core of the matter was Peking's insistence on becoming an independent nuclear power;[79] and the crucial decisions in Peking may well have been taken in the spring of 1958 leading to the withdrawal of Soviet nuclear assistance in June 1959. The crisis moved into overtly documented polemics after the Cuba missile crisis in late 1962. It was translated thereafter from polemics into a slow but substantial build-up of forces on both sides of the Sino–Soviet frontier, notably after the Chinese Communist nuclear explosion of October 1964.

Turkey

Turkish security objectives during its take-off period and beyond, in the 1960s, remained loyal to the decision of 1923 that it should seek its destiny through modernization within its borders, at peace. It has thus far managed to do so amidst the turbulent twists and turns of four decades.

In the 1930s there were stabilizing agreements with Greece (1930); Russia (1931); Persia (1932); the Balkan states (in 1934, with Greece, Rumania, and Yugoslavia); the Middle Eastern neighbors (in 1937, with Iraq, Iran, and Afghanistan). Uneasiness concerning Italy led in 1934 to the beginning of Turkish rearmament. In the wake of the Ethiopian crisis the Montreux Conference (1936) permitted Turkey to refortify the Straits. Down to 1939 Turkey leaned to Britain and France, concluding a mutual security pact with the former on the eve of the Second World War.

The awkward but successful Turkish neutrality of the war years gave way to wholehearted association with the United States, in the face of Russian postwar pressure. The first major United States–Soviet confrontation occurred over continued Soviet occupation of Northern Azerbaijan. Turkey's security as well as the disposition of Iranian oil helped determine Truman's decision to resist. It was out of the diplomatic pressure on Turkey, as well as the Communist guerrilla effort in Greece, that the Truman Doctrine was later enunciated.

As the Cold War unfolded, with Turkish membership in both NATO and CENTO, a new strand began to emerge in Turkish policy, in the 1960s: increased emphasis on regional cooperation and self-reliance. Three forces have contributed to this trend which is still at an early stage:
— increased confidence in Iran and Pakistan as well as Turkey, as they moved forward with some success in economic and social modernization;
— a sense of diminished threat from the Soviet Union after the Cuba missile crisis and the exacerbation of the Sino–Soviet split;
— a sense that the United States was seeking to reduce the scale of its commitment in that part of the world.
This development was accompanied by some uneven, limited, movement towards normalization of Turkish–Soviet relations. Only the aching problem of Cyprus from time to time opened historic wounds and threatened to bring Turkish forces into the field against old enemies.

Mexico

The years of the Second World War saw the mood of the oil nationalization of 1938 give way to a remarkable and sophisticated stabilization of United States–Mexican relations.

The essence of the transformation lay in growing Mexican pride and confidence engendered by its sustained economic and social progress, combined with a lively appreciation among Mexico's leaders of its need for a steady and viable relation with the United States. This need stemmed from flows of trade, tourists, and public and private capital, as well as for the kind of ultimate protection required during the Second World War and the Cuba missile crisis.

Mexico's progress in terms of its revolutionary creed and consensus lifted, to a degree at least, the sense of inferiority and humiliation for long built into its relations with Washington. By and large, American diplomacy encouraged that sense of Mexican dignity and achievement by its recognition of the legitimacy of the Mexican Revolution as a forerunner, in objective at least, of the Alliance for Progress and in dealing sensitively with bilateral trading issues and the Chamizal.

The problem of Castro's Cuba briefly cut across this pattern of reconciliation. Castro evoked initially in Mexico some resonance with its own revolutionary past. And United States policy – notably, the Bay of Pigs adventure – evoked the worst memories of interventionism. But the reality of Castro's impact on the Hemisphere, and its unsettling impact on the Mexican economy in the early 1960s, produced a hard-headed sobriety in Mexico City. This was confirmed by the Cuba missile crisis and its outcome. Even earlier in 1962 it was the Mexican Foreign Minister's remarkable address at Punta del Este which created the formula of 'incompatibility' on the basis of which Cuba was banned from the Organization of American States; although Mexico, having done the essential diplomatic job, retreated into legalist obscurities to avoid difficulties at home with the left.

Within the Hemisphere the new modernizing Mexico has moved with caution. It is conscious that in Central America it could easily be regarded by these smaller, less advanced states as another colossus of the North. Its role in Latin American economic integration, and in OAS affairs generally, has been forthcoming but not a role of leadership. It remains conscious that it is part of North America, not South America; that it is solving tolerably well its problems of transition to the new leading sectors of the drive to technological maturity (steel, engineering, chemicals, electronics, etc.); that the political system it evolved at such human cost and effort is unique; and it judges there may not be much profit for Mexico in enlarging its responsibilities.

It enjoys the respect it has earned on the world scene; but at this stage of history Mexico is more deeply taken up with the dynamics of its own modernization than it is with an effort to project itself abroad. It has come far in giving a distinct modern character to its complex and difficult heritage; but it knows many problems lie ahead. Its foreign policy is designed to conserve its energy and resources for those domestic tasks.

CONCLUSIONS

With the take-off and drive to technological maturity, the process of industrialization itself becomes the center of politics. The accompanying charts catch something of the degree of uniformity and variation – past and present – as men and resources move from agriculture to industry, and real income rises.

Depending on the timing of take-off, what was relatively uniform were the technologies absorbed and the sequence of their absorption. The efficient absorption of technologies carries with it powerful imperatives, social and political as well as economic. But those imperatives do not produce political and social uniformity; and their economic impact varies as well with the scale and resource base of particular economies. We are confronted – in this mixture of uniformity and uniqueness – with a classic problem of biological science.

176

Two facets of the process had particular meaning for the political process.

First, more or less regular growth provides, through both the workings of the economy and the market place of politics, the possibility of increased real incomes to the expanding proportion of the population engaged in the modern economic sectors or brought into effective political participation. The fatalism of the traditional society and the confusions and frustrations of the preconditions period give way to the pursuit of increased welfare which is now, palpably, a realistic possibility.

Second, the changing shape and structure of the society, with increased urbanization and industrialization, lays on the agenda a succession of pressures to allocate the outputs of government in new ways.

In this chapter we have, in particular, traced the following:

— the claim of the new expanding industrial and commercial middle class for a central role in the constitutional system;

— the claim, usually granted only subsequently, of the industrial working class and the less advantaged citizens in modernizing rural life for participation in politics through the right to vote;

— the claim of the industrial working force for protection against excessive hours of work and other burdens and hazards of factory life – initially, women and children, then the working force as a whole;

— the claim of the less advantaged for an expanding range and scale of social services;

— the competing claims of agriculture and industry for protection and the urban consumer for low prices for essentials;

— the claims of the growth process itself for increased allocations to infrastructure, education, and other forms of governmental assistance.

One could construct from these experiences – no two alike, but marked by a similar succession of problems – a dynamic equilibrium model in which the inevitable tensions and pressures built up around constitutional, growth and welfare issues are resolved peacefully by invoking the great central advantage that take-off brings about: an enlarging pool of resources available for allocation. In a society enjoying regular industrialization and growth (including the modernization of agriculture), the old harshness of traditional (and even of most preconditions) societies is lifted: the pie to be divided is increasing; what one group gains need not be what another group loses; both may gain.

It is one thing to struggle over a fixed volume of resources. It is a different matter to argue over the relative size of increments to be shared. Debate may be hot; but it is less likely to be bloody. On that basis, the carrying forward of industrialization itself as a communal venture can be a healing, unifying,

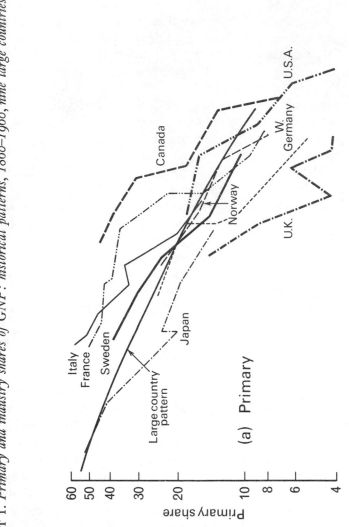

CHART 1. *Primary and industry shares of GNP: historical patterns, 1860–1960, nine large countries*[a]

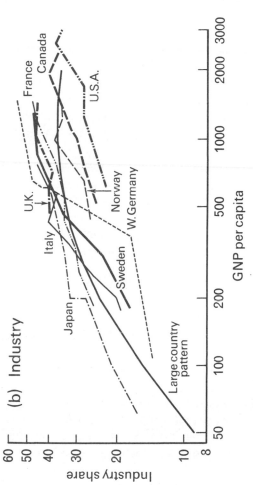

(b) Industry

Industry share

GNP per capita

France
Canada
U.S.A.
U.K.
Norway
W. Germany
Italy
Sweden
Japan
Large country pattern

ᵃ From Hollis B. Chenery and Lance Taylor, 'Development Patterns: Among Countries and Over Time', *The Review of Economics and Statistics*, November 1968, p. 401. The 'Large Country Pattern' averages incorporate observations on nineteen contemporary nations with populations of more than 15 million. The historical data are derived from P. Temin, 'A Time-Series Test of Patterns of Industrial Growth', *Economic Development and Cultural Change*, January 1967. GNP per capita are approximations in 1960 U.S. dollars. The concepts of take-off and drive to technological maturity do not translate automatically into GNP per capita. They are based on the degree of diffusion of then existing technology. For example, nations enter take-off at different levels of GNP per capita, depending on population, resource balances, exportable surpluses, etc.; and there can be technologically mature rich and poor countries. GNP per capita can only be related, therefore, to the stage of growth by a range; and it is a range difficult to work out historically because of problems in comparing income over long periods. Nevertheless, if the reader wants a rough benchmark to indicate the end of technological maturity in the contemporary world, I suggest something like $500 GNP per capita when, if consumer sovereignty reigns, the automobile–durable-consumer-goods' sectoral complex appears to take over leadership in growth.

widely shared objective. This is true in theory; and it is, in part, true of the experience of political communities.

But history affords no pure models of dynamic equilibrium. The softening influence of increased resources available for private and public allocation is there; but even the smoothest case of progressive adjustment – say, Britain from 1783 to 1914 – is marked by acute tensions and moments of crisis short of constitutional breakdown. And most other cases are not as smooth as Britain.

What caused these crises which, in most cases, yielded domestic violence, revolution, and discontinuous constitutional change?

First, there were disruptive movements within the economic system itself; for example, cyclical fluctuations, post-take-off structural crises, bad harvests, and other forces affecting the rate of growth and the level of employment. The observation of William Matthews before a parliamentary committee in 1832 is not the whole truth; but it is an abiding part of the truth in industrial societies: '. . . you cannot get them to talk of politics so long as they are well employed.' Unemployment, for example, played a part in European political unrest of 1830–2 and 1848. It was part of the background to the Russian Revolution of 1905; and wider disarray, as well as the burden of war, played a role in 1917. In post-1945 years, deceleration in growth rates – for example, in Turkey in the late 1950s – has played a significant role in political disequilibrium, as it often has in Latin America.

In general, then, the process of industrialization at a rapid and regular rate creates problems and tensions in political life as the dynamic struggle for new allocations of power and resources proceeds. When the economy turns down or stagnates, breaking hopeful expectations and reducing relatively or absolutely the resources available to governments for allocation, the underlying tensions may take – and often have taken – violent form.

Second, there was war. The tricks of industrialization, progressively applied, lifted the ceiling on real per capita income within nations which entered take-off. But they did not alter geography, except to make more distant places more easily accessible. The growing nations still lived in a world where, strategically, what one nation gained, another lost or believed it lost. The old inherently competitive tensions of mercantilism and earlier times remained – even when barely held within bounds short of major war between 1815 and 1914.

Moreover, the impact of economic and political modernization, coming as it did at different times to different nations, shifted the real or apparent relative military potential of nations, opening up new ambitions, fears, or both. And so, wars continued.

For the losers, war – as in earlier times – damaged or broke the sense of legitimacy attached to the existing constitutional dispensation and encouraged other contenders for power to emerge: France, after 1870 and 1940; Germany, after 1918 and 1945; Russia, after 1905 and 1917; Japan, after 1945.

For the winners, war, in the short run, could strengthen the hand of the existing constitutional dispensation: Germany, in the period 1864–71; Japan, in the 1890s and after 1905. But these exercises in limited aggression during take-off had their long-run cost: they fostered grandiose illusions which, when translated into action at the close of the drive to technological maturity, yielded tragic results.

Even without discontinuities in growth and welfare – and wars – one would not, of course, expect the political process to adjust without friction to the structural changes and new demands generated by industrial growth. Each of the issues involved gains for one group, real or believed losses for others (the shortened work-week, up to a point, probably produced gains for both). The widened sharing of power and resources was accomplished by conflict and struggle of greater or lesser intensity, despite the softening influence of the enlarged pool of resources. These occurred in phases of activism and consolidation similar to those delineated by A. M. Schlesinger, Sr. for the United States (see above, pp. 20–1).

The adjustments were generally accomplished with less violence in societies where suffrage had been widened and democratic institutions operated to a greater or lesser degree. This was true not only of Britain but of post-1870 France, Imperial Germany, Japan between 1890 and 1931. Even when changes came from the top, the existence of potentially strong popular pressure played its part, as in Bismarck's social welfare reforms of the 1880s. There was an important strand of Alexander II's famous dictum of 1856 running through the adjustments – in democratic as well as autocratic societies: 'It is better to abolish serfdom from above than to await the time when it will begin to abolish itself from below.' It operated not merely through the fear of violent revolution but through the fear of a shift in voting patterns. *Noblesse oblige* came easier – in the style of Disraeli, Bismarck, and Theodore Roosevelt – when there was a popular electorate to be faced.

In general, the take-off and drive to technological maturity proved an environment more conducive to movement towards democracy than the period of the preconditions for take-off. We shall leave the discussion of democracy to chapter 7. Nevertheless, certain observations on the range of cases examined here may be useful background for that chapter:

— The capacity of each society to move towards democratic politics was affected by the sweep of its pre-industrial history.

— The political problems of industrialization formed an agenda which, in part, lent itself to democratic compromises, in part to ideological confrontation. A high and steady rate of growth helped tip the balance towards pragmatic compromise.

— On the other hand, ideological fragmentation of democratic political groups – where it existed – weakened the capacity of parties and parliaments to influence the course of policy as pursued by the executives and the bureaucracies; for example, in France, Germany, post-1905 Russia, and Japan.

— More generally, the effectiveness of the democratic element in politics was weakened by the fragmentation of parties, whether that fragmentation reflected ideological or other differences of view.

— There was some tendency for democratization to move forward in a sequence of three steps: movement towards freedom of speech and assembly, improvements in the administration of justice, etc.; the creation of representative parliamentary bodies based on a progressively widened electorate, with powers short of control over the budget; the winning of budgetary control by the parliament. In pre-1914 Russia the third stage was not achieved; and the effective power of the Mexican House of Deputies over the president's budget is, at best, marginal.[80]

Clearly, also, the disruption of war, against the background of unresolved political and social problems of early phases of industrialization, permitted purposeful, disciplined political parties to seize power in Russia and China; and the techniques of modern communication and control have permitted these parties to maintain their primacy over substantial periods of time.

On the other hand, the defeat of dictatorships in more advanced societies (Germany and Japan) permitted democratic forms of government to emerge and, thus far, to survive, when an environment of steady economic and social progress and security was maintained.

The vicissitudes of political life during the preconditions period – and, in some cases, during the take-off and early phase of the drive to technological maturity – produced political revolutions. New social as well as political objectives and modes of organization were proclaimed for society, including commitments to elevate rapidly the level of life for all citizens – thus, for example, Mexico and Turkey in the preconditions, and Russia in the early stage of the drive to technological maturity. Many of the newly independent nations of the post-1945 era began their political life under such hopeful banners.

In these cases what one can observe is that significant expansion in social welfare has, in fact, been largely a function of the rate of growth itself. The revolutionary objectives and commitments were not without some meaning in terms of policy and allocations of resources. And, even when they remained mainly commitments of rhetoric and principle rather than of substance, they had political meaning in the society, to some extent attaching the poor to the regime.

But without regular growth to provide the requisite enlarged inputs to government, the scale on which these commitments to popular welfare could be met was relatively limited.

CHAPTER 5

AMERICAN POLITICS: A NOT SO SPECIAL CASE

INTRODUCTION

Three Special Initial Conditions

American life was initially colored by three special characteristics which have left abiding marks on the political scene.

First, the sense of America's special meaning and moral responsibility. This arose from the counterpoint between values and institutions brought from Tudor England and the primitive setting of a continent rich in arable land and natural resources. Out of the terms inherent in the arrival of seventeenth-century English colonists on an almost empty continent, an American political life evolved which tended progressively towards self-government in the townships and counties, the primacy of the colonial legislatures, and, utlimately, the principle of one-man one-vote.[1] This bent was heightened by the physical exigencies and opportunities of seventeenth-century North America, which permitted – even required – a high degree of individual freedom and individual enterprise.

With the passage of time this interplay between a peculiar political and economic environment yielded, in Tocqueville's phrase,[2] the 'magnificent image' which 'does not meet the gaze of the Americans at intervals only; it may be said to haunt every one of them in his least as well as in his most important actions and to be always flitting before his mind'. The converging visions of America as a place of unique human sanctuary, of unique material opportunity, and of transcendent democratic mission are the basis for what Gunnar Myrdal once described as the nation's 'moral overstrain'[3] and for Sartre's observation on Americanism:[4] 'Americanism is not merely a myth that clever propaganda stuffs into people's heads but something every American continually reinvents in his gropings. It is at one and the same time a great external reality rising up at the entrance to the port of New York across from the Statue of Liberty and the daily product of anxious liberties.'

184

As Reinhold Niebuhr observed, the Puritan and Deist traditions came together on this point:[5]

Whether our nation interprets its spiritual heritage through Massachusetts or Virginia, we came into existence with the sense of being a 'separated' nation, which God was using to make a new beginning for mankind. We had renounced the evils of European feudalism. We had escaped from the evils of European religious bigotry. We had found broad spaces for the satisfaction of human desires in place of the crowded Europe. Whether, as in the case of the New England theocrats, our forefathers thought of our 'experiment' as primarily the creation of a new and purer church, or, as in the case of Jefferson and his coterie, they thought primarily of a new political community, they believed in either case that we had been called out by God to create a new humanity. We are God's 'American Israel'.

Since, in fact, neither Deity nor nature decreed that the virtue of individual Americans would differ from that of others, American politics has been suffused with the counterpoint between 'the magnificent image' and the mundane struggles of interest and of power which are the universal working materials of organized life. The most distinctively American figures – say, Lincoln and Mark Twain – have been those who accepted and even underlined the moral imperfections of America, while not abandoning 'the magnificent image', often bridging the gap with the solvent of humor.

The second special condition that imprinted the American mind lay in the economy. American life as it gradually unfolded was marked by a set of economic characteristics that were to help give a particular form and thrust to industrialization when it came:

— a high rate of population growth (accelerated by immigration) and, generally, in growth of real income per head;

— a relative abundance of good land in relation to the supply of labor, especially of skilled labor;

— consequently higher real wages for industrial labor and higher average real incomes in agriculture than in Europe;

— an agriculture which lent itself to maximizing output per man rather than output per acre outside the cotton south – and, to some degree, even within the pre-1860 south, given the rising price of slaves;

— a social structure and income distribution which encouraged production for, relatively, a mass market;

— great distances and obstacles to transport to be overcome before an efficient national market could be created.

All this set the stage for large-scale production, financing, and marketing organizations once a continental market emerged after the Civil War, and posed distinctive problems in reconciling industrial concentrations of power with democratic politics.

The third distinctive strand was the double bar-sinister which cut across the fabric of American life: the pushing back, decimation, and ultimate segregation of the American Indian; and the joining of the English colonists in the African slave trade, notably after 1689, when the monopoly of the Royal African Company was ended. The first yielded a nagging moral, human, and social issue, still alive in contemporary America; the second, the greatest of America's social and political problems as a national society.

THE POLITICS OF THE PRECONDITIONS FOR TAKE-OFF

Dating

As in chapter 3, the preconditions period for the United States is dated in terms of both a long sweep and a shorter period, culminating in take-off. The take-off itself could be dated from the 1820s and the rapid growth of a viable cotton textile industry in New England with familiar spreading effects within the region; but that surge is regarded as a limited geographical phenomenon, and the take-off as a more clearly national phenomenon is dated in the two decades before 1860, when efficient intra- and interregional market connections were brought about through the northern railways and the foundations for American heavy industry were laid.

The preconditions period, on short term, is dated from 1788 and the formation of the nation under the Constitution. As in other cases, the dating of the long sweep of the preconditions period is inherently more arbitrary. One could begin with the founding of initial colonies in Virginia and Massachusetts. Or, one could take as a benchmark the surge in the value of foreign trade from the late 1740s. But given the intense, formative role after 1763 of the struggle with London over taxation in the emergence of American political life, the date chosen is the end of the Seven Years' War.[6]

The Key Questions

Following the pattern used in chapter 3, the analysis here will focus on these three questions:
— Did intrusion by a more advanced power play a part in the preconditions period? If so, did a mood of reactive nationalism contribute not only to modernization but also to military or diplomatic effort to expand abroad?
— Were there major constitutional changes during the preconditions period and to what extent were they related to intrusion from abroad or to economic and social change within the society?
— Did public policy play an active role in preconditioning the economy for take-off?

186

The Role of External Intrusion and External Adventure

External intrusion – or its threat – played three distinctive roles in the American preconditions for take-off: in bringing about the Revolution itself; in shaping and achieving acceptance of the Constitution; and in tipping the balance of national policy towards encouragement of industrialization itself.

As the first of the European colonies to seek and achieve political independence, by definition external intrusion played a part in the emergence of modern America; but it was, of course, a different kind of colonial struggle than those cases where European rule was imposed on non-European peoples.[7] It arose from a discontinuity in British policy which ruptured a permissive dynamic equilibrium successfully maintained for a century and a half between London and the colonies.

There was, over the colonial years, a gradual growing away of the colonies from British patterns of life, which accelerated during the eighteenth century. It yielded a gradual gathering of self-consciousness and sense of distinctiveness. There was also, however, English acquiescence in the evolution of increasingly strong colonial legislatures. Thus, a continuing colonial identification with England persisted against a background of significant changes in colonial outlook. This made a revolutionary response to post-1763 transatlantic tensions slow to emerge and unpalatable to many when it did emerge.

The accumulating, incremental widening of the gap between English and colonial life was sufficient to lead Benjamin Franklin to propose as early as 1759 an imaginative new constitutional dispensation in the Albany Plan. But the proposed leap was too great, lacking circumstances of urgency and an awareness in London of the process under way in the colonies.

The issue was brought to crisis, as often in constitutional history, by the problems of war and postwar adjustment. The issue was joined as the result of the effort of Parliament, at a time of straitened finances, to force the growing colonies to assume a greater share of the costs of their own defense – via taxation rather than (mainly) by trade regulation, as in the past. Thus opened the protracted constitutional struggle of 1764–76.

It is unnecessary to rehearse here the various social, political, and regional interests within the colonies that finally converged sufficiently to yield the Declaration of Independence, as George III and his ministers vacillated but, in the end, pressed as a matter of principle their constitutional prerogative as they understood it. The fundamental point is that the evolution of the colonies over their first century and a half of life – including a sense of enhanced capacity and confidence induced by colonial exertions during the

Seven Years' War – had yielded a *de facto* situation, not fully perceived on either side of the Atlantic until the final test of 1774–6, where the powers London understandably assumed as legitimate could not be peacefully implemented. And this was true even though a strong loyalist spirit survived and many were apathetic rather than ardent at the prospèct of independence.

Tax measures judged natural, prudent, and equitable in London were, on balance, taken in the colonies to be an unacceptable and repressive regression – a retrogressive intrusion of external power in the form of the violation of Englishmen's rights assumed to be firmly established out of the Tudor past.

The American Revolution emerged, then, from a clash between security and welfare considerations within the British colonial system. The clash was brought on by enlarged defense expenditures, yielding, in turn, a constitutional crisis centered on differing views as to the legitimate terrain of authority and power in the colonies under the English constitution.

The removal in 1776 of the royal authority in London, and its agents in the colonial capitals, threw power back on the states where a lively democratic political life had evolved in the legislatures. After 1776 it was not difficult to substitute American for English executive figures in the states. There is a high degree of continuity between colonial and post-colonial state politics.

The Articles of Confederation provided an initial minimum substitute for British executive authority for the new nation, sufficient to muddle through the war and early postwar years. But difficulties compounded to a point where a number of responsible political leaders in the states came to the judgment that a new constitution was required. Their sense of purpose converted a discussion of revision of the Articles into a constitutional convention.

The Constitution of 1787 represented an effort to provide adequately for the three abiding strands of government in the light of weaknesses revealed under the Articles of Confederation.

The allocation to the President of the role of commander-in-chief, as well as responsibility in foreign affairs, reflected security anxieties stirred both by the military presence and pressures of Britain and Spain on the frontiers agreed at Paris in 1783 and by the unsatisfactory state of foreign relations in general.

The allocation to the federal government of control over the currency and customs, as well as the power directly to raise tariff revenues, reflected the disarray caused by paper currency issues in the states, the barriers to trade raised between the states, and by the unsatisfactory state of the servicing of domestic and foreign debts. Important leaders came to feel that neither welfare nor growth was assured under the Articles.

The complex constitutional balance between big and small states, the independence of the Supreme Court, and the guarantees of the first ten amendments were the exactions of 'Justice' to achieve acceptance of a government that might also be strong enough to assure unity and 'tranquility'.

Putting aside the 'Blessings of Liberty' as a special but not unique statement of constitutional aspiration, the formal objectives of the Constitution are a classic grouping of the three tasks of government: security, 'the common defence'; 'the general Welfare', embracing policy towards growth as well as welfare policy in the narrower sense; 'Union', 'Justice', and 'domestic Tranquility,' the constitutional objectives.

The acceptance of the Constitution by the special conventions was, in some states, a close thing; and among all the factors that tipped the balance towards ratification, it is not possible confidently to single out one as critical. But the fear of strong central government in a post-colonial nation was so substantial and the welfare issues were so contentious that it seems unlikely that the Constitution would have been accepted if they were not balanced by a security fear. Such fear was uneven in its regional strength but still pervasive. It centered on the possibility that the nation under the Articles of Confederation could not cope successfully with a strong and disdainful Britain and the larger world of nation states and empires whose presence was felt on the nation's ambiguous borders as well as in its economic and political relations across the Atlantic.

This sense of vulnerability – notably to Britain – suffused, as well, the debate on national economic policy. In 1783 Lord Sheffield published, and Americans morbidly read, *Observations on the Commerce of the American States with Europe and the West Indies*. Sheffield took the view that the commercial prospects for the new nation were dim outside the British Navigation System and that America could never establish extensive manufactures. A standard subject for collegiate debate in the late 1780s and early 1790s was: 'Does the National Security depend on fostering Domestic Manufactures?' And the Hamiltonian position rested squarely on what was to become the abiding doctrine of aspiring under-developed nations: 'Not only the wealth but the independence and security of a country appear to be materially connected with the prosperity of manufactures.'

As Jefferson was about to take over in 1801 he encouraged Eli Whitney to continue his efforts, under his contract with the Adams administration, to manufacture his guns with interchangeable parts to free the United States from dependence on the French arms supply; and Jefferson's Embargo, of December 1807, designed to insulate the nation from involvement in European war, produced a Hamiltonian surge of manufacturing enterprise. The link of manufactures to 'independence and security' was further underlined, of course, in the War of 1812.

The period of the preconditions saw the United States engage in one exercise in what might be called reactive aggression; that is, the clumsy and ill-fated effort to clear the British from Canada during the War of 1812.

As American trade and shipping were whipsawed by Napoleon's Continental System and the British Orders in Council, war hawks emerged who saw in a successful struggle with Britain the opportunity to acquire Canada, reduce the Indian menace on the Western frontier, and open more forest land for settlement by American pioneers. Although the case for Madison's declaration of war of June 1812 was based formally on the assertion of American rights to freedom of the seas, it was generally understood that the operational objective would be Canada.

Thus, less than a month after war was declared, General Hull, having marched from Dayton, Ohio, led his force across the river at Detroit and offered the Canadians liberty under the American flag. With his flank on Lake Erie dominated by Canadian ships, the Canadian militia unmoved by the prospect of liberation, and with the threat of Indian massacre dangling before him, Hull surrendered his expeditionary force on 16 August 1812. A series of further probes into Canada was little more successful, yielding long remembered outrages at York and Newark, on the Canadian side, and Niagara, across the American border. The unpopularity of the war and the weakness of Madison's administration prevented from developing any substantial army or adequate strategy for its use. And, with Napoleon's abdication in April 1814, Britain was able to release to the Canadian–American front increased forces. The United States was then thrown on the defensive. Macdonough's victory on the lake at Plattsburg was probably decisive in avoiding a serious British incursion in September 1814. And Jackson's post-treaty victory at New Orleans permitted an inglorious war to end with a glow of national satisfaction.

The net result of the tragi-comic stalemated war was to strengthen the sense of Canadian unity and attachment to London, while providing the United States a national anthem, a future President, and an enlarged naval tradition. But the rebuffed American offer of liberation also left continued anxiety in the north and hurt feelings to the south, which subsequently colored the U.S.–Canadian relationship with a wariness and apparent indifference which have proved quite compatible with a long, quiet frontier.

Constitutional Change

The progression from colonial rule to the Articles of Confederation to the Constitution is, of course, the formal constitutional sequence from 1763 to the 1840s.

Within that framework, however, three substantive strands of constitutional evolution can be detected: the expansion of popular participation in politics; the expansion of the powers of the central government and rising sense of nationhood; the alteration of the role of slavery in the economy of the South and the emergence of the problem of balancing the political power of slave versus non-slave states in an expanding continental nation. The problem of slavery is a relatively unique element in the American story; although there are parallels in Russian serfdom. The issue of the regional balance of power in a new nation, however, is by no means unique, as the cases, say, of Germany, Nigeria, and Pakistan suggest.

Interwoven with the constitutional conflict with Britain in the period 1763–75 was the question of access to political power within the colonies themselves. The colonial assemblies derived, in principle, from the popular franchise which emerged naturally at local levels of government. The franchise was subject to a variety of restrictions: women and slaves could not vote; religious restrictions applied in certain colonies; and a property qualification was almost universal, although a qualification generally not difficult to meet given the availability of cheap, good land. As the population expanded into new lands within the colonies and the cities grew, both back-country districts and urban mechanics and workers found themselves and their interests, in degree, under-represented, as those colonial groups earlier entrenched held to their prerogatives.[8]

This undercurrent of tension in local politics among the colonists themselves converged with a feature of the British tax program which would have undercut the powers of the colonial assemblies as they were, in fact, constituted. A good deal of colonial history is the story of the 'winning of the initiative' by the legislatures. Their leverage over the colonial governors rested substantially on their power over the sources of revenue to defray provincial expenses, including the salaries of the governor and most of the royal officials. In 1764 London provided that the new customs receipts could be used directly to pay such salaries. The reaction of the colonial assemblies was particularly acute because they had gathered strength in the generation of conflict in North America before 1763.

Vital questions of the locus of political power in the colonies were, then, part of the developing revolutionary ferment.

The protracted debate with London from 1764 and the mobilization of American opinion which occurred in the years immediately before the conflict brought the colonial community closer together and gave the less powerful and less privileged an enlarged voice and status. And the Revolutionary War itself to some extent shifted the young nation's social and political balance, as Loyalists departed and the exigencies of war, wartime inflation, and wartime politics brought forward new men to whom the confiscated property of tories and crown lands were cheaply available. To some extent the conflict with Britain strengthened those working for popular government in America: '. . . they might never have been strong enough to dictate the future of American politics if the Revolution had not played into their hands.'⁹

But there was, on balance, more continuity than change in the movement from colonial government to the new state constitutions under the Articles of Confederation to the Constitution.

The property qualifications survived in almost all of the state constitutions; but R. E. Brown is almost certainly correct in his judgment that it was not onerous for white males and in underlining the assessment of the men at Philadelphia that their document would have to run a highly democratic gauntlet.¹⁰

The Constitution itself, while broadly measuring the political weight of the states by population (with slaves at three-fifths), left the franchise to each of them. Property and religious qualifications withered away as the nation moved west and the cities grew, leaving white manhood suffrage (or taxpayer's suffrage) the rule by 1826, except in Rhode Island, Virginia, and Louisiana.¹¹ It was not this modest democratizing evolution but rather the movement to the West and to the cities that yielded the Jacksonian watershed in mood and policy. Above all, there was the march of the successive American generations undergoing a lively version of the preconditions for take-off, taking for granted the great architectural settlements of the previous generation and plunging into debate on specific issues of policy – notably, the tariff and internal improvements.

The tensions and uncertainties of the 1790s – about the centralized powers the American people would find acceptable – gave way to Jefferson's 'We are all Republicans, we are all Federalists' in a more solid way than his gracious conciliatory phrase of 1801 had, perhaps, envisaged.

The external environment vindicated and consolidated the role of an energetic national government: the exigencies imposed by war in Europe and the War of 1812; the opportunities and problems thrust on the federal government by the Louisiana Purchase; the problems of the Canadian border, Florida, and of the new Latin American Republics. Federalist–Republican tension persisted to a degree in the domain of economic policy. But by 1840 a half-century of successful political experience under the Constitution – of accumulated common memories of crises weathered, of recurrent elections, of power peacefully passed to the opposition – gave to the Union, under federal government, a substance which John Marshall's decisions reinforced but did not create.

In contemporary parlance, the United States moved during the preconditions period from a precarious statehood towards nationhood. But this trend itself contributed to the coming of regional crisis rooted in the diverging dynamics of the cotton South and the industrializing North.

The clash between the rhetoric of the Declaration of Independence and the fact of slavery had proved sufficient to set in motion a movement to end the trade in slaves, to end slavery north of the Mason–Dixon line, and to prohibit slavery in the Northwest Territory. But the interplay between the cotton textile revolution in England and Whitney's cotton gin made slavery profitable over wide areas of the South. The half million slaves of the 1790s increased to some 4 million on the eve of the Civil War.

Both North and South expanded during the preconditions period, in territory and population, as well as in income and ambition. But in the House of Representatives the North began to pull ahead by 1820, in part because of the manner in which slaves were counted under the Constitution. The Senate became the center of the struggle of the South to prevent its interests from being overwhelmed in the Congress; and the number of slave and free states became critical. Thus, the ingenuity of the Missouri Compromise in 1820 was required to buy time; but its provision of no slavery north of 36°30′ guaranteed that time would run out and Jefferson's 'fire bell in the night' would again be heard.

The next great constitutional issue arose from South Carolina's claim to nullify the tariff of 1828. As in 1820, compromise was necessary to surmount it – in this case, Clay's liberalized and de-escalating tariff schedule of 1833; but, like the 1820 reaffirmation of the Northwest Ordinance, Jackson's proclamation and the Force Act, redoubtably reaffirming the overrriding authority of the federal government, laid the basis for future confrontation which Jackson perceived would be on 'the Negro or slavery question'.

Economic Policy

Few contemporary developing nations have experienced a more self-conscious and persistent debate on the politics of the preconditions for take-off than the United States between 1788 and 1843. In part, this resulted from the postwar sense of continued challenge from Britain. But the interweaving of economic policy with the appropriate functions of federal versus state governments gave the matter political, constitutional, and, even, philosophic status, from the initial debate of Hamilton and Jefferson to Jackson's War on the Second National Bank and the concurrent clash of North and South over the tariff.

Hamilton's Report on Manufactures of 1791 is a fundamental extension of the *Wealth of Nations* to the case of a relatively underdeveloped nation intent on catching up with an already existing industrial front-runner. In that particular sense, it is the beginning of the modern literature on development. Washington occasionally had his doubts about Hamilton's policy, as over the constitutionality of the first National Bank. But, in the end, he gave Hamilton his head: with the funding of the debt; the Bank itself; the import duties and domestic taxes necessary to set the national fiscal system into motion; the mint; and, indeed, the opportunity to put his case for industrialization to the Congress and the people.

And over the half-century that followed, public policy – federal or state – fulfilled its role with respect to each of the classic headings of the preconditions for take-off:

— A Hamiltonian interpretation of the powers of the federal government gave the nation an initially sound basis for dealing financially, and otherwise, with a potentially threatening external environment.

— A stable political base and public climate at home were maintained and encouraged a concentration of the nation's energies, talents, and resources on economic development.

— A complex mixture of federal, state, and private enterprise gradually broke the transport barriers to the creation of an efficient national market through a succession of surges in turnpike, canal, steamship and railway investment – the latter fundamental in multiple ways to the American take-off.

— The cotton gin, initially fostered by the new patent system, yielded a capacity to earn enlarged foreign exchange to finance necessary imports.

— A tariff system, at first for revenue and then for protection, encouraged men to take the plunge into modern manufactures in the face of relatively expensive labor; but its moderation did yield an industry still capable of international competition.

— The social and political evolution of the North encouraged popular education and an approximation, at least, of equality of opportunity – a characteristic reinforced by the availability of good, cheap land under federal policy.

— The federal government generated an independent arms supply which contributed techniques of interchangeability and fine machining to American industry as a whole.

— The U.S. Army, and its military academy, was biased by federal policy towards tasks of engineering and then put to work in exploration and in certain critical public works.

Behind these limited but active measures of public policy, the expansion of domestic and foreign commerce developed a corps of entrepreneurs and institutions of finance capable of moving over to industry when opportunity offered; and it generated, even in pre-industrial years, expanded cities, which could serve as the broader matrix for industrial development.

As with other nations, the American preconditions for take-off unfolded unevenly – and also with a certain irony. The 1790s proved a decade not of industrial development, as Hamilton hoped and sought to induce with his ill-fated scheme in New Jersey. It was a decade of enormous expansion in exports of agricultural products in response to European wartime needs. These developments encouraged urbanization, expanded the banking system, and diffused high profits; but it was more a vindication of Jefferson's than Hamilton's vision.

When Jefferson came to power he and Gallatin for a time could behave as good Republicans. They cut the excise taxes and reduced the debt. But against this background the Embargo so cut customs duties as to dissipate the possibility of Gallatin's farsighted national transport scheme of 1808. It also plunged the nation into a phase of concentration on manufactures, carried forward during the War of 1812. With the failure of Jefferson's fiscal base in the Embargo, a perhaps unique opportunity was lost to build the American transport infrastructure on a federal base; for, except for the Cumberland Road which Jefferson initiated, the post-1815 balance of political interests in the nation severely restricted the federal role in public improvements.

Recognizing the meaning of his experience, and the nation's, by 1816 Jefferson was fully a Hamiltonian with respect to industrialization:[12]

... there exists both profligacy and power enough to exclude us from the field of inter-change with other nations: that to be independent for the comforts of life we must fabricate them ourselves. We must now place the manufacturer by the side of the agriculturalist ... experience has taught me that manufactures are now as necessary to our independence as to our comfort...

This mood yielded national consensus on the protective tariff of 1816, but did not prevent the collapse of most of the uncompetitive factories developed under wartime circumstances.

The steady balance between agricultural and manufacturing development, which Hamilton, and then Jefferson, came to envisage, proved hard to achieve: industry surged ahead in New England of the 1820s against a background of falling agricultural prices; but the 1830s was cotton's decade, as British and Eastern capital was caught up in the land boom that followed the rise in the cotton price, induced by a shortage of acreage relative to demand throughout the Atlantic world, until Jackson blew the whistle in 1836 with the Specie Circular.

Biddle's desperate scheme to keep the induced flood of cotton from further breaking the cotton price (and the transatlantic financial network based on it) briefly worked down to the spring of 1839. A credulous London accepted for a time short-term American notes rather than bullion in repayment of earlier debts; while, at home the Biddle syndicate extended credit to the planters so that they could keep their crop off the market. But the cotton price could not be held. Depression came, and the stage was set for the critical transition to industrialization in the generation before 1860.

There is, then, a rough shifting of economic priority by decades from agriculture to industry in the nation's first half-century, in response to the international military, commercial, and price environment in which the American economy evolved. But through these vicissitudes, federal and state policy helped move American life to a point where sustained industrialization could occur.

THE POLITICS OF THE TAKE-OFF AND DRIVE TO TECHNOLOGICAL MATURITY

The Data and the Questions

The grand sweep of American growth set out in table 30 is familiar and well studied.

The exact anatomy of the American take-off was the subject of lively debate in the 1960s;[13] but the industrial surge of the 1840s and 1850s is sturdily established.[14]

We deal in this section, as in chapter 4, with the take-off and drive to technological maturity together, to permit the following political questions to be posed in ways which emphasize their continuity as well as their sequence.

— What constitutional problems of justice and order arose?
— What policies were adopted towards growth and welfare?
— How did security policies alter during the sweep of industrialization, particularly in the two classic times of temptation to expansion: during the take-off and towards the end of the drive to technological maturity?

Constitutional Change

The great constitutional issues of the periods of take-off and of drive to technological maturity centered, in part, on matters typical of other nations experiencing these phases of development, in part, on matters peculiar to American history.

There is, for example, the widening of the electorate through the Fifteenth Amendment (1870) and the effort to enlarge the electorate's power, through the direct election of Senators, in the Seventeenth (1913).

196

TABLE 30. *Basic data: U.S., 1790–1963*

Year	Urban proportion of total population[a] (%)	Annual rate of growth: total population[b] (%)	Quinquennial rate of growth of GNP[c] (%)	Annual rate of growth: real net national product[d] (%)	Annual rate of growth: industrial production[e] (%)	Proportion of labor force in: farming[f] (%)	Proportion of labor force in: manufacturing[f] (%)	Proportion of national product (current prices): agriculture[g] (%)	industry[g] (%)	services[g] (%)	Government expenditures as proportion of GNP[h] (%)
1790	5.1	..									
1800	6.1	3.1				73.7					
1810	7.3	3.2				80.9	2.8				
1820	7.2	2.9				78.8					
1830	8.8	3.0				68.8					
1840	10.8	2.9	1834/43–1839/48 24			63.1	8.8				
1850	15.3	3.1	1839/48–1844/53 31			54.8	14.5				
1860	19.8	3.1	1844/53–1849/58 30			52.9	13.8				
1870	25.7	2.4	1866/78–1874/83 31		1860–80 4.3	52.5	19.1	1866–79 20	33	47	
1880	28.2	2.3	1874/83–1879/88 26			51.3	18.9				
			1879/88–1884/93 20								
1890	35.1	2.3	1884/93–1889/98 13	1880–99 4.5	1880–1900 4.5	42.7	18.8				1890 7.1
1900	39.7	1.9		1899–1909 4.3		40.2	20.3				1902 7.9
1910	45.7	2.0		1909–19 3.8	1900–13 5.2	31.4	22.2				1913 8.5
1920	51.2	1.4		1919–29 3.1	1913–1925/29 3.7	25.9	26.9	1919–28 11	39	50	1922 12.6
											1927 11.7
1930	56.2	1.5		1929–37 0.2	1925/29–1938 0.9	21.6	20.2	1929 9	42	49	1932 21.3
1940	56.5	0.7		1937–48 4.4		17.0	20.1				1940 22.2
											1948 23.0
1950	64.0	1.4		1948–53 4.7	1938–58 5.3	12.0	23.9				1957 28.5
				1953–57 2.2							
1960	69.9	1.7				8.1	23.2	1961–3 4	43	53	1962 33.2

[a] Data for 1790–1810 from W. S. Woytinsky and E. S. Woytinsky, *World Population and Production*, New York, 1953, p. 124; for 1820–1960 from Abram Bergson and Simon Kuznets (ed.), *Economic Trends in the Soviet Union*, Cambridge, Mass., 1963, pp. 72–3.

[b] Elizabeth W. Gilboy and Edgar M. Hoover, 'Population and Immigration' in Seymour Harris (ed.), *American Economic History*, New York, 1961, p. 248.

[c] Robert E. Gallman, 'Gross National Product in the United States, 1834–1909' in *Output, Employment, and Productivity in the United States after 1800*, Studies in Income and Wealth, Volume Thirty, New York, 1966, p. 22.

[d] John W. Kendrick, *Productivity Trends in the United States*, Princeton, 1961, p. 79.

[e] S. J. Patel, 'Rates of Industrial Growth in the Last Century, 1860–1958' in *Economic Development and Cultural Change*, April 1961, p. 319.

[f] Stanley Lebergott, 'Labor Force and Employment, 1800–1960' in *Output, Employment, and Productivity in the United States after 1800*, Studies in Income and Wealth, Volume Thirty, New York, 1966, p. 119.

[g] Simon Kuznets, *Modern Economic Growth*, New Haven, 1966, pp. 90–1.

[h] Richard A. Musgrave, *Fiscal Systems*, New Haven, 1969, p. 94.

Again, in close parallel with the British crisis over enlarged welfare outlays and their financing, the income tax amendment was finally ratified in 1913, after almost four years of debate in the states – an act typical of the late stage of the drive to technological maturity. The appropriate status and rights of labor organization weave through the legal and legislative history of these years down to the Clayton Act (1914) and beyond.

But these, and other, familiar constitutional issues of industrialization interact with three special aspects of the American political scene:

— the endemic debate, from 1787 to the present, on the relative powers of the federal and state governments, including, of course, the pivotal pre-Civil War debate on the constitutional character of the Union itself;

— the problem of slavery and the post-Civil War rights of the Negro citizen;

— the issue of monopoly, which, while by no means unique, took on a special cast in the post-Civil War period as the size and momentum of the American market encouraged large-scale business units which the majority finally judged to be potentially in violation of the competitive ground-rules of American life.

Slavery and the status of the negro citizen

The two pre-Civil War decades of American take-off were marked by a simultaneous push to the West and acceleration of industrial development on a wide front. The latter exacerbated the southern sense of economic inferiority, dependence, and distinctiveness. The former posed the truly critical question: the future of slavery in the balance of a Union whose clearly emerging continental shape ruled out the possibility of a natural balance between slave and free states. The South looked to politics and the law to redress the balance decreed by climate and geography, railroad technology, and squatter sovereignty.

By and large, the Compromise of 1850 was uneasily accepted in the North given the prize of California; although the tight, new fugitive slave law stirred the abolitionists and posed for many more a deep moral issue. The Dred Scott decision of 1857, accompanied by the battle over the Kansas constitution, brought that issue to still sharper focus: should the powers of the federal government assert the legal legitimacy of slavery throughout the Union? The assertion of legitimacy collided with the morally ambiguous balances which had thus far held the Union together: the Missouri Compromise, the Ordinance of 1787, and the consensus of the Founding Fathers that slavery was a fact of life, but an evil fact of life to be limited and which, hopefully, would wither away.

198

The politics of the take-off and drive to technological maturity

In his Freeport Doctrine, Douglas sought with ingenuity to save the Union by giving the South its formal victory at a national level, while permitting the state legislatures to negate slavery by inaction where it did not command majority assent. But this policy of *de facto* nullification was too much for the North – a resistance heightened by fear that the rise of the price of slaves in the South during the cotton boom of the 1850s would soon lead to a demand for the re-opening of the slave trade.

Lincoln's drawing of the line on the extension of slavery into the territories in the spirit of 1787 won him the Presidency in 1860, in the face of a fragmented opposition; and this proved too much for the South to accept, given its illusory hopes that the leverage of King Cotton would both weaken the North disastrously and render Britain a firm ally. The South did not appear to understand the full implications of the dramatic developments of the 1850s: the linking of the Northeast to the Northwest, where population expanded from 3.3 to 5.4 million in a decade; the logistical thrust the railways would give to the inevitable drive of the Northwest to keep the mouth of the Mississippi within the Union; the diffusion of industry beyond the Northeast and the drawing into American life of the German and Scandinavian immigrants; and the tempering effect on British foreign policy of its requirement for northern wheat.

Thus, the dynamics of the take-off both helped precipitate and determine the outcome of the Civil War.

The constitutional structure of modern America – like the constitutional structure of modern Germany – was settled by war. The coming of the railway and accelerated industrialization undercut the relative power of the South, in the one case, of Austria, in the other.

Lincoln had drawn a difficult line, separating the paramount constitutional question of Union from the moral issue of slavery – a separation which permitted him to hold the critical border states in the Civil War. He was under constitutional oath to maintain the Union: he regarded slavery as an evil, but its destruction was for him a secondary tactical issue, and the long-run future of the Negro in America a tragic puzzlement. Out of the painful realities of Reconstruction, the nation drew a similar line, separating the formal rights of the Negro under the Thirteenth, Fourteenth, and Fifteenth Amendments from the actual status he was to enjoy as a citizen in the several states. The North simply did not have the sense of purpose, priority, endurance, and, perhaps, the administrative machinery to continue to impose and enforce on the South the laws that might have continued to give substance to these amendments. As between a permanently occupied South and *de facto* violation of the Negro's constitutional rights, the North opted for the latter evil. And so, in 1877 the troops were withdrawn and the

Negro's status left, for almost eighty years, mainly in the hands of white southern political and social life and the wider economic and social dynamics of the nation. But the Fourteenth Amendment stayed on the books and on the American conscience.[15]

On short term, the outcome of the Civil War – as measured from 1877 – thus granted to the South a version of Douglas' Freeport Doctrine in reverse: the law called universally for full Negro citizenship, but the nation acquiesced in its *de facto* nullification in the South.

Since, by 1840, universal white manhood suffrage had been virtually achieved, the substantial negation in the South of the Negro's political power after 1877 left the electorate essentially unaltered in structure from that time down to the granting of women's suffrage by the Nineteenth Amendment (1920).

The status of organized labor

As John R. Commons perceived in his classic study of American labor, the essentially universal story of the worker's efforts to defend his position in the world of modern industry was, from the beginning, colored by special characteristics of the American scene. Cheap, good land was available. The vote came at an early stage of industrial development and with it the possibility of political participation and influence. The states, rather than the federal government, had power, until relatively late in American history, over many of the issues which directly concerned labor. It was harder to organize labor on a continent-wide basis than it was to organize industry. And, finally, large-scale immigration had a major impact on the labor market and labor organization.

The impulse of American labor to organize raised – as in other societies based on individual private property rights – formal constitutional questions. Were such collective, quasi-monopolistic groupings legitimate? Could labor properly be withheld from the market? What techniques could labor use within the law in attaining its goals at the expense of employers and the public in general?

The legal history of American labor is diffuse until events of the 1930s brought the issue squarely under federal legislation with the Wagner Act. But two rough phases can be distinguished.

Phase One: 1794–1842. Starting with the famous Philadelphia Cordwainers, the labor movement moved forward sporadically as industrialization gradually took hold. Its fortunes fluctuated with periods of pressure on real wages from rising prices and with the rhythm of the business cycle. It was harassed from time to time by the doctrine of conspiracy brought over from English common law: '. . . a confederacy of two or more, by indirect means to injure an individual or to do any act, which is unlawful or prejudicial to the community'.

Despite running warfare with the courts, and the tendency of organizations to collapse during cyclical depression, the trend of union membership was upward. Techniques of collective bargaining were painfully learned as well as the possibilities and limits of the strike and boycott. Notably in the 1830s, efforts were made to group and briefly, even, to nationalize the labor movement. And with the overturn of a lower court ruling in the Massachusetts Supreme Court in 1842 (Commonwealth v. Hunt), the doctrine of *prima facie* conspiracy was firmly set aside by Chief Justice Shaw:[16]

We think, therefore, that associations may be entered into, the object of which is to adopt measures that may have a tendency to impoverish another, that is, to diminish his gains and profits, and yet so far from being criminal or unlawful, the object may be highly meritorious and public spirited. The legality of such an association will therefore depend upon the means to be used for its accomplishment.

It was natural that this assessment should emerge first in Massachusetts which already had a generation's experience with rapid industrialization.

Phase Two: 1842–1914.   Although Shaw's ruling was broadly accepted in the courts, it did not end the union's struggle for status. The legitimate 'means' for conducting labor relations proved quite as fruitful a terrain of debate and conflict as the issue of collective labor organization itself. As industrialization accelerated and widened after the Civil War, the Knights of Labor made its bid for a national labor movement with broad political objectives. The effort failed for multiple reasons, of which the attempt to hold skilled and unskilled workers in the same organization was probably most basic; but its decline was accelerated by the revulsion against the Haymarket riot of 1886. In that year the narrower, more solid, less overtly political American Federation of Labor was formed.

The critical legal issue for labor became the use of the court injunction to uphold contracts between employer and employee which would prevent the latter from joining a union, or, even (as in the Pullman strike) prevent union leaders from inciting members to strike.

In addition, the Sherman Act of 1890 was interpreted for a time as applying to the unions as a form of monopoly.

To alter this interpretation became a major aim of organized labor. The AFL expanded in the pre-1914 trend period of rising prices and pressures on real wages. Gompers finally achieved his rhetorical 'Magna

Charta' in the Clayton Act: 'The labor of a human being is not a commodity or article of commerce.' But the legitimacy of the yellow dog contract survived in the courts; and the debate on the nature and limits of action by organized labor rolled on. Symbolically, however, the Clayton Act, like the overthrow in Britain of the Taff-Vale decision, was an historical benchmark, reflecting, as it did, the strong wave of pre-1914 feeling that the powers inherent in modern industry justified the granting of legitimacy to organized labor.

The control of monopoly

The issue of industrial concentration was more acute in the United States than in Europe or Japan, for reasons reaching deep into the American political system and the character of the post-Civil War industrial economy.

The debate over the First and Second National Banks had revealed the antagonisms within the nation against great concentrations of economic – as of political – power. But aside from John Jacob Astor's fur empire, economic units tended to be small down to the 1850s. Daniel C. McCallum's dictum on the organizational reasons for failure of some of the early long-distance railroads foreshadowed a good deal of future industrial history:[17]

A Superintendent of a road fifty miles in length can give its business his personal attention and may be constantly on the line engaged in the direction of its details; each person is personally known to him, and all questions in relation to its business are at once presented and acted upon.

In the government of a road five hundred miles in length a very different state exists. . . I am fully convinced that in the want of a system perfect in its details, properly adapted and vigilantly enforced, lies the true secret of their [the large roads'] failure.

On this perception a group of imaginative railroad engineers designed the organizational structure for the first large-scale American industrial enterprise. It was based on the centralized management of specific functions, broken down by departments. Its unity was maintained by the prompt and uniform reporting and standardized operating instructions permitted by the telegraph.

The half-century after the Civil War saw the United States move from the modest but sturdy industrial base, created in a predominately agricultural society before 1860, to an urban society dominated by industry. The American economy rapidly absorbed the new technologies generated on the world scene: steel and chemicals, electricity, refrigeration, and the internal combustion engine, rubber and oil. And it organized itself to make the most of the unique, rapidly expanding continental market which emerged.

There were men still in the inventive tradition of Whitney and the cotton gin: Edison and Berliner and the Wright brothers, for example. But the era was dominated by those who perceived possibilities of large profit by some marriage of existing technology and the immense national market, through new forms of industrial organization: thus, in 1882 the Standard Oil Trust; Swift and his meat empire; Duke and his mass manufacture and distribution of cigarettes; Gary and his vast steel holding company; the transcontinental railway nets themselves.

As these and other massive new units emerged, they experimented with various forms of consolidation, horizontal as well as vertical. The central problem was to combine the advantages of scale – with respect to the cost of acquiring raw materials, efficiency of plant operations, mobilization of labor supply, marketing, and working capital – with the imperatives of unified management. The railroads, especially the Pennsylvania, provided the model adopted most often. And sometimes railroad executives moved over directly to apply their management and accounting experience to other fields. Central operational units related to each function were created, with general managers for each such department. Coordination and broad policy-making fell to a group of commanding figures supported by small staffs.

It was in the struggle against the power of these units – which drove the American economy to technological maturity – that the constitutional basis was laid for the Progressive Movement and much that lay beyond for the role of the federal government in the economy.

The legal and constitutional history of American organized labor is, even down to the present, the story of an unfolding process in which the drift towards acceptance of its rights is marked by a counterpoint of balancing constraints arising from particular situations, methods, and confrontations of power. It is as if American society felt its way uncertainly forward in fitting this collective instrument into a society whose underlying pre-suppositions were atomistic and competitive.

Much the same can be said of policy towards monopoly and concentrations of industrial and financial power. As J. W. Hurst emphasizes, the initial role of the law in nineteenth-century America was to release private energies, including those channelled into commercial, social, and political associations.[18] As the power of the post-Civil War railway and other industrial concentrations made itself felt, the political life of the nation came slowly to the acceptance of Calhoun's old dictum: 'Power [could] only be resisted by power – and tendency by tendency.'

Munn v. Illinois (1876) was for the constraint of corporations what Commonwealth v. Hunt was to the balancing power of organized labor. The Supreme Court upheld the right of the State of Illinois to regulate the grain elevators, denying blanket protection by the Fourteenth Amendment where a public interest was at stake:[19]

... when private property is devoted to a public use, it is subject to public regulation.

... it is difficult to see why, if the common carrier, or the miller, or the ferryman, or the inn-keeper, or the wharfinger, or the baker, or the cartman, or the hackney-coachman, pursues a public employment and exercises 'a sort of public office', these plaintiffs in error do not. They stand, to use again the language of their counsel, in the very gateway 'of commerce', and take toll from all who pass. Their business most certainly 'tends to a common charge, and is become a thing of public interest and use'. .... Certainly, if any business can be clothed 'with a public interest and cease to be *juris privati* only', this has been. It may not be made so by the operation of the constitution of Illinois or this statute, but it is by the facts.

The application of this doctrine out of the Granger cases came slowly. First in the states, then through the Interstate Commerce Act (1887), and the Sherman Anti-Trust Act (1890). On the basis of the latter, protracted political and legal struggle yielded (after setback in the Knight case (1895) and victory in the Northern Securities case (1904)) the Wilsonian climax: the Federal Reserve System and the Federal Trade Commission, as well as the Clayton Act.

In dealing with the fact of concentrations of power in a mature industrial society, America evoked all the tools of politics available: legislative, administrative, and legal – as well as the rhetorical and educational power of the post-1900 presidents. In trying to solve a theoretically insoluble problem in a society formally committed to competitive individualism, Holmes' dictum held: 'The life of the law has not been logic: it has been experience.'

Industrial concentration may not have proceeded to the degree that it might have done in a different legal environment; but, clearly, the trend continued as the DuPont and, then, General Motors pattern of organization brought wider and more diversified production units under effectively unified central management. The relative power in the society of these concentrations was hedged about and balanced, although Gabriel Kolko's conclusion is essentially correct that the society, as a whole, reluctantly, complacently or eagerly accepted their existence.[20] In the balancing process two factors outside the range of political instruments played a part:

— a climate of opinion that rendered business leaders increasingly hesitant in exercising the more egregious monopolistic powers they technically commanded;

— the coming of the stage of high mass-consumption which made industry increasingly sensitive to the attitudes of the consumer and to public relations in general.

But it was ultimately in exploiting the most revolutionary development of the pre-1914 years – the progressive income tax – that American political life found the most effective ways to soften the exigencies of a modern industrial system.

Policy Towards Growth and Welfare

The sequence of economic and welfare issues faced and decided in American political life during the take-off and drive to technological maturity is essentially similar to that faced in other societies examined in chapter 3, notably those of Western Europe: tariff policy; the control of hours and conditions of work in the factories, mines, and railroads; a reallocation of resources through politics and government towards social services. Excepting the federal role in subsidizing the trans-continental railroads and the land grant colleges, the direct role of government in the economy's development was minor.

The tariff

The story of the American tariff, from 1842 to 1913, appears to share the broad shape of tariff history elsewhere. An initially low tariff position gave way, with the acceleration of industrialization, to a high tariff phase, ameliorated in the years of rapid trade expansion and rising cost of living before 1914. But the state of the federal revenues, of cyclical fluctuations, of north–south and, then, Republican–Democratic party politics, gives the American tariff story certain special dimensions.

The constitutional settlement with the South yielded the compromise tariff of 1833 which called for a lowering of rates to a 20 per cent level of 1842. But a shortage of federal customs revenues, at the bottom of a depression, led Congress to acquiesce in protectionist pressures. There followed a brief period of high duties, moderated in 1846, and further scaled down in 1857 in the face of a revenue surplus.[21]

With the South out of the Congress, tariffs were raised radically during the Civil War years. Protectionist interests converged with revenue requirements and the need to avoid granting preference to imports in the face of high domestic excise taxes. The average rate on dutiable commodities was 48 per cent in 1865, more than twice the level four years earlier.

The high rates on protected articles generally survived the repeal of most of the excise taxes down to the tariff of 1883. Protectionist interests managed to frustrate rising popular sentiment against the tariff with minimum concessions, aided by the built-in biases of the newly formed Tariff Commission.

In the course of the 1880s the two major parties lacked clear-cut issues on which they could safely disagree without fragmenting their constituencies. In an instinctive rather than rational process they came to polarize around the tariff issue, as the Whigs and Democrats had done in the 1840s. They gambled, in effect, that popular sentiment could be led by political argument to assess the diffuse, complex, and unmeasurable consequences of high tariffs, positively or negatively, and voters would come to identify themselves primarily as either nationalist producers or exploited consumers. On that basis, Cleveland bluntly challenged the Republicans in 1887 on the tariff; and they responded by advocating still higher tariffs, which they proceeded to implement after their victory the following year.

But it was one thing to reject lower tariffs, a different matter to support still higher tariffs. In the Tariff Act of 1890 the Republicans overplayed their hand and the voters responded by bringing Cleveland back in 1892. The consequent moderations in the Tariff Act of 1894 were minor. Cyclical depression then weakened the case of the tariff liberals, and the Republican victory of 1896 brought another increase in protection the following year.

The post-Civil War protectionist victories were won in an environment of a falling secular trend in prices which granted real wage increases to the urban worker through the market process. It could be – and was – argued that tariffs elevated the cost of living beyond the level it would otherwise attain; but that sophisticated argument could be countered successfully by appeals for protection against low wage levels abroad. From 1896 the trends in the world economy shifted. For a generation the rising cost of living and pressure on urban real wages became a central political and social fact in the United States as in Britain and Germany. And it converged in the United States with the notion that tariffs encouraged concentrations of private industrial and financial power, the most dramatic political issue of a period where still the rural population was in the majority.

Protectionist interests and habits, however, were deeply entrenched in the Congress and yielded only slowly. The 1909 Tariff Act brought no substantial change; but protectionism was by then clearly on the defensive. Only with Wilson's victory did America move strongly in the direction of lower duties, for the first time since the Civil War.

Although Schattschneider's classic study is of the tariff revision of 1929–30, his dictum on the post-Civil War era as a whole is valid:[22]

... the dominant position of the Republican party before 1932 can be attributed largely to the successful exploitation of the tariff by this party as a means of attaching to itself a formidable array of interests dependent on the protective system and intent upon continuing it ... it must be rated as one of the most notable political achievements in American history.

... American tariff history is the account of an unsuccessful attempt to set up a beneficently discriminatory set of privileges, resulting in legislation so indiscriminately broad as to destroy the logic and sense of the policy. The very tendencies that have made the legislation bad have, however, made it politically invincible.

It was the tariff's pervasiveness and deep political roots that made the revisions of 1894 and, even, 1913 relatively so modest. It took the full traumatic weight of the Great Depression of the 1930s to set the United States on a different course; and, even now, the protectionist beast in American politics can be kept at bay only with eternal vigilance and effort.

Welfare policy

The welfare issues of American industrialization centered on hours of work; public education; and workingmen's compensation. With minor exceptions, these matters were left with the states, where diverse economic and political circumstances decreed a wide variety of outcomes. The relatively declining tendency of agricultural prices in the two decades after 1873 raised more strongly in the United States than in Europe the question of bimetallism; but the movement died without issue, as prices turned up again in the mid-1890s and the American farmer subsided into a more conservative posture.

The pre-Civil War labor movement can be roughly dated from its emergence in Philadelphia in 1827. It concentrated initially on the demand for shorter hours of work, but soon constituted itself a lobby for expanded public education.[23]

With the vote available in the North, political pressure for universal, tax-supported public education proved an easier issue on which to make progress than a restricted work-day. The demand for public schools rallied a wide constituency which accepted the connection between popular education and democracy, on the one hand, productivity, on the other. New England already had its public school system in the 1820s; Pennsylvania acted in 1834; New York City in 1842; New York State in 1849. Labor's role in pressing the North to universal public primary education was its greatest achievement before 1860.

The ten-hour movement, paralleling that in Britain, yielded some uneven results. In 1840 the federal government led the way symbolically in the navy yards; and the issue was pressed to legislation in Pennsylvania, New Hampshire, Maine, Ohio, California, and Georgia. These initial acts were, however, subject to evasion. In New York and Massachusetts the rising agitation failed to produce formal results, although the question of conditions of work, notably for women and children, was laid successfully on the public agenda and the public conscience.

The post-Civil War period was a turbulent era for labor, marked by cyclical fluctuations, the absorption of massive immigration, occasionally, bloody labor–management struggles, organizational experiments with national and then craft unionism, and flirtations with various ideological doctrines derived from Europe or home grown. But the market process granted labor real progress, through falling prices and the introduction of new industrial technologies which raised both labor productivity and real wages.

Against that background, the battle for humane conditions in the factories went forward slowly. In 1866 Massachusetts led the way with a law forbidding employment of children under ten and requiring an eight-hour day and six months of schooling for employed children between ten and fourteen. After a further decade, this law was enforced, setting a pattern for other states. By 1900 half the states or more set a minimum of twelve years of age in manufacturing industries and a maximum of ten hours a day for women and children. Legislation began to regulate conditions of work and safety in shops, mines, and the railroads. In 1892 the eight-hour day was made the rule in the federal government; and from the 1880s a federal role was sanctioned in railroad disputes. And by 1902 Maryland passed the first state compensation law reflecting the gradual rise of the doctrine of employer responsibility when industrial accidents were not caused by the worker's negligence.

The changed economic environment of the late 1890s and the pre-1914 years accelerated the gathering trend towards government action to civilize by political means mature industrial society. American unions had often turned to politics when cyclical unemployment denied them bargaining leverage in the labor market; but the pre-1914 generation in the United States was not generally a period of severe unemployment. Labor turned both to organization and to politics to combat the erosion of real wages through rising prices.

Average union membership rose from 447,000 in 1897 to 2,716,300 in 1913.[24] But the percentage of the total working force unionized was still low; and, as the British experience demonstrated, labor organization itself was not capable of overcoming the weight imposed on real wages by the rise of living costs. American real wages, as measured by Alvin Hansen, drifted slightly downward in trend over these years, and never attained the 1897 level again until 1920,[25] despite substantial increases in money wages. There was a quite marked shift in the distribution of national income away from labor to profits, interest, and rent, as the calculations in table 31 suggest.[26]

The rapidly enlarging urban working force in these circumstances turned naturally to politics to seek redress. It gave strong support to the Progressive Movement which swept through city, state, and federal governments, leaving behind not merely some reforming mayors, governors, and presidents but a residue of legal instruments and institutions for the control of industry and finance and that truly revolutionary social tool, the income tax.

The legacy was imperfect, but it kept in social and political equilibrium a

The politics of the take-off and drive to technological maturity

society undergoing severe structural strain. Part of the solvent was rhetorical and a matter of mood which Theodore Roosevelt articulated as well as anyone: 'This New Nationalism regards the executive power as the steward of the public welfare. It demands of the Judiciary that it shall be interested primarily in human welfare rather than in property, just as it demands that

TABLE 31. *A functional distribution of American income, 1870–1910*

	(per cent of total income[a])				
Period	Employee compensation	Entrepreneurial net income[b]	Dividends	Interest	Rent
1870 and 1880	50.0	26.4	15.8		7.8
1880 and 1890	52.5	23.0	16.5		8.2
1890 and 1900	50.4	27.3	14.7		7.7
1900 and 1910	47.1	28.8	15.9		8.3

[a] Detail may not add to total because of rounding.
[b] Includes income of unincorporated businesses, farmers, and other self-employed persons and undistributed corporate profits.

the representative body shall represent all the people rather than one section or class of the people.' That this view was stated by the leader of one wing of a split Republican Party – which had dominated American politics since 1860 – rather than by the victorious Democratic candidate of 1912 made it more, rather than less, significant for the temper of American politics in the sixty years that followed.

In terms of the reallocation of resources, however, the Progressive Movement (including its increased attention to conservation) leaves only a modest mark on the national accounts, as table 32 indicates.[27]

TABLE 32. *United States government expenditures by functions as per cent of GNP (all levels of government) 1890–1913*

			Civilian			
	Total	Defense	Law, order, adminis- tration	Economic and environ- mental services	Social services	Public debt
1890	7.1	1.4	1.2	2.0	1.8	0.7
1902	7.9	1.5	1.1	2.1	1.9	0.5
1913	8.5	1.1	0.9	2.6	2.1	0.4

The 1913 figures for social service outlays were 4.1 per cent for the United Kingdom, in the wake of the Liberal reforms; 5.1 per cent for post-Bismarck Germany. The balance of American life was relatively tilted still towards the maximization of private income and towards private rather than public responsibility for insurance against the risks of life.

Security Policy

Manifest destiny and the take-off

From 1840 to 1914 the United States experienced two decades when the fever of manifest destiny briefly gripped the nation's foreign and military policy: the 1840s and the 1890s – the first during take-off, the second towards the end of the drive to technological maturity.

The Mexican War began in May 1846 and ended with the Treaty of Guadalupe Hidalgo about two years later. It resulted from the convergence in Polk's mind of a passionate desire to round out the nation to Oregon and California and a fear that the great prize – California – might be seized or bought from the Mexicans by England or France. This joining of material and security considerations had been inhibited, down to the very end of Tyler's administration, by a constitutional consideration: the problem posed by Texas' joining the Union as a slave state and upsetting the delicate North–South balance. After the election of 1844, acting in the spirit of Polk's apparent mandate, Tyler bypassed the two-thirds Senate majority he could not get for a treaty of annexation in favor of 're-annexation' via a joint resolution of both houses, which carried.

Polk found that Mexico would swallow the annexation of Texas and the border at the Rio Grande, but could not bring itself to sell California. He manœuvred for war and ended up with the continental nation secured from the British and French; a Mexico that would never forget the gallant death of its young cadets; and a constitutional crisis which the 1850 Compromise could not assuage and which the discovery of gold in California tended to accelerate. A more massive fact lay behind the diplomacy of the 1840s, the cut and thrust of domestic politics, and the single-mindedness of Polk. There welled up in large segments of the American community a strongly felt sentiment that, come what may, the United States would stretch to the Pacific at least along the boundaries that did, in fact, emerge. There was also a considerable articulate opposition, based on the question of slavery in Texas and on the issue of war itself. But the doctrine of manifest destiny was sufficient to carry a dark horse candidate to a narrow, popular majority against the great figure of Henry Clay. A stronger Mexican government with a longer perspective might have found a way to accede without war.

An accident of politics might have elected Clay. But a tide was running, notably in the West and South, that would have been difficult to stem.

As Americans looked west, they did so in a competitive international arena. To the northwest and in the Pacific Britain was still an active, imperial power. France was seeking to retrieve in the Far East something of what it had lost in the eighteenth century and gained and lost under Napoleon. To the south, Mexico was struggling to achieve the stability and administrative energy to consolidate the large empire it had inherited from colonial Spain. It was not difficult in this setting to generate a sense of at least relative righteousness about the American thrust to the Pacific. The alternative solutions could claim, in American eyes, no higher legitimacy than Polk's manifest destiny. Americans had denied a balance of power solution to the affairs of the Western Hemisphere a generation earlier; and, despite the strong reservations of some, they felt rough justice as well as power on their side as Polk extended the principle to the Far West. What was not clearly calculated was that the elimination of the balance of power threat on the continent upset the regional balance of power in domestic politics. And this issue moved to the center of politics in the 1850s.

Thus, American policy in the 1840s belongs with Bismarck's policy of the 1860s; Japan's and Russia's, of the period 1890–1905; and with that of Mao, Nasser, and other ambitious regional expansionists in the 1950s and 1960s. Americans of the 1840s were not unique in seeking to redraw the arbitrary lines on maps, inherited from a colonial past they did not make. But they were luckier than some in seeking territories that were not thickly settled and confronting resistances that proved manageable through diplomacy, violence, or both.

Imperial temptation at technological maturity

Some historians enjoy finding large principles, foreshadowing great events, in minor episodes.

The Samoan affair, climaxed by the need for a conference in Berlin in 1899, is an example. Starting in the 1830s one can trace American whaling and missionary interests in Samoa; by the 1860s a commercial interest; by 1872 a lively naval interest in the harbour of Pago Pago. Although the United States was willing to take some military risk to assert its rights in the islands, it was for a decade (1889–99) unwilling to accept direct imperial responsibility. Complications with Britain and Germany finally led to a settlement which gave the navy the harbor it had long wanted.

Similarly, the annexation of Hawaii was accepted in 1898 after five years of acute (and almost a half century of chronic) vacillation.

Finally, there was Cuba and its insurrection. Colonial unrest in Cuba had stirred the United States, on and off, since 1868. But it moved the nation into war with Spain when a powerful set of forces converged between 1895 and 1898: a peculiarly cruel suppression of insurrection; the generation of widespread interest and heat through the popular press; the blowing up of the *Maine*; a sluggish Spanish diplomacy; and an American President both weaker than his predecessor and burdened with a higher proportion of expansionists in his party.[28]

These problems had in common four elements. First, the nation's sentiment or prestige was caught up in the area by old ties of commerce or missionary effort. Second, there was an actual or potential challenge from an imperial power, raising the question of a vacuum which some potentially unfriendly power might fill if the United States remained aloof. Third, there was an ardent and articulate minority urging that American duty, American interest, and American destiny all required the acceptance of new responsibility. Finally, both before and after the event, the nation confronted and openly wrestled with the problem of reconciling its new ambition and responsibility with its abiding commitment to the principle of national self-determination. An American commercial interest was present in each case; but in none does it appear to have been decisive.

When in the election of 1900 the ideological concepts of the new imperialism clashed with those of the old virtuous hemispheric isolation, McKinley successfully defended the new empire with a negative rather than a positive formula: 'Don't haul down the flag.' And, however cynical the Teller Amendment – disclaiming intent to annex Cuba – may have been regarded by some, the self-denying ordinance built into American history and values, which it represented, was, on balance, to prove immensely powerful in the subsequent half-century.

Further to the west in Asia, the United States moved, in the wake of the British incursion into China in the 1840s, to assume equivalent commercial advantages and initiated in the next decade the opening up of Japan. As Russia, as well as the Western European states, pressed into the area and Japan moved to join the imperialist club in the mid-1890s, the United States sought to hold the ring with the enunciation of the Open Door policy in 1900, a doctrine with balance of power as well as commercial implications. The former were reflected, but only dimly understood, in Roosevelt's role at Portsmouth in 1905. Like Bismarck in 1878, Roosevelt leaned against an up-and-coming power, denying the Japanese what they regarded as the full fruits of victory. Like the Russians after Berlin, the Japanese remembered.

To the diplomatic incidents in the Pacific and Caribbean can be added the early suggestion of a possible new American relationship to Britain resulting from the rise of Germany. The vigor with which the German consular and naval units played the game in Samoa in 1889 for the first time defined Germany as a potential threat to identifiable American interests. Although the Berlin negotiations ended the affair in reasonably good order, the flare-up left some memories in the United States. In July 1895 Cleveland and Olney asserted an American right, under the Monroe Doctrine, to insist on arbitration of the boundary dispute between Venezuela and British Guiana; and they did so in language designed at least as much to assert a general rise in American power *vis-à-vis* Britain (and to outflank Republican expansionists) as to achieve a successful resolution of the dispute. The long-delayed reply from London brought about a flare-up of anti-British feeling in the United States, which was evidently dangerous to the peace. Moderates on both sides were aided, however, by the Kaiser's famous telegram to Kruger which, by reminding Britain of the growing pretensions of Germany in Eurasia, made easier the acceptance of arbitration in Latin America.

The emergence of the possibility of armed clash with Germany forced on both sides of the Atlantic a re-evaluation of the contemporary significance of Anglo–American relations which helped prepare the way (certainly in Britain, perhaps also in the United States) for the alliance of the first half of the twentieth century.

Meanwhile, the navy and the army were responding in different ways to the new technical and international environment of the United States.

In 1875 a naval officer was dispatched to Europe to survey the state of naval architecture. His report in 1877 posed a vivid contrast between the rapidly evolving European navies, using the new technology permitted by steel, and the American coastal fleet made up primarily of wooden sailing vessels of Civil War construction. For the next two decades successive administrations and the Congress were torn between an instinct to maintain some kind of naval parity with the European powers and a concept of the nation's strategic position in which coastal defense was virtually the only abiding naval task the Congress was prepared to acknowledge as legitimate. The upshot was a series of expanded naval appropriations, starting in 1883, which permitted the United States to have in hand a fleet of five capital ships at the outbreak of the Spanish–American War.

Over the fifteen years between 1883 and 1898 there was some acceptance of the concept that the Navy's usefulness might extend beyond a rigid adherence to coastal defense. It was acknowledged that the fleet might be required to protect American citizens and commercial interests abroad; and, indeed, during the 1890s the new, longer-range vessels moved about the hemisphere and the world, Dewey being at Hong Kong when war with Spain began.

Nevertheless, the development of the new American Navy in the 1880s and 1890s reflected a considerable gap between professional and popular thought. The first American battleships were rationalized and initially presented to the public as instruments for coastal defense. Aside from Captain Mahan, the men advocating a new navy were not primarily interested in a new American military and naval strategy based on a new concept of the American national interest. They were interested in being first-rate operating professionals, playing a role of dignity on the world scene. They sensed, vaguely but surely, that the self-evident maturing of the American economy would somehow result in the nation's taking its place among the great powers, and that this required an enlarged and modernized navy at the earliest possible moment. But their concerns were primarily tactical and technological rather than strategic; and their primary goal was enlarged appropriations. In this setting, a combination of ardent support from a purposeful minority, a vague tolerance for a somewhat bigger and better navy within the Congress, and the self-evident need to replace obsolescent vessels ultimately yielded the Great White Fleet.

Thus, the trends which made a naval victory in Manila the most striking engagement in a crusade to free the Cubans from Spanish oppression were discernible well before the event; but, on the whole, the evolution of modern technology probably accounted as much for the vitality of the Navy at the close of the century as the emergence of new doctrines of the national interest and of the Navy's role in protecting it.

Like the naval officer, the professional American soldier emerged from the Civil War knowing that he had met with success a test at the limits of then modern war. He resented the rapid collapse and subsequent neglect of the military establishment; and, like his fellow American scientists and scholars, his mind and aspirations were stirred by post-1865 developments in Europe – notably the rise of Germany and the General Staff concept.

In Upton the army produced not a Mahan but a professional who carried forward ardently the organizational principles of Washington's 'Sentiments', and in Colonel Wagner an officer who gave vitality and distinction to the new, essentially tactical school at Leavenworth. Unfortunately for the soldier, however, there was no technological development in ground warfare equivalent to steel, steam, and the torpedo; there were merely a new rifle and smokeless powder. There was no ground force equivalent for the navy's elastic claim for an enlarged order of battle to cover commercial interests abroad. No ground-force enemy could be identified in these decades except the Indian; and by the 1890s even the Indian Wars were over. In consequence, the Army entered the Spanish–American War grossly unprepared and served with little distinction; but it emerged with enlarged permanent garrison responsibilities in the new American empire.

The strand of naval romanticism was important and powerful because it was associated with the articulation of the first new conceptions of the nation's relation to the world since Washington, in which process the writing and influence of Captain Mahan played a unique role. Mahan's work developed from the requirement of teaching naval history at the Naval War College, and he used the occasion of preparing his lectures to present a whole series of propositions about sea power: mystical, geo-political, economic, strategic, and tactical.

The ambiguity of Mahan

The principal elements in Mahan's thought can be rearranged and summarized in the following sequence:

1. The balance of the world's power lies in the land mass of Eurasia; and it is subject to unending competitive struggle among nation states.

2. Although the balance of world power hinges on the control of Eurasian land, the control over the sea approaches to Eurasia has been and can be a decisive factor, as the history of many nations, most notably Britain, demonstrates.

3. In the end, naval power consists in the ability to win and to hold total dominance at sea, which, in turn, requires a naval force in being, capable of meeting and defeating any likely concentration of counterforce. A naval power must, therefore, maintain, as a concentrated tactical unit at readiness, an adequate fleet of capital ships with adequate underlying support.

4. Support for such a force includes forward bases, coaling stations, a merchant fleet adequate for overseas supply, and, perhaps, certain territories whose friendship is assured at a time of crisis. It follows, therefore, that naval power should be prepared actively to develop an empire as well as a substantial foreign trade and pool of commercial shipping.

5. The United States stood at a moment in its history and in its relation to the geography of world power when its full-scale development as a naval power was urgent.

6. The pursuit in times of peace of the prerequisites for naval power would have the following ancillary advantages: the challenge of commercial and imperial competition would maintain the vigor of the nation; acceptance of responsibility for Christianizing and modernizing the societies of native peoples within the empire would constitute a worthy and elevating moral exercise; and the whole enterprise would be commercially profitable.

Before 1900, at a time when the Germans had still not moved seriously towards continental dominance, and when the Japanese had not yet defeated the Russian fleet, it was difficult to dramatize the underlying shifts in power

215

within the Eurasian land mass that were taking place; and it would have been even more difficult to make Americans accept consciously the notion that the build-up of naval strength was ultimately required in order that American influence could be exerted not merely defensively in the Atlantic and the Pacific but also on the structure of power within Eurasia. In Mahan's own writing the full significance of propositions 1 and 2 were thus obscured and slighted; for, if they were taken seriously, what was called for was not an exuberant American effort to assert itself unilaterally on the world scene but an expansion in its total military power – army as well as navy – in alignment with those other nations which shared its interest in avoiding a dominant concentration of power at either end of the Eurasian land mass.

Mahan was, it is true, steadily an advocate of Anglo–American under-standing. As the First World War approached, he helped articulate the nature of the American power interests in its outcome. Generally speaking, however, propositions 3 through 6 became detached from 1 and 2, leaving Mahan, in his net influence, mainly a propagandist for the expansion of the American Navy and its forward bases; for the creation of the Isthmian Canal; and for the concentration of the battle fleet. He did not emerge as a consistent philosopher of the nature of the American interest and expositor of its strategic position on the world scene.

Projected out into national policy, the comfortable ambiguities left in the exposition of Mahan and his followers had an important consequence. Whereas the technical requirements of the American strategic position called for the rapid development of the concepts and attitudes of alliance, the new doctrine was shaped to fit the mood of national assertiveness which welled up towards the end of the nineteenth century. Not only such figures as Senator Lodge but also many key American naval officers permitted them-selves, for example, the luxury of being both advocates of Mahan and twisters of the lion's tail.

Despite the inevitable concealment of the full implications of major power status for the nation in the emerging new world power structure, Mahanism was only partially accepted as national doctrine after the Spanish–American War. The proportion of American GNP allocated for military purposes did not rise from 1902 to 1913: it fell from 1.5 per cent to 1.1 per cent. Despite the rise in prices, military outlays for the services only rose in absolute terms from $165 to $250 million between 1902 and 1913. There were hard and nasty problems to be faced in the Philippines and elsewhere, leading to a revulsion against imperial responsibilities. Wilson's election in 1912, with Bryan as Secretary of State, appeared to reverse the nation's verdict of 1900; and that verdict was not, in fact, a vindication of imperialist policy but a decision not to withdraw from the Philippines. Perhaps more important, the advocates of the Large View had to compete for public interest and attention with domestic problems and the values brought to bear on them in the Progressive period. The balance of public interest shifted from problems of security to those of welfare; and this fact was reflected in both policy and the allocation of public resources.

The Stages of Growth and the American Security Position in the Twentieth Century

America's role on the world scene in the twentieth century did not stem, then, from the brief phase of old-fashioned imperialism that welled up in the 1890s on the basis of a partial acceptance of Mahan's propositions 3 to 6. It arose from the march of the stages of growth, yielding particular situations which were to enforce on Americans a sense of vulnerability and danger arising from Mahan's propositions 1 and 2 – in 1917, 1940–1, 1947, 1950, and 1965.

In the three decades after the Civil War, four great areas – Germany, Japan, Russia, and the United States – moved rapidly forward in industrialization: Germany and the United States to industrial maturity, Japan and Russia into take-off. The interplay among them was to determine the world's balance of power in the first half of the twentieth century. Each pursued (or was about to pursue) policies of limited regional expansion, but down to the mid-1890s they were at stages which did not lead to major efforts to seize the European or Asian balance of power.

The twentieth-century arena, clearly beginning to form up in the latter decades of the nineteenth century, assumed, then, this form. Stretching east from Britain were new major industrial powers in Germany, Russia, and Japan, with Germany the most advanced among them. Towards the end of the nineteenth century Italy and parts of the Austrian Empire moved into take-off; but their lag behind Western Europe decreed a secondary role. In the face of this phenomenon, Britain and France were moving uncertainly towards coalition, with Britain also beginning to look west across the Atlantic for further support. And, poised uncertainly on the rim of the world arena, groping to define a position consistent both with its tradition and with its new sense of world status, was the enormous young giant, the United States, its economic maturity achieved.

But the sweep of industrialization across northern Eurasia was not uniform. A good part of Eastern Europe and China did not move into take-off. They were still caught up in the early, turbulent, transitional phases of the preconditions; and they were to provide peculiar difficulty.

Why should this have been so? Each of these two regions, if attached to any major power, had the geographic location, population, and long-run potential capable of shifting radically the power balance in Europe or Asia; but, lagging behind their neighbors in the growth sequence, they lacked the political coherence and economic strength to defend themselves.

In the end, it was the relative weakness of Eastern Europe and China, when flanked by industrially mature societies – their vulnerability to military, political, and economic intrusion in their protracted stage of preconditions – which provided the occasion for the great armed struggles of the first half of the twentieth century. Put another way, it is unlikely that the world arena of competitive power would have yielded major continental struggles to the death if colonial stakes and the impulses for local and regional aggression alone were at work. Indeed, the Italian experience at Adowa, the British experience with the Boers, the American experience in the Philippines turned men's minds away from imperial grandeur at the turn of the century. It was not Joseph Chamberlain but the Liberals who won the British election of 1906. Germany – not empire – mainly concerned British and French leaders. It was the structure of Eurasia, where the control over Eastern Europe and China threatened to determine the destiny of all the major mature states, that primarily shaped war and diplomacy after the turn of the century.

But in America of the 1890s the implications of the differential stages of growth in a competitive world arena were still latent. Despite occasional gunfire from the Yalu to Cuba, from South Africa to Manila Bay, it was not too difficult to view the world as still held in balance by a British relationship to Eurasia, which prevented any one power or coalition from dominating or threatening to dominate that area. And, excepting the Western Hemisphere, Americans felt free to concentrate on the issues and debates of the Progressive era.

THE POLITICS OF HIGH MASS-CONSUMPTION

Growth and Welfare

The automobile sectoral complex

In retrospect, Henry Ford's public announcement in 1909 was like the enunciation by a single instrument at the opening of a complex symphony of its central theme. He said his aim was to produce and sell a cheap, reliable, single model 'for the great multitude' so that every man 'making a good salary' could 'enjoy with his family the blessing of hours of pleasure in God's great open space'. When men came to a point where they could afford and were permitted to buy these instruments for a family's mobility in privacy, the appeal proved virtually irresistible in every corner of the globe, in every culture and political setting.

Thus far the mass production, sale, and use of the automobile has been the most powerful innovation of the twentieth century – like the nineteenth-century railroad – because of its multiple effects. It became a significant, if not dominating, market for steel and engineering products, rubber, glass, oil, and light electronics; it restructured life along suburban lines; it linked rural to urban markets in new, more flexible ways; it created a requirement for large-scale sales and servicing industries; it set up massive social overhead requirements for roads and parking facilities; it played a critical role in a social revolution touching patterns of life from courting habits to the getaway methods of bank robbers. It was accompanied by – and, in various indirect ways, related to – a surge in the production of various durable consumers goods and processed foods which came to fill homes, as rising incomes and suburban life made personal service expensive and inaccessible: washing and drying machines; vacuum cleaners; the electric ice box; the oil furnace and, then, air conditioning; canned and, then, frozen foods.

The revolution can be technically dated from 1913 and Ford's moving assembly line for the model T. But it was the rise in the number of American private automobiles from 8 million in 1920 to 23 million in 1929 which marked the first full experience of a society in the stage of high mass-consumption. Not until the mid-1960s did the number of private automobiles in use per million population in Britain, France, and Germany approximate the American figure of 1929 (177,000), by which time the American ratio had more than doubled (385,000, 1965).

Except for building roads and providing conventional infrastructure in the suburbs, this is a stage of development that apparently does not evoke great enterprise on the part of governments, so long as real income regularly expands.[29]

In the 1920s Americans were caught up in the drive to the suburbs and all that went with suburban life, a massive 44 per cent increase in suburban population.[30] Down to the depression most Americans were prepared to acquiesce in Coolidge's dictum: 'The business of America is business.' Governmental allocations to economic and environmental services – having risen sharply from the pre-1914 level – were about constant as a proportion of GNP in the 1920s; and, for social services, the proportion fell from 3.5 per cent to 3.2 per cent, despite the expanded outlays for education required in urban and suburban areas – outlays which rose from $1.1 to 2.5 billion between 1920 and 1930, mainly from state and local government revenues.

The great depression: the shift to welfare outlays

But the inherent placidity of American political life depended on the maintenance of the high rate of growth which permitted the progressive diffusion of the automobile and the new way of life. For this neither American economic thought nor public policy had provided.

And when depression came, it proved peculiarly intractable due to the technical character of the stage of high mass-consumption itself.

When in earlier historical stages the momentum of growth hinged on the continued extension of railroads, or on the introduction of other cost-reducing industrial processes, on the side of supply, investment could be judged profitable at relatively low levels of current consumers' demand. Investment in new technology, in a depression environment of low labor and raw materials costs, could pull the economy up from the bottom of the cycle. But when investment comes to be centered on industries and services based on expanding consumption, full employment is needed, in a sense, to sustain full employment; for unless consumption levels press outward, capacity in consumers goods industries and those supplying them with inputs will be underused, and the impulse to invest will be weak. Thus, the horizons of American industry, now geared to the economics of high mass-consumption, lowered radically in the 1930s, and appeared almost to stabilize at a low level. It took a rise in consumers' income per capita – brought about by the dynamics of the Second World War – to set the automobile sectoral complex again in motion.

In a sense, the multiplier, operating on the basis of the introduction of new technologies on the supply side, could no longer initiate expansion from the trough of depression: the accelerator – that is, increased investment derived from an expansion in consumption – was needed. Keynesian doctrine and policies were, then, a proper product of the coming of the age of high mass-consumption.

The depression brought to power Franklin Roosevelt with an initial mandate to act in almost any direction he chose, so long as he lifted the nation from the trough of depression. But, so far as unemployment was concerned, he lacked a program. He had campaigned on the principle of a balanced budget; and his program was uncertain in other directions, as well. In a deeper sense, however, the concept of a program of action had quite concrete meaning, given Roosevelt's administrative method; for he gathered around him in the Executive Branch – and released in the Congressional Branch – every variety of activist. There was no national plan; but there was a competitive contest to apply every partial insight or national experience which seemed relevant to the nation's crisis. Roosevelt's first term was a climactic bringing together – an orchestration – of men, ideas, and policies formed over the previous half-century's national debate, study, experiment, and experience.

The New Deal broadly combined the mood and heritage of the Progressives and that of the War Industries Board of 1917–18. Looked at closely, however, one can detect more particular elements: from the Grangers and bimetallists to labor leaders; from the disciples of Veblen and Wesley Mitchell to those of Irving Fisher; from social workers to bankers. Men who learned how to operate in the setting of state capitals, who had operated in Wall Street, who had never operated before outside a college campus and academic politics, who had never before held a job – all were put to work side by side in the feverish setting of Washington in 1933. Roosevelt released and organized in the New Deal the American gift for action in the face of palpable problems, guided by *ad hoc* theories of limited generality.

In two specific respects the New Deal can be regarded as a major success of the national style. Leaving the problem of massive unemployment aside, the nation made a series of limited, specific innovations, each with a substantial history of prior thought, debate, and, in some cases, state-level experiment behind it. This was so with respect to farm policy, social security legislation, banking and securities legislation, the Tennessee Valley Authority, and even the enlargement of labor's rights to organize and bargain collectively. Behind what sometimes appeared to be the hasty and casual labors of the Executive Branch and the Congress were men with long-accumulated knowledge and concrete particular purposes which were shared by substantial constituencies and backed by serious staff work. It is for that reason that so much of the legislation passed in a flood during the first New Deal phase proved, with minor modification, acceptable in the subsequent generation. The New Deal altered the balance of power between the Federal Government and the private markets and among the major social groups competing for shares in the national income along lines that conformed to powerful trends of thought and feeling which – the depression of 1929–33 having occurred – could have been further frustrated only at increasing danger to the society's stability.

Technically, the New Deal performed successfully a second task. It strengthened the institutional foundations of the economy in such a way that it was likely to be less vulnerable to a cyclical downturn. The government became committed automatically to cushion declines in farm incomes as well as income losses due to unemployment; the banking structure was given an adequate insurance basis; and the capital markets were put under rules and a surveillance that were to prove wholesome. The institutional floors within the United States, which had caved in during the decline of 1929–32, were not only repaired, they were also strengthened. The measures that accomplished their repair were also, of course, measures of reform, and, as such, they involved the alteration or extension of familiar institutions or the creation of institutions long canvassed. Here, too, then, the New Deal was at home with its problems, and it could draw on the concepts, men, and experience directly relevant.

With respect to the problem of recovery policy, there was no equivalent body of experience or consensus. In his 1933 mood of mixed determination and profound intellectual uncertainty, Roosevelt reached back to the last great national crisis the nation had faced, the First World War, and created the National Recovery Administration on analogy with the War Industries Board. Its underlying conception – that price stability and wage increases achieved by negotiation would stimulate recovery – was incorrect, tending to raise costs without in fact increasing the level of effective demand. The NRA absorbed and dissipated in the course of 1933 a good deal of the nation's initial emotional response to the new President's mood and probably slowed down the process of recovery. It was removed from the scene by the Supreme Court in 1935, leaving behind the Wagner Act and a substantial additional heritage of reform, but otherwise only relief that the way was cleared for a more rational and effective approach to revival. Gradually, however, out of the maze of debate and experiment it did emerge that the central task was to increase effective demand; and the national budget was used in various ways to this end. The powers of government were never used, however, on a scale and with a conviction capable of bringing the economy back to full employment.

As the 1930s wore on, government and private economic institutions appeared to settle into a kind of acceptance of substantial unemployment as a way of life. With no clear understanding of the deflationary impact of current government policies, and with 14 per cent still unemployed, leaders in and out of Washington appeared to panic in 1937 at a modest tendency of prices to rise; and the nation plunged into a sharp recession, from which it had fully recovered by September 1938. But it took the war – and the war in its most desperate stage (1942–3) – to make the nation rediscover its full economic potential and to alter the dour expectations on which private investment decisions in the 1930s appear to have been made.

The upshot of the depression and the New Deal for the national accounts was a sharp relative shift of the nation's resources to public purposes.

With the Social Security Act of 1935 the United States at last implemented principles accepted in Germany and Britain before 1914; and the Act survived the test of its constitutionality in 1937. It embraced pensions to needy aged, old-age insurance, unemployment insurance, benefit payments to the blind, dependent mothers and children, and crippled children, and appropriations for work in public health.

Thus, in the short run the failure of the dynamics of high mass-consumption to yield steady growth led to a radical increase in relative outlays for social welfare.

TABLE 33. *United States government expenditures by functions as per cent of GNP (all levels of government), 1927–1940*[31]

			Civilian			
	Total	Defense	Law, order, and adminis-tration	Economic and environ-mental services	Social services	Public debt
1927	11.7	1.2	0.8	3.6	3.2	1.4
1932	21.3	2.8	1.6	6.0	6.3	2.3
1940	22.2	2.3	1.2	7.2	6.9	1.7

In Roosevelt's second term, however, the legislative flood was stemmed by a coalition of Republicans and conservative Democrats; and the Second World War brought the economy back to full employment and resumed growth.

The resumption of high mass-consumption

The Employment Act of 1946 confirmed the responsibility of the federal government for the level of employment already registered by the voters of the 1930s; and the lessons learned from the new Keynesian consensus and practical experience, buttressed by the stabilizers built into social security legislation, permitted the stage of high mass-consumption to roll on for another decade after 1945.

Private automobiles in use per million population had increased only from 189,000 in 1929 to 200,000 in 1939, to 201,000 in 1945. The figure was 323,000 in 1956, at the cyclical peak. The drive to the suburbs was resumed at full throttle and the wide range of industries and services linked to the diffusion of the automobile resumed their momentum of the 1920s.

As in the 1920s, the impulses to reform waned. President Truman fore-shadowed, in his proposals to the Congress, some of the critical issues of the 1960s: civil rights, conservation, medical insurance. Except for a considerable extension of the social security system, however, he could not move beyond the narrow limits of Executive authority. President Eisenhower did not share his ambitions. He explicitly took the view that in domestic matters this was a time for reducing the role of the federal government in economic and social life; and in this, he articulated the mood which had prevailed in the Congress since the late 1930s. There was, nevertheless, some forward movement in the 1950s: a national highway network; and like President Truman, President Eisenhower extended the social security system to still another ten million citizens. But, essentially, the dynamics of the private sector was left to work itself out; and a water pollution bill that would have placed some responsiblity in Washington was vetoed in 1960.

There was, in short, an interval of thirty years between the New Deal and the next major legislative revolution, as there had been a generation's gap between Wilson and Franklin Roosevelt. The stage of high mass-consumption seemed enough, when it worked.

But there was a limit to its capacity to provide growth and momentum to the economy: by 1957, 75 per cent of American families owned an automobile; 81 per cent (in wired homes) a television set; 96 per cent a refrigerator; 78 per cent a washer; 67 per cent a vacuum cleaner. It became clear that the now enormous automobile and durable consumers goods complex was waning as the basis for American growth in the 1950s.[32] In fact, the lowered growth rates of the 1950s would have been still less without the rise in state and local expenditures to support the expanding suburbs; the road-building to sustain intensified use of the automobile; and the progressive expansion in social security outlays. The proportion of GNP going to public outlays did not rise in the 1950s as fast as during the depression years; but it did rise. Social security outlays were 6.2 per cent of GNP in 1948. Within the framework of existing legislation they were lifted to 8.0 by 1957. Outlays on economic and environmental services, which had doubled between 1927 and 1940 (3.6 per cent to 7.2 per cent of GNP) and had fallen to 3.4 per cent by 1948, were at 5.1 per cent by 1957.

Constitutional Issues

Putting aside the Eighteenth Amendment, the formal constitutional issues of this era centered, in effect, on one issue out of the past, another that belonged to the future: that is, the legitimacy of the federal role under New Deal interpretations of the interstate commerce and general welfare clauses of the Constitution; and the problem of bringing the Negro to *de facto* full citizenship. Except for the NRA, which was struck down by the Supreme Court, to widespread relief, the other New Deal innovations survived constitutional test and became part of the nation's institutional furniture. Classic reservations on federal authority were lifted as problems of depression and reform emerged on a scale palpably beyond the capacities of state and local government. The question of the appropriate balance of power within the federal system did not disappear from the political agenda; but the United States accepted, in a sense, a more European role for the national government than in the past.

The issue of civil rights emerged in the war and the post-1945 years on an accelerating curve whose pace was underestimated. Roosevelt imposed in the federal government and in war contracts a non-discrimination clause; and under full employment circumstances Negro employment in war industries increased from 3 per cent to 8 per cent, while Negro federal employees increased from 40,000 to more than 300,000. In 1948 Truman ended segregation in the armed forces and the exigencies of the Korean War gave the Negro an expanded role in combat as opposed to service units. In 1948, also, he presented to Congress a strong civil rights bill designed to expand the Negro's economic opportunities, increase his access to the vote, and to extend more effectively the protection of the law. In 1954 and 1955 came the school desegregation decisions; and in 1957–8, the law was tested at Little Rock and in the courts and was strongly reaffirmed. A Civil Rights Act passed through the Congress in 1957 – the first in eighty-two years – creating a Civil Rights Commission, setting up a Civil Rights Division in the Justice Department, strengthening the legal machinery to assure the Negro's right to vote.

Rural vs. urban Negro population[33]

Year	Urban (millions)	Rural (millions)
1910	2.7	7.1
1920	3.5	6.9
1930	5.2	6.7
1940	6.2	6.6
1950	9.4	5.6
1960	13.8	5.1

But these were only opening moves in a struggle that was to mount in the 1960s and expand over a wide front in terms of issues and geography. For a new, more active generation of Negro Americans was coming to maturity and the effects were at last to be felt of the new men who had drifted to the cities and to the North.

Between 1940 and 1960 Negroes in the South remained about constant, but had increased in the North from 2.8 to 7.2 million.

What the Negro wanted was, essentially, what the white American citizen was getting from his society: the amenities of the stage of high mass-consumption, including an equal education for his children, an equal right to vote, an equal right to jobs and housing, an end to social segregation in all its forms. In that sense, the drive for civil rights – gathering strength as the stage of high mass-consumption was losing its power to drive forward the economy – was to produce in the 1960s an element of paradox: while American politics was caught up in the effort to meet the Negro's demands, it was also seized of the public problems that lay beyond high mass-consumption in the search for quality.

As suggested in chapter 6, that stage had several dimensions; but one was, simply, that the United States had been consuming capital rapidly during the surge of the automobile age: the pollution of the air; the degradation of the countryside; the destruction of values in the central cities, where the Negroes congregated. But the cumulative gap between the market economics of the stage of high mass-consumption and its welfare economics came strongly on to the American political agenda only in the 1960s.

Security Policy

The most important proposition about security policy and the stage of high mass-consumption – in the United States and, thus far, elsewhere – is that it appears to be associated with a disinclination to engage abroad beyond minimum requirements for national security as these are perceived.[34] The progressive diffusion of high standards of living to the bulk of the population appears, when successfully in progress, a process that absorbs national energies and attention in a quite thoroughgoing way. And when the process broke down in the 1930s, the effect in the United States was to turn the nation not to external adventure but still further inward.

The enlarged American role on the world scene in the two generations before the mid-1950s arose from external pressures and challenges, reluctantly and belatedly accepted. These pressures and challenges can be related to the march of stages of growth elsewhere, but not to the kind of inner imperatives which marked earlier American military and foreign policy in its rare active phases.

Wilson was elected in 1916 on the slogans: 'He kept us out of war' and 'Too proud to fight'. It was the threat to the balance of power represented by unrestricted German submarine warfare (heightened by the Zimmerman letter) that brought the United States into the First World War.

America then proceeded to reject not only the League of Nations but the French plea that American military weight be steadily felt in the European balance. Until the great international crises came after 1929, the United States did not, of course, wholly withdraw. It sat as a major power in the Nine Power Treaty of 1921; the Naval Treaty of 1922; the Dawes and Young Plans of 1924 and 1929; and the Pact of Paris outlawing war in 1928. But the underpinnings for this global role were shallow in public opinion and among political leaders. There was little will to sustain this role amid the mounting crises of the 1930s – as Stimson's failure with Hoover and Roosevelt's with the Congress demonstrate. Only the fall of Paris and a beleaguered Britain in 1940 and the Japanese movements of 1940-1 to consolidate its hegemony in Southeast Asia as well as in China brought America to draw a line at the final takeover of Europe or Asia by potentially hostile powers.

After 1945, the impulse to withdraw unilaterally was strong again, as Roosevelt told Stalin it would be, in his opening statement at Yalta. It was only with reluctance and in the face of stark and costly alternatives that America turned about in Europe in 1947 and in Korea in 1950, in the face of palpable threats to the Eurasian balance of power.

The military pacts of the postwar years simply asserted the truth which the United States had reluctantly come to accept, as Britain's power waned relatively in the face of the rise of industrial Germany, Russia and Japan: the United States regarded itself as endangered if a single potentially hostile power should seize effective control over the balance of power in Europe or Asia or intrude into the Western Hemisphere.

Only a rich and confident nation could make this policy effective; and it could only do so if the smaller powers of these regions also felt themselves threatened by the emergence of potentially dominating powers in their regions. But neither in concept nor in spirit nor in execution was this an imperial venture. It was a recurrent, painful acceptance of a fact of life in an arena of power radically re-shaped by the diffusion of modern science and technology to others who, in one way or another, had come to accept the doctrines of Hamilton's *Essay on Manufactures* and progressively moved ahead.

A NOTE ON HIGH MASS-CONSUMPTION ELSEWHERE

The accompanying chart projects something of the surge of the automobile age and all its works in postwar Europe and Japan of the past twenty years. The nature of recent growth in the nations of the Atlantic is the subject of a substantial, sophisticated, and sometimes contentious literature.[35] But it is not a gross over-simplification to regard their remarkable development as rooted in the achievement of levels of income per capita which released efficiently the stage of high mass-consumption, with all its powerful spreading

CHART 2. *Diffusion of the private automobile: 1900–66, seven countries*

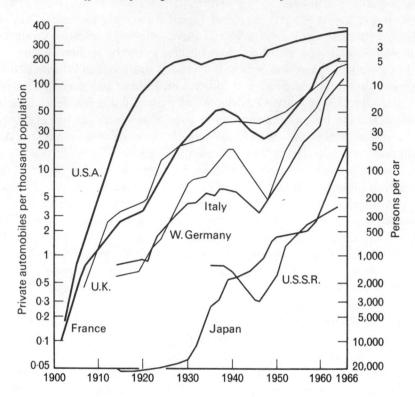

effects. As Svennilson perceived, it was the failure to make this transformation which essentially distinguished America from Europe in the 1920s.[36] And, after a careful analysis of the growth equations in aggregate terms for the two regions during the postwar period, Denison concludes:[37]

What distinguishes postwar Europe is that increases in output in the fast-growing countries have systematically been particularly marked in those products that Europe produced only on a small scale and at high cost *compared to the United States* in the early 1950s, and for which techniques for lowering costs with an increase in the scale of production already existed in the United States and did not need to be developed gradually and expensively as markets expanded. . .

Automobiles and consumer durables provide classic and obvious examples of the process but it was quite pervasive and, I believe, applied to a great range of detailed products.

Like Americans, Europeans and Japanese seem relatively content with the stage of high mass-consumption when it operates strongly and steadily. Periods of social unrest and of major expansion in allocations to social

228

welfare came at times when its dynamics were not effectively at work: in Europe between 1918 and 1925 and during the depressed years of the 1930s; in Europe and Japan in the immediate postwar years when political life was being reorganized and accumulated popular pressures for social change were felt, and strengthened, in the defeated nations, by the occupying authorities.

For example, in the case of Britain there is a sharp rise in the proportion of GNP allocated to social services from 4.1 per cent in 1913 to 12.9 per cent in 1932; the figure declines to 11.3 per cent in 1938; moves to a postwar peak of 18.0 per cent in 1950; and declines to 16.3 per cent by 1955.

For example, in the case of Germany there is a remarkable rise in the troubled interwar years: from 5.1 per cent in 1913 to 14.3 per cent in 1925 to 24.8 per cent in 1932. The subsequent increase to 1958 is modest – to 27.9 per cent.

These figures can only be suggestive; and, of course, they reflect fluctuations in GNP as well as movements in absolute social service outlays. We have a good deal more to do before the allocation of national resources through governments can be confidently related to political and social history. Certainly we must disaggregate them into their major components before they can be linked fully to political and social analysis. But even casual observation of postwar Europe and Japan of the 1960s cannot fail to catch the authentic absorption of large parts of the population in the great equalizing social revolution that comes with the stage of high mass-consumption – a revolution whose inadequacies are only strongly felt by those who have fully enjoyed its benefits.

And, clearly, this turn of affairs has greatly cushioned the inherently painful postwar adjustments in status on the international scene which these nations have experienced. For a time, at least, high mass-consumption has proved for most citizens a quite satisfying alternative to frustrated dreams of past glory and the burdens of empire. It has, in fact, been difficult for political leaders in Western Europe and Japan to generate the resources required to minimize risk and danger in a treacherous world arena.

CHAPTER 6

THE POLITICS OF THE SEARCH FOR QUALITY

BEYOND THE AUTOMOBILE AGE

Writing a decade ago, I had this to say about what lay beyond the stage of high mass-consumption:[1]

... the life of most human beings since the beginning of time has been mainly taken up with gaining food, shelter and clothing for themselves and their families. What will happen when the Buddenbrooks' dynamics moves another notch forward, and diminishing relative marginal utility sets in, on a mass basis, for real income itself?

Will man fall into secular spiritual stagnation, finding no worthy outlet for the expression of his energies, talents, and instinct to reach for immortality? Will he follow the Americans and reimpose the strenuous life by raising the birth-rate? Will the devil make work for idle hands? Will men learn how to conduct wars with just enough violence to be good sport – and to accelerate capital depreciation – without blowing up the planet? Will the exploration of outer space offer an adequately interesting and expensive outlet for resources and ambitions? Or will man, converted *en masse* into a suburban version of an eighteenth-century country gentleman, find in some mixture of the equivalent of hunting, shooting and fishing, the life of the mind and the spirit, and the minimum drama of carrying forward the human race, sufficient frontiers to keep for life its savour?

A decade later we know a little more than we did about the problems and possibilities of this further stage of growth which might be called: the search for quality.

We shall deal with this new stage mainly in terms of the American scene; but offer, also, some observations on the transition in the same direction to to be observed elsewhere in the societies of richer nations.

What we are considering here, of course, is a brief and early phase – a fragment in time and place – of the ultimate problem posed for man by the Newtonian perspective and the industrial revolution: What will he make of his life in an environment where material scarcity is progressively lifted from him?

The political issues of this stage – as we can now perceive it – may be usefully grouped under the familiar headings of growth and welfare; justice and order; and security.

GROWTH AND WELFARE

The Shift to Certain Services: Private and Public

The economics of the search for quality raises substantial problems in both the private and public sectors of the American economy. These stem from the character of the emerging leading sectors.

A shift in outlays and in the working force has for some time been under way to what are called the service sectors. As V. R. Fuchs states in the opening passage of his book *The Service Economy*:[2]

> The United States is now pioneering in a new stage of economic development. During the period following World War II this country became the world's first 'service economy' – that is, the first nation in which more than half of the employed population is not involved in the production of food, clothing, houses, automobiles, or other tangible goods.
>
> In 1947 total employment stood at approximately 57 million; by 1967 it was about 74 million. Virtually all of the net increase occurred in institutions that provide services – such as banks, hospitals, retail stores, schools. The number of people employed in the production of goods has been relatively stable; modest increases in manufacturing and construction have been offset by declines in agriculture and mining.

Fuchs finds that employment grew 0.9 per cent per annum faster in services than in industry from 1929 to 1965, and that none of this increase can be explained by an overall shift of final output to services. He allocates half the differential to relatively shorter hours, lower labor quality, and less capital per man in services: the other half of the differential he attributes to lesser technological change and economies of scale.[3]

The shift in employment is compounded of two elements: the slow rate of increase of productivity in the service sector taken as a whole; and the high income elasticity of demand for certain services. It is to the latter that we must look to understand the economics of the search for quality.

Over the whole sweep of this period a good many of the service sub-sectors with high rates of growth in real output (rather than merely in employment) are linked to the automobile–durable consumer goods complex; e.g. auto repair, automobile dealers, gasoline stations, furniture and appliances.[4] And these sub-sectors, associated with the stage of high mass-consumption, decelerate with the passage of time.

On the other hand, there is a marked acceleration in the share of the consumers' real resources going to medical services, recreation equipment, foreign travel, education, religious and welfare expenditures.[5]

It is the rise of these service sub-sectors that helps define one aspect of the search for quality.

On the public side, outlays for purposes other than defense rose disproportionately in the 1960s, despite the remarkable sustained surge in the economy as a whole and the fiscal burden of war in Vietnam: non-military federal purchases of goods and services were 1.7 per cent of GNP in 1960, 2.4 per cent in 1968; state and local purchases 9.1 per cent in 1960, 11.3 per cent in 1968.[6] In money terms, transfers by the federal government doubled in these years, moving relatively from 7.5 per cent to 9.9 per cent of GNP. In this process, grants-in-aid from the federal government to state and local governments rose from $6.5 billion in 1960 to $18.4 billion in 1968.

TABLE 34. *Changing structure of U.S. federal budget outlays, 1964 and 1970*[7]
(fiscal years: in $ billions)

	1964 actual	1970 estimate	Change 1964–70
National defense	53.6	81.5	+28.0
(Special Southeast Asia support)	—	(25.4)	(+25.4)
Major social programs:			
Social insurance trust funds (excluding Medicare)	22.7	37.2	+14.4
Welfare payments and services	3.4	6.1	+2.6
Education and manpower training	1.6	7.2	+5.6
Health (including Medicare)	1.8	13.0	+11.2
Low and moderate income housing	a	1.1	+1.1
Community and regional development	0.8	3.3	+2.4
Subtotal, major social programs	30.4	67.8	+37.4
Interest	9.8	16.0	+6.1
Veterans benefits and services	5.7	7.7	+2.0
All other programs	22.1	24.9	+2.8
Allowances for pay increase and contingencies	—	3.2	+3.2
Undistributed intragovernmental transactions	−2.9	−5.7	−2.8
Total	118.6	195.3	+76.7

[a] Less than $50 million.

The rapid rise of GNP in these years masks a movement of resources to welfare purposes which, by normal standards of American politics, must be judged remarkable.

The revolutionary legislation of this period laid the foundations for still larger increases in education, social welfare, housing, and medical assistance in the years ahead, if the Congress backs the commitments of policy American law now incorporates.

Table 35 exhibits the outcome for the 1960s for government expenditures as a whole.[8]

In short, the numbers show that, in the search for lives of higher quality, Americans have increasingly sought education, health, travel, and other forms of recreation in disposing of their private resources; and through the political process their representatives acquiesced, at least, in radical legislative measures to expand public outlays for education, health, housing, and other forms of social welfare.

TABLE 35. *Federal, state and local expenditures as proportions of gross national product*

	1959	1963	1968
	(%)	(%)	(%)
National security (including space, foreign aid, and veterans)	11.0	10.9	10.7
Interest payments	1.4	1.4	1.4
Law, order, and administration	2.2	2.5	2.5
Economic and environmental services	4.4	4.4	4.6
Social services	9.7	10.9	14.2
Total	28.7	30.1	33.4

Possible Implications for Productivity, Balance of Payments, and Wage–Price Discipline

In terms of growth and its stages, this shift in resources and manpower to certain private and public services raises the question of whether the earlier and more massive movement of the United States than other more advanced nations into these service sub-sectors will damp the relative increase in American productivity in such a way as to exacerbate already substantial balance of payments difficulties.

The entrance of the United States into the automobile sectoral complex in advance of others brought with it leadership in a range of industries, embracing relatively new technologies, that helped support American productivity and the American balance of payments position. The absorption of these technologies under conditions of market efficiency by Western Europe and Japan has already put severe pressure on the United States trade surplus.

The question arises: Will the shift to services, in the international sequence in which it is now taking place, raise further major balance of payments problems for the United States?

This question has not yet been subjected to systematic analysis; and no dogmatic answer to it is yet possible.

For example, the possibilities for introducing new technology into the service industries are not, by any means, exhausted. And in an economy as vast and resourceful as that of the United States, there may well be untapped potentialities for increasing productivity in services, as has already been demonstrated in American agriculture. There are, for example, potentialities for the use of television and other mass educational devices whose surface has only been scratched; and there may be in medicine and in the layout of hospitals significant possibilities for economy in resources and personnel. And the transatlantic race in a new generation of commercial aircraft may determine where the balance of payments burden falls in the face of the almost universal impulse of people to travel abroad as soon as they can afford it.

This shift in leading sectors has implications that go beyond the course of productivity in the sectors themselves. American business organization has been built around the special scale and momentum of private markets in a rich continent. The relative movement towards services has not rendered irrelevant the American industrial structure. Automated data processing, for example, is revolutionizing banking, insurance, and other services; and the International Business Machines Corporation and other firms producing the new equipment are structured along the now classic balance between centralized executive leadership and decentralized, diversified divisions. But in areas such as education and medicine, there is not only a need for innovation and pioneering, but also for new patterns of business organization, given the peculiar institutional nature of the markets.

One may devise and manufacture – as is now happening – all manner of imaginative teaching devices, based on modern technology, designed to improve the quality of instruction in an age of mass higher education. It is a quite different matter to induce schools and teachers to adopt them and to use them well. The Lockheed Aircraft Corporation, for example, has designed a hospital of greatly increased efficiency, which has been applied experimentally; but it is likely to be accepted only slowly by the medical profession.

Moreover, the actions and policies of government interweave these new dynamic sectors, quite aside from the government's enlarged role in medicine. The race in new aircraft hinges on a partnership between government and private enterprise. Various private firms are geared to apply modern analytic and data processing methods to education and urban problems, among others; but they must find their markets in an intricate public–private maze of institutions, not by direct appeal to a mass market. Similar public–private links may have to emerge if the clearing of air and water pollution is to be accomplished and rational transport schemes devised for the great cities.

In short, some of the most dynamic elements in the private sector of the economy may have to build their enterprises in relation to institutions and public bodies quite unlike the private markets associated with the classic American industrial giants. Patterns of industrial organization devised for supplying military and space programs, may come to characterize widened areas of more conventional civil activity as well. And these patterns will have to demonstrate their efficiency.

The new phase of American growth raises a second problem of enterprise; that is, the great skewness in the allocation of creative, innovating talent within the American economy. Three major American industries grew with substantial research and development components built deeply into their initial structures: chemicals; electricity and electronics; and the aircraft industry. Others followed in various degrees. But it was for long true in many industries that directors and managers who were comfortable and skillful with problems of finance and marketing, labor and plant efficiency, were awkward and uncertain in dealing with the organization of creativity involved in research and development departments. It was harder there to reduce policy issues to a palpable problem to be solved. Great industries, absorbing vast resources, have gone their way with relatively minor attention to institutionalized invention and refinement of techniques; for example, steel, construction, textiles, automobiles, railroads and mass transit in general.

Table 36 reflects the distortion in research and development outlays.[9] In 1960, 83 per cent of all research and development expenditures in the industrial sector of the American economy was undertaken in five industries: aircraft and missiles; electrical equipment and communication; machinery; chemicals and allied products; motor vehicles and other transport equipment. Something like this pattern had persisted over the previous thirty years.

Thus, as the technologies of high mass-consumption are efficiently absorbed in Western Europe and Japan – and managerial devices are learned there for combining strong executive leadership with ample working capital, modern research and development, and efficient diversified production units – the American primacy will have to be maintained, if it is maintained, by innovations in certain service sub-sectors (including innovations of organization) and by spreading the potentialities of modern science and technology out over a much wider front than in the past.

There is the possibility, then – or likelihood – that the shift of employment services in general, combined with a high income (and political) elasticity of demand for certain particular services, may damp the average increase in American productivity;[10] and this would complicate a problem already severe – the problem of reconciling a high and stable rate of growth with relative price stability.

TABLE 36. *Product orientation of applied research and development by industry, United States, 1960.*

Industry	Expenditure in all product fields	Product field								
		All product fields	Guided missiles	Communication equipment and electronic components	Aircraft and parts	Chemicals except drugs and medicines	Machinery	Motor vehicles and other transportation equipment	Atomic energy devices	All other product fields
	($ million)	(as a percentage of total product expenditures in each industry)								
All industries	10,161	100.0	22.0	21.2	11.1	7.7	7.3	5.5	5.5	19.7
Aircraft and missiles	3,577	100.0	48.9	15.1	19.1	0.4	a	0.6	3.1	12.8
Electrical equipment and communication	2,355	100.0	5.8	51.6	10.5	0.4	a	a	14.1	17.6
Machinery	927	100.0	13.7	17.4	2.5	0.6	51.5	2.7	1.7	9.9
Chemicals and allied products	882	100.0	a	a	a	61.7	a	a	2.9	35.4
Motor vehicles and other transportation equipment	844	100.0	6.6	10.3	9.1	0.6	4.6	58.2	0.7	9.8
All others	1,576	100.0	n.a.	n.a.	n.a.	12.9	n.a.	n.a.	4.1	n.a.

a Not available separately but included in 'All other product fields'.
n.a. Not available.
SOURCES: National Science Foundation, *Funds for Research and Development in Industry*, 1960, p. 80; The Conference Board.

The argument about wage–price guidelines and their role in this reconciliation is familiar enough to us all.[11] I would simply assert my view rather
than argue it here: I do not believe that in the United States (and in other
advanced democracies) conventional fiscal and monetary policy, operated
without wage–price guidelines, can steer successfully within the narrow path
bounded by a politically unacceptable level of unemployment and an economically unacceptable rate of inflation. I see no other viable course than to
create, as soon as dogged education and advocacy make possible, the deep
understandings within our societies required for carrying out appropriate
wage and price policies. To attempt the reconciliation by fiscal and monetary
policy alone is to try to sit on a two-legged stool.

Economists find it difficult to weave together wage–price guidelines,
fiscal and monetary policy. They prefer instinctively to stay with the decorous
debate on the relative advantages of fiscal and monetary policy, with antece-
dents reaching back to Malthus and Ricardo. This is not because the guidelines are some kind of vague exhortation (or 'jawboning') but because they
require an extremely difficult political negotiation. The object of the negotiation is not only to assure that average money wage increases approximate the
average increase in productivity but also to assure that the balance of power
is not upset among competing union leaders; that such fragmented and
difficult organizations as the construction workers are corralled; that business
does not exploit labor self-discipline to shift the proportion of income going
to profits; etc. Viable wage–price guidelines cannot be negotiated once and
for all. They require continuing negotiation. They cannot be easily achieved,
because they require changed attitudes on the part of industry, labor, and
government. They are not – even when accompanied by intelligent fiscal
and monetary policy – a panacea; for they cannot be held when the level of
employment is so high and demand for labor so strong that non-union labor
can negotiate substantially higher wage increases than the wage–price
guidelines would allow.

But the difference between politically and socially acceptable and unacceptable levels of unemployment may be precisely in this range; that is, the
range as determined at the lower level by stop-and-go policies under a regime
of fiscal and monetary policy alone, and, at the upper level, by the escalation
of non-union wage rates, under a regime of wage–price guidelines plus
fiscal and monetary policy.

It may be more convenient and aesthetic for economists to evade the
issue of wage–price guidelines. But good economics requires that they
face it, because neither wages nor prices are set in wholly competitive
markets. They are not pure dependent variables, as the whole bias of
classical economics leads us to teach our students. The quasi-monopolistic

environment in which they are set gives them, in degree, an independent power to determine the outcome affecting the level of effective demand as well as costs.[12]

But more than industry–labor understandings on wage and price guidelines is involved. The government's budget is a critical variable, notably at a time when welfare and security outlays are both high and under pressure to expand. Unless labor, industry, and government – as well as the Congress – can find at least rough consensus on the nation's purposes and priorities, as a whole, incorporated in the national budget – as well as on wage–price guidelines in the narrow sense – the political result is likely to be inflation and a progressively undermined balance of payments; stop-and-go policies which, on the urban American scene, could be socially explosive; or risk-taking with American security and the security of those who depend on its dispositions with respect to military strength and foreign aid.

Great constitutional issues are, then, involved in wage and price policy with which American political life has not yet come successfully to grips.

A Crowded Public Agenda

In short, the search for quality has ended in America the phase when the central task of politics was to maintain relatively full employment, build roads, and let the private markets diffuse the satisfactions of high mass-consumption. The public agenda is now crowded with contentious issues of growth and welfare; at a time when security issues of great moment are also there; when the balance between justice and order is under the most intense and sensitive debate of the past century; and when the question of justice raises among other things a requirement for large additional public outlays.

The test of the capacity of the democratic process to achieve a consensus, which will permit government allocations consistent with political stability, may be as severe in developed as in developing nations, as they move forward in the search for quality in the years ahead. Certainly it is so – and will be so – in the United States.

Thus, the year 1968 saw in America each of the abiding elements of politics enflamed and in mutual conflict: a debate on security policy and security outlays, focused around Vietnam, but implicit with a general isolationist sentiment; a debate on a tax increase which could only be obtained from the Congress by constraints on welfare outlays – a tax increase required not merely to maintain orderly government in the United States but to stabilize an infirm international monetary system; a debate on the appropriate constitutional balance between justice and order, with respect to race and the cities.

The Bill for Prior Capital Consumption

On the domestic side, behind the debate lay the fact of enormous capital consumption[13] that occurred during the stage of high mass-consumption, in the form of air and water pollution, the degradation of the central cities, and the emergence of a sector of the population (white as well as black) which had fallen beyond the reach of the institutions societies use to make man an effective social animal in our times: the family, church, schools, welfare, police, and an economy which had a diminishing role for raw, unskilled labor. The backlog was recognized and politically confronted at a time when America had to run pretty fast to stay where it was.

Reliable estimates of the cost of correcting both the past and the built-in forces of deterioration, operating relentlessly from day to day, do not yet exist.[14] From what we do know, however, the outlays generated in the 1960s are inadequate; and the political challenge for the future, formidable.

In one case, the challenge may be met. The best estimate of the cost of correcting for water pollution by the late 1970s requires federal expenditures of about $1 billion annually, matched by state and local expenditures of $1.5 billion. This compares with 1969 annual federal outlays of about $200 million plus about $250 million in state and local outlays.[15] The shortfall in 1969 was of the order of $2 billion annually. President Nixon's proposals of 10 February 1970, are based on precisely these estimates and would, if accepted, both provide the federal component (for four years) and ease the problem of generating matching local resources.

In the more massive field of housing, however, prospects are less good. In a critique of the Housing and Urban Development Act of 1968, Anthony Downs examines the implications and feasibility of its heroic target:[16] 'the construction or rehabilitation of twenty-six million housing units, six million of these for low and moderate income families' in the 1970s. He notes that the rate implied is about double that achieved in the recent past, 42 per cent higher than the American peak. It implies a rise in the proportion of GNP for residential construction from the current range of 3.0–3.3 per cent to 3.9 per cent in 1970, 5.1 per cent in 1980. Aside from the massive shift in resources, he notes the change in attitude required to meet problems of relocation and the opening up of the suburbs. And he is not sanguine that the target will be met.

Priority for Law and Order Over Welfare, Growth, and Justice

At just this time, American politics has taken a conservative turn, in the classic manner delineated, in general, by Plato and more narrowly by Arthur

Schlesinger, Sr. (see above, pp. 20–1). In a law-and-order reaction against techniques of black and white protest and against the rise of crime in the cities, public policy has moved – in the states as well as in Washington – into the hands of those reluctant to expand the allocation of resources to welfare purposes. The rhetoric and tactics of small radical minorities shifted the attitudes of critical marginal voters from acquiescence in what seemed both necessary and morally right for the community, to a reluctance one associates with congressional attitudes towards foreign aid for assertive and disruptive developing nations.

Meanwhile the Nixon Administration in its first sixteen months has publicly foresworn wage–price guidelines, thus risking a lower rate of growth, continued inflation, or (as in the 1950s) both. A disproportionate reliance on monetary policy is likely to result in interest rates incompatible with a rapid increase in housing construction; and pressures for tax reduction may further damp the rate of increase of public revenues.

In the short run, the prospects for dealing adequately with the public dimensions of the agenda of the search for quality cannot be rated as promising. The Great Society surge of public effort left a groundwork of legislation and yielded substantial shifts in resources in the right directions; but the scale of the shift was not sufficient to match the scale of the problems; and the temper of American politics has, for a time at least, resulted in a drawing back rather than in a reinforcement of its ardor.

Thus, American political life runs the risk of the kind of polarization which France has long known, with the hard-pressed urban areas playing the role of a volatile Paris in relation to a more complacent suburban and rural majority.

But much more is involved here than political arithmetic: that is, the level of taxes, the proportioning of welfare and security outlays; the pattern of housing and other relevant outlays in the private sector. As always, the numbers help pose the issues but do not explain them. The search for quality has raised in the United States profound questions of justice and order and of security policy. It is the substance of these which account for the passion of the debate over the arithmetic and the present disposition of the nation's resources.

PROBLEMS OF JUSTICE AND ORDER

The Problem of Race and the Latest New Men

Behind the new terms in which American political life is being conducted are two impulses, related at a number of points, but basically distinct: the Negro revolt and the unrest among a modest but significant proportion of the

240

TABLE 37. *The economic and social position of whites and non-whites: U.S. 1960 and 1967*

	1960		1967	
	Non-white	White	Non-white	White
Median income of non-white families as per cent of white families	55%		62%	
Persons below the poverty level[a] (number in millions)	11.4	28.7	8.3	17.6
Persons below the poverty level (per cent)	55%	18%	35%	10%
Proportion of population receiving welfare	—	—	14%	3%
Proportion of non-white families with income of $8,000 or more (in 1967 dollars)	13%		27%	
Proportion of non-white families with female head	22.4%		26.4%[b]	
Proportion of non-white families living in 'poverty areas', i.e. large cities	77%		56%[b]	
Educational attainment of persons 25 to 29 years old (median years of schooling)	10.8	12.3	12.2[b]	12.6[b]
Proportion males 25 to 29 years old completing four years of high school	36%	63%	60%	75%
Unemployment rates	10.2%	4.9%	6.8%[c]	3.2%[c]
Unemployment rates for married men	7.9%[d]	3.1%[d]	3.3%[c]	1.7%[c]

(SOURCE: *Recent Trends in Social and Economic Conditions of Negroes in the United States*: Department of Labor, Washington, D.C., July 1968.)

[a] As applied to 1967 incomes, the poverty threshold for a non-farm family of four was $3,335, as defined by the Social Security Administration.
[b] 1968.
[c] First six months, 1968, seasonally adjusted.
[d] 1962.

white youth. Each is focused for public attention by an articulate minority; but each poses issues which suffuse political and social life on a wider scale.

The shift of public resources to education, welfare, and housing is, in fact, substantially – not wholly, but substantially – a response to the acuteness of the race problem in the United States. It is easier to get funds under such functional rubrics than, more explicitly, to elevate the life of the Negro community. Despite the advances of the 1960s the Negro's relative state of underdevelopment cuts across every objective measure of social advance, as table 37 indicates; and remedy evidently requires attack on the broadest possible front.

Behind the rise of the race issue in American politics during the 1960s lay a dynamic process with six elements at least:

— The massive movement of the Negro from rural to urban areas (notably since the 1930s) and his progressive concentration and entrapment in the central cities from which whites were moving to suburbia – a trend the Negro began to share a little only in the past few years.

— The stirring – and then the dashing – of Negro hopes by the Supreme Court decision on desegregation of 1954, its slow implementation, and the evidently limited possibilities of school desegregation to deal with the full range of Negro inequities.

— The wars in Korea and Vietnam – requiring full Negro participation in the ultimate responsibilities of citizenship – stirring a demand for full rights of citizenship: as Louis Lomax has written, 'War, if American history is to be believed, is the great integrator'.[17]

— The emergence in the course of the 1960s of a new assertive mood and a new assertive leadership within the Negro community as economic, educational, and political progress made credible the concept of full equality of citizenship and, at the same time, made less bearable the large gaps that remained.

— The impact on American Negroes of the entrance of the New African nations into the world arena of politics, with full sovereign rights – most notably, via the United Nations in New York.

— And, perhaps, the pervasiveness of television, dramatizing inescapably the gap between suburban and ghetto life.

To these forces, operating on the outlook of the Negro, must be added the growing sense among many whites that passive acceptance of the ghettos was morally intolerable at a time of unexampled, sustained prosperity.

American Negroes are, then, a classic example of New Men lifted partially from rural poverty, fragmentation, and passivity by the workings of a progressive industrial society, pounding now on every dimension of the constitutional process for full equality. Their story belongs with the rise in the

242

past two centuries of repressed middle classes, industrial workers, and land-less peasants whose demands yielded fundamental constitutional changes by peaceful means, bloody revolution, or both.

The Three Negro Problems

Three dimensions of the Negro problem can be roughly distinguished.

First, there are those – perhaps 20–25 per cent of the Negro population – who have, as it were, fallen out of American society in the sense that neither family life nor education nor motivation fit them for employment unless extraordinary, complex, and expensive efforts are made to recruit, train, and rehabilitate them for jobs that might bring a normal round of life. Without such efforts they will continue to live in a sub-culture marked by frustration, violence, and crime. We are talking here about perhaps 5 million men, women, and children.

Second, there are perhaps 75–80 per cent of the Negro population moving forward in terms of average levels of income and education, with expanding opportunities in industry and government opening to them. For these, the absorptive capacity of American society is working tolerably well – not without continued pain, inequity, and frustration – but well enough for the process to yield the most essential of stabilizing hopes; namely, that the life of the children will be better than that of the parents. The process of integra-tion – in human terms – out of school, as well as within, has probably moved more slowly. In any case, its pace and frustrations have set in motion a new strand of Negro separatism – and pride in separatism.

Third, there is among both groups a statistically small (say, 2 per cent) but politically and psychologically significant group who are actively drawn to some form of ideological rather than pragmatic resolution of their situa-tion: self-segregation; violence; or the revolutionary overthrow of American society as now constituted.

The success of American democracy in dealing with this new explosive phase of its oldest and most acute social problem depends on the fate of all three segments of the Negro community: the pace of action gradually to bring the ghetto dweller into a working relation to the society, so that he feels he has the capacity to shape his destiny; the pace of economic and social escalation for those already geared to the workings of American society; and the outcome of the soul-searching among the radicals.

The scale of the allocation of public resources, combined with the imagina-tion and persistence of private industry, will strongly affect the fate of the first group; and the rate of growth of the American economy, the second. The trends in the 1960s were in the right direction. But, on short term,

243

there is little basis for optimism given the conservative bias of the Congress and the cast of current U.S. policy designed to deal with inflation. And in the sweep of the past, acute social and political unrest has often been triggered by deceleration in the wake of prior progress; e.g. 1789, 1830–2, 1848, 1905, and the convulsions after 1929. But looking at the 1970s as a whole, assuming an average real rate of growth of 4%, assuming a continuation of the favorable trends of the 1960s in narrowing the educational and income gaps between whites and non-whites, the prospects are reasonably good.

Andrew Brimmer's estimates, based on these assumptions, can be put in the form of the following table:[18]

TABLE 38. *The economic prospect for American Negroes: 1980*

	Whites	Non-whites
Average per capita money income, 1967	$2,590	$1,510
Average per capita money income, 1980 (1968 prices)	$3,648	$2,277
Per capita increase	41%	51%

In real life, this is probably as rapid a rate as one might expect such a gap to be narrowed, given its deeply rooted causes. And this limited but real rate of progress assumes that the economic growth rate for the economy will remain reasonably high and that the forces working for social amelioration generated in the 1960s will continue to operate steadily.

With respect to the third group – the radicals – something more needs saying; for they, like the radical minority in other explosive situations, have articulated feelings which suffuse the minds and feelings of many who draw back from their prescriptions.

The Curse of Slavery: the Problem of Negro Self-respect

It is the radicals who have gotten most explicitly at the dimension of the problem which distinguishes the American Negro revolt from, say, the British Chartists, the Parisians of 1848 and 1870, the Russian revolutionaries of 1905: the overcoming, at last, of the psychological heritage of slavery and of the second-class citizenship that followed. And, in this, they speak for a wider segment of the Negro community.

One cannot read, for example, *The Autobiography of Malcolm X* or Eldridge Cleaver's *Soul on Ice* without knowing how central to the resolution of this problem is the Negro's finding his own self-respect.[19] Their ultimate charge against the American white man is that he created a setting which humiliated the black man – in his relations to his women and his family, and in his own eyes as a unique human being. It is no accident that, as Malcolm X worked his way out of a broken family and the ghetto underworld to find himself a proud leader of his race on the world scene, he moved away from total racial war to more humane ground on which to fight the Negro's battles. It is the pride of this passage which underlay his critical transition:[20]

I believe that it would be almost impossible to find anywhere in America a black man who has lived further down in the mud of human society than I have; or a black man who has been any more ignorant than I have been; or a black man who has suffered more anguish during his life than I have. But it is only after the deepest darkness that the greatest light can come; it is only after extreme grief that the greatest joy can come; it is only after slavery and prison that the sweetest appreciation of freedom can come.

Cleaver's ultimate human message – not his rather conventional radical political message – is in these three passages:[21] 'We shall have our manhood. We shall have it or the earth will be leveled by our attempts to gain it'; 'The price of hating other human beings is loving oneself less'; 'But put on your crown, my Queen, and we will build a New City on these ruins.'

Whitney Young – a leader of the moderate, determined, harassed Negro majority – poses the issue as follows:[22]

Denying black citizens even the most elementary control over their lives results in more than economic and social handicaps; it causes psychological wounds that go far deeper and are far more disabling than any other form of hurt. The scars of oppression are seen in the faces of jobless men and in the deteriorating buildings of the ghetto, but the real damage is to the hearts and souls of black people, who must put up with a thousand daily hurts and indignities from a society that brands them inferior. The cry 'Black Power' is the expression of the black man's frustration and anger at his powerlessness. It is a cry for recognition, a chant of desperation, an appeal for participation in his own destiny.

And on this basis, he makes central to his program a proposal for community control within the ghetto. It is a proposal based on the same ultimate faith in the capacity of free men to make responsible choices as that which shapes the conclusion of chapter 7 on the long-term prospects for democracy in the developing world; and it shares also the technical judgment in chapter 7 that development, in the end, must basically be a self-help proposition.

And, indeed, the psychological dimension of the Negro revolt occasionally suggests an assertive new post-colonial nation rather than a rising class within a national society. For example, one can observe the search for a cultural identity that often marks the period immediately after the formal end of colonialism; the language, if not the actions, of some Negro radicals has evoked at times the mood of the romantic post-colonial expansionist – an identification explicit among some radical Negros; and, perhaps –

245

although it is too soon to be sure – the pragmatic modernizing strand in the Negro leadership is winning out, as the Negro radicals have confronted on the American scene versions of the same three forces which have gradually attenuated the outward thrust of revolutionary romantics on the world scene:

— the resistance of other social groups, notably, ethnic urban groups, intent on protecting their own interests as the Negro moves to equality (on the world scene, the resistance of other people's nationalism);

— the resistance to violations of law and order by local, state, and federal governments, backed by a popular majority (on the world scene, resistance of major nations to shifts in the regional balance of power);

— the urgency of the pragmatic tasks of housing, education, and health, now overshadowed by the more conservative cast of state and national legislatures (on the international scene, the cumulative cost of domestic welfare neglect within developing nations and the cut-back in foreign aid in certain of the more advanced).

The analogy of the American race problem with post-colonial radical nationalism may illuminate a little; but it should not be pressed far, because the overwhelming majority of American Negroes, despite the rage with which they have lived, remain committed to fight out the struggle within the structure of American society:[23]

Black people aren't going to solve the problem by moving back to Africa or retreating into some fantasy-world of a separate state. We are Americans; our forefathers' blood, sweat, and tears watered every blade of grass, every inch of land of this country. America belongs as much to the black man as to anyone else. America's wealth was built by slave labor and, later, by the ruthless exploitation of the black caste which was denied its fair share of the wealth it created.

The two Americas must realize that the fate of each is tied to the other. We can work together to create an Open Society which brings dignity to all men, or we can die together in an agony of hate and violence. The choice is ours.

Whether the Negro's gathering pride in his separateness becomes a platform from which he can, with greater dignity, find his place in American society; or whether it becomes a base for progressively more acute race confrontation in America is, ultimately, the question posed by Malcolm X, Cleaver, and Young.

Limited Elements of Hope

If a radical policy is to be set aside by Negroes, it will be not merely because it is judged to have been counter-productive but also because something like Whitney Young's vision of an Open Society proves to have enough substance from day to day to justify the struggle to make American society move on its own terms. And here there are, at least, elements of hope, aside from Andrew Brimmer's projections.

Despite evident intense racial friction, powerful long-run social solvents are at work in American society. There is, for example, the increasing mutual acceptance of white and Negro children and the increased sanctioning of that acceptance in public and commercial life. It is clear that the struggle over school desegregation has intensified as well as eased the race question in America. The balance cannot yet be struck with confidence. But it is the author's impression that, on balance, taking the generations as a whole, the net movement is towards more natural as well as widened contacts between the races. There has also been an end to Uncle Tom casting in cinema and television; and the cumulative consequences of Negro elevation to posts from the Supreme Court, Federal Reserve Board, and Cabinet on down.

And there has emerged a tremendous demand for talented and trained Negroes in government, industry, and education which provides for, say, 25 per cent of the Negro population more opportunites for rapid advance than for whites.

The changes under way are neither universal nor complete; but, as any American in middle life can attest, they are substantial. They have demonstrated that the root psychological problem can be reduced from both sides: by white acceptance of Negroes as full and unique individuals as well as by Negro attainment of that self-assessment, sometimes against heroic odds. Negro pride in his history, culture, and distinctiveness could strengthen this process, depending on the forms it assumes.

The long-run ameliorative trends in the society were reinforced by the cast of national political leadership down to 1969. The political balance of the Nixon Administration – and of the Congress – then shifted, with wide consequences including the composition of the Supreme Court. It is too soon to assess how the reining in of political support for these underlying trends will, in fact, shape the rate of *de facto* progress of the Negro towards full citizenship.

The outcome will be determined, in part, by the pace of continued expansion of Negro participation in politics – an expansion which yielded an increase of Negro voter registration in the South from 2.2 to 3.1 million between March 1964 and May 1968, plus a Negro Senator and several mayors. To the extent that this route yields results, the American Negro – his problem and its resolution – returns to the more conventional family of problems posed by the elevation of New Men in responsive democratic societies.

In a sense, the American Negro faces the kind of choice confronted by

American labor in the post-Civil War drive to technological maturity: should he throw his energies into radical politics or into ameliorative change? Should he seek constitutional change, if necessary by violent means, or concentrate on improvements of welfare within the existing constitutional framework? Like the choice of American labor, the outcome will depend on his assessment of the realistic options he perceives to be open to him.

The prospects, then, for a gradual peaceful accommodation of the Negro thrust for full equality in American society are mixed. The deceleration of growth in the economy and of the flow of public resources to ghetto problems threatens to heighten tensions – if, in fact, such deceleration occurs. The conservative reaction against white and black radicals could lead to either polarization in American politics or a regathering of moderate forces; but, in the short run, we must count the political environment a negative factor in the equation. The growing sense of Negro distinctiveness could – as some Negro radicals hope – work towards polarization. On the other hand, longer-run psychological, political, and social forces are working to bring the Negro problem more fully into the framework of the American system – notably the rise of the Negro in political life. And these could converge in a benign, mutually reinforcing process with the dynamics of growth delineated by Brimmer.

It is not certain American democracy can reconcile peacefully the tension between justice and order in its midst, centered on the Negro; it is certain that it will take time and involve friction and setbacks as well as progress; but a solution is not to be ruled out.

The Affluent White Youth: New Version of an old Story

There are certain links between the Negro revolt and the volatility of a proportion of American youth. But, basically, their problems are profoundly different: the Negro overwhelmingly wants the full benefits of high mass-consumption;[24] the affluent white dissident is in revolt against the round of life, institutions, and attitudes he associates with high mass-consumption.

In the sweep of recorded history there is no more recurrent theme than the reaction of sensitive and articulate youth against the world created for them to enter. Plato, for example, analyzed the transition from the money-seeking oligarchs to the licentious democrats of Athens in these terms:[25]

Oligarchy was established by men with a certain aim in life: the good they sought was wealth, and it was the insatiable appetite for money-making to the neglect of everything else that proved its undoing. Is democracy likewise ruined by greed for what it conceives to be the supreme good?
  What good do you mean?
  Liberty.

248

... perhaps the insatiable desire for this good to the neglect of everything else may transform a democracy and lead to a demand for despotism. A democratic state may fall under the influence of unprincipled leaders, ready to minister to its thirst for liberty with too deep draughts of this heady wine; ... Law-abiding citizens will be insulted as nonentities who hug their chains; and all praise and honour will be bestowed, both publicly and in private, on rulers who behave like subjects and subjects who behave like rulers.

... The parent falls into the habit of behaving like the child, and the child like the parent: the father is afraid of his sons, and they show no fear or respect for their parents, in order to assert their freedom ... the schoolmaster timidly flatters his pupils, and the pupils make light of their masters as well as of their attendants.

... the citizens become so sensitive that they resent the slightest application of control as intolerable tyranny, and in their resolve to have no master they end by disregarding even the law, written or unwritten.

... Insolence they call good breeding, Anarchy freedom, Waste magnificence, and Impudence a manly spirit.

... So he spends his days indulging the pleasure of the moment, now intoxicated with wine and music, and then taking to a spare diet and drinking nothing but water; one day in hard training, the next doing nothing at all, the third apparently immersed in study. Every now and then he takes a part in politics, leaping to his feet to say or do whatever comes into his head ... His life is subject to no order or restraint, and he has no wish to change an existence which he calls pleasant, free, and happy.

Plato's image of the contending generations in Athens is an inexact portrait of the contending generations in America, for both pursue objectives better balanced than Plato's stylized caricature would suggest; and, as suggested below (p. 252), for this generation of radical youth the revolt appears to be less against standards of their families than those of the society as a whole.

But Plato does describe clearly one version of an enduring dynamic force in history: the determination of the young to free themselves from the memories, burdens, and priorities of the previous generation and to strike out on new paths. The frustrations and failures of the older generation are left by the roadside. What the older generation achieved is taken for granted: what remains to be achieved is raised on the new banners – be they personal or collective.

Without some such process, political life – already heavily weighted towards the *status quo* – would be intolerably sluggish and unresponsive to new problems and possibilities.

In the evolution of societies since modern industrialization began, the predominant progression has been for the young to seek higher incomes, more education, higher status in the society than their elders. And statistically this is almost certainly still the case for the American young, taken as a whole. For example, of the seven million Americans now undergoing higher education – beyond secondary school – (as opposed to 1.5 million in 1939–40) one can assume a very high proportion look to a life better than their parents, defined in quite conventional ways. And the same is almost certainly true in the other more advanced nations. But radically expanded advanced education ceases to provide automatic entrance into the elite and becomes a more conventional technical training for an intensely competitive labor market. In fact, a major component of youthful discontent, from Paris to Tokyo, arises from what are judged archaic systems of education and from uncertainties about prospects in the active world beyond.

There has always been, however, a contrapuntal theme to be observed, mainly in the life of individual families – a shift in objectives with the generations from, say, money-making, to social status, to social service, or, merely, to the enjoyment (and even dissipation) of the family's accumulated assets.

For an economic historian, this sequence, which I have called the Buddenbrooks dynamics (after Thomas Mann's novel), is a familiar component in the rise and fall of firms and, even, industries.

The Changing But Gathering Revolt: 1920–70

In America of the 1920s the Buddenbrooks dynamics could be seen at work on a modest statistical scale for the society as well as within families. Some children of the affluent looked back at American participation in the First World War as romantic or criminal folly, rejected the life of Babbitry for Greenwich Village and the Left Bank, bathtub gin and, as the saying goes, explicit sex. Depression rubbed out the decade of social and psychological revolt by the comfortable and talented, picking up their remittances at American Express in Paris or elsewhere. That revolt gave way to the more conventional leftist and pacifist political aspirations of the 1930s.

Over the next generation sustained prosperity laid the foundations for an even larger revolt against Babbitry and the society that produced it – foundations which can be traced, for example, in the almost obsessive focusing of American war and postwar novels on the relation between man and bureaucracy. In the 1950s a consensus developed among American leaders in many fields that prosperity was not enough; that massive public efforts would be required in education, welfare, race relations, and urban rehabilitation. This consensus was expressed in 1960, for example, in the Rockefeller Brothers Fund Panel Reports[26] and the President's Commission on National Goals;[27] and the original context of the phrase the New Frontier was the following:[28] '. . . what to do when the increase in real income itself loses its charm? Babies, boredom, three-day week-ends, the moon, or the creation of new inner, human frontiers in substitution for the imperatives of scarcity?'

In the 1960s several phenomena converged to yield a reaction by a significant margin of the more affluent American young which combines elements evocative of both the 1920s and 1930s:

— A sense that the age of high mass-consumption was drawing to an end; that its virtues could be taken for granted where they were not flatly rejected in favor of private retreat; and that the ample deficiencies in contemporary American society required prompt correction if, indeed, they did not justify the society's overthrow.

— A sense, particularly marked since the Cuba missile crisis, that the Cold War, as it had existed since 1945, was drawing to a close; that the menace of the fragmented Communist world had diminished; and that peace either ought to be attainable by unilateral American action or, if not, that the world could be left to its own devices while the United States concentrated, in safety, on its unresolved domestic problems. The American role in the war in Vietnam appeared, in this light, a peculiarly painful, wicked, and wrong-headed anachronism.[29]

— The Negro revolt dramatized the scale of America's unresolved problems; permitted engagement by many active and ardent young in successful social action; and introduced them to techniques for pressing their case by methods which brought them into confrontation with the law.

The Style and Method of the Radical Youth

In a society entering the complex transition from high mass-consumption to the search for quality – in a world in unresolved transition from Cold War to the chaos or order that lies beyond – there emerged voices demanding urgently, at once: a domestic life of quality and justice; a wider range of freedoms for the individual; and world peace. They took for granted or rejected the affluence which had been cumulatively achieved in their society and struck out in new directions: from language, music, and dress to generalized revolt against bureaucracy, technology, and the maintenance of national military strength. The style of the disaffected young has been one of outraged total rejection of every manifestation of the values and institutions and policies cherished or supported by the preceding generation.

The problem of American youth is not confined to the ardent, radical, affluent, and politically activist minority. There are those who have entered colleges – in the great wave of expansion in higher education – without essential intellectual capacity, interest, or motivation. Their unease in academic life and anxiety about the future are major factors in the passivity with which the majority in universities have often permitted small radical minorities to act without opposition.[30] The radicals expressed discontent even if it was not their discontent. There are also many who are concerned with the same problems that engage the radicals but reject violence and search for other ways to reshape their environment. There is a mass of secondary school students who, in a highly conformist generation, imitate the fashions set in hair and violence, beads and drugs. But the radical, or alienated, youth are worth special attention both because their behavior has affected the tides of national political life and because, like the radical Negro, they express attitudes more widely diffused in more dilute forms.

We now know a good deal about the kind of young American who has engaged in recent radical politics.[31] Many recent studies confirm the conclusion of Richard Flacks:[32]

In sum, our data suggest that, at least at major Northern colleges, students involved in protest activity are characteristically from families which are urban, highly educated, Jewish or irreligious, professional and affluent. It is perhaps particularly interesting that many of their mothers are uniquely well-educated and involved in careers, and that high status and education has characterized these families over at least two generations.

Activists are more 'radical' than their parents; but activists' parents are decidely more liberal than others of their status . . .

Activism is related to a complex of values, not ostensibly political, shared by both the students and their parents . . .

In pressing their case, the contemporary radical youth went beyond their parents and sympathetic faculty friends in a particularly important respect. They became enamored of the device of confrontation; that is, finding an issue of limited popular appeal; arranging a violation of the law which would result in a bloody clash with police before television cameras; and achieving a widened base of support among those who dislike seeing students bloodied by night sticks. The method had old anarchist and communist theoretical roots but took on a new vitality in the age of television and the environment of the struggle for civil rights. And it has found its contemporary philosophers and theorists.

Only a few hardened leaders of American youth understood from the beginning that many more Americans are concerned with the instigation of violence than with students paying the penalty of violence. The bulk of protesting American youth did not seek the conservative reaction which resulted in American politics, or the polarization of society still sought by some leftist theorists and agitators. The evolution of American political attitudes and policies since the election of 1968 has puzzled and fragmented the New Left.

But, whatever the fate of the technique of confrontation, the issues posed by the radical youth remain central to the politics of the search for quality. Offering few, if any, prescriptions, they have, like many radical minorities in the past, both complicated the political, social, and institutional life of their nation and underlined the changing character of their society's agenda. Thus far, on balance, they have set back the objectives they profess to support. It is still to be seen whether they will strengthen the pursuit of those objectives on longer term.

A Prescription and a Critique

Kenneth Keniston has produced as good an analysis as any of alienated American youth, and it is worth quoting his judgment of the underlying cause of their discontent and his proposed remedy.[33]

After tracing the American pursuit of expanding income through what I would call the drive to technological maturity and the stage of high mass-consumption, he says:

In the past two generations, then, we have moved closer and closer to the millennial goal of prosperity.

Thus, paradoxically, at the very moment when affluence is within our reach, we have grown discontented, confused, and aimless ... If we are to move toward a society that is less alienating, that releases rather than imprisons the energies of the dissident, that is truly worthy of dedication, devotion, idealism, and commitment, we must transcend our outworn visions of technological abundance, seeking new values beyond technology ...

The 'unfinished business' of technological society is, on a historical scale, increasingly vestigial, a 'mopping-up operation'. Revolutionary causes lose their impact when they have been largely accomplished; men are seldom stirred to arms in a cause already victorious ...

But most important, the fallacy of unfinished business overlooks the crucial questions for most Americans today: what lies beyond the triumph of technology? After racial equality has been achieved, what then? Abundance for all for what? Full employment for today's empty jobs? More education that instills an ever more cognitive outlook? ...

... human wholeness means a capacity for commitment, dedication, passionate concern, and care – a capacity for wholeheartedness and single-mindedness, for abandon without fear of self-annihilation and loss of identity ...

Only if we can transform the technological process from a master to a servant, harnessing our scientific inventiveness and industrial productivity to the promotion of human fulfillment, will our society be worthy of commitment. And only the vision of a world beyond technology can now inspire the commitment of whole men and women.

I have little quarrel with Dr Keniston's definition of the source of the problem. The shift from high mass-consumption to the search for quality is a real discontinuity in the life of man in industrial society – in one sense, the first major discontinuity since take-off. And his passionate evocation of the whole man living the good life is rooted in the best values of our civilization: a psychological balancing of the state within us which would yield a kind of platonic – but still democratic – politics.

But there are four observations to be made on this prescription.

First, his dismissal of 'unfinished business' is too casual. The ardent affluent and alienated young are a small minority in American society. Their concerns may foreshadow issues which will increasingly engage the political and social life of the nation; but there is a vast majority, white and non-white, which still have much to ask of the economy, the affluence, personal fulfillment and status it potentially affords.

Put another way, the stages of growth is a kind of marginal analysis: it arises from an isolation of new sectors with high momentum rising as the older sectors decelerate. It defines, in effect, the new directions an economy and a society are taking. But politics in a society based on one-man one-vote is an averaging and balancing process. And the tension between the margin and the average is acutely felt when those at the margin strike out in a direction sharply different from that in which the average is still moving.

For the United States – and other nations moving forward into the search for quality – 'unfinished business' will remain central to the political agenda for some time to come; and that business must be conducted through familiar instruments of government and bureaucracy and by exploiting all that modern technology can afford.

Second, many items of 'unfinished business' relate directly to a society of quality many of the alienated young profess to seek. The bringing of the Negro to full citizenship, correction of air and water pollution, slum eradication, provisions of education for all the talented, and medical care for the poor and old – these will not solve private human dissatisfactions of men in a modern world. But they are, surely, part of the task of making a good life, not merely a mopping-up operation.

Third, the transition to a world made safe for the pursuit of human fulfillment and diversity requires transition also from a world in tenuous equilibrium, with blood spilled every day in Southeast Asia and the Middle East, to something more nearly approximating stable world order. And that transition is not to be achieved either overnight or by a unilateral American abandonment of all the pedestrian devices of diplomacy and force.

Fourth, the suffusion of public and private life with increasing strands of zest and spontaneity, skill and dedication, passion and care, need not and should not await the apocalyptic day when all are affluent and the world is in stable peace. The tasks of reconciliation within America (and within other national societies) and the tasks of human welfare and reconciliation on the world scene need these qualities now. And many who enter the social and political institutions designed to achieve them – doctors and lawyers, architects and economists, bureaucrats and diplomats – find it possible to express all they have to offer in human as well as in technical capacity. (It is a global phenomenon that the alienated radical youth – and faculty 'liberals' – are drawn disproportionately from fields such as sociology and philosophy which, in some incarnations, provide few technical tools for changing the character and content of society.)[34]

But it is the methods rather than the objectives of the alienated radical youth which are distinctive. In a review of statements by the so-called Chicago Eight, Philip Green had this to say:[35]

... the liberty *they* wish to exercise is not at all the same as that liberty of speech which is (at times) constitutionally protected in the United States. On the contrary, they wish to do much more than merely register dissent, as a few quotations will illustrate.

'What the present system will not tolerate is the continued functioning and growth of a protest movement ... which relies ... on direct confrontation either between the oppressed and their oppressors or between an aroused and disillusioned people and their government' (David Dellinger); '... what happened in the streets of Chicago was a people's insurrection against a government we had been told was our own' (Lee Weiner); 'We should stand on the right to self-defense and revolution as protected by the Bill of Rights and Declaration of Independence' (Tom Hayden, in 'Rebellion and Repression').

Clearly, this asserted 'right to rebel,' to defy the constituted authorities if they continually ignore one's demands, is much more profound than the mere right to dissent, with its implication that one must be prepared to be a 'good loser'. It suggests that the rightfulness of democratic 'law and order' is accepted only contingently, rather than unquestioningly. And such a philosophy signals a willingness – our willingness, more correctly, since this is also my own position – to live with a constant threat of anarchy.

Since the death of Socrates, the individual's relation to the law has been one of the most intensively explored moral issues posed for man as a social animal. Like other moral issues, it can be settled only as a matter of private conscience and judgment. If men feel the laws and conditions they confront are, in some sense, intolerable, they clearly have the right and power to act with violence against them outside the law; and they have often done so in history with greater or lesser success, reward, or penalty.

But the matter does not end there for society.

In a democracy – even in an imperfect democracy – based on the principle of one-man one-vote and majority rule, Jefferson's warning remains germane:[36]

The first principle of republicanism is that the *lex majoris partis* is the fundamental law of every society of equal rights; to consider the will of the society enounced by the majority of a single vote, as sacred as if unanimous, is the first of all lessons in importance, yet the last which is thoroughly learnt. This law once disregarded, no other remains, but that of force, which ends necessarily in military despotism.

Clearly, the majority of Americans understand the challenge built into the technique of confrontation and are prepared to resist it. While their reaction of 1968–70 did not yield 'military despotism', it did produce a sharp alteration in national political priorities away from the issues American radicals profess to support. We have not seen a transformation from Plato's 'democracy' to his 'tyranny'; but we have been able to observe something of the process he envisaged. We have seen a little of what happens in a society when 'fear comes to dominate the political atmosphere, and policy turns to a reliance on repression rather than on social progress as the primary instrument of order'.[37]

Socrates posed the question in terms of the individual's obedience to the law. But there is a version of this problem posed for the political activist rather than the philosopher; for example, Marx' dilemma after the failure of the First Internationale and Lenin's in 'What is to be Done?' of 1902: What does the radical politician do if he cannot persuade the majority to follow his lead? Does he seek power by means of conspiracy and violence, against the will of the majority, in the name of historical legitimacy or higher truth? Does he seek to wreck what he cannot dominate or alter within the law, in the hope that his objectives of substance will be advanced in the process?

If his answer to one of these latter two questions is affirmative, the radical – be he communist, fascist, or anarchist – then confronts the question of ends and means. In politics they are not clearly separable: the political results actually achieved – whatever the formal objectives – are in part a result of the methods employed: the outcome of the French Revolution did not conform to the hopes and banners of 1789 and the early revolutionary days; nor did the outcome of the communist revolutions in Russia and China conform to the aspirations of the peasants, workers, and intellectuals who lent them support at critical phases.

If the revolutionary minority loses its ostensible cause, it is set back; if it wins, it may be led to maintain power by means of repression and terror which distort and mock its professed objectives.

Barrington Moore, Jr., has recently explored this dilemma, emerging with a net indictment of gradualism.[38] But he is too good a scholar not to recognize the dilemma:[39] 'The gradualist argument seems shattered. But precisely at this point the revolutionary argument also collapses. It is clear beyond all shadow of doubt that the claims of existing socialist states to represent a higher form of freedom than Western democratic capitalism rest on promise, not performance.'

What of the anarchist position? What of devotion to violence and revolution for its own sake? If men find some decisive private satisfaction in orgiastic opposition to existing institutions, their choice can be challenged only when they violate the law – even if embroilment with the law is an object they seek.

In moral terms, however, there have been few less persuasive performances in modern times than men professing love and peace, brotherhood, humane personal relations and widened participation in the society's institutions proceeding to their objectives by violence and hatred; by efforts to mock and destroy the values of others; by efforts to destroy the institutions they profess to see changed. It is proper that they have been judged by their means rather than their professed ends.

But clearly, the struggle of men for equality of political, social, and economic opportunity, against entrenched non-democratic structures, has involved violence in the past. And it is incontestable that violence played a part in moving societies from where they were to where they are. From that fact, however, it does *not* follow that:

— gradualism would not have yielded better results, if autocratic rulers had permitted it to occur (for example, in tsarist Russia);

— use of violence did not have severe short-run and long-run human, social, and political costs (for example, the traumatic scars on French political life of 1789, 1848, and 1871);

— violence is an appropriate and productive tool to advance worthy causes in contemporary American society.

Evidently, American democracy is far from perfect. If one takes as basic criteria, for example, equality of opportunity and one-man one-vote, there are substantial elements of injustice in its laws and institutions. But it is not an unyielding autocracy like late eighteenth century France, tsarist or Communist Russia. The case for abandoning gradualism and ameliorative change is weak.

At their core, communism and fascism hold that the majority are lazy and apathetic fools; and power – or important pieces of power – can be seized and held by a shrewd, purposeful, hard-working, disciplined minority.

At its core, anarchism holds that the destruction or weakening of imperfect institutions will lead to their humanization.

There is no reason to believe that American society at this stage of history is incapable of defending itself against both doctrines and the actions that flow from them. But the cost of that defense may come high in terms of precisely the objectives the radicals profess.

The Quality of Life and the Limits of Politics

So far as the quality of life in private terms is concerned, what modern society has had to offer is, on balance, a widened range of human choices. From the flow of the agricultural laborer to Manchester at the close of the eighteenth century, to the flow of the Negro to the American cities, the widened choices have been hedged about by the constraints of industrial civilization. But with all the costs of city life, men on every continent for two centuries have demonstrated by the tramp of their feet how they voted in making the rural–urban choice. Moreover, the constraints of urban life have been – and can be – widened. How, within these widened choices and widened constraints, men have disposed their private lives and resources has been, within the law, a private matter: whether by a family trip to national parks or a quiet Sunday afternoon before the television screen; whether in joining a string quartet or in apathetic boredom; whether in passionate pursuit of scientific or aesthetic excellence or at the auto race track.

Private happiness is not to be defined or legislated by public policy, which can only widen or narrow the range of choices men command in its pursuit. Or, as Bernard Crick has put it:[40] 'Politics cannot make men good, but they can make it easier or harder for us to be good.'

So far as the current generation of alienated young is concerned, a great deal hinges on choices they still have to make: to opt out of the society they reject for a simpler life, closer to nature and man, if not into the private, lonely world of drugs; to convert their present psychological rejection into sustained professional efforts to overthrow the constitutional structure; or to dedicate their talents and concern to the unfinished business of transitions in domestic and international life which evidently will not take place simply by asserting the need for them.

American society will tolerate the social losses of the first; its inherent toughness and resilience will cope with the second; and, although the data are not yet in, it may well draw the bulk of the dissidents of talent to the third choice.

PROBLEMS OF SECURITY

The Fall-back to Partnership and Fair Shares

The revolt of the flaming youth of the 1920s ended with the Great Depression. The ardor of the isolationist radicals of the 1930s was overtaken by the Hitler–Stalin Pact and the Second World War.

Neither a recurrence of the Great Depression nor the coming of a third world war is inevitable. But neither the state of the American economy nor the state of the world is likely to permit the United States a simple concentration on the improvement of the quality of American life.

With respect to the economy, as we noted, the problem of mastering inflation is acute; the balance of payments remains precarious; and the shift to certain private and public services could damp the rate of American productivity increase relative to other advanced nations.

As for security, the inherent character of the search for quality – in both its private and public manifestations – is likely to lead men to look inward and diminish attention, concern, and the allocation of resources to the world scene. This phase comes at a peculiarly sensitive interval in the history of American foreign policy. The United States is seeking to engineer a transition in the balance of world responsibility, long foreshadowed, essential, but precarious.

From President Truman's decision to support European unity rather than to play a classic game of divide-and-rule, American policy looked to the day when its responsibilities on the world scene would diminish as strong partners emerged. In the wake of the Cuba missile crisis and the intensified Sino–Soviet split, President Johnson moved on a wider front towards what he called a policy of partnership and fair shares: the United States fell back in the Alliance for Progress to junior partnership status at the summit meeting in 1967, as Latin American integration came to the fore; it threw its weight behind African regionalism and sub-regionalism; it encouraged Asians to look to increased management of their own affairs through regional cooperation – the central theme of President Johnson's Asian tour in the autumn of 1966; it dealt quietly, almost passively, with the phenomenon of de Gaulle and left to Europeans their dispositions with respect to unity, seeking relations of balanced partnership in the Kennedy Round negotiations, the workings of the international monetary system, and aid to the developing world. Relations with Japan moved in parallel to those of Europe. 'Vietnamization' began in earnest in May 1967 when General Abrams arrived in Vietnam as General Westmoreland's deputy, with full-time assignment to work with the ARVN on its improvement. In November 1967 General Westmoreland expressed the view in public that within two years some American troop withdrawal might begin.

President Johnson summed up these developments as follows, in New Orleans on September 10, 1968:[41]

We have always hoped and believed that as our friends and allies grew in strength, our burden would grow less lonely. We have been moving over the last few years toward a long-term position in which the United States would be able to assume its responsibility in enterprises of common concern, but our partners would be able to assume theirs.

After summarizing developments in this direction in Asia and Europe, he went on:

We must look to the further enlargement of Europe's assumption of responsibilities of their own in the future. In monetary affairs, in trade negotiations, in emergency food problems – across Asia and Europe and Latin America – the shift to partnership effort has already, I assure you, been substantial. Our relative burdens, as the years go by, become lighter.

I believe the day will soon come – which we have been building toward for 20 years – when some American President will be able to say to the American people that the United States is assuming its fair share of responsibility for promoting peace and progress in the world, but the United States of America is assuming no more or no less than its fair share.

This shift corresponded both to strong pressures in American life and to strong desires on the world scene for nations and regions to take a larger hand in their own destiny as their strength and confidence grew and the world arena increasingly lost its bipolar cast. Both trends are likely to persist, as President Nixon's report on foreign policy, of 18 February 1970, suggests.

Some Limits of Safety

But, as chapter 8 indicates, the pace at which this process can proceed, without risking a rupture of the European and Asian balances of power, is limited, given:
    — the unresolved debates in Moscow and Peking on the orientation of their future foreign policies;
    — the unresolved conflicts in Southeast Asia and the Middle East;
    — the irreducible role of America as a nuclear guarantor in the non-communist world – a role heightened by movement towards a non-proliferation treaty and one which requires for its credibility a degree of military commitment on the ground.

Despite the rise of neo-isolationist voices in the United States, there is nothing in U.S. interests or the balance of national opinion to suggest that America would not act promptly and with great strength in the face of an actual disruption in the balance of power in Europe or Asia – the pattern of convulsive reaction to be observed in 1917, 1940–1, 1947, 1950, and 1965. The march of the stages of growth in Asia will increase its relevance to American security in the generation ahead, as the bulk of the world's population which lives there moves forward towards technological maturity. Military technology and modern communications have heightened, not reduced, the interdependence of the United States and other continents. Thus, the bedrock position of Presidents Kennedy, Johnson, and Nixon on Vietnam is that a failure to hold there would foreseeably risk a larger war in a nuclear age.

Less dramatically, the precarious equilibrium on the world scene could be upset by excessive unilateral reductions in the military or foreign aid budgets; by substantial troop withdrawals from NATO; or a rise in protectionist forces which set in motion beggar-thy-neighbor policies elsewhere.

In short, American politics in the age of the search for quality – with its heightened demand for the allocation of energy, talent, and resources to the domestic scene – operates within constraints imposed by the state of a world structure which, if ignored or dealt with casually, could yield security dangers which, as in the 1930s, might overwhelm the effort to find new balances between growth and welfare, justice and order at home.

The outcome hinges, in part, of course, on whether the frustrated pressures for high mass-consumption and a world arena increasingly resistant to Moscow's old dreams lead the USSR towards arms controls and policies of moderation – notably in the Middle East; and whether the tormented debate in Peking finally yields a decision to concentrate on domestic growth and to resume a take-off now aborted for a decade. But those decisions, in turn, will be affected by the image in Moscow and Peking of the United States: of its capacity to play its role steadily as the critical margin in world equilibrium – hopefully a declining margin – while seeking to master the heightened domestic problems of the search for quality.

The Danger of Empty Rhetoric

Of all the dangers confronted by the United States, perhaps the greatest is the belief or pretence that there are easy answers to the dilemmas of this stage of American history. A commentator recently defined a workable national government in the United States as one that 'can deal generously and effectively with dissent in a deeply divided unpopular war; that can re-order domestic priorities and come to terms with poverty and the blacks and the campuses'.[42]

To ignore the fact that the heart of the American division now lies in differing views on the appropriate balance between justice and order; to ignore the judgment of three presidents who have concluded, against interest, that disengagement from Southeast Asia, without a firm and honorable settlement, risks a third world war in a nuclear age; to ignore the razor-sharp issues of economic, social, and educational policy involved in 'coming to terms with poverty and the blacks and the campuses' – this is unhelpful. If American democracy successfully finds viable balances among the contending issues of security, growth and welfare, and the constitutional order now on its agenda, it will do so by avoiding any pretence that there are soft options available and accepting the ironic fact that the search for quality is posing, in its early phase at least, as complex and contentious problems as America has faced since the 1850s.

When we can achieve a reasonable perspective on America in the 1960s, it will emerge, I believe, as a decade of almost unique political difficulty. Wilson and Franklin Roosevelt faced in sequence major tasks of welfare and, then, of security. But gathering in 1963 – and then exacerbated over the years that followed – were simultaneously: pressures to round out the classic agenda of the welfare state, foreshadowed at least since Truman's time; the new contentious agenda of the search for quality; and the hard reality of the struggle for the destiny of Southeast Asia. Taken all together, they put every dimension of the political process under acute strain. To deal with all in reasonable balance – denied the luxury of sequence – has been and remains a major test of the American constitutional system.

The politics of the search for quality

Canada came into the stage of high mass-consumption only slightly in line astern the United States in the 1920s. Western Europe and then, at an extraordinary pace, Japan, moved to enjoy its ambiguous blessings in the past twenty years. It is quite possible that the diffusion of the automobile on a mass basis will decelerate at a lower level than in North America, given the geography and levels of population density in other regions.

And one can, in fact, already observe in these countries versions of the problems associated in the United States with the search for quality. A substantial body of literature, for example, now documents the shift of manpower and income to services in Western Europe, in a pattern similar to that in the United States;[43] and there is little reason to doubt that, in its own way, Japan will follow. Certainly, like the United States, these nations have consumed capital during the sweep of the automobile age on a massive scale, yielding problems of air and water pollution and urban congestion, which will have to be faced by the public sectors.

In different ways, the problem of reconciling high rates of growth with price stability is central to the economic and political life of each – although damped by special factors in Germany and Japan.

Theoretically, if all the advanced nations suffered inflationary pressures beyond the capacity of their politics to contain, they might move forward together in parallel disarray, with none experiencing balance of payments constraints. In fact, their inflationary crises have come at different times and intensities, forcing phases of reduced growth rates and of reduced tax inputs to governments. In turn, these posed difficult choices between welfare and security outlays – excepting Japan, where security outlays are minimal. In the 1960s the result has been a piecemeal reduction in relative security outlays and commitments by Canada and Western Europe, throwing strains on the United States judged by most Americans as abnormal in the short run, intolerable for the long pull.

At first glance, the race problem in the United States is a unique phenomenon. And, indeed, the flight to the suburbs in Western Europe and in Japan has not left explosive racial ghettos behind. But in Canada, Belgium, and Northern Ireland the environment of spreading affluence has contributed, at least, to a new assertiveness of relatively disadvantaged segments of the population and produced demands for an altered political, social, cultural, and economio equilibrium.

No American reader, for example, of the *Preliminary Report of the Royal Commission on Bilingualism and Biculturalism* in Canada can fail to be struck by certain analogies with the race problem in the United States;[44] for example, the fact that many of the problems posed by French Canadians were 'a direct consequence of urbanization and industrialization'; the tendency of the French Canadian community to regard 'itself in the position of a proletariat in relation to the English-speaking minority' in Quebec; the disproportionate influence of the small separatist minority and the tendency of the moderate majority to 'abandon the public arena to the "angry" and the "rough" men because they are afraid of being no longer "in the stream of history"'; the simultaneous existence in Quebec of two trends: to take 'a very hard look at itself' and 'a very clear determination to achieve "liberation"'.

The statesmanship required to master these problems within the democratic process, without violence or schism, is only in degree less than that demanded in America as the Negro moves to full equality.

And in Italy, the drawing down of the pool of labor available to the north has, at last, ended the Two Kingdoms, increased labor's bargaining leverage, and opened a new unified but contentious phase of Italian economic and social, as well as political, history.

As in the United States, a radical youth exists in the other advanced nations, which tends to believe that the Cold War is outmoded and a bore. They find the war in Vietnam not only ugly but anomalous. Even before the bulk of the citizens of their societies have come fully to share in high mass-consumption, they are drawn to revolt against its values. At the same time, they exhibit concern for their own future, as educational systems have rapidly expanded, the quality of teaching become more dilute, and their professors, caught up increasingly in American-style research, more remote.

In each nation there are distinctive variants and proportions as among those seeking private retreat from a bureaucratic and technological society; those in active political revolt; and those anxious for their destiny in the world beyond the university. But all three strands can be detected – sometimes within the same individual.

Raymond Aron has summarized the mood and posed the question:[45]

So far student rebels have neither invented nor developed anything. Their themes of protest, their visions of the future seem to be borrowed from writers long-since buried in obscurity like the pre-Marxist Socialists, especially the French ones, Proudhon or Fourier. ... Thus the rebels no longer dream of collective ownership of the instruments of production but of a new mankind and a cultural transfiguration.

... Nostalgic for a bygone culture, they are reviving old utopias, but they act according to methods incompatible with democratic rules, methods which stir sad memories in men of my generation. Must we tolerate these methods because these young people are disturbing calm certainty and intellectual complacency, because in spite of everything they are expressing not only the dissatisfactions of spoiled children but a hope for spiritual liberation beyond submission to the necessities of science as applied to production?

... Can a revolt of the violent in the name of a libertarian ideal society, open the way to the future? Can it help to humanize the authoritarian organizations of a liberal society? Or will it lead, directly or indirectly, either of itself or by the reaction it will bring about, to a repetition of the tragedies of yesterday, even before they have ceased to haunt our minds? Those who want to go beyond liberalism always run the risk of returning to a previous stage.

Aron, like Plato, fears, then, that the libertarian revolt of the young will generate demands for despotism: for policies of reaction which risk not only the democratic process but progress in the search for quality itself. The student revolt has yielded measurable reactions in this direction only in France, Japan, and the United States; thus far these have been relatively moderate. It is too soon to assess whether they represent movements along a stable equilibrium path or deviations behind which will build up explosive problems for another day.

To Aron's I would add a second danger: that the universally heightened concern with the domestic agenda produce security policies which unhinge the balance of power and lead to major conflict: either directly or by inducing an accelerated pull-back of the United States, as American isolationists profit from the unwillingness of others to play what is judged a fair role in NATO and other joint ventures.

For Western Europe and Japan, avoidance of this outcome requires a freeing of minds from the simple image of a now dominant United States, committed to look after the world's problems out of its own interests and natural hegemony – a freeing of minds also from the traumas of the Second World War, the painful liquidation of colonialism, Suez, etc. – and a joining in the greatest piece of 'unfinished business', the building of world order. To this transition, a resolution of Britain's role in an enlarged Europe could substantially contribute. The general presumption has been well stated by Angus Maude:[46]

People will only do great things if they see the possibility of great things to do. Once they see the possibility of creative action – *their own* action – they may regain the confidence that has begun to desert them. When they have regained their own self-confidence, they will recover a confidence in their country. When they have rediscovered a role for themselves in their country, they will rediscover a role for their country in the world.

There are, evidently, great things for Western Europe and Japan to do – above all, in helping move the world community from where it is to a better approximation of stable peace, a task discussed in chapter 8.

WILL THE SEARCH FOR QUALITY SUCCEED?

As for the ultimate question posed by the search for quality – the enrichment of private life – we still know little, and what we do know is not decisive.
　— We know that many men and women have found private fulfillment (as

well as frustration) by bringing their talents and training to bear within modern industrial and governmental life.

— We know that we have only begun to examine these bureaucratic structures to see how they might be modified in ways which give to individuals within them widened opportunities for expressing their talents and capacity for responsibility; and we have only begun to examine the universities to see how they might be modified to produce in this age of mass higher education both excellence in the abiding sense and citizens better prepared to fashion more humane lives for themselves and others. From what we do know, there is no reason to despair that these institutions can be rendered more humane; but there is, equally, no reason to believe these goals will be achieved by incantation rather than by laborious effort.

— We do not know the proportions in which the coming generations will choose among the three major options: private retreat from the organized modern world; purposeful revolution; and dedication to its step-by-step improvement.

— We have not yet come in the advanced societies to a point where the private and public demand for resources permits radically reduced hours of work; and, therefore, we know little about how men would use a substantial expansion of leisure. (In the United States, at least, the combination of increased claims for public resources, the clamorous pressure for all to share the full benefits of the stage of high mass-consumption, plus the costs of recreation, travel, etc. is likely to make the early phase of the search for quality one of intense national economic effort.)

— Above all, we do not know whether societies caught up in the search for quality will avoid the self-indulgences Plato perceived in his stylized 'democracy', which marked the vicissitudes of Rome in decline, and the down-side of the Chinese dynastic cycles. There may or may not be 'outer barbarians' beyond the modest enclave of advanced nations (about 20% of the human race) now gripped or becoming gripped of the new agenda. But there are certainly nations and peoples striving for the things and the status the more advanced nations now enjoy. As in the past, the unfolding of history is not likely to see vacuums of power long unfilled.

If we turn inward and grow lax in the laborious struggle to move from Cold War to stable world order, if we fail to reach out in brotherhood to those coming up behind us, notably those who have not yet completed successfully the take-off, if we fail to respect the vulnerability of this precarious global community, with its national components at very different stages of growth and aspiration, living in the shadow of nuclear weapons – then, surely, we face evils greater even than those generated during high mass-consumption, pressing hard upon us now during the early phase of the search for quality.

In *40 Years On*,[47] the headmaster's speech at the end evokes the mood that drives us all in the search for quality – and, also, the underlying danger.

In our crass-builded, glass bloated green-belted world Sunday is for washing me car, tinned peaches and Carnation milk.

A sergeant's world it is now, the world of the lay-by and the civic improvement scheme.

Country is park and shore is marina, spare time is leisure and more year by year. We have become a battery people, a people of underprivileged hearts fed on pap in darkness, bred out of all taste and season to savour the shoddy splendours of the new civility. The hedges come down from the silent fields, the lease is out on the corner site. A butterfly is an event.

Tidy the old into the tall flats. Desolation at fourteen storeys becomes a view.

Who now dies at home? Who sees death? We sicken and fade in a hospital ward and dying is for doctors with a 'phone call to the family.

Once we had a romantic, old-fashioned notion of honour, patriotism, chivalry and duty but it was a duty that didn't have much to do with justice – with social justice anyway. And in default of that justice and in pursuit of it, that was how the great words came to be cancelled out.

The crowd has found the door into the Secret Garden. Now they will tear up the flowers by the roots, strip the borders and strew them with paper and broken bottles.

Honor, patriotism, chivalry, and duty may have different meanings now than they once did, in this post-nationalist world, struggling through clumsy multilateral efforts to tame violence, bring forward the poor, and create stable balances we have not known since 1914. But without them the prospects for all of us are dim.

CHAPTER 7

POLITICS AND DEMOCRACY IN THE CONTEMPORARY DEVELOPING WORLD

DEMOCRACY

The Change in Expectations

On the eve of the First World War, it was not unreasonable for men to believe that parliamentary democracy was the natural – and probably universal – outcome of economic and social progress. The English-speaking world, France, Scandinavia, and Germany had all evolved in this direction. In their own way, even the more exotic latecomers – imperial Japan and Russia – had taken steps down this road. Vast China had just formed a Republic whose banners included the democratic aspiration. Latin America, with all it vicissitudes and imperfections, had been committed for almost a century to the common doctrines of a democratized West. And the colonial world was almost wholly under the tutelage of nations which had long practiced democracy.

All this changed with the First World War and its aftermath. Since the 1920s and the failure of Woodrow Wilson's simplistic crusade to make the world safe for democracy, the concept of democracy has been on the defensive. The world of Mussolini, Lenin, and Harding – then of Hitler, Stalin, the Japanese militarists, and Chamberlain – did not suggest that democracy, as classically conceived, was the wave of the future. Nor did the Great Depression and Franklin Roosevelt's impotence in the face of American isolationists.

In the end, the effectively mobilized power of the British Commonwealth and the United States saw the Allies through the Second World War; but the global political community since 1945 was not a setting which revived facile ideological optimism.

In the midst of war and postwar chaos, mainland China fell, like Russia in 1917, under Communist grip; the postwar dispensations left power in Europe and Asia closely balanced between Communist and non-Communist worlds. A Castro appeared in Latin America, challenging the continuity of the heritage from Bolivar. By, say, 1960 it was not unreasonable for men to question whether democracy was to be the natural outcome of modernization in the twentieth century. And to this result the endemic failure to make democracy work in the developing regions has contributed.

Political scientists, viewing the contemporary scene, have grappled with the question of democracy in terms mainly derived from modern sociology. They have looked for ways to measure democracy as a relative matter in which such variables as the degree of popular participation in the political process, the degree of freedom of the political opposition and the press, the degree of competitiveness among political parties, the degree to which the individual citizen regards it possible to leave his imprint on public policy, are observed and roughly measured. They have probed at the cultural and social substructure of politics to see what kind of behavior inhibited democracy or made it a more viable possible system.

In viewing democracy as a matter of degree and of direction of movement, they have surely been right. And in keeping open their minds to the possibility that history will not automatically yield democracy as its universal end product, they have been equally right.

Accepting these propositions, this chapter examines the character of politics and the prospects for democracy in the contemporary developing world.

A Definition

I take it that democracy begins with a set of propositions something like these:

1. Individual human beings represent a unique balancing of motivations and aspirations which, despite the conscious and unconscious external means that help shape them, are to be accorded a moral and even religious respect; the underlying aim of society is to permit these individual complexes of motivations and aspirations to have their maximum expression compatible with the well-being of other individuals and the security of society.

2. Governments thus exist to assist individuals to achieve their own fulfillment; to protect individual human beings from the harm they might do one another; and to protect organized societies against the aggression of other societies.

3. Governments can take their shape legitimately only from some effective expression of the combined will and judgments of individuals, on the basis of one-man one-vote.

4. Some men aspire to power over their fellow men and derive satisfaction from the exercise of power aside from the purpose to which power is put. This fundamental human quality in itself makes dangerous to the well-being of society the concentration of political power in the hands of individuals and groups even where these groups may constitute a majority. *Habeas corpus* is the symbol and, perhaps, the foundation of the most substantial restraint – in the form of due process of law – men have created to cope with this danger.

It follows, ideally, that:

— the democratic constitution should provide for free expression of political views, rights of assembly, *habeas corpus*, and the other basic protections of the individual as he confronts government and law;

— the actions of government should be subjected to regular scrutiny, criticism, and debate by the people, their representatives, and by an unmonopolized press;

— the majority will of individuals should, in the end, determine the scale and incidence of the inputs to government and the balances struck in allocations to the three abiding tasks of government.

A good deal of constitutional history consists in the successive achievement of each of these elements of democracy.

Virtually all systems of government claim the consent of the governed; but some count on raising the cost of dissent to such a high level, by repression or other sanctions, that consent consists merely in submission – the absence of open revolt or of massive public disorder. Democracy lowers the cost of dissent to the minimum and creates lawful procedures for the active and explicit registering of consent, so that opposition will always know that its views and interests can be heard and can be given effect, within the constitution, if it achieves majority status.

Democracy is, thus, a method which forces government to seek and then to reflect the active majority will – rather than the passive consent – of the governed.

The Relativity of Democracy

The democratic concept recognizes from the beginning that the talents, tastes, and interests of citizens are not identical: government can provide only equality of opportunity and equality before the law. As Gabriel Almond and Sidney Verba have underlined,[1] there are in all societies those who are politically apathetic or otherwise inactive; and this proportion varies and can be roughly measured. Even among the active and interested citizenry in a vigorous democracy, the expression of consent goes forward by a process of representation which places important powers in the hands of those who lead the major groups in a society.

Some of the most delicate and least explored problems of democracy arise from the differing intensity of political interest and feeling among individual citizens. At one extreme, the relative apathy and disinterest of many can lead to a rationale for dictatorship by a purposeful, energetic, and politically interested minority. At the other extreme, the apathy and callousness of a majority to a deeply felt injustice, inflicted on a minority, can lead to explosive tensions, even where the formal rules of democracy are reasonably well observed.

In short, government by consent of the governed and majority rule are concepts of meaning; but they are not simple. The welfare economist's puzzlement as he confronts the problems of inter-personal comparisons has its counterpart in politics.

The pure democratic conception is, then, compromised to some extent in all organized societies: by the inescapable process of representation; by the need to protect individuals from each other; by the need to protect the society, as a whole, from others; by inequality among individuals in both political interest and in the weight they bear from the political environment. Thus far, at least, one can only measure democracies we have known in terms of the degree to which their goals have been fulfilled.

From Plato on, political scientists have recognized that men may not understand their own best interest, and, in particular, that they may be short-sighted and swayed by urgent emotions in their definition of that interest. As between the individual's limitation in defining wisely his own long-run interest and his inability wisely to exercise power over others, without check, democratic societies have broadly chosen to risk the former rather than the latter danger in the organization of society, and to diminish the former danger by popular education, the inculcation of habits of individual responsibility, and by devices of government which temper the less thoughtful political reactions of men. Aware of the abiding weaknesses of man as a social animal, the democrat leans, nevertheless, to the doctrine of Trust the People rather than Father Knows Best. And he is committed to refine and develop the degree of democracy within his society rather than seek refuge in one form or another of philosopher kings.

The Conditions for Successful Democracy

But democracies only survive if they provide effective government. The successful working of democracy appears to require three connected conditions.

First, that there be a relatively broad majority agreement within the society on the main directions of policy towards security, growth, and welfare; that is, on the substance of the first two basic tasks of government. The ability of a society, through its representative leaders, to find effective majority agreement on the great issues, while permitting factional competition and compromise to settle lesser issues, is perhaps the most fundamental condition for stable democracy.

The second condition is constitutional and limits the power of the majority: it is to guarantee to the minority that their basic rights will be protected as well as their ability to continue to express freely and effectively their dissident views, within the law, as part of a living political process.

Third, the whole political process must be underpinned by a widespread loyalty to democratic values and to the continuity of the democratic process itself, notably among those who lead the society's major groups.

Breakdowns in the continuity of democracy have come about in the past, and in recent times, in advanced as well as in developing nations, when consensus was broken – when some purposeful minority within a population revolted in response to what it believed to be a gross failure under one or more of the three basic categories of national policy: policy toward national security; domestic welfare; or the provision of justice under existing constitutional arrangements. Such ruptures have been brought about by a volatile, organized minority, when the majority was probably against the active minority; with the minority; or simply apathetic, disorganized, or uncertain.

To hold up some such definition of democracy and the conditions for its successful operation (and for its rupture) is virtually to define how difficult a task it is to manage stable democracy in the semi-modernized settings of developing nations – even the most advanced among them; and how easy it is for democracy to break down. And in this they share the experience of nations at similar stages in the past, as chapters 3 and 4 suggest.

Putting aside Britain and the United States as special cases, France only achieved effective parliamentary government after the take-off, in the 1870s; the powers of Parliament in technologically mature Germany were limited until after the First World War; only beyond take-off did Russia achieve the limited degree of democracy it did after the Revolution of 1905; like Germany, the achievement of full parliamentary democracy in technologically mature Japan awaited defeat in war; pre-1949 China, in the preconditions, provided at times vigorous political debate and significant degrees of personal freedom, but this was rather more a product of chaos than of effective democratic government; Turkey moved into a recognizable (but unstable) pattern of

271

democratic life only post-World War II, after the take-off was under way; and Mexico, in the early stage of the drive to technological maturity, lives with a special pattern of semi-democratic government.

The Survival of the Democratic Aspiration

But, despite its evident vicissitudes since 1914, democracy, as a goal – an aspiration – has never been more alive than in the contemporary developing nations not under Communist rule – and, perhaps, if we knew more, in societies under Communist rule. As David Apter notes:[2]

Whether in the Burmese constitution, or in the Turkish, Ghanaian, or Tanganyikan, liberal individual rights and values are expressed, whether as aspirations or as immediate conditions. (That they are most often observed in the breach is not really to the point here; they still have an element of sanctity about them.) There remains a *potentiality* for constitutional government in the classic sense of this term . . .

That the libertarian tradition is not dead in modernizing nations is revealed by the fact that departures from the spirit and letter of the law are almost always justified on grounds of expediency rather than doctrine.

Modernization in the third quarter of the twentieth century – outside the Communist world – is generally believed to require movement towards democratic government. It is the thing to do – or to try to do.

Many of these first urgent efforts to create democratic rule did not succeed. And the concept of democracy itself has been interpreted in pragmatic ways which sought to reconcile autocratic government with a commitment to popular participation which proved, in fact, beyond the society's capacity to manage in an effective and orderly way.[3] But the pressure to move in this direction remains, nevertheless, more urgent than in the past, when the presently more advanced nations were at equivalent stages of growth and social modernization. Despite all its imperfections and the challenges to it, democracy is more than ever regarded as a touchstone of dignity and modernity.

THE ENVIRONMENT OF POLITICS IN THE CONTEMPORARY
DEVELOPING WORLD: SIX DISTINCTIVE FEATURES

Before looking at some actual patterns of politics, democratic or otherwise, it is worth listing six pervasive characteristics of the situation and performance of the contemporary developing nations, as opposed to parallel circumstances in the past. Later we shall distinguish these nations and societies in terms of stages of growth; but for the moment we shall treat them as a group.

The Cold War

Protracted hostility between Communist and non-Communist states has been, of course, special to our times; although the latter stages of American colonialism and early preconditions period were somewhat similarly colored by the Anglo-French rivalry.

The Cold War environment has had four major consequences:

— Its strictly military dimensions diverted attention, talent, and resources away from domestic tasks of development, notably in areas located close upon the borders of the Communist world; but, in some cases where the challenge was not excessive, the external threat heightened the effort at modernization; for example, Turkey and Iran, South Korea (after 1953), Thailand, Malaysia and post-Castro Latin America – a pattern familiar from the past.

— Its ideological dimensions introduced an explicit sense of choice concerning the appropriate political and social techniques for modernization, raising, in particular, the question of whether Communist methods should be followed – a problem present in the modernizing world since, say, 1848, but palpably more intense and explicit in our time.

— In its political manifestations it drew some portion of the literate elite into efforts totally to supplant existing constitutional systems rather than to modernize them gradually; and this complicated the task of building an effective national consensus – again, a problem familiar in the past but heightened in our time.

— The availability of modern arms from more advanced powers, with cold war political interests, encouraged war. It made efforts appear more feasible to alter resented international boundaries left arbitrarily from colonial times or by the accident of postwar international agreements or events. A high proportion of the major post-1945 crises arose from this setting of frustration and the temptations of fancy military hardware from without; e.g. Korea, Quemoy-Matsu, Laos and Vietnam, the Malaysia confrontation, the India-Pak war, the Middle East wars of 1956–7 and 1967. The Cuba missile crisis was a special version of this problem.

The Big Backlog of Technology

The most profound difficulty of the contemporary developing world flows directly from a fact which also provides its most substantial potential advantage; namely, an enormous backlog of technology which includes the technology of public health. Modern public health and medical techniques are extremely effective and prompt in lowering death rates; they require relatively low capital outlays; and they meet relatively little social and political resistance. Thus, the rates of population increase in the presently developing areas are higher than those that generally obtained in the early stages of growth in the past.

Historically, annual population rates of increase during the take-off decades were generally under 1.5 per cent. France was as low as 0.5 per cent; Germany, Japan and Sweden, about 1 per cent; Britain as high as 1.4 per cent only in the two decades preceding 1820. Nineteenth-century United States (over 2.5 per cent) and pre-1914 Russia (over 1.5 per cent) are the great exceptions; but in both cases these rates occurred in societies rapidly expanding the area under cultivation. Aggregated annual rates for the major developing regions of the contemporary world have run about as follows in the 1960s: Latin America, 2.9 per cent; South Asia, 2.1 per cent; the Middle East, 3.0 per cent; the Far East, 2.6 per cent; Africa, 2.3 per cent.

The compensating advantages from the large international pool of technology have been real but limited to a relatively few sectors: for example, transport (e.g. aircraft and motor vehicles); communications (e.g. satellites); and, in agriculture (the new rice and wheat strains, pesticides, and modern fertilizers).

One of the most important potential technological advantages of the contemporary world has been little exploited; namely, the educational possibilities of radio, videotape and television.

On the whole, however, what is striking in the developing world is the extent to which the technologies most immediately relevant are relatively old-fashioned; for example, roads, power stations, food and drink industries, textiles, iron and steel, chemical fertilizers, etc.

Foreign Aid

The emergence of systematic development aid within the international community, notably in the 1960s, has, of course, been a partial compensation for the burdens and tensions imposed by the Cold War, the more powerful commitments to democracy and social justice, and to high rates of population increase. However insufficient the flows of assistance may appear when set against standards of what might be desirable, it is a considerable achievement of the international community to transfer (as it did in 1968) some $6.4 billion in various forms of net official development aid, within a total net flow of resources (official, multilateral, and private) of $12.7 billion.[4] This statement is not to be taken as a judgment that these flows are adequate, notably in the light of the debt burdens of the developing world. Foreign aid is, simply, a new – and, historically, rather remarkable – fact of international life.

Higher Rates of Growth

More intense international communications, including the cumulative effect of positions taken in international organizations, have increased pressures for immediate gains in economic and social welfare for the majority of the people. They have placed demands on many of the developing nations which they have not been in a position to meet, given their stage of growth and the rate of expansion of their economies. On the other hand, this environment has yielded an international consensus on what growth requires and a body of men trained in the tasks of economic development capable of

TABLE 39. *Average annual rate of growth in gross domestic product, 1960–7: Developing and Industrial countries*[5]

	(%)
Developing countries	5.0
Africa	4.0
South Asia	4.1
East Asia	5.6
Southern Europe	7.1
Latin America	4.5
Middle East	7.2
Industrialized countries	4.8

SOURCE: World Bank.

carrying forward the process within their own societies. Historically, one could observe slowly emerging out of the process of modernization itself the groups of men who, in the end, concentrated their attention and talents on economic development in, say, France, Germany, Russia, Japan, Turkey, and Mexico. The postwar international environment – and the internationalization of post-graduate education – has accelerated the development of such men. And governments in the developing world have been inclined to give the technocrats of growth their head, in part at least.

Under these pressures and with the foreign aid available, we have seen higher average rates of growth than were typical of the developing world before 1914 (Table 39).

Pre-1914 real product in Britain increased at a rate of, say, 2.8 per cent;

France, at under 2 per cent; Germany averaged about 2.6 per cent; and pre-1914 Russia, about 2.75 per cent. Japan and the United States were higher at about 4 per cent.

Higher rates of population increase have, of course, reduced the rate of growth in income per head to an average of 2–2.5 per cent per year. By historical standards, also, this is a reputable performance.

These contemporary growth rates average cases running as high as 8–10 per cent (e.g. Taiwan, South Korea, Iran) with others moving forward at lesser rates or, even, stagnating. There is, evidently, still plenty to do before self-sustained growth is even approximately universal. Political stability in the developing world in the decades ahead will depend, in part, on the maintenance of high and steady rates of growth, where they exist; on the achievement of such rates where they do not exist (e.g. India, Indonesia, black Africa); on the achievement of steady rates of growth where they have been erratic (e.g. much of Latin America). For the developed world, this requires: enlarged net assistance, including debt roll-overs; liberalized trade (which would be of mutual benefit); and the finding of terms on which private capital flows can make a rational contribution to development. The development agenda of the 1970s is more complex than that of the 1960s, in part because progress had been made and we know more about the problems, as well as the widened possibilities; and it is, at least, as urgent politically, because no situation is more explosive than one of deceleration in the wake of prior progress.

But it is a heartening fact of modern history that every nation can see that sustained growth is possible – and possible on terms consistent with its own culture, political independence, and ambitions.

As the Pearson report says:[6] 'The most encouraging feature of the progress in the poorer countries is the wide dispersion of good development experience. It is not confined to countries of any particular geographical area, topography, race, religion, or population size.' Forty-one countries are then listed which have achieved a minimum increase of 2 per cent per head for ten years or more since 1955.

There is no reason to despair that sustained growth is an achievable goal in non-totalitarian societies. Looking back to the anxieties and debates of the late 1950s, that is a good sentence to be able to write.

The Larger Relative Role of Governments

The upshot of all this is that governments have generally undertaken a relatively more active role in growth and welfare functions than in the past, at similar stages. Table 40 suggests this general difference; but, probably, the case of pre-1914 Russia (if we had the data) and certainly Japan (included here) indicate that the patterns for Western Europe and the United States were not universal even at earlier times.

The United States, the United Kingdom, and Germany in 1913 were relatively more advanced (in terms of then existing technologies) – more highly urbanized and industrialized – than most of the contemporary developing nations covered in the 1966 regional averages presented in this table. Japan as of 1910 (at an early phase of the drive to technological maturity) exhibits a pattern more nearly like that of contemporary developing nations, marked, however, by a distortion in military outlays shared only by certain countries in the Middle East.

TABLE 40. *Government expenditures as a proportion of gross national product: pre-1913 and 1966 (developing regions)*

	'Security'	'Welfare and Growth'		'Constitutional Order'	
	Military	Social Services	Public Gross Investment	Other	Total
	(%)	(%)	(%)	(%)	(%)
U.S. (1913)	1.1	2.1	2.6	1.3	8.5
U.K. (1913)	3.7	4.1	2.2	2.4	12.4
Germany (1913)	3.3	5.1	2.2	3.1	14.8
Japan (1910)	11	4	4	6	25
Latin America[a] (1966) average	1.5	5.5	5.4	9.4	21.8
Asia[a] (1966) average	3.3	3.3	5.2	6.2	18.0
Middle East[a] (1966) average	8.5	8.2	13.1	7.6	37.4
Africa[a] (1966) average	2.1	4.1	5.3	10.4	21.9

[a] Derived from United Nations statistics for the year 1966.
For Japanese data, see above, pp. 129 and 150–2.

The following particular features stand out:
— the exceedingly high – indeed, pathological – security outlays in the Middle East;[7]
— the larger relative role of public investment;
— the higher relative outlays for the 'other' functions of government which reflect the more important part played by government, in all its dimensions, in the contemporary developing world as compared to its role in earlier times; although abnormally high salaries for public servants and inflated bureaucracies may distort outlays under this heading in a good many of the poorer nations.

Endemic Political Instability

It is also true that governments in the developing world have been notably unstable – a lesson to be read in Fred von der Mehden's array of coups in modernizing countries from their time of independence to early 1964, set out in relation to the kind of political systems they have experienced[8] – a relationship examined later in this chapter.

TABLE 41. *Coups or attempted coups: Developing countries*

System	Number of countries	Countries with coups
No effective parties	17	14 (83%)
Proletariat	3	0 (0%)
One-party	18	2 (11%)
One-party dominant	12	4 (33%)
Two-party dictatorial	4	2 (50%)
Two-party democratic	7	3 (43%)
Multiparty	22	15 (68%)

A STATISTICAL APPROACH TO MODERNIZATION AND DEMOCRACY

The question then arises: Can we link the degree of economic and social modernization in developing nations to their capacity to sustain representative government?

The task has been attempted, among many others, by Irma Adelman and Cynthia Taft Morris.[9] Using factor analysis on seventy-four developing nations of the contemporary world, they have measured their degree of economic, social, and political modernization in terms of some forty-one variables, as of the year 1961. They conclude by grouping these nations in three categories: 'countries at the lowest level of socioeconomic development'; at an 'intermediate development level'; and at a 'high' development level.

Any such effort to achieve a typology by statistical averaging will conceal as well as illuminate. (I would disagree, for example, on the categories into which some of the nations have been placed.) Nevertheless, the interesting and industrious work of Adelman and Morris broadly confirms the reality within the contemporary developing world of nations at differing degrees of development; and these degrees bear a family relationship, at least, to the notion of early and late preconditions for take-off; take-off; and the drive to technological maturity.

So far as democracy is concerned, they find what others have found before: there is a long-run but not a short-run relationship between levels of economic and social development, on the one hand, and the capacity of societies to sustain representative government, on the other:[10]

It will be recalled that there is very little short-run association between the form of government and economic growth for countries at any of the three levels of government. Our results for countries at the 'high' level, however, show a significant positive association between long-run economic performance and the establishment of representative political institutions.

Broadly, their conclusion conforms to the lesson of history as seen in chapter 4: the possibilities for democracy increase when take-off emerges from the inherently contentious period of the preconditions, but democracy is by no means a certain political result of rapid industrialization.

And, clearly, such broad statistical associations cannot take us far forward in understanding a world where, at under $100 per capita GNP, India has maintained for more than a generation a recognizable working democracy and Brazil and Argentina (at, say, $300 and $750 per capita GNP) are under military dictatorship.

To probe behind the averages embedded in the statistical correlations, we shall look briefly at four kinds of cases: the politics of the Revolutionary Romantics; the mainly autocratic politics of the preconditions; failures of Latin American democracy in the drive to technological maturity; and the relatively successful democracies of the developing world.

THE POLITICS OF THE REVOLUTIONARY ROMANTICS: THE DISTORTION IN OUTPUT ALLOCATIONS

The politics of developing nations has been marked in the generation since 1945 by a group of autocratic or totalitarian leaders who have chosen, in differing proportions and under differing influences, to build their domestic politics on 'anti-imperialism' and to channel a high proportion of the limited energies, talents, and resources available to them into external expansion: in Asia, Mao, Ho, Kim and Sukarno; in the Middle East, Nasser and the other radical Arab leaders; in Africa, Nkrumah and Ben Bella; in Latin America, Castro.

In some cases the nations were new, and these dispositions represented an effort to solve the problem of achieving national unity in continuity with the politics and banners of colonial struggle (Indonesia, Algeria, and Ghana); in other cases the leaders represented a revolutionary victory in an older state and moved to translate ideological momentum into an expansion of territory or political influence (China, Egypt, Cuba); in North Vietnam and North Korea, the two circumstances combined.

What we have seen in our time is something of the ideological expansionist zeal which colored Athens' thrust towards empire in the fifth century B.C., after the defeat of the Persian imperialists; which suffused the Revolutionary and Napoleonic external adventure of France; and which touched, even, the American sorties towards Canada during the War of 1812.

Fully to understand these cases, one must understand the character and history – the formative experiences and dreams – of each of the leaders and their principal revolutionary associates; for no two are identical. What they have in common are these elements:

— as political leaders, their initial moments of glory arose from one form or another of revolutionary success;

— they each faced the problem of consolidating revolutionary victory in settings of inherent political fragmentation and turbulence, and they accorded primacy to that political task;

— although in each case the possibilities of moving forward in economic development were real, the mundane tasks ahead were judged less attractive, in terms of their previous experiences, skills and biases – and less attractive also in terms of rallying their people – than a conversion of the anti-imperialism of their revolution into national policies;

— in each case there was a terrain for expansion, physical, political, or both, which was initially judged not beyond their capacities.

Only in the case of Sukarno was economic development wholly, or almost wholly, neglected; although Ben Bella's and Castro's efforts were almost as feeble, and Ho's performance from 1954 to the resumption of the effort to take over South Vietnam and Laos in 1958, was undistinguished. In China and Ghana grandiose development schemes were set in motion beyond their capacity to sustain; in North Korea after 1953 there was considerable industrial progress, persuasively outmatched in South Korea only during the 1960s; in Egypt intelligent development planning went forward, but in an environment of commitment and allocations to external effort which strained and frustrated the ambitious domestic effort.

Some of these leaders are gone and the fate of others – and their policies – is still to be determined. In general, however, they encountered three forces which have tended to frustrate them, like their predecessors in history.

First, they encountered other people's nationalism. Their revolutionary doctrines had a certain resonance in other lands within their regions; but it is one thing to be a radical nationalist Arab, a believer in Black African unity and assertiveness, or to hold that the social ills of Latin America require radical solutions: it is a different matter to take your orders from Cairo, Accra, or Havana.

Second, they have encountered the resistance of those who, for their own reasons, have not wished to see the regional balances of power upset. Although the United States has carried in our time the major burden of supporting those under pressure of regional aggression, the British and Australians stood with Malaysia; fifteen nations with South Korea; six with South Vietnam.

Third, the distortion in the allocation of scarce resources and the relative neglect of domestic welfare gradually imposed attrition on domestic political support for policies of external grandeur which failed to yield decisive results.

It was in such settings that Nkrumah, Ben Bella, and Sukarno gave way to successors who elevated the priority of growth and welfare; the great debate proceeds between Mao and his opposition; and the North Vietnamese begin to surface their inner debate on the priority of victory in the South versus 'building socialism' in North Vietnam.

It is no easy thing for a group of political leaders to abandon a vision to which their mature lives have been committed and which, up to a point, granted them success. Mao, evidently, has refused, and will probably refuse to the end, to acquiesce in the pragmatic bent of his 'revisionist' opponents who would encourage policies based on 'objective economic laws' at home and external policies such that 'the world can bask in the sunlight of peace' and 'infants can slumber in the cradles, and mothers and wives may no longer live in nightmares'.[11] Kim's dream of ruling all of Korea from Pyongyang will die hard as will the dream of the men in Hanoi that they alone are the proper successors to the French colonial empire in Asia. Castro will never find in producing sugar a substitute for his vision of converting the Andes into the Sierra Maestra of South America. And, tragically, Nasser could not hold for long to the idea that occasionally engaged him: that Cairo will only be great when Egypt, by its performance in economic and social development, helps lead the Middle East by example in overcoming its heritage of poverty and reconciling an intractable Arab culture with the exigencies of the modern world.

In the case of Hanoi, Pyongyang, Cairo, and Havana, the availability of large external resources permits postponement of the decision to shift from expansion to growth and welfare.

And before these dreams are abandoned, we can expect final desperate acts to fulfill them. In Sukarno's 1965 connivance with the Indonesian Communist party to destroy the army leadership we saw one such act. It may well be that Mao's Cultural Revolution and Ho's Tet offensive will emerge, in historical perspective, as two others. There is at this writing a little hope – no more – that the radical Arab obsession with Israel and its related intent to destroy the Arab moderates has run its course, having peaked with the Fedayeen explosion of 1970.

But, in the end, soon or late, Napoleon's minute to his finance minister in December 1812, when he abandoned the Continental System, is likely to prevail:[12] 'Undoubtedly it is necessary to harm our foes, but above all we must live.'

THE MAINLY AUTOCRATIC POLITICS OF THE PRECONDITIONS: EARLY AND LATE PHASES

As chapter 3 demonstrates, the preconditions for take-off – the interval between the fracture of the traditional society and the first sustained phase of industrialization – can take a long time. In China a century and a quarter of piecemeal modernization has passed; and the mainland is still not organized to complete its take-off.

The intense pressures of modern communications may foreshorten the period in this century. Nevertheless, as in the past, one can still roughly define nations at early and late phases of the preconditions. There are today, for example, societies touched with elements of modern life but still far from a situation where movement into sustained growth is an early realistic possibility; for example, Cambodia, Nepal, Yemen, Haiti, Mali, Malawi, and a good many other of the less advanced African states. In various combinations, they lack the men, institutions, and resources to move forward to that point, and in some cases they lack political leadership seriously engaged in the economic tasks of the preconditions period.

Socially, such nations are characterized by low levels of urbanization, literacy, communications, and other indicators of modernization.

Politically, they are heterogeneous, ranging from a vicious dictatorship in Haiti to traditional monarchy in Nepal; from Sihanouk's studied ambiguities, when in power, to the nominally radical nationalist rule in Yemen and Mali. In some cases the writ of the central government runs to the regions and villages; in others, there is considerable tribal or other local autonomy on a traditional basis. In all cases, the bureaucracy is weak.

Generally, these early preconditions cases are marked by a low degree of democracy, although African and other tribes evolved, within their round of life, forms of government by consent of the governed which still persist to a degree.

By technical indexes of modernization, Afghanistan belongs at this lower end of the spectrum; but it is engaged, within the narrow limit of its resources, in an active process of modernization and, even, an interesting, if precarious, experiment in movement towards parliamentary government.

In such nations, the general rule might be drawn from the inscription on the pedestal of a statue of Kwame Nkrumah that once stood in front of the Parliament House in Accra: 'Seek ye first the political kingdom, and all other things shall be added unto it.' As in the past, what are here called the constitutional functions of government are primary in the politics of the early preconditions.

Rulers in such nations generally take their most urgent task to be the consolidation and extension of the powers of the central government in an environment of regional, tribal, and factional fragmentation.[13] There is a good deal of sense in the contemporary political scientist's emphasis on the achievement of an effective sense of nationhood as the first challenge following upon the legal establishment of statehood; and if nationhood is described in terms of effective rule, running from the center to the regions, the task remains even in long established states such as Liberia and Ethiopia.

In Africa, Irving Markovitz perceives three political stages: the struggle for independence; the consolidation of power; and, then, the issues of technology, democracy, and the bringing of the people as a whole into the development process.[14]

Economic progress tends to be relatively slow in such nations, except when blessed with both large exportable natural resources and governments prepared to use such revenues for rapid build-up of the economic infrastructure, including education. Political leaders are denied the benefits of popular exhilaration, the sense of momentum, and the enlarged flow of tax resources that come with the take-off. They are also spared, to some extent, the strain of new demands and expectations, as a high proportion of the people outside the capital pursue their traditional round of life and are only drawn gradually into the network of modern markets, communications, and expectations.

Such leaders look to a variety of devices to bind up in unity a society still marked by many traditional features: the projection of their own hopefully charismatic personalities: xenophobic nationalism; the slow build-up of administrative competence; hardhanded security forces.

A good many countries at this early preconditions stage also evoked the device of a large national political party, often monopolistic. I shall have more to say later about political parties. But the most important observation to be made about them on the contemporary scene in developing nations is that generalizations are likely to be misleading: they fulfill very different functions in different nations at different stages of political development.

At this early preconditions stage their primary initial purpose has been to link the people to the new government – to evoke their loyalty, to induce a sense of participation and nationhood. The party was, in effect, a party of the state.

In some cases, the initial party structure began to assume important abiding functions; for example, the recruitment of talent for government as well as for the party itself; patronage; propaganda that went beyond the attempt to generate initial enthusiasm; for example, this happened in the course of the 1960s in Guinea, Mali, Tanzania, and Tunisia. In the Ivory Coast, Houphouet-Boigny has, even, been able to use the party structure to draw some of the political opposition into his party and the government. But writing in the mid-1960s Wallerstein was able to entitle an essay: 'The Decline of the Party in Single-Party African States'.[15]

Where the party did not move forward to such new functions, it tended to wane or lapse. Governments, slowly gaining administrative strength and confidence, operated without them – using, or not using, other devices for inducing popular participation or seeking the assent of major politically active groups.

There are also, of course, nations at a more advanced stage of political and economic development, but still short of take-off.

Economically, the build up of infrastructure (including trained administrators and technicians) has come to a point where take-off can be contemplated in the decade ahead for some of the larger African nations.

When, in 1959, the United Nations Department of Economic and Social Affairs surveyed Africa since 1950, its analysts identified the major industrial groups with forward momentum in the period 1948–57, as: food, beverages, tobacco, cement, and bricks.[16] These typical industrial sectors of the preconditions period – not powerful enough in their direct and indirect effects to initiate a take-off – constituted at that time, along with such infrastructure sectors as transport, education, electric power, and the traditional mineral and agricultural export sectors, the basis for forward movement in Africa. The survey concluded:[17]

The economic development programmes at present in operation are essentially preindustrialization programmes. They aim at providing the proper framework of basic facilities and social services (accounting together for 80 per cent of expenditure under the plans) in the hope that this will induce spontaneous private investment, particularly in industry, but also in agriculture and other directly productive fields.

This pattern has persisted, with increasing emphasis on import substitution industries which might, in the time ahead, help move the more advanced African nations into take-off, notably in an environment of regional and (more realistically) subregional markets. As a recent analyst has said:[18]

The mainly autocratic policies of the preconditions

Countries like Cameroun, Democratic Republic of Congo, Ethiopia, Ghana, Ivory Coast, Kenya, Nigeria and Senegal have already installed a certain range of industries, although mainly consumer goods industries. In the remaining independent countries south of the Sahara, industrialisation can hardly be said to have started ... It follows that the task is not free trade in what exists so much as to build up, through economic cooperation, new industry. It is the stimulus that common markets can give to the creation of new productive capacity and greater diversity in manufacturing industry that makes them of critical importance in the development of Africa.

Although import substitution industries are likely to provide an important sectoral basis for the take-off of the African nations, the pace and character of industrial growth in, at least, the more fortunate among them is likely to depend on whether they also emulate the pattern of which Sweden is the best historical example; namely, to move systematically up the chain of processing with respect to their industrial and agricultural raw materials for export.[19] The export of sawn timber rather than logs not only left additional value added in Sweden, it also diffused the technology of the steam engine through the Swedish economy. The export of pulp and paper not only added a profitable new source of foreign exchange, it forced the pace of chemical engineering on a wide front. The repetition in the contemporary world of something like this way of progressively absorbing new technologies requires not merely agreement between the countries concerned and the foreign firms which now usually participate in the exploitation of their raw materials but, even more, a concentration of their educational policies on the development of scientists, engineers, and managers capable of mastering and administering the more advanced processing stages.

But, as Ndegwa suggests, regional cooperation will also be necessary for the African nations to achieve and maintain a high rate of industrial growth. Such arrangements offer a way of tempering the heritage from colonial history which decreed that a good many new nations would be very small. Economically, they should permit infrastructure to be built at a critical formative stage in the fields of transport, communications, electric power, and education on a more rational and efficient basis than national frameworks would permit. With respect to industry, the option is created of locating plants to supply the regional market in the various participating countries on a scale which could not be sustained by small national markets. And the lesson of the Central American Common Market in its early years has been that there are larger potentialities for intra-regional trade than might *prima facie* be estimated among countries of similar structure at so early a stage of industrialization.

But politically, too, economic regional efforts can have significant consequences. The collaboration of economic ministers and technicians in regional institutions (e.g. development banks) and the agreements they reach tend to strengthen their hand within their governments and to increase the weight of growth policies in the total complex of their governments' dispositions.

Indonesia, having conquered inflation since 1965 and having moved forward in agriculture, is consciously designing a policy for its first wave of industrial expansion. It will also face problems with import substitution as the basis for take-off – not because its market is small but because smuggling is so easy. And it has the need – as well as the possibility – of developing along the Swedish path of raw material processing.

The slow but critically important rhythm of modern education is yielding in both Africa and Indonesia a new generation of men with a capacity to increase the efficiency of government and private enterprise.

What one can observe in these more advanced preconditions cases is a tension which earlier marked, also, some of the nations which moved into the take-off during the 1960s.

As communications improve – and the habits of national politics – factional parties or groups form up which, if they are permitted, assert their narrow interests against the government, but with little or no sense of responsibility for a balanced national policy.[20]

As Lucian Pye notes, in Pakistan and Indonesia such parties 'made a shambles of parliamentary government' by their 'endless inter- and intra-party maneuvering' laying the basis for Ayub's decade of rule and Sukarno's experiment in guided democracy.[21] Much the same could be said of the South Korean civil politicians between the downfall of Syngman Rhee and the military coup of 1961.

The political history of the developing nations over the past generation is littered with such breakdowns of parliamentary governments, rooted in the existence of small factionalized parties capable of protest, pressure and manoeuvre, but not structured to assume responsibility for negotiating within themselves the compromises on which a national policy could be based, often not even linked closely to an orderly election process. Ayub Khan's words of October 1958, as he decided 'to clear up the mess', have been spoken, in effect, by many soldiers as they moved – with reluctance or otherwise – into the presidential palace: 'We are not like the people of the temperate zones; we are too hot-blooded and undisciplined to run an orderly parliamentary democracy.'

But another soldier, in a temperate zone, warned in a similar speech against the factional party spirit a hundred and sixty-two years earlier, in another experimental democracy:[22]

... One of the expedients of party to acquire influence within particular districts is to misrepresent the opinions and aims of other districts. You can not shield yourselves too much against the jealousies and heartburnings which spring from these misrepresentations;

they tend to render alien to each other those who ought to be bound together by fraternal affection . . .

This spirit, unfortunately, is inseparable from our nature, having its root in the strongest passions of the human mind . . .

It serves always to distract the public councils and enfeeble the public administration. It agitates the community with ill-founded jealousies and false alarms; kindles the animosity of one part against another; foments occasionally riot and insurrection. It opens the door to foreign influence and corruption, which find a facilitated access to the government itself through the channels of party passion . . .

As we shall see, Ayub's and Washington's judgments are not the last word on political parties in the preconditions period and beyond; but they reflect accurately the strains on the unity of the state and the ability of governments to perform their essential functions when democratic political participation assumes the form of multiple party factional strife.

As Apter has said:[23] 'Fear that opposition will produce factionalism, corruption, and separatism is pervasive in new nations'; and the fear has often been justified.

The political tensions that come as the preconditions proceed are likely to be heightened by the relatively modest economic progress of this stage. Modern concepts and expectations are easier to diffuse than substantial movement forward in economic growth. Weak quasi-democratic states are, in particular, vulnerable to inflation as factional pressures pile up on a distracted government that can neither mobilize the real resources to meet them nor negotiate moderation through the political process.

As in the sweep of the past, then, the politics of the preconditions period has proved in our time turbulent and not usually conducive to democratic practice.

Some of the new African nations, derived from both British and French colonialism, have moved through this stage thus far in tolerable order under autocratic governments, in which single party systems (or virtually single party systems) have been used not merely to generate a wave of national sentiment but also to provide channels for the recruitment of talent, two-way communication, patronage, and the bringing of opposition within the range of consensus. The Thais have exploited their old sense of national identity to move through this phase into take-off, transforming their government structure along the way into what Fred Riggs calls 'a bureaucratic polity';[24] and they now feel confident enough to begin to experiment, even if grudgingly, with competitive politics. And there are other subtle cases of political modernization which have gone forward on the basis of essentially autocratic government; for example, in Morocco and Iran.

But conventional, competitive parliamentary politics has been hard to reconcile with the underlying realities of such transitional societies.

Politics in Take-off

Take-off brings both easement and further political problems. The focus of politics moves, in degrees at least, from the constitutional tasks of making a nation to the tasks of growth itself. Take-off brings a heightened sense of national achievement and national identity. Abstract debate over competing ideologies begins to fade in the face of the pragmatic imperatives and possibilities of growth. Economic planning and the distribution of government investment resources – from foreign as well as domestic sources – gives the center a certain new leverage over the regions. Thus, South Korea since 1963; Taiwan's stability despite grave unresolved political problems; the confident evolution of a still vulnerable Thailand; the relative steadiness of the small nations of the Central American Common Market in the 1960s. But the political leader's problems remain acute. The struggle over fair shares is likely to intensify: rural versus urban, one region against another; conflict between growth versus welfare allocations are likely to arise; and abstract ideological commitments from the past die hard and slowly.

On balance, the political tasks become easier in this stage than in the preconditions – and more susceptible of meeting the underlying conditions for democratic government; but the political process remains vulnerable in the face of fluctuations in the rate of progress, increasingly felt inequities in the distribution of the benefits of progress, as well as to excessive military allocations.

And the inevitable growth in power of the central authority, required by modernization of the society, may bring latent unresolved regional conflicts to a dangerous point – as once happened in the United States, as has recently happened in Nigeria, and as has been threatened in divided Pakistan.

The Meaning of Communist Takeover

For those who believe in government by the consent of the governed – and in democracy as a goal – the outcome for democracy in the preconditions and take-off societies has not thus far been tragic in the non-Communist world.

There is promise of adjustment and change, of experiment and learning in the turbulent vicissitudes of the contemporary developing nations at an early stage. Democracy, although often set back, lives to fight another day.

In the developing nations under Communist rule, it is a different story. Such single party dictatorships can produce political order. They can master regional and factional contention. They can shake the traditional ways and habits. They can set up institutions for mobilizing the people and connecting them to the central government, through instruments of control and of endless propaganda. But they perform these familiar tasks of political modernization at the cost of foreclosing other more natural paths of evolution. And they do a poor job in economic and social development. Their natural advantages in being able to mobilize a high proportion of resources in the hands of the state are negated by exaggerated allocations for security purposes and by the incompatibility of their compulsion for total control with the conditions for rapid increase in agricultural output. Communism has proved to have a gray thumb; and this is no trivial matter in societies where 70 per cent or more of the working force is in agriculture. It remains, in fact, a serious weakness of the Soviet Union where Communism had the advantage of coming to power after the economy had moved beyond take-off and was generating a large agricultural export surplus.

But totalitarian regimes have demonstrated an important and painful truth: it is possible to clamp on a society a single party regime which, if supported by security resources on a sufficient scale and with sufficient unity and determination within the party, can perpetuate the monopolistic hold of that party against many pressures, over long periods of time. And in terms of democratic values and concepts of government, an overriding priority in public policy accorded to maintenance of a single party's rule over a nation is not good. The tragedy of Communism is not so much its initial dictatorial character as its capacity to deny future choices to those who fall under it.

FAILURES OF LATIN AMERICAN DEMOCRACY IN THE DRIVE TO TECHNOLOGICAL MATURITY

Latin America is worth special attention because democracy continues there to labor under great difficulties although the bulk of the population lives in nations experiencing the drive to technological maturity.

Mexico and a few other Latin American nations have reconciled steady growth with a reasonably stable political life (or phases of stability), embracing a substantial degree of democracy as we have defined it. But Latin America as a whole has presented to the world a recurrent pattern of frustrated democratic aspiration, uneven rates of growth, and inflation, marked at the present time by military dictatorships in Argentina, Brazil, and Peru, endemic instability even in Uruguay and Chile with more deeply rooted democratic institutions and habits.

The economic phenomena to be explained are suggested in table 42 (showing inflation and growth data for Brazil and Chile) and the accompanying chart[25] which contrasts the steadiness of growth in Mexico, its relative

TABLE 42. *Annual growth and inflation rates: Brazil and Chile, 1962–8*

	Brazil		Chile	
	rate of inflation	rate of increase in GDP (real terms)	rate of inflation	rate of increase in GDP (real terms)
1962	55.3	5.4	13.9	4.9
1963	80.6	1.6	44.3	4.7
1964	86.6	3.1	46.0	4.1
1965	45.4	3.9	28.8	5.0
1966	41.1	3.4	22.9	6.1
1967	24.5	4.9	18.1	2.0
1968	24.0	6.0[a]	25.6	3.5

[a] Estimated.

CHART 3. *GDP of selected Latin American countries, 1950–67, constant prices*

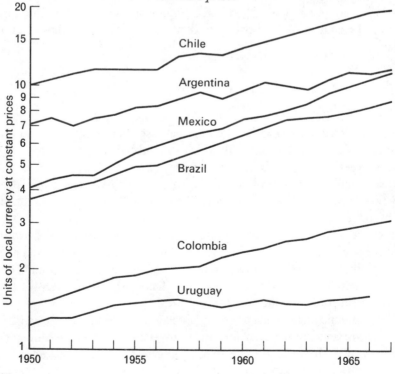

steadiness in Colombia, with its erratic course in Brazil, Chile, Argentina, and Uruguay.

Three factors interact in Latin America to yield erratic growth rates, political instability, and recourse to military dictatorship:

— the long term political heritage of Latin America;

— the specific economic and social problems of moving from take-off into a steady drive to technological maturity in the Latin American context;

— inflation, which is both a result and a further cause of political, social, and economic instability.

Each Latin American nation is, of course, unique – like all others. Some have faced deeply rooted problems of race – others not. The Portuguese cultural heritage of Brazil differs from the Spanish heritage elsewhere. They vary over a wide range in resource endowments, in the timing and degree of modernization, population growth rates, and income per capita.

What they have shared are these things:

— a political culture marked by a counterpoint between paternalistic government and extreme individualism, with little instinct for voluntary cooperation or assumption of communal responsibilities by the citizen, beyond the heritage of the rural Indians;

— a political style that was rhetorical and legalistic rather than operational and pragmatic, leading to much abstract ideological debate, mainly derived from old European banners, which has heightened the inherent tendency to social and political fragmentation;

— a long experience of political domination by landholders and the church, gradually broken by a rise of urban groups under circumstances which led to a rather systematic relative neglect of modernization in rural life;

— a relative freedom from military intrusion by more advanced powers (excepting Mexico and some of the Caribbean and Central American states), permitting a tolerably peaceful evolution since independence without the external challenges which in other cases have heightened a sense of nationhood.

Clearly, the Latin Americans have had to fashion – and will have to fashion – their own versions of democratic life, for they did not derive from Tudor England.[26]

Despite vicissitudes which John Quincy Adams perceived[27] and Bolivar experienced[28] from the earliest days of independence, Latin America has moved forward to make its own kind of modern societies.

As noted earlier, the bulk of the population of Latin America lives in nations which have moved beyond take-off into the drive to technological maturity.

The take-off in the more advanced South American nations can be dated from the mid-1930s; although elements of modern industry were introduced earlier. The Great Depression cut export earnings drastically; and, behind extreme protectionist barriers, import substitution industries were built in textiles and other consumer goods. By the late 1950s these sectors decelerated and movement began into the key sectors of the next stage: steel and metal-working; fertilizers; pulp and paper; the less sophisticated electronics; etc.[29]

But the take-off left a most difficult heritage.

Without competition at home and with continued reliance on traditional agricultural exports to earn foreign exchange, industry developed habits of inefficiency. Unlike the Japanese, South Koreans and Taiwanese, for example, there was no drive for quality control and exports in the new manufacturing sectors. Prices were set, under monopolistic circumstances, on the basis of large mark-ups and low rates of turnover. Idle capacity was accepted as normal. In some cases markets were small; and little effort was made to expand them by modern distribution methods that would reach the poorer segments of the population. As the middle class – which generally failed to pay its taxes – reached income levels compatible with automobile ownership, assembly plants were introduced for many models, yielding high cost operations. The number of models limited local production of components, which might have stimulated intermediate industries, virtually to tires and batteries.

Meanwhile, a series of political leaders emerged, on the Peronist model, who shifted the center of power from the old landowners to the rapidly growing cities; for example, Jiminez, Batista, Vargas and Kubitschek. They represented in a peculiarly Latin American way, the kind of change in the balance of political power which occurred more decorously in Britain through the Reform Bill of 1832. And a part of the labor force was organized under unions which pursued for their limited clientele as outrageously narrow monopolistic policies as the new industrialists, both at the expense of the farmer and the urban working class as a whole.

Pressed by their urban constituencies, governments engaged in welfare policies which, except for massive administrative outlays, could not be translated into significant transfers of resources at existing levels of government income, with erratic rates of growth. And the enterprises owned and operated by government were used for political purposes, operating often at heavy subsidy.

Finally, the modernization of rural life was neglected: as a source of food, foreign exchange earning, and as a market for industrial products.

This environment made difficult the introduction on an efficient and rational basis of the capital-intensive industries required for the drive to technological maturity. It is one thing to have an inefficient textile plant: a quite different matter to have a white elephant steel mill or chemical fertilizer plant.

It is increasingly clear, then, that for Latin America to move forward with sustained high momentum in the key sectors of the drive to technological maturity, radical improvements in efficiency are required. The framework of tariff protection inherited from the import substitution stage of industrialization, combined with the small size of many Latin American national markets, inhibits rational investment, production, and market policies in these capital-intensive industries.[30] The lack of clear and reliable policies towards the role of private foreign investment has also inhibited progress in those sectors, since, in many cases, the rapid, efficient introduction of these technologies requires a phase of foreign capital imports and, at least, elements of foreign management.

In a rough and ready way there has been progress in these directions during the 1960s, notably in Brazil since 1965, and in Argentina under Ongania. But, even under military rule, the heritage of the past yields slowly and unevenly.

A perception that the structural shift to the heavy industry and fabricating complex is urgently needed is the basis of the drive of many Latin American leaders for economic integration, since that appears the least painful common route to enforce the degree of competitive efficiency, quality control, and export-mindedness required. Overcoming the protectionist and monopolistic heritages of the first phase of its industrialization – and finding acceptable terms both ways for the exploitation of foreign capital, management and technology – will clearly be a major test of Latin American economic policy in the 1970s, determining, in part, the pace and regularity at which the drive to technological maturity moves forward.

The problem of efficiency in the new capital-intensive industries and of moving towards regional economic integration is compounded by the inflation problem.

Inflation distorts the direction of investment; it sets up exchange rates which tend to lag behind their real level and thus make exports difficult; it tends to make men seek in business not to maximize their output at low prices but to find that type of output and that price level which is the best hedge against inflation. It creates an atmosphere within which the worker loses a sense of connection between productivity and wages as he struggles blindly to hedge against inflation.

In political and social terms inflation sets every element in the society against the other. It prevents that coming together of people around a national objective and a national program which is essential for the modernization of the society in reasonable order. In an environment of inflationary expectations, men are driven inevitably to take out the best insurance policy they can. The fact that this effort to take out insurance policies leads and forces further inflation is a phenomenon that each individual and group, operating alone, is in no position to take into account.

Latin American inflation is like a dog chasing his tail. At the present time it is less an economic phenomenon – given increased tax collections and flows of external resources – than the reflex of social and political fragmentation and the habit of price and wage setting that grew out of that background.

In short, Latin American economic growth has been slower than it might be at this stage and marked by stop-and-go phases of inflation and constraint. These deny to the political life of Argentina, Brazil, Chile, Uruguay, and, now, Peru a major solvent – high and regular rates of growth in the private sector and in public revenues.

Behind this failure is the fragmentation of social life reflected in and then exacerbated by the factional character of the political parties. The setting in which Illia and Belaunde were overthrown by the military – and Frei's efforts ran into the ground – was marked by two characteristics. First, well-meant policies could not be carried steadily forward in the face of inflationary and other economic pressures that were not politically mastered; second, a fragmented civil political life (in Chile, within the Christian-Democratic party) denied the President the day-to-day support he required to meet his commitments to the citizens who elected him.

In effect, the moderate Peronistas and moderate members of the Argentine business community behaved as if they would rather have military government than help Illia achieve the particular substantive objectives of policy they, in fact, shared; and Illia, loyal to his minority party, did not know how to seek a majority consensus.

After a lifetime of advocating what Belaunde sought to do, Haya de la Torre denied him the APRA support needed for solid progress. Belaunde, desperately anxious to achieve as much of his dream as he could in his term as President, forced the pace on inflationary terms, with the usual chaotic result; and he thus opened the way to a military takeover aimed more at Haya than at the IPC.

In Brazil in 1965 all these elements of frustration and factionalism were present, plus the Sukarno-like strand in Goulart.

Thus, the way has been opened, in one country after another, in recurring crises of inflation and deceleration of growth, for the military to step in as guardians of the state, initially against little resistance and with much popular relief.

The civilian politicians, by their self-interested factionalism, by their attachment to rhetoric irrelevant to the actual tasks of security, welfare, growth, and a humane but orderly constitutional balance, had lost the respect of the people.

But, the inherited raw materials of Latin American political life need not lead to this outcome, as the evolution of affairs in Venezuela, Colombia, and Costa Rica – as well as Mexico – suggests.

THE RELATIVELY SUCCESSFUL DEMOCRACIES OF THE DEVELOPING WORLD

The social and political fragmentation inherent in the political life of societies making their way to modernization is not confined, of course, to Latin America. Nor is the inherent tension between the imperatives of effective government and the excessive pressures upon government arising from untempered, factionalized political life. It is not surprising, therefore, that where a significant degree of democracy has been reconciled with effective government in the developing world, there is a similar pattern in political life.

In essence, this reconciliation has occurred where large, but not monopolistic, political parties – or coalitions – have emerged capable of conducting the ultimate function of political parties; that is, to effect compromises among various regional and other factional interests on the basis of which governments can conduct a reasonably orderly policy within the limit of their resources.

Since, as we have noted, political parties perform a variety of different modernizing functions, it is worth underlining what function is here judged to be critical. These large national parties, or coalitions, are driven to effect the necessary minimum compromise agreements as a condition for seeking the advantages of political office on a national level. Because they are large, they cannot be content to constitute themselves merely as bodies of special interest or protest. They provide, therefore, an initial foundation on which an elected president can carry forward a national policy. And once in office, the existence of the party tie helps maintain a certain minimum discipline over the members of his party, since they have to face foreseeably an election together.

This is the function which, until its recent vicissitudes, the Congress party in India performed. It is the function performed by the PRI in Mexico. It is the key to the limited but real reconciliation of progress and elements of democratic practice, effected by Park through the Democratic Republican party. It is the basis for the reconciliation of progress and elements of democracy in Malaysia through the Alliance party which, as a kind of holding company for lesser parties, has thus far prevented the groups within it from performing in the usual factional way.

In Colombia and Venezuela the reconciliation has been achieved, again, through more or less stable party coalitions and understandings which have given the presidents a minimum foundation on which progress and order could be reconciled with significant elements of democracy, under circumstances of severely limited inputs available to the state.

In Chile, the victory of the Christian-Democratic party under Frei appeared to offer a solid foundation for his administration; but its inner factionalism made this base more apparent than real.

Costa Rica, after three cycles of constitutional government, chaos, and dictatorship, emerged in July 1953 with solid popular support for the National Liberation party, which remains dominant, although it experienced the peaceful loss of the presidency to a coalition candidate in 1958. Its initial leader, Figueres, returned to the presidency in 1970.

In a more advanced society facing somewhat different problems, the Liberal party in Japan has been the foundation for a generation of successful democratic experience in an environment of rapid progress.

Most of these cases are still fragile. In different degrees the Congress party, the PRI, and the Liberal party in Japan are each under strain. They appear to have difficulty absorbing younger men and adjusting to the emergence of new, assertive groups thrown up by the process of modernization itself. And since there is no other large national party (as in the United States or the United Kingdom) which can take over if the major party fragments, national political life in these three countries is shadowed by the possibility of factional disintegration. The coalitions in Colombia and Venezuela show, from time to time, signs of acute strain; and challenge to the coalition in the presidential election of April 1970 brought the former to dangerous political crisis. They must be maintained by endless negotiation and endless widening and renewal, to avoid precisely the kind of fragmentation that Colombia has experienced and which threatens the Congress party in India. President Park judged that the Democratic Republican party was not yet a solid enough base for him to permit the transfer of power safely to another president. The Malaysian Alliance, sitting astride a tense racial situation, has been recently put to the test of civil disorder, and remains under strain.

Aside from their fragility, most of these parties and coalitions have a special history in which the need for consensus among the civilian politicians was painfully learned. The Congress party, after all, was founded in 1885 to seek Indian independence. The PRI only came to its present functions and policy after Mexico had known a bloody decade of civil war, in which the need for compromise and reconciliation was learned by Mexicans in the hardest possible way, and they had had a further generation to reflect on the operational meaning of their revolution (1920–40). The coalition in Colombia only emerged after much domestic bloodshed; and the civil politicians in Venezuela make their compromises with the memory and in the shadow of possible military dictatorship. The Costa Rican civil politicians cooperate responsibly in the sure knowledge that chaos and dictatorship are possible outcomes in their land. The statesmanship of the Malaysian Alliance was also built in the certain knowledge of what might happen to them all if the forces of racial tension were unleashed.

In short, one cannot offer to all the developing nations the formula of large, but not monopolistic, parties or coalitions as a panacea. Special circumstances mark the emergence of each.

And this is, of course, true also of the classic two-party systems of Britain and the United States. After all, there are few more bloody civil wars in recorded history than the British blood-letting of the seventeenth century and the American blood-letting of the nineteenth. And both have a great deal to do with a subsequent national instinct to avoid excessively hard ideologies and clearcut confrontations, and to seek pragmatic agreements on particular issues within and between their two party systems.

On the other hand, it is an important and central fact that we can see from democratic successes of the past as well as the present the direction in which the answer can be found to the inherently acute tensions between democratic politics and effective government in developing nations; and that the relief of this tension has taken similar form in different cultural settings.

Those who believe in civil government and who believe in the reconciliation of orderly progress and government by consent of the governed ought to read every morning, at least, the words of Benjamin Franklin: 'We must, indeed, all hang together, or most assuredly we shall all hang separately.'

Surely, sometime, the civil political leaders in, say, Argentina, Brazil, and Peru; in Pakistan and Indonesia; in Iran, Thailand, and South Vietnam; in Greece, Spain, and, even, in the contentious Arab world, ought to be able to learn that the right road ahead, if they believe in orderly civil rule, is: to put aside the slogans and conflicts of the past; to create party institutions that force negotiation of a broad consensus; and to discipline within it their personal and factional differences.

On the basis of modern history, in quite different cultural settings, they can say it is a difficult thing to do; but they cannot say it is impossible.

In seeking the difficult line between consensus and the area of legitimate hot debate, the politicians of the developing world have a great potential asset. Latent in all developing nations, and explicit in some, is the idea that modernization of the society in ways loyal to its culture and tradition – and loyal, also, to its own visions of the future – is the correct ultimate response to the humiliations of the past; and, in fact, it is the only viable road to the status of dignity on the world scene which their peoples seek. Once accepted in these terms, modernization can be a unifying objective – in fact, an ideology – which places in manageable perspective inevitable conflicts over the distribution of its benefits.

Articulate politicians of the developing world tend to fashion their speeches from rhetoric out of the past: clerical, anti-clerical; government versus private ownership; free trade versus protection; the Second versus the Third Internationale; the struggle against colonialism; etc. But the real issue of life in developing nations now centers about the best way for that nation to modernize in its own fashion. And to this question the old slogans and battle cries are largely irrelevant.

For the fundamental fact about modernization is that it is a great national venture. It is not a job for any one group. It is not carried forward successfully by unrestrained class struggle, but by restraining compromises in terms of perceived larger national and human interests.

In the end, of course, democracy must be more than a tactical agreement among some political leaders to temper factionalism within the framework of a consensus centered on modernization. Democracy must, finally, embrace all the people and reflect the faith that the people know best.

Just as the healing role of modernization as an ideology makes democracy more possible, modernization, in its most technical sense, is assisted by the spread of democratic process and responsibilities to the people – when done in the right way.

The modernization of a society requires strong leadership and, even, a measure of planning at the center; but it will not succeed unless it engages the energies and the commitment of the citizens themselves.

The advantage of democracy – that it diffuses responsibility as well as power – has a special meaning in agriculture which engages the lives of most citizens in the developing world. If we have learned one lesson about development in the postwar generation, it is that collective agricultural systems are grossly inefficient; and they are inefficient because they withdraw from the farmer the incentive and the responsibility for getting the most out of his land. The slow, grinding drama of agriculture under communism demonstrates day after day, year after year, that there are simply not enough police in the world to follow the peasant about to make sure he does the things he must do to make food grow efficiently.

On the other hand, where governments have created for the farmer a local setting of choice and responsibility, he has exhibited admirable good sense – as the Green Revolution now proceeding demonstrates.

In an essay on Asian political parties, Lucian Pye observes:[31]

298

The relatively successful democracies of the developing world

There is already considerable evidence that in Pakistan, as everywhere else in Asia, whenever the common people have been asked to make their choices as to what the government might best do to improve the conditions of their daily life, they have come up with remarkably sober, restrained, and responsible suggestions – a bridge here, a new road there, a new village school this year, and a delay until next year for the new wall. It is precisely these choices within the context of the immediate realities of Asian society which may prove to be far more important in generating sustained economic and social development than the showpiece projects, such as new airports and the like, which fascinate the more insecure nationalist politicians who would avoid the test of popular preferences.

In 1965 I saw, high in the Andes, Indian villages under the aegis of the tragically frustrated Cooperación Popular – then perhaps the best single development project in Latin America. Citizens of the villages had to choose the projects they would conduct and commit their labor to the effort. And together with a small margin of government resources, they were building roads and schools, churches and bull rings, irrigation ditches and rural electrification lines. Similar projects have been conducted with success in urban slums – covering housing, water, and sewerage projects. Literally thousands of such projects were prepared and the commitment of labor made, only to be frustrated by the byzantine working of Peruvian party politics.

Pope John XXIII once said this: 'Special effort . . . must be made to see to it that workers in underdeveloped areas are conscious of playing a key role in the promotion of their personal socioeconomic and cultural betterment. For it is a mark of good citizenship to shoulder a major share of the burden connected with one's own development.'

There is, then, a double truth here: first, the engagement of the people as a whole in responsibility and effort is required for rapid, efficient modernization – the job cannot be done by edict or political cadres or cops. Second, this kind of participation – including but going beyond participation in free elections – is required if the movement towards democracy in the developing world is to advance from its present narrow base.

Politics in the contemporary developing world, as it was in the seventeenth, eighteenth, and nineteenth century world of Europe and Japan, is a profession for a narrow political elite with access to education, information, money, and the institutions which actually manipulate political power. In degree, it was a wider terrain in the United States in the nineteenth century; and it has widened in the twentieth century for all the advanced nations committed to a democratic track.

Even when politics was elite business, it made a considerable difference whether the elite leaders had to face honest one-man one-vote elections, or not.

But what is being demonstrated in the life of the contemporary developing nations goes beyond the old truth that elections help keep even a corrupt politician more honest, and a complacent bureaucracy more attentive to the people's needs. It is that the people – when they can become engaged – are at least as wise, if not wiser, than the elites who would speak for them.

There is reason for understanding and compassion in viewing these elites. They arose in many cases from settings half local, half international: half part of developing nations, half part of a more advanced world. Few of their members spent much time in the villages of their nations. They had feelings of guilt towards their own people, a mixture of hostility and attraction for the world outside. They were vulnerable to xenophobic, nationalist, and Marxist slogans and doctrines which eased their sense of guilt and ambivalence. If faith in democracy had to be built on this transitional generation alone, that faith would have weak foundations. What justifies such faith is the demonstration in one part of the developing world after another that the people, as a whole, are capable of a role of serious citizenship – not merely to be members of howling mobs bussed in to throw rocks at embassies or to strew flowers before favored foreign dignitaries.

Democracy was always conceived as a combination of liberty and the assumption of responsibility.

The rule has not changed in the past twenty-five hundred years; and the peoples of the contemporary developing world appear capable of living by it – if given half a chance by their leaders.

Challenged (as I have been by my students) to set down the operating lessons of history and the contemporary world for making democracy work in a developing nation in the last third of the twentieth century, I would offer these six rules:[32]

1. Concentrate the nation's scarce energies, talents, and resources on the modernization of the society rather than on external adventure.

2. Develop modernization in loyalty to the society's culture, traditions, and ambitions as a national ideology – as the appropriate response to past humiliation and weakness on the world scene.

3. Generate a high and steady rate of growth in the economy and in resources available for public purposes.

4. Develop a large but not monopolistic national political party, or coalition of parties, containing legitimate representatives of the key groups within the society, among which compromise agreements must be reached before an effective national policy can be pursued by the government.

5. Pursue a policy of widening democratic participation and responsibility out to the citizenry as a whole, notably in rural areas.

6. Pursue in foreign affairs a policy of cooperative regionalism to

strengthen the nation's and region's capacity to avoid external intrusion and to play a role of dignity and effectiveness on the world scene.

I believe that something like these rules will, in time, be learned and applied, if the developing nations do not permit themselves to be trapped in single party, police state dictatorships.

A STATEMENT OF JUDGMENT AND FAITH

This judgment is made with reasonable awareness of the heritages of the past and the problems of the present and future which must be overcome.

It is not difficult to write with skepticism or pessimism about the prospects for democracy in the developing world.

And surely a hopeful outcome will take time. Surely the political life of these nations will see many crises before stable patterns of democracy emerge.

My temperately optimistic judgment emerges not merely from faith but from knowledge of how men and women have voted, with dignity and conviction – and sometimes at risk of their lives – in honest elections of Latin America and Asia, when given a chance; by having looked often – and in many countries – into the shrewd and passionate faces of men and women who have grasped the possibilities offered them for making, through their own responsible efforts, a better life for their children than the life they and their parents knew in the villages of the developing world; by having seen – in one place after another – the beginnings of a reconciliation between the young and privileged in these developing nations and the disadvantaged in the slums and neglected villages – from the Andean highlands to the Iranian plateau; from the slums of Caracas and Rio to the villages of Vietnam; and from having observed the slow erosion of anachronistic and divisive ideologies.

That the political life which emerges from the cauldron of our times in the developing world may differ from the particular forms of democracy we know in the Atlantic world, I have no doubt. But, equally, I have no doubt that the men and women of these nations will fashion, in time – in their own way – democracies that evidently belong in the political family we now easily recognize; for a sense of the dignity and fellowship of man is no monopoly of the Atlantic world. And, as Dr. Busia of Ghana has made clear, it is not only Anglo-Saxons that can learn the lesson that 'no man or group of men is virtuous enough to be permitted to hold absolute power'.[33]

CHAPTER 8

WAR AND PEACE IN THE GLOBAL COMMUNITY

INTRODUCTION

This final chapter examines the prospects for the community of human beings, taken as a whole, in terms of the three tools whose use has shaped this book:
— The concept of government and politics as the effort to resolve the three abiding but often conflicting imperatives of security, welfare and growth, and the maintenance of an acceptable constitutional balance between justice and order.
— The concept of the stages of growth as the process which, in modern times, has thrown up for political decision many of the critical issues, under each of these three headings, with which government and the political process has had to deal.
— And, behind it all, the concept of man himself, containing in the state within him impulses of spirit, appetite, and reason – id, ego, and super-ego – which are the ultimate raw materials of organized social life.
What emerges as man's prospects if these three tools are successively applied to the world community?
In the exposition that follows, it is assumed that stable peace does not imply or require world government in the simplistic sense. But it does imply a system of arrangements which would more or less effectively constrain international friction to the terrain of diplomacy and international politics. It also implies effective communal action on behalf of the general welfare of humanity. And, finally, it implies accepted concepts for dealing with problems of justice and order – and the balance between them – in the world community.

THE THREE TASKS OF GOVERNMENT

The United Nations Charter

Looked at through this prism, the Charter of the United Nations can be seen as an effort to define the security, welfare, and constitutional objectives of a community which announced itself, in 1945, as 'determined to save succeeding generations from the scourge of war, which twice in our lifetime has brought untold sorrow to mankind. . . .'

The central security objective of the Charter is the avoidance of war itself, in a world where sovereignty still reigns; but, as considered below (pp. 321–2), problems of international conflict interweave, as well, with the Charter's constitutional criteria.

The welfare objective is 'to promote social progress and better standards of life in larger freedom. . . .'

The constitutional objectives are incorporated in the following statement of aspiration, further developed in Article 1: 'To reaffirm faith in fundamental human rights, in the dignity and worth of the human person, in the equal rights of men and women and of nations large and small, and to establish conditions under which justice and respect for the obligations arising from treaties and other sources of international law can be maintained. . .'

It may seem naive – and it is certainly painful – to evoke these hopeful words which have been so imperfectly fulfilled after a quarter-century of effort. But it may be useful to stare at what we have – and have not – accomplished in fulfillment of pledges to one another which still represent what most of humanity would like to see happen on this small and vulnerable planet.

SECURITY

Stalin's Decision

The wartime dream of continued concert among the major powers was to have been the basis for fulfilling the security objective of the United Nations Charter. Such negotiated concert, which neither the United States nor Russia had the capacity or will to impose on each other by force, was to have made the Security Council work, despite its veto provision. That dream was violated by Stalin's choice, publicly announced in his uncompromising electoral speech of 9 February 1946, which made inevitable conflict between the communist and capitalist worlds the premise of his domestic and foreign policies, a premise soon given substance by his actions at many points.

Stalin chose to consolidate and extend, where possible, the power he might directly exercise from Moscow rather than to assume a more dilute great power role on a global basis.

Three Communist Offensives

We have since seen three tolerably clearcut waves of Communist external effort.[1]

There was Stalin's thrust of 1946–51 (in association with Mao, from 1949); Khrushchev's, of 1958–62; and, finally, the offensive conducted over recent years by Mao and those who accepted his high-risk doctrines with respect to so-called 'wars of national liberation'.

Starting in early 1946, Stalin moved to consolidate into Communist states those countries of Eastern Europe where Soviet troop positions provided leverage, while pressing hard against Iran, Greece, Turkey, and then, via the Communist parties, in Italy and France. His effort in Europe reached its climax in the Berlin blockade of 1948–9.

The West would not risk war with Russia to defend the hard-won wartime agreements on political freedom for Eastern Europe, a fact Stalin cautiously established between 1945 and 1948; but it did respond with the Truman Doctrine, the Marshall Plan, and the creation of NATO as Western Europe came under threat. A stalemate developed after the success of the Berlin airlift in 1949.

As this duel in the West proceeded, Stalin launched an offensive in the East which can roughly be dated from Zhdanov's Cominform speech of September 1947. The subsequent activist phase involved guerilla warfare in Indochina, Burma, Malaya, Indonesia, and the Philippines. And after the Chinese Communists came to power in November 1949, the offensive in Asia reached its climax with the invasion of South Korea. It ended in May 1951 with the successful United Nations defense at the thirty-eighth parallel against a massive assault by the Chinese Communists, although costly fighting continued for two further painful years of negotiation.

From the opening of truce talks in the summer of 1951 to the launching of the first Soviet Sputnik in October 1957, there emerged what passes in postwar history for a relatively quiet interval. It was, of course, interrupted by the Suez and Hungarian crises in 1956; but these resulted less from the tensions of the Cold War than from the dynamics of change within the non-Communist and Communist worlds, respectively. During this time, the Soviet Union was mainly engaged in its post-Stalin redispositions – political, economic, and military.

Meanwhile, Communist China turned, for a time, primarily to tasks of domestic development. Only in Indochina did local conditions favor major Communist momentum; but the North Vietnamese settled at Geneva in 1954 for half the victory they had sought.

Khrushchev's domestic changes represented a limited but significant softening of Stalin's harsh regime – and for Soviet citizens, historic gains. His foreign policy style was different, too, and, in its way, more flexible. Nevertheless, considerable ambitions remained embedded in Moscow's foreign policy. And with the launching of Sputnik, a new phase of attempted Communist expansion got under way.

Khrushchev sought to exploit two new facts on the world scene: first, the emerging Soviet capacity to deliver thermonuclear weapons over long distances as a means of forcing the West to make limited diplomatic concessions; second, the marked acceleration of nationalism and modernization in Asia, the Middle East, Africa, and Latin America, yielding an environment of endemic turbulence on those continents.

It was in this post-Sputnik period that Moscow laid down its ultimatum on Berlin; the Communist party in Hanoi announced it would undertake to revive guerilla warfare in South Vietnam; Castro took over in Cuba; and Soviet military and economic aid arrangements were extended to increase their leverage not only in the Middle East, where the process had begun in 1955, but, also, in Indonesia and elsewhere. It was then that Mao announced, 'The East Wind is prevailing over the West Wind'; and, in that spirit, he initiated in 1958 the crisis in the Taiwan Straits.

There was a good deal of opportunistic enterprise, rather than a majestic grand design, in all this; but it was clearly a phase of Communist confidence and attempted forward movement.

In 1961–2 Khrushchev's offensive was met by the West, as a whole, at Berlin; and a further dramatic test of nuclear blackmail was faced down by President Kennedy in the Cuba missile crisis. For the time being at least, that latter crisis answered a question which had greatly engaged Khrushchev: whether the Free World would surrender vital interests through diplomacy, under the threat of nuclear war.

The answer to the second question – concerning the ability of the West to avert successful Communist exploitation of the inherent vulnerability of the developing area – had to be given at many points by many devices, negative and constructive, from the de-fusing of the Congo to the Alliance for Progress and the World Bank's India–Pakistan consortium.

By the end of the Cuba missile crisis the momentum had largely drained from Khrushchev's post-Sputnik offensive; but Moscow's move towards moderation, symbolized by the negotiation of the Atmospheric Test Ban Treaty in 1963, had no echo in Peking.

The Sino–Soviet split was gravely aggravated after the Cuba missile crisis and became increasingly overt as recriminations were exchanged and inter-party documents revealed.

The Chinese Communists sought to seize the leadership of the Communist movement, notably in the developing areas, and to unite it with the radical nationalists of Asia and Africa. They thrust hard against Soviet influence within Communist parties on every continent, fragmenting some of them;

sought to bring Castro aboard; moved boldly, over-playing their hand, in Africa; probably played some role in triggering the attempted Communist takeover in Indonesia; and struck an aggressive pose during the Indo–Pakistani war of 1965. As a result of the problems they created, the Afro–Asian conference at Algiers in 1965 never materialized.

At one point after another this Chinese Communist offensive in the developing world fell apart, leaving the war in Vietnam as perhaps the last major stand of Mao's doctrine of guerrilla warfare. That war was revived by Hanoi on a new basis in 1964 with the introduction into South Vietnam of regular North Vietnamese forces, in the wake of political disintegration in Saigon, beginning in May 1963.

The convergence of enlarged military pressure from without and disintegration within brought South Vietnam close to defeat; and President Johnson decided to meet the situation by introducing substantial American forces.

There is a certain historical logic in this outcome.

For the better part of a decade, an important aspect of the struggle within the Communist movement between the Soviet Union and Communist China had focused on the appropriate method for Communist parties to seize power. The Soviet Union had argued that the crossing of frontiers with arms and men should be kept to a minimum and the effort to seize power should be primarily internal.[2] They argued that it was the essence of 'wars of national liberation' to expand Communist power without causing major confrontation with the United States and other major powers. The Chinese Communists defended a higher risk policy; but they were militarily cautious themselves. Nevertheless, they urged others to accept the risks of confrontation with United States and Western strength, against which the Soviet Union warned.

Although Hanoi's effort to take over Laos and South Vietnam proceeded from impulses which were substantially independent of Communist China, its technique constituted an important test of whether Mao's method would work even under the optimum circumstances provided by the history of the area. As General Giap has made clear, Hanoi is conscious of this link: 'South Viet Nam is the model of the national liberation movement in our time . . . if the special warfare that the United States imperialists are testing in South Viet Nam is overcome, this means that it can be defeated everywhere in the world.'[3]

So far as Peking was concerned, its stake in the war in Vietnam was not merely doctrinal vindication: American failure would lead to a withdrawal or dilution of commitment to Thailand and the Asian mainland, in general, thus removing the major obstacle to an extension of Peking's power and influence – a fact of which Moscow was acutely aware and a dilemma to which Hanoi was not wholly insensitive.

Moscow on the Defensive

So far as the Soviet Union is concerned, what we have seen since the Cuba missile crisis and Khrushchev's removal is a policy increasingly motivated by anxiety and concern rather than hope and vision of ideological satisfaction. There was an authentic exuberance about Khrushchev's vision of the future. He may not have been so sure that nuclear blackmail would work; although he gave it a good and mortally dangerous try. But he did believe – as nearly as we can guess – that the Soviet Union would soon catch up with the United States in economic performance. He did believe – as nearly as we can guess – the developing world would prove a promising terrain for Communist expansion.

But since 1962 Soviet economic prospects resumed a more Russian cast; that is, of a society moving forward at a conventional rate but lagging, as traditionally, the West. China has become once again in Soviet policy and in the minds of the Russian peoples a problem and an anxiety, stirring deeply rooted ancestral fears – not the vindication of an ideological dream. The developing regions of the world, even the Middle East, the most proximate and promising, where the problem of Israel has provided continuing Soviet leverage, have demonstrated a capacity to go their own way, following a variety of non-Communist patterns in their economic, social, and political life, motivated ultimately by a sturdy nationalism.

Finally, of course, Stalin's empire in Eastern Europe, step by step, has shown an assertiveness which has forced Moscow to put aside the question of how it could be used as the base for a westward thrust and has raised again an old Russian question: How can Eastern Europe be managed so that it is not a threat to the security of Russia?

Out of this protracted and disruptive duel of power and ideology two things emerged.

The Common Law of the Cold War

First, there arose an implicit common law for the conduct of the struggle across the truce lines of the Cold War: in Europe, at Berlin and on the Elbe; in Asia, at the 38th and 17th parallels. The rule was this: if A obtruded with military force or the threat of military force over B's side of the line, it was acceptable for B to bring to bear whatever defensive power he could mobilize against A's intrusion; but it was not acceptable for A to take B's defensive action as an occasion for escalation.

On this basis, Azerbaijan, Greece, and the two major crises in Berlin (1948–9 and 1961–2), were weathered in the West without progressive escalation. The rule also governed the denouement of the Cuba missile crisis and Korean war, including the defensive American response to Chinese intervention when United Nations forces moved north of the thirty-eighth parallel. And thus far, at least, the rule has governed the behavior of both sides in the war in Vietnam: Hanoi, despite its propaganda, accepted the bombing of North Vietnam as a defensive counter to the presence of its regular forces in the South, and paid a considerable price for its conditional cessation on 31 October 1968, while the United States neither invaded North Vietnam nor obstructed its sea routes.

There has been nothing automatic or explicit about this rule. It flowed, simply, from the perceived danger of total war in a nuclear age. If a defensive reaction to a Communist intrusion were to be taken as the occasion for increased Communist offensive thrust, or if Communist intrusion were taken as the occasion for conquest of the land from which the intrusion was launched, where, short of nuclear war, would the cycle of violence end?

It is a hopeful irony that, after experimenting extensively with the unfolding powers of the industrial revolution when applied to warfare, men were capable of peering over the edge and drawing back to something like the limited war conventions of the eighteenth century, in the face of the quantum jump in destruction provided by nuclear weapons.

Regionalism

The second response to Stalin's, Mao's and, then, Khrushchev's policy was to build a series of regional security arrangements as provided under Article 52 of the United Nations Charter.

In Latin America the arrangements included the United States. There was a consensus in Latin America after the Second World War that such arrangements could provide to Latin America two advantages: inhibiting the intrusion of extra-hemispheric powers into the region; and also inhibiting the United States in the kind of direct intrusions into Latin American affairs which had marked earlier times. The memories of colonialism; of the French in Mexico of the 1860s; of the Axis role in the Second World War; and then, from 1959, Castro in Cuba – these have been sufficient to keep the Rio Treaty system alive.

Its effect has been to limit allocations of resources to military purposes in Latin America below that in other regions;[4] to mute the military expression of conflicts inside Latin America; for example, Argentina–Chile, Peru–Ecuador, Peru–Bolivia, El Salvador–Honduras.

The Cuba missile crisis and its outcome strengthened the system. The crisis in the Dominican Republic at first strained the system; but its outcome, as seen by most Latin Americans, was, on balance, finally seen to be salutary.[5]

In Western Europe NATO emerged initially as an instrument of psychological reassurance – as a kind of security underpinning for the Marshall Plan. But the Communist willingness to undertake the offensive on the ground in Korea, combined with the development of the Soviet nuclear capability, brought SHAPE to life. An integrated allied command, including substantial German ground forces, was built. Khrushchev's post-Sputnik evocation of nuclear blackmail and the 1958–62 ultimatum which hung over Berlin then brought the issue of United States–Western European nuclear arrangements to the center of the stage, including proposals for the Multilateral Nuclear Force and the Atlantic Nuclear Force. This phase of allied exploration and negotiation gradually subsided after the Cuba missile crisis and in the face of British and French as well as Russian resistance to these proposals. Allied attention came to focus on intensive and serious nuclear consultation within the Alliance and on the possibilities of detente to the East.

The Soviet invasion of Czechoslovakia fractured more naive views concerning the ease and length of time that would be required for reconciliation in Central Europe; but it did not wholly destroy the concept that NATO might shift from a role simply of defense to a role of negotiation and, even, arms control in concert with the Warsaw Pact and its members.

The United States was an integral part of the security arrangements created in Latin America and Europe. But the new nations of Africa devised in 1963, through the Organization of African Unity, a regional system from which the major non-African powers were excluded. The early stage of Africa's political and economic development and the recurrent crises over the Congo, Rhodesia, South Africa, as well as the civil war in Nigeria, have masked the promise, while underlining the incompleteness, of the African system. Building on habits and patterns of inter-tribal negotiation, the Africans have displayed a gift for settling their problems among themselves; notably, Ethiopia–Somalia; Morocco–Algeria. The insistence that the tragic Nigerian question be left to Africans dramatized the depth of their will to forge their own destiny, while limiting the security role of the non-African powers.

The road ahead for African regionalism is obviously long, given the fact that Black African regional sentiments must compete with more conventional nationalism and nationalism with tribalism; but what the Africans have accomplished not only in politics but in the emergence of regional and subregional economic institutions may have substantial implications for the future of the continent.

In Asia, too, arrangements are emerging which may cast a long and, hopefully, benign shadow. The initial American role in Asia was essentially to fill vacuums of power on an *ad hoc* basis where the cost of not undertaking responsibility outweighed the pain and burden of accepting responsibility: the occupation of Japan itself; the bloody return to South Korea after an unwise withdrawal; the security arrangements with Taiwan after the flight of the Nationalists in 1949; SEATO, after the Geneva Conference of 1954 and the French withdrawal; ANZUS, to protect two somewhat lonely nations, as British power in Asia waned.

As the North Vietnamese brought their regular forces into Vietnam via Laos in 1964, and the military and political situation in South Vietnam deteriorated, Asians knew that their destiny was in balance. Would the United States honor its treaty commitments in that part of the world; or would mainland China inherit suzerainty in the wake of American acceptance of Hanoi's success in South Vietnam and Laos? However obscure their public announcements, this assessment of the options was as real to responsible leaders in Karachi, New Delhi, Rangoon, Djakarta, and Tokyo as it was in Seoul, Vientiane, Kuala Lumpur, Singapore, and Saigon.

The American commitment of major forces in 1965 produced a profound change of sentiment and perspective throughout Asia. Asians began to think seriously about their future, and to act as if they had a future of their own to shape. They began to behave as if they agreed with the judgment of Lee Kuan Yew, speaking 22 June 1966 to students in Singapore about Vietnam:

If South Vietnam disappears, can you imagine the problems of Prince Souvanna Phouma? He already has enough problems.

And what about so many of our other friends in Southeast Asia? And the point which I made, I hope not without some effect, was – 'Do you believe that Pakistan is a lackey of the Americans?' They are friends of China. There are the Burmese – they are the best neutralists in Asia. How is it that none of them have really said that 'this is a crime against humanity committed by the Americans?' Of course! Hundreds of Vietnamese are dying every day – for what? For Vietnam? No! To decide that Vietnam shall not be repeated. That is why they haven't raised their voice in protest with the same indignation and rage.

But whilst we buy time, if we just sit down and believe people are going to buy time forever after for us, then we deserve to perish.

Asia since 1965 has begun to use the time that was being bought for it in blood by the South Vietnamese and those fighting beside them. Asia, which, more than any other region – even the Middle East – lacked a sense of common experience and destiny, has begun to behave like a region with long-run common interests.

There was, for example, the meeting of the Asian and Pacific Council

(ASPAC) in Seoul in June 1966. That meeting accepted the Australians and New Zealanders as full members. It thus responded to the vision and policy of Harold Holt who had told his people that, while ties to London and Washington would persist, their destiny was as part of Asia and the Pacific. The Asian Development Bank came briskly to life under the leadership of the distinguished Japanese, Takeshi Watanabe. Asian central bankers, transport experts, educators, and others began to meet together, as their European counterparts did twenty years earlier. Despite the war, action, as well as planning, was undertaken by the Mekong Committee with the building of the Nam Ngum dam in Laos and the start on Prekh Thanat in Cambodia.

In this more hopeful environment, the Indonesians struggled out of the grip of Sukarno and the Communists, in October 1965, to begin serious economic recovery and development, joining with Malaysia, the Philippines, and Thailand to revive in 1966 the dormant Association of Southeast Asian Nations (ASEAN).

Perhaps most important of all, the Indonesians, the Japanese, and others in Asia began to discuss quietly among themselves their responsibilities for the stability of a post-Vietnam settlement in Southeast Asia.

In short, we have seen in the non-Communist world a remarkable rise of regional structures and spirit over the past generation, in each case responding to special and particular circumstances, but suffused by a desire of men to free themselves from an initially bipolar world and shape their own destinies and by an awareness that conventional nationalism would not suffice.

The Organization of American States was built on a consensus that the major extra-continental powers should be excluded from a security role in the Western Hemisphere, and the United States restrained from inappropriate political and military intervention in Latin America; NATO was built to insure an effective nuclear deterrent against the Soviet Union, in an environment in which Germany could safely makes its contribution, thus providing a secure base from which the Atlantic could proceed towards peace with the East as fast as history might permit; the regional institutions of Africa have been built to keep Africa for the Africans; in Asia regionalism emerges as a way of providing cohesion in the face of the potential threat of a nuclear Communist China, under circumstances where it is clear that Asians must do more for themselves if the American component in their security is reliably to be available.

In the Middle East regionalism has been obstructed by unresolved, multiple schisms: not only the Arab versus Israeli tension, but that between radical and moderate Arabs and between Arabs and other Muslims, notably Iran and Turkey. Only time will tell whether the political leadership of the area will come to the realization – and act upon it – that their dignity and status in the modern world depend on so grouping together – and solving their own problems – that major external powers cannot manipulate them for their own purposes.

Efforts at peacemaking

Major war has been avoided, then, and the temptation to aggression reduced by these two reactions to the Communist thrust; that is, by a common law rule to damp escalation and by the beginning, at least, of regional organization, excepting the Middle East. Those have been minimum conditions for survival and for the possibilities of progress in the non-Communist world. But peace, evidently, requires a reaching across the barriers of the Cold War.

From the offer in June 1946 of the Baruch Plan, the West never ceased to hope – and to try – to reach accord on a method to remove the danger of nuclear weapons and of nuclear war itself. And from Potsdam and, then, Byrnes' offer of a fifty-year German disarmament treaty (September 1946), the West has continued to grope sporadically towards a resolution of the German problem which would bring security and peace to Central Europe.

Formerly, all the twists and turns of diplomatic exchanges over the years centered, in the one case, around the problem of mutual inspection, in the other, around the problem of free elections in East Germany. It is not easy to penetrate with confidence the balance of hopes and fears which determined for so long Moscow's rigidity on these two issues.

But in the 1960s that balance – whatever it may have been – has shifted, at least a little. A number of factors have elevated fear and anxiety in Soviet policy:

—the Sino–Soviet split and the evident determination of China to become a nuclear power;

— the outcome, in Berlin and the Cuba missile crisis, of Khrushchev's technique of nuclear blackmail;

— the rising assertiveness, against this background, of the peoples of Eastern Europe.

These were the three main elements, but there were others; for example, the slowing down of the Soviet economy which eliminated, for the time being, Khrushchev's vision of a Soviet Union surpassing the United States in production by 1970; and the Communist failure either substantially to expand power or to produce striking examples of progress in the developing regions of the world among its protégés.

President Kennedy, and then, with great persistence, President Johnson, sought to translate this new environment into positive movements towards order and stable peace. And some progress was made: the Atmospheric Test Ban Treaty; the agreement to keep weapons from outer space; some normalization of United States–Soviet bilateral relations, including an intensive and temperate dialogue on the Middle East and Vietnam; agreement to proceed with the Non-Proliferation Treaty; agreement to launch talks on offensive and defensive nuclear weapons systems. And President Nixon has pursued these efforts in continuity with his predecessors.

The Non-Proliferation Treaty is not, of course, a United States–Soviet negotiation or an exercise in 'bridge building'. It is a constitutional arrangement of the greatest significance for the world's future political and security structure. Its fate will be settled not in Washington and Moscow but in Tokyo, New Delhi, Jerusalem, Rome, and Bonn; and perhaps, also, in Canberra, Berne, Stockholm, Rio and Buenos Aires.

The proposition being put to the world's parliaments is that they deny themselves the ambiguous option of a national nuclear weapons capability and seek their security through collective means based on existing – mainly United States – commitments. They are not likely to accept and sustain the proposition unless the United States is judged a stable and reliable factor in the equation of security and unless Washington and Moscow make progress in taming their bilateral arms race.

Taken together, the Non-Proliferation Treaty and the missile talks are certainly the most important – and, potentially, the most hopeful – efforts to move across the barrier created by Stalin in February 1946. But clearly, the nuclear question is only beginning to be approached; and Bonn's dialogues with East Germany, Poland, and the Soviet Union are only limited first steps on a long road.

Soviet fear and anxiety about an external environment which, day by day, is becoming less capable of control from Moscow, is not a sufficient basis for stable peace, as the mortally dangerous situation in the Middle East underlines every day. Some positive changes may have to occur in Soviet society – and its view of its destiny in relation to the world – before the foundations of something like world order can emerge. And this, evidently, will take time.

And we must await, as well, the outcome of the great debate in Communist China.

With Mao we have observed an effort unique in modern history – indeed, an effort for which it is difficult to find parallels in history: the grandfather evoking his grandchildren to defeat his children. The grandchildren were the volatile, energetic, ambitious youth whom Mao could bring into the Red Guard. The children in this case are the pragmatic generation of soldiers and technicians who emerged in post-1949 China, who wished to get on with the unfulfilled task of modernizing that old and remarkable civilization.

Mao perceived that the consequences of modernization would lead China towards a bureaucratic and increasingly moderate regime in both its domestic and foreign dispositions. He used his powers in the 1960s to try to stem the tide, as he saw it, via the Cultural Revolution. He produced an economy whose production in 1970 is only marginally higher than that of a decade earlier; but an economy that contained within it a nuclear weapons complex amidst continuing poverty and relative industrial and agricultural stagnation.

There is so much unique about the story of China's modernization that one can only predict with diffidence. But whether mainland China turns, in the years ahead, to a more conventional effort at modernization and whether it develops less pathological relations with the rest of Asia, the Soviet Union and the United States, are critical issues for peace. Just as a stable and secure West is a force for detente with the Soviet Union, a movement towards regional consolidation in Asia could help future Chinese leaders decide, at last, that internal development and a normalization of external relations was the proper course.

An Interim Conclusion about Security

We can conclude, then, that the world community, viewed as a political system, has succeeded in surviving for a quarter-century without major war but has moved only a little way towards building a system of stable peace in the security terms envisaged in the United Nations Charter. This negative achievement is not trivial. The environment of this quarter-century has been the most dangerous man has ever known: a convergent struggle for power and ideology; the nuclear sword of Damocles; the bringing into the world political system of all the continents largely neutralized or out of play between 1815 and 1914 – continents which had all the explosive potential of the Balkans before the First World War.

By historical norms of human behavior, this equation could have been expected to yield major war.

Major war has been avoided by self-limiting common law rules of attack and defense; by the building of regional security arrangements which reduced the attraction of aggression; and by the gathering strength and assertiveness of nations and peoples which have destroyed the initial bipolarity of the world arena for power, posing for Moscow and Washington increasingly the question: How can this community of diffusing power and authority be organized without excessive danger?

These forces have permitted the human race to survive without major war; they have yielded some tentative groping towards accord across the lines of the Cold War; and they have produced a structure of global and regional arrangements which, potentially, could be one foundation for movement towards peace. But another generation's effort, at least, will probably be required to fulfill the real but precarious promise of what has been accomplished.

GROWTH AND WELFARE

Wartime Beginnings

On the whole, the world community has done better than ever before in its history in acting communally to perform the growth and welfare functions of government. The effort began at Hot Springs in 1943 with an examination of the food and agriculture problems of the postwar world, leading to the creation of FAO. Then there was Bretton Woods – a rare effort to avoid remembered mistakes of the past. It has been a great asset that those who have borne responsibility in government are old enough to remember what happened between 1929 and 1933.

European Recovery and Unity

Of course the World Bank and the International Monetary Fund were not enough. Nor was UNRRA. The United States had to undertake the Marshall Plan as a special venture.

In the context of the Marshall Plan, the United States made a fundamental decision. The decision was to throw its full weight behind European efforts at economic and political unity. There were those who argued that European unity could pose a danger for the United States in the long pull. They argued it would be wiser to continue a policy analogous to that which Britain had long conducted toward the Continent – a policy of divide and rule. President Truman rejected this argument, as did his successors. They have taken the view that the United States wanted partners, not satellites, for the long future; and they were prepared to gamble on the underlying long term parallelism of American and Western European basic interests.

President Kennedy, after de Gaulle's press conference in January 1963, initiated a complete review of this strand in American policy. But the upshot was a sturdy reaffirmation of United States support for European unity, articulated in Frankfurt in June. President Johnson's ultimate faith that this course would again commend itself to France, played a part in his determination to do nothing to exacerbate relations with France in the period 1963–9. And the post-de Gaulle resumption of discussions on the enlargement of the European communities to include Britain appear, *ad interim*, to justify that faith.

The Developing Areas

The remarkable and prompt recovery of Europe led men, as early as the winter of 1948–9, to turn their minds to the problems of assistance to the developing world. It was during the meeting in Paris of the United Nations General Assembly – with the Berlin blockade and the airlift in effect – that a resolution was passed which helped induce President Truman's fourth point in his Inaugural Address of January 1949. It was becoming clear to those concerned with international policy that the next great common task in the field of the general welfare would be to accelerate economic growth in Asia, the Middle East, Africa, and Latin America. The Korean war cut across these efforts; and the Eisenhower Administration was divided on its wisdom and appropriate scale. But towards the end of the 1950s the foundations for the Alliance for Progress and the India–Pakistan consortium arrangements were laid. And President Kennedy, supported by a gathering consensus in the Western world, launched the 1960s as the Decade of Development.

Looking back from 1970 at what has happened in the 1960s, one cannot help feeling that there has been a fundamental breakthrough in human experience.

As noted in chapter 7 in all the developing continents there are countries which have demonstrated to their own satisfaction that they have the capacity to move forward on a fairly regular basis at rates which substantially outstrip the rate of population increase; and that such growth can be translated into improved welfare that can be seen and felt by the people. Confidence that the children will live better than the parents matters more than the closing of some abstract and statistically ambiguous gap between rich and poor nations.

The list of success stories is quite impressive, even though some may still be fragile: South Korea, Taiwan, Thailand, Malaysia, Pakistan, Iran, Turkey, Tunisia, Mexico, the Central American Common Market, Colombia, Venezuela, Paraguay; and, despite current vicissitudes, one can rightly add India, Brazil, Peru, and Chile.

None of these countries is rich in terms of income per capita by the standards of Western Europe, Japan, or the United States. All face real and difficult problems in maintaining the momentum they have established. But the most important demonstration of all has taken place; namely, that by their own efforts, with a margin of international support, they have the capacity to move into sustained growth and begin to fashion modern societies, capable of applying the best in contemporary science and technology, on terms which are consistent with their own history and culture and their own visions of the future.

That inner confidence – the confidence that, to a significant degree, the nations and peoples of the developing world have the capacity to shape their own destinies in a modern environment – is the most important single component for successful economic and social development.

Meanwhile, in a remarkable and unexpected surge, a breakthrough in agricultural yields has proved feasible, buying time many of us feared we did not have for policies of population control to take hold. There is a decent hope, at least, that the Malthusian crisis we feared would certainly occur in the course of the 1970s and 1980s can be avoided; although the birth rate in the developing world remains a formidable barrier in the path of progress.

In short, there is a serious sense in which we – that is, all those everywhere who have worked at the task – have succeeded in making the 1960s the Decade of Economic Development; although the agenda for development in the 1970s remains formidable, as the Pearson Report suggests.[6] And even its agenda may not suffice.

Constitutionally, we have moved, much more than is generally understood, towards multilateralizing our procedures of assistance – converting them to an explicit communal effort, rather than a reflex of conventional national foreign policy.

The typical aid negotiation is no longer merely a bilateral arrangement between an advanced and a developing nation. It is a communal negotiation in which responsible men from the developing nation sit around the table with representatives of the World Bank, the International Monetary Fund, a regional development bank, and representatives of, say, Great Britain, Germany, France, Canada, Japan, the United States, and others.

This quiet international revolution has been little noted – and it is two-sided. Negotiations may be stiff; but they are focused on whether or not a nation's self-help measures justify the allocation of resources from abroad.

Typical questions are these:

— Are tax collections rising fast enough?

— Is the developing nation putting enough resources into agriculture?

— Is the educational system being modernized to serve the nation's needs for the future?

No one would deny that such questions have political meaning and sensitivity within a developing nation. They are an intrusion on sovereignty – as is the pressure to vote tax money from one nation to assist another which is less advanced. But if we are to act as an international community in granting assistance, they are legitimate questions to ask.

Money and Trade

In monetary affairs and in trade the achievement among the more advanced nations is also creditable. We have seen for a quarter-century an astounding and steady increase in the volume of international trade, conducted under quite liberal policies. And this has been underpinned by monetary policies which, while bringing us from time to time to the edge of disaster, have, nevertheless, proved consistent with the maintenance of a viable international monetary system, despite the waning capacity of gold as a medium of reserve.

This achievement goes back, of course, to Bretton Woods.

And the story of the Bretton Woods institutions begins with Article VII of the Lend-Lease agreement negotiated between the United States and Great Britain in 1941, signed in February 1942. Article VII did not commit Britain to abandon empire protection; but it did commit the two countries jointly to seek greater freedom of trade in the postwar period and to undertake wartime negotiations looking to this end.

With Article VII agreed, economists began to formulate schemes for a better world.

Although marked national differences ultimately emerged, economists and their governments agreed that low tariffs were a good thing; but they understood that more than increasingly free trade was involved in remaking an international economy. Between the wars, at various stages, nations had faced severe balance-of-payments deficits both in general and in terms of specific currencies; and they had been led to institute all manner of national practices to defend their balance of payments against such deficits. Moreover, it was a central fact of the interwar years that London had ceased to perform adequately this crucial international function. Financial power passed substantially to the United States; and the United States, unaware of its new international responsibilities, or unwilling to acknowledge them, had not effectively performed London's old functions. The economists of the West looked, therefore, to the creation of an international institution from which nations could borrow on short term, cushioning balance-of-payments deficits. Thus, vicious spirals of protective financial and trade policies would be avoided and the foundations maintained for a neo-classical international economy.

In one sense the new international institution was designed to guarantee that the United States, inevitably the largest and most powerful contributor, would this time behave responsibly as the ultimate source of international short-term capital. This, roughly, was the background of thought which ultimately yielded the International Monetary Fund.

The intellectual ancestry of the International Bank was mixed. In part, it was designed simply to supplement UNRRA and aid nations in long-term reconstruction projects which promised to yield returns sufficient to justify loans rather than grants. But at Bretton Woods the Latin Americans, speaking for the underdeveloped world, threw their weight towards the concept of the Bank as a source of capital for long-term development projects; and this notion was accepted, within the limits of the Bank's resources and its dependence on private capital markets.

In a larger sense, the International Bank, like the Fund, represented an effort to assure a degree of American responsibility with respect to long-term capital supply. The captious withdrawal of American capital from Europe in 1929 and after had played a memorable part in driving downward the spiral of international depression; and the Bank was designed to supply a more stable flow of (initially) American capital to the international economy.

Incorporated in the Bretton Woods agreements, moreover, was a provision which represented an American lesson from the past, painfully learned. Nations were permitted to defend their balance of payments when a foreign currency became 'scarce'. The United States had failed to acknowledge between the wars that creditor as well as debtor nations had responsibilities to the international community; and American tariff policy combined with the irregularity of American capital movements had created between the wars a mild version of the 'dollar shortage' that was to obsess the post-1945 world economy. The 'scarce-currency' provision in the Bretton Woods agreements, volunteered at American initiative, represented not merely an important concession to the views of other nations but also a frame of mind and level of international understanding among responsible Americans that were to contribute to later, more substantial American efforts to set the international economy on its feet.

So much by way of aspiration and conception.

But, of course, the resources made available to the International Monetary Fund and the World Bank were not sufficient to do the job by themselves. And the United States had to assume more directly some of the responsibilities implicit in the Bretton Woods arrangements.

Specifically, the Marshall Plan and the United States willingness purposefully to run a balance of payments deficit provided both a flow of capital to the world and a means for building up monetary reserves depleted during the war. And the fact that Marshall Plan allocations were made in terms of dollar deficits rather than overall deficits permitted Britain and France to maintain a flow of capital to their currency areas.

By the end of the 1950s, however, the United States deficit began to become an anxiety to the United States and the world community rather than a simple blessing. Through the 1960s we have had to build slowly the attitudes and the policies required for the long pull in a world where deficits and surpluses are bound to shift as among the major monetary powers, imposing adjustment responsibilities on both deficit and surplus countries.

In recent years we have scrambled through the adjustments to the British devaluation of November 1967, the two-price gold system of March 1968, and the French crisis of November 1968. In every case the international community confronted situations which, if not handled with loyalty to the international monetary system, could have led us down the road of 1929–33. In each case a rational *ad hoc* solution was found on a common basis.

But, evidently, this is not good enough. The stability of the international monetary system requires urgently not merely the IMF Special Drawing Rights but a deeper commitment to the principle of adjustment by surplus as well as deficit nations on behalf of the international system. Whether those adjustments are via trade, limited exchange rate flexibility, or both, is of secondary importance. And it is also clear that the international monetary system will not prove viable unless nations are prepared to treat their domestic dispositions with respect to wage and price policy as a matter of international responsibility. It is not difficult to understand the German feeling in the summer of 1968 that they were being put under international pressure, because their wage–price discipline was better than that of certain other nations. The advanced democracies have no other rational course than to create, as soon as persistent education and advocacy make possible, the deep understandings within their societies required for carrying out wage–price guidelines, in which wage increases are effectively linked to the average increase in national productivity. These sensitive domestic issues will have to become, in an important sense, international issues before the world monetary system is firm and stable.

In a community of sovereign governments, the non-Communist world has, then, moved some distance down the road to fulfilling the functions which governments perform. However imperfectly, there is a recognition in the parliaments of the developed world that a communal duty exists to the developing nations. As noted above (p. 274–5), it is a remarkable fact that the net official flow of financial resources from the sixteen nations on the Development Assistance Committee (DAC) to less-developed countries and multilateral agencies dedicated to their support was some $7 billion in 1968. The criterion of 1 per cent of GNP to be allocated for development purposes has not been met by the DAC nations as a whole. Development aid is clearly not what it ought to be – notably in the United States where official aid flows have declined from 0.65 per cent of GNP in 1961 to 0.47 per cent of GNP in 1967.[7] But in the sweep of human history, it is a considerable achievement that we have come as far as we have towards a global conception of responsibility and interdependence transcending nationhood as it has been known, reaching deep into the most intimate problems of national households.

And so, also, with the trade and monetary arrangements we have devised, goaded on by the memory of how we nearly destroyed each other in the 1930s.

But the achievements are all precarious, all vulnerable. In development, monetary affairs, and trade, we are – as a community – still walking a tightrope across a deep chasm.

CONSTITUTIONAL ISSUES

Objectives

Article 1 of the United Nations Charter defines the key constitutional objectives of the system as:
— prevention and removal of threats to the peace;
— suppression of acts of aggression;
— respect for the principle of equal rights and self-determination of peoples;
— promoting and encouraging respect for human rights and for fundamental freedoms for all without distinction as to race, sex, language, or religion.

Arms and Men Across Frontiers

The greatest of these constitutional problems of the world community has been, of course, the problem of aggression itself; that is, deterring or dealing with efforts to alter the territorial or political *status quo* by one form or another of violence (or threat of violence) applied across international frontiers. We have discussed some of its Cold War dimensions as constituting the central problem of security for the world community; but it has wider-ranging constitutional dimensions as well.

The problem of violence across frontiers was exacerbated by the two quite arbitrary processes which shaped those frontiers.

First, there emerged *de facto* or *de jure* lines of demarcation between the Communist and non-Communist worlds. These lines resulted principally from the disposition of military forces at the end of the Second World War, although they were also affected by events in the early postwar years – notably, Stalin's consolidation of his position in Eastern Europe, the Chinese Communist victory on the mainland, and the Geneva Accords of 1954, reaffirmed with respect to Laos in 1962.

Second, a series of new states emerged from the process of decolonization. Most of their boundaries were products of colonial history; but in the Indian subcontinent, the Middle East, Southeast Asia, and elsewhere, the birth of new nations produced new lines on the map.

A great deal of the first postwar generation's history consists of efforts to frustrate those who sought to alter those international boundaries and truce lines by force: Communists, because they felt that they had the ideological right and duty to move their power forward beyond them; certain new nations because they felt a sense of historical grievance over the lines which had emerged or simply because they developed ambitions across those boundaries. At certain points the two efforts became linked, as Communists acted to enflame post-colonial ambitions, frictions, and discontents.

Self-determination

The issue of aggression interwove also with the constitutional question of how 'self-determination' was to be defined; for example, in Budapest in 1956 and in the Dominican Republic in 1965–6. It linked, as well, to the constitutional question of 'freedoms for all without distinction as to race' in the case of Angola and Rhodesia.

The meaning of 'self-determination' has been a searching, ambiguous, and unresolved issue in the international community. The facts of political life and political development rendered the imposition of one-man one-vote secret ballot elections by the international community an impossible universal rule. The Charter would not have been agreed if 'self-determination' had been so explicitly defined. But the question then arose: when should the overthrow of a government by force be recognized as a matter for international action and when accepted as part of an authentic domestic process of 'self-determination'?

At best, we have created only an uncertain body of common law in answer to that fundamental question. Generally, tolerance reigned: coups and revolutions were accepted as constitutionally legitimate if they were, essentially, a product of domestic political life. The critical issues were those related to the balance of Communist versus non-Communist power.

The Communist takeover of the Chinese mainland was accepted, in the West, for example, as an authentic domestic event, as was Castro's takeover of

Cuba. It is true the Bay of Pigs operation was mounted; but President Kennedy held his hand, in the face of its failure, avoiding full national commitment to Castro's removal on simple ideological grounds.

Moreover, with no great sense of pride, the West accepted as beyond the reach of rational and legitimate military action the Soviet response to the Hungarian uprising of 1956 and the Czechoslovak movement towards liberalization in 1968 – in both of which 'self-determination' by any reasonable interpretation of the United Nations Charter was denied.

As noted earlier, contentions within the Western Hemisphere have been dealt with, in the end, on a regional basis, although they have also occasionally emerged for debate at the United Nations.

In Africa, some conflicts have been dealt with regionally, some globally; notably, the Congo, South Africa, Rhodesia, and the question of the Portuguese colonies.

Without a relevant and viable regional framework, the Middle East conflicts and the Indo–Pakistani war of 1965 were dealt with through United Nations machinery, supplemented by great power diplomacy.

What can we conclude, in general, from this tangled, unshapely, pragmatic experience?

First, the Cold War struggle has not only posed directly basic constitutional (as well as security) issues, it has also suffused in varying degrees and generally heightened constitutional issues whose roots were essentially independent of the Cold War.

Second, where, for whatever reasons, the United States and the Soviet Union moved in parallel, the danger was reduced; for example, in the Indo–Pakistani war, out of common intent to frustrate Communist China's efforts to intrude into the Indian subcontinent through its tie to Pakistan; via the hot line exchanges, to achieve a Middle East cease-fire in June 1967, as the forces unleashed threatened to engage the major powers.

Third, to the extent that regional machinery could grip and resolve issues in contention, the dangers of larger confrontation and conflict were reduced; although the recent Soviet interpretation of the limits of 'self-determination' in Communist states poses a major constitutional problem for the future.

This is the case because it is difficult to envisage serious and sustained movement towards peace if the Soviet regime continues to regard as a mortal threat to Soviet security the kind of modest movements towards national assertiveness and liberalization sought by the Dubcek regime. The judgment here is pragmatic, not moralistic. As one weighs the balance of forces operating within Eastern Europe, it is hard to escape the conclusion that the forces of nationalism and liberalism are on the rise and that a rigid

323

effort to constrain them will yield progressively more severe crises, potentially more dangerous and disruptive in East–West relations than the Czechoslovak crisis of August 1968.

A curious, anxious, almost tsarist uneasiness now pervades Moscow's approach to its liberals at home as well as abroad. And this is a cause for hope as well as concern. Before 1914 Russia knew phases of flexibility and forward movement as well as of absolutist orthodoxy.

Regionalism: Solution to an American Dilemma?

As for the United States, President Johnson, starting in 1966, launched a purposeful policy in support of regionalism beyond Europe, extending to Latin America, Africa, and Asia the same underlying faith that has suffused United States policy towards Western Europe since the time of President Truman; that is, the faith that minimum American interests in the structure of power could be met if the regions became strong and moved towards unity; and that the American role within them could be reduced with the passage of time. That was, from Washington's point of view, the meaning and purpose of the summit meeting of American Presidents at Punta del Este, with its new emphasis on Latin American integration; of the policy of support for African regional and subregional institutions articulated to the Ambassadors of the member states of the Organization of African Unity, in May 1966; of the support for a New Asia, during President Johnson's travels of October–November 1966.

Behind all this was a recognition not only of the fact that the peoples of these regions wished increasingly to shape their own destiny, but also that the people of the United States, while not isolationist, were in a mood to let others do more and America less, after a generation of sometimes lonely filling of vacuums of power. Regionalism commends itself as a half-way house between excessive direct United States responsibility and an American isolationism for which there is no rational basis in the world of modern weapons and communications.

It is American support of regionalism – from President Truman to President Nixon – which distinguishes its policy from empires of the past, recent and ancient. Consciously rejecting the alternative of divide and rule, President Truman set a pattern of support for regional unity in Western Europe which conformed to the American instinct that its interests in the world's structure were real and abiding, but did not require intimate control and manipulation for the long pull, and could largely be met if others generated the strength and coherence increasingly to defend their own independence. The risks in following this federal path can only be fully assessed in the longer future; but they promise to avoid the certain vicissitudes of a more Periclean course.

Reconciliation: The Locus of Responsibility

In terms of the constitutional issues treated here, this mood and policy offer an opportunity for reducing the Cold War dimensions of certain contentious constitutional issues, leaving the way open for reconciliation and settlement on the basis of the local and regional forces at work.

But this possibility has a corollary, if it is to be fulfilled. It demands a growing sense of regional responsibility and increased capacity to take these matters in hand. For too long peacemaking has been regarded as business for the major powers, while lesser powers felt free to indulge, with acts of force across international frontiers, their resentments and painful memories from the past. If the next generation is to move from where we are towards stable peace, peacemaking must become everyone's business: from the borders of Cambodia to those of Israel; from Kashmir to Ecuador.

All of this is not certain; but it is conceivable.

The hardest reconciliation of all – the most intractable of the constitutional issues of the world community – may lie in white–black relations in the southern part of Africa. The presently limited power of the blacks to apply force has permitted, for the time, a policy of international gesture. And this is not wholly evasive; for no one can prescribe what a humane and peaceful evolution of the region would be. And there is at least the possibility that the imperatives of rapid industrialization will erode from within the grip of apartheid dogma. So we accept the gift of time and hope that those who live there will prove wiser than those who do not.

An Interim Balance Sheet

Having held the mirror of the United Nations Charter to the struggles, failures, and achievements of the human community over the past quarter-century, what can we conclude?

The image in the glass, like the human condition, is confused and imperfect. It is a different looking world than the optimists at San Francisco believed it would be. But there has been, perhaps, more will to survive the nuclear age; more capacity to rebuild and to build; more determination of nations to remain independent and men to be free; more ability to learn from past tragedy – than pessimists would have credited.

One thing the common achievements share: they are all fragile. But what has been accomplished constitutes a base from which we could go forward.

The tasks appear to be these.

First, moving from the mere frustration of aggression to a phase of settlement, reconciliation, cooperation with respect to endemic disputes arising either with Communist regimes or between non-Communist states.

Second, moving forward in the tasks of growth in the developing regions and, especially, coming to grips – as a world community – with the food–population problem where the danger of catastrophe has been postponed but not removed.

Third, carrying forward, refining, and consolidating the movements towards regionalism – in Western Europe and elsewhere – as well as the global cooperative enterprises in the field of aid, trade, money, and various technical fields which lend themselves best to universal effort.

Fourth, moving towards a liquidation of key issues of the Cold War in Europe, and towards arms control, while working to bring a more moderate Communist China – if and when it emerges from the current great domestic debate – into a normal and stable relationship to Asia and the world.

Taken altogether, they would – if accomplished – bring the major powers back to something like the relationship envisaged among them in 1945 and permit the United Nations structure an opportunity to fulfill its initial purposes – supported by a sturdy, federal regional substructure which might keep within bounds conflict between nations – insulated from great power interventions – where it could not wholly prevent them.

THE STAGES OF GROWTH AND THE PROSPECTS FOR PEACE

A Hopeful Possibility

What insight do stages of growth analysis provide in assessing the prospects for progress on this agenda over the next generation and beyond?

So far as war is concerned, the central fact in recorded human history is the ease with which nations (or tribes) can reach the conclusion that war is a correct and morally justifiable course, when they confront apparent weakness on their borders – or beyond, if they command the logistical reach. Governments have, perhaps, not abhorred vacuums of power; but they have certainly been systematically tempted by them. The Athenian delegation was historically correct when it told the Spartans:[8] 'We have done nothing extraordinary, nothing contrary to human nature in accepting an empire when it was offered to us and then in refusing to give it up.'

The diffusion of modernization has given this abiding characteristic of man as a social animal a particular shape and sequence.

Even before sustained industrialization, it permitted the scramble for colonies by Spain and Portugal, Britain, the Netherlands, and France. And by the end of the nineteenth century the vacuums of power were virtually all filled, with Belgium, Germany, Italy, and the United States also in the field.

Aside from colonialism, we have also seen nations succumb to the temptation, at an early stage of modernization, to move against neighbors judged less strong; for example, Revolutionary and Napoleonic France; the United States in the War of 1812 and the Mexican War; Germany in the 1860s; Japan and Russia in the decade after 1895; and the Romantic Revolutionaries of the post-1945 era.

Finally, we have observed the major efforts of the twentieth century, by technologically mature powers, to seize the balance of power in Europe or in Asia: the Kaiser's and Hitler's; the Japanese militarists'; and those of Stalin and Krushchev.

Perhaps the most hopeful fact on the world scene is that the march of the stages of growth is operating to reduce all three types of temptation or palpably to raise the cost of succumbing to them. There is no automaticity here: the changing framework of the world arena in the past, brought about by the relative movement of nations through the stages of growth, did not, in itself, cause wars; and further changes will not guarantee peace. But changing power relationships in the process of growth increased the likelihood of war over the past two centuries, and could increase the possibilities of stable peace in the future, if men and governments are prepared to exploit them to that end.

The Balance of Power in Europe and Asia

As noted earlier, the forces at work in the environment confronted by the Soviet Union make less likely than it may have appeared even a decade ago that the seizure of the European or Asian balance of power is a realistic objective of policy for Moscow; although the Middle East and the warm waters of the Mediterranean and the Indian Ocean still, evidently, beckon.

The movement of Western Europe and Japan from postwar chaos and impotence to high mass-consumption; the gathering pressures in Eastern Europe to follow in that path, on the basis of national traditions which have survived a generation within Stalin's empire; the evident potentialities of China – with the nuclear seed implanted within it – if China turns to modernization; the emergence of a powerful Japan, with industrial capabilities that could foreseeably match those of the Soviet Union; the limited Soviet logistical, political, and economic potentialities in Southeast and South Asia – all tend to encourage, if rationality reigns, a Moscow more prepared than Stalin was in 1946 to seek a manageable and safe environment for the Soviet Union rather than one directly dominated by the Soviet Union.

And this tendency could be strengthened if Soviet policy unleashes the stage of high mass-consumption in the decade ahead. Again, there is no guarantee that the automobile age will lead Soviet foreign policy in any automatic way to a more peaceful cast; but Soviet life, in its widest sense, is likely to be substantially absorbed by the satisfactions and exigencies of its version of that stage; and this could have, by one route or another, its dampening effects on external ambitions.

Something similar can be said of mainland China and its abortive take-off. A concerted and sustained and wholehearted effort at the modernization of China is long overdue. Chinese leadership has, since 1949, experienced frustration in pursuing its external objectives: against Taiwan and South Korea; in the offshore islands; in its tortured, initially fraternal, now envenomed, relation to Moscow; in seeking leadership among the world's Communist parties and the non-Communist romantic revolutionaries. With respect to India, China's forays of 1962 and posturing during the India–Pak war of 1965 managed to generate an attitude in New Delhi evocative of Paris after 1870, without even acquiring an equivalent for Alsace–Lorraine.

Meanwhile, the contrast between their own relative economic stagnation and the vitality of Japan and South Korea, Taiwan and Hong Kong, Malaysia and Singapore has not been lost on some, at least, of the Chinese leadership.

It is not to be ruled out, then, that, post-Mao, mainland China turns, at last, to the process of modernization for which the Chinese elsewhere have demonstrated they are so gifted.

In the calculus of its leaders, the outcome in Southeast Asia, in the months and years ahead, may play a substantial part. If American policy should open a vacuum there, one must expect Peking to concentrate on filling it. But if a Southeast Asian equilibrium is maintained, by a concert of local and external efforts, the chances are good that mainland China will turn, for a generation at least, to the completion of its take-off and the drive to technological maturity.

There is no guarantee, of course, that round about the turn of this century a monstrously large and technologically competent China will not turn again to grandiose external objectives. But the forces within Asia itself, if harnessed in regional cooperation, could also present to such a China at such a time a posture of poise and strength sufficient to discourage expansionist adventure. The mass and momentum are potentially there, as well as American and, perhaps, Russian interests in their harnessing in cooperation. To build that kind of Asia is, evidently, a central task of the coming generation – not as China's enemy, but as a neighbor prepared to live in peace, determined to avoid the offering of temptation.

Regional Aggression and the Romantic Revolutionaries

In the short run the forces of attrition operating against the romantic revolutionaries – set out in chapter 7 (pp. 380–2) – promise potentially a phase, at least, of respite; although it should be underlined that, in the Middle East and elsewhere, the world community may face dangerous crises before the leadership, in those nations they now dominate, turn wholeheartedly from external adventure to unfulfilled tasks of growth and welfare.

Whether their pragmatic successors survive, and move their nations forward for a protracted period in sustained modernization, depends in part on whether the more advanced nations are prepared adequately to assist them in economic and social development. The successors to Sukarno and Nkrumah, for example, are laboring mightily against not merely the inherent problems confronted by nations at their early stage of development but also to make up the massive dissipation of exceedingly scarce capital and resources conducted by their predecessors. They need help.

If the world community is to enjoy the stability that can come when a nation finds that it can successfully move forward in modernization, enlarged resources will probably be required for capital assistance – notably, for India, Africa, and Indonesia. The preconditions for take-off is an inherently difficult and volatile process that can easily attract or induce external violence.

If a sustained shift in priority from external adventure to the tasks of growth and welfare is agreed to be a part of building a stable peace, the lengthy unfulfilled agenda of development should not be taken casually in the more advanced nations of the world community.

Some Caveats

The general argument for the increased possibilities for peace comes to this: with the age of colonialism coming to an end, and the movement forward in stages of growth of new nations and old, the temptation of stronger nations to extend their power against weaker nations is being reduced. This negative fact could be reinforced by the positive attractions of the next stage of growth in certain critical areas. Aggressions of the past have induced reactions of modernization and nationalism that are now rendering the world community potentially more stable in this dual sense.

In part, modernization is a military fact: China and South Korea have more technical capacity to resist attack than they had in, say, 1842, 1895, or 1950. But, in part, the growing inhibition against military aggression is psychological. It is one thing to move into a passive traditional society or a distraught society in the preconditions for take-off. It is a different matter to try to conquer – or otherwise take over – a modernizing society which has begun to define itself as a nation and which promises protracted resistance to sustained occupation or external control.

But, evidently, this process is no guarantee against violence across international boundaries:

— Russian fears of a mature nuclear China of the future could lead to a Sino–Soviet war in which Russia seeks to deny China a nuclear capability.

— Russian fears of nationalism and liberalism in Eastern Europe have already produced three major interventions with military force: in 1953, in East Germany; in 1956, in Hungary; in 1968, in Czechoslovakia.

— Failure to produce a stable Southeast Asian settlement could tempt China to intervene there on a larger scale, risking a major Asian war.

— The turn away from radical expansionism is not yet visible on the horizon in the Middle East.

— Frustration of growth in important parts of the developing world could induce a shift of policy from a concentration on modernization to external adventure.

— Above all, the problems of the more advanced nations, as they move beyond high mass-consumption to the search for quality, could induce excessive withdrawals of commitment and resources from the world scene that would unhinge areas of relative equilibrium and yield not movement towards stable peace but to chaos and enlarged areas of violence and international conflict.

We have come a long way in the quarter-century since Stalin's speech of February 1946: in Western Europe and in East–West relations; in the balance of forces at work in Asia; in the dynamics of modernization in the developing regions. But it would not be difficult to envisage future movement not towards order and reconciliation and progress but towards disruption, fragmentation, mass hunger, and renewed danger in a fragile nuclear world.

What can be said, on the basis of a quarter-century's effort against considerable odds, is that the task of moving in the next generation towards more stable peace does not appear impossible.

And those are about as good odds as man is ever granted in great enterprises.

THE STATE WITHIN US

A favorable outcome must be rooted in the emergence of new balances of power – regional and global – that make the use of force across international frontiers – direct and indirect – increasingly less attractive as compared to the pursuit of growth, welfare, and an improved quality of life within societies. Order within national societies has been built – often over centuries of bloody interregional struggle – not by ignoring the fact of power but by organizing power in ways which limited violence over larger areas. And, in the end, this is likely to be true of any degree of order achieved by the human community.

But one would hope that there could be more to it than that.

This has been an extraordinary two centuries in human experience. Doctrines of nationalism and human liberty, of revolutionary egalitarianism and manifest destiny have combined with the diffusion of modern science and technology to transform the world, for the first time in history, into a single, sensitively interacting community. This transformation was not mainly the result of an antiseptic diffusion of knowledge or search for profit. It occurred through an interacting series of intrusions from abroad and convulsive transformations of societies at home, in reaction to those intrusions. The working ideologies of men – the way they look at themselves and their societies and the external world across their borders and beyond the seas – are the product of that cumulative, bruising reactive experience.

The question is this: As memories of past humiliation fade, as efforts to achieve domination of others lead to frustration, as old ideologies prove themselves irrelevant, is it possible that more humane perspectives will develop among men across international boundaries?

Out of an understanding of his own cumulative experience will man come closer to balance within himself and in his nation's public policies, not through the installation of philosopher kings, but because he perceives more clearly the realistic possibilities open before him – those which are unprofitable; those which are dangerous; those which best promise a decent fulfillment of his private talents and tastes in a community with others at different stages of growth?

The thrust and counterthrust among nations and among groups within societies, as the tricks of modern technology were unevenly diffused, has tended to elevate those parts of man which Plato described in terms of 'spirit', Freud in terms of the 'id'. To use the phrase Lorenz evokes in a similar context,[9] 'militant enthusiasm' has not been difficult to generate as nations and peoples fought back against external intrusion and new men fought their way up within societies against powerful resistances, as modernization proceeded and they sought the benefits and prerogatives they felt to be theirs. To return to Kurt Vonnegut's observation (p. 11), men may be led by unfolding experience to teach a bit less 'savagery' to their children.

The aggressive instinct in man will surely survive; but we have demonstrated within national societies – and are hopefully demonstrating within such communities as the Atlantic and Western Hemisphere – that they need

331

not lead to violence across international frontiers. Indeed, one fundamental conclusion of this book is that modernization has been, above all else, a creative response to one form or another of prior aggression or intrusion.

The meager or negative returns from international aggression and the unfolding potentialities of modern growth could lead men to elevate relatively benign and temperate versions of 'appetite' and 'ego' as well as 'reason' and 'super-ego' in their dispositions with respect to one another, within and among nations.

Or, as Freud expressed it, at the close of *Civilization and Its Discontents*:

Men have gained control over the forces of nature to such an extent that with their help they would have no difficulty in exterminating one another to the last man. They know this, and hence comes a large part of their current unrest, their unhappiness and their mood of anxiety. And now it is to be expected that the other of the two 'Heavenly powers', eternal Eros, will make an effort to assert himself in the struggle with his equally immortal adversary.

But Ardrey's 'unanswerable question' is not trivial nor cheaply answered: 'Whether morality without territory is possible in man . . .'[10] Indeed, the diffusion of responsibility for certain critical security and welfare functions from national capitals to alliances – and to such international bodies as the IMF and the Common Market – may have altered already in some of the more advanced nations the kind of nationalism which evoked from men some of their best as well as worst qualities. But in the sweep of history the nation state, as we know it, came late. The territorial imperative initially operated over areas smaller than the nation state. Man has exhibited a certain federal gift in distributing his loyalty to family, town, state, nation, and to common causes beyond.

Certainly, we have to see if this capacity can be extended; for we still surely need the catalogue of virtues Ardrey finds rooted in the territorial imperative:[11] 'Our capacities for sacrifice, for altruism, for sympathy, for trust, for responsibilities to other than self-interest, for honesty, for charity, for friendship and love, for social amity and mutual interdependence. . .'

Behind it all is the fact that modern science and technology have rendered all men brothers whether they like it or not; by creating a network of intimate interaction which links the domestic life of nations to their external dispositions as never before, quite irrespective of distance and ideology, postures of amity or hostility or indifference. One can hope that this fact would gradually strengthen the theological and humane counsel in our cultures that human brotherhood is, in fact, the ultimate reality.

But if higher precept does not suffice, hard experience may lead men to find livable compromise on the basis of the dictum of Charles Curtis:[12] 'It may be that truth is best sought in the market of free speech, but the best decisions are neither bought nor sold. They are the result of disagreement, where the last word is not "I admit you're right," but "I've got to live with the son of a bitch, haven't I?"' Written about race relations in the United States, it contains the kernel of wisdom most needed in diplomacy to take the human race through the generation ahead towards stable peace.

The better balancing of the state within us can be strengthened not only by returning, as Lorenz suggests, to the old precept 'know thyself',[13] but also, perhaps, by a fresh view of history – of where we have come from; of the role of violence in our story; the dangers to which dreams and passions from the past might take us; and the humane possibilities open if we can generate sufficient perspective, balance, and moderation.

To contribute to that end is one purpose of this book which arrives by a long and private route at the judgment long incorporated in the concepts of the golden mean and Confucian balance: it is unwise and dangerous for man to press excessively one strand in his nature and for nations to press excessively one strand in their interests.

No one can teach and write the story it encompasses without a sense of the irony and, even, the humor of the human experience in these past two centuries in seizing, harnessing, and seeking to exploit the Newtonian perception. There is an element of clownishness in the ardors and postures, triumphs and pratfalls that have brought us to where we are. But laughter, too, is part of finding the balance that will permit us to survive and go on, as Joyce Cary perceived when the dying Gulley Jimson gaily reviews his life to the concerned nun on the way to the hospital:[14] 'It's dangerous for you to talk, you're very seriously ill.' '. . . I should laugh all round my neck at this minute if my shirt wasn't a bit on the tight side.' 'It would be better for you to pray.' 'Same thing, mother.'

THE VIEWS OF OTHERS IN RELATION TO THE APPROACH TAKEN HERE

Reasons for this appendix

A book stands on its own feet. It is judged useful by others to the extent that it illuminates problems that interest them. Those engaged in the study of politics are thoroughly capable of assessing this book in relation to their concerns.

This Appendix presents the view I have formed of the present state of the study of political development; and the relation of this book to that rich and lively literature. The treatment here of that literature will be illustrative rather than encyclopedic. This Appendix is an essay in ideas rather than bibliography.

The rationale for this Appendix is the following. First, I have been for many years a friendly and respectful observer of modern political science, especially of that part of it focused on political development. In the 1950s at M.I.T., for eight years in government, and in writing this book and teaching its substance, I have read and profited from the efforts of those who have sought to use new methods in studying the oldest of man's problems: how to rule himself. It is possible that the perspective on those efforts of an historian and economist, who has also had the occasion to study and participate in political life, may prove marginally helpful to those fully engaged in the field.

Second, it is my impression that the field is now fragmented but capable of greater unity than it has thus far attained. I believe I understand the reasons for that fragmentation. I would hope that the approach used in this book might contribute something to movement towards a unity which, as the Introduction suggests, might permit the insights of modern political science better to illuminate practical problems of the contemporary world. (I am also aware that the only unity I may encourage is united opposition to my views; but even that kind of debate can be fruitful.)

Third, in writing this book I have sought to solve much the same problems with which contemporary political scientists appear to be wrestling; and an explicit comparison of our respective methods, however different they may be, could, perhaps, contribute something to the ongoing discussion of method in political science. Indeed, *Politics and the Social Sciences*, edited by Seymour Lipset, touches on many of the issues raised in what follows – an effort independently undertaken but which can be regarded as one man's attempt to resolve the problems raised in that interesting symposium.

Social theory and politics

Although many minds and methods are now at work in political science, it is, I believe, fair to say that the major revolution of the past generation, notably in the study of political development, has been to bring the General Theory of Action to bear on the field – the body of concepts with which Talcott Parsons and Edward Shils are particularly associated, but to which a host of others have contributed. They have influenced us all, even those who have disagreed with their approach, or with aspects of it.

Modern social theory was evoked in the study of politics for an excellent reason. Political scientists were turning away from the methods and categories used in the study of the advanced democracies of the Atlantic world. They, like their colleagues in economics, were captured by the drama and the challenge of Asia, the Middle East, Africa, and Latin America, as they moved forward to modernize their life in the widest sense. In these regions few of the implicit assumptions about politics derived from the contemporary Atlantic world applied. One had to look afresh at the cultural, social, and institutional underpinnings of the political process to understand what was going on, just as economists had to go beyond the world of Keynesian income analysis if they were to understand and prescribe for the process of growth in what came to be known as the developing world.

It is natural, therefore, that the major studies of political development of the past generation tend to have built into them the concepts and language of modern sociology. In the widest sense, their projects and their conclusions have been governed by the questions posed by modern sociology.

This is true, for example, of the distinguished Studies in Political Development sponsored by the Committee on Comparative Politics of the Social Science Research Council. Their subject matter suggests the areas of interest that flowed from social theory: communications, bureaucracy, education, political culture, and political parties. The underlying sub-structure of social theory is suggested by the common headings used in Almond and Coleman's path-breaking survey of 1960, *The Politics of the Developing Areas*: processes of change; political groups and political functions; governmental structures and authoritative functions; political integration. A similar theoretical matrix lies at the base of David Apter's *The Politics of Modernization, Old Societies and New States,* edited by Clifford Geertz, and other efforts of lesser generality in the field of political modernization.

The turn of economists to fundamental problems of economic development in nations where not much of modern technology has been absorbed led them to look afresh at economic history as the story of growth. Similarly, the new interest of political scientists stimulated a fresh look at political history as the story of political development. And this yielded the comparative study of *Political Modernization in Japan and Turkey,* edited by Robert E. Ward and Dankwart A. Rustow, and many other retrospective studies, including Cyril Black's *The Dynamics of Modernization,* S. N. Eisenstadt's *The Political Systems of Empires,* Robert T. Holt and John E. Turner's *The Political Basis of Economic Development.* Samuel P. Huntington's *Political Order in Changing Societies* is also rich in its interweaving of historical and contemporary cases.

Limitations of the general theory of action

But, like any method, the General Theory of Action has its limitations. It is from the character of these limitations that the shape of contemporary political science – and its fragmentation – derives.

The editors of *World Politics* once prevailed upon me to review *Towards a General Theory of Action* (Talcott Parsons and Edward A. Shils, ed.). If I return to that review (July 1953) seventeen years later it is only because I find in the contemporary literature of political development precisely the limitations I then defined in this structure of thought – a structure much elaborated over intervening years but rooted still in the concepts defined in that book.

I shall proceed by first indicating the problem areas; and then – once they are arrayed – consider how each has been dealt with in the contemporary literature on political development and in this book.

First, the role of culture (pp. 536–8 of the *World Politics* review article). The anthropologists among the authors of *Towards a General Theory of Action* were uneasy about the role assigned to culture. Culture was introduced from outside the theoretical structure; but it played the essential role of giving substance to the cognitive, cathectic, and evaluative modes of orientation which led men to act in particular ways in particular circumstances, with respect to the objects of orientation. And culture itself was one of the objects of orientation. This led Professor Kluckhohn, speaking for the anthropologists, to dissent as follows (quoted, p. 537): . . . 'the present statement does not give full weight to the extent to which roles are culturally defined, social structure is part of the cultural map, the social system is built upon girders supplied by explicit and implicit culture.'

This genteel debate among mutually respectful colleagues engaged in a common enterprise underlined both the problem of how to introduce culture into social analysis and the limited sense in which the General Theory of Action was general. I concluded (p. 538): 'It is a general theory [of action] in that it sets a frame for analyzing all particular decisions by action units; it is not a frame for the general analysis of whole societies.' I noted that it was, in fact, a form of Marshallian partial equilibrium analysis (pp. 537–8), where tastes are given from outside the system in the case of the consumer, and the market and cost environment are externally given, in the case of the producer.

In the General Theory of Action, individuals (or other action units) are seen as maximizing their gratification (or minimizing their deprivation) by making a series of choices among the alternatives they perceive to be open to them. They act, however, in a social context in which they perform a range of functional 'roles'. From this notion flow concepts of individual and social equilibrium, achieved through complementarity of expectations of performance. The individual is well adjusted when his perception of his environment and his evaluation of various alternatives converge with his cathectic judgments (or feelings) about gratification. Since his environment embraces other individuals and the social system, this, in turn, implies that his expectations of gratification conform to what others expect of him in his various roles. A social system is harmonious when the roles which define it, for purposes of a theory of action, correspond to the expectations of the various role-players concerning their respective performances. Given the determinants of action, these optimizing conceptions, in turn, imply widely shared concepts for defining situations, shared expectations of gratification, and shared conceptions of value: in short, a common culture.

Parsons and Shils developed another tool: five pattern variables. They are an effort to define and to relate the dilemmas men and social units confront in action. By definition, action is a choice among alternatives, and the three modes of orientation need not lead to action in the same direction. The five choices are designed to be exhaustive, and thus to embrace every conceivable kind of human or social action: (1) the choice between gratification and evaluation, pleasure or duty (affectivity *vs.* affective neutrality); (2) the choice between a personal view of an object and a view in terms of its significance for the society or social unit (self-orientation *vs.* collectivity-orientation); (3) the choice between an evaluation of the object in terms of its relation to the actor and an evaluation in terms of its relation to the whole social structure, or some lesser entity larger than the actor (universalism *vs.*

particularism); (4) the choice between seeing the object in terms of its performance qualities rather than in terms of some believed inherent qualities (ascription *vs.* achievement); and (5) the choice between conceding to the object of orientation an undefined but general set of rights and conceding only a clearly specified set of rights (diffuseness *vs.* specificity).

The pattern variables represented an hypothesis of substance. After commenting on their limitations I observed: 'They underline the fact that individuals, social units, and societies, in their widest, most conventional sense, can elevate one human quality or relationship only at the cost of another; and they thus dramatize the unavoidable problem of choice that men confront in coping with their total environment – a choice that extends even to the heart of their value system.'

The pattern variables have been, I believe, the conscious or unconscious framework within which most analysts of non-western societies have viewed the psychological, social, and political transition from traditional to modern societies.

Now, what problems are raised by this Theory of Action?

One is the difficulty of re-assembling the whole individual, once he is dismantled into his component roles. Harold Lasswell's observation, quoted in chapter 1 (p. 8), applies, after a fashion: 'Political science without biography is a form of taxidermy.' Individuals play their roles – and react to them – as whole personalities, not as stylized, abstracted components. 'Equilibrium' of an individual in one role tells us little of his situation in others – or of his general state of contentment or desire for change in his total setting.

A second problem is the inherently static character of the equilibrium that emerges. The authors of *Towards a General Theory of Action* were conscious of the problem (see, for example, pp. 6, 26, 47, 76, 230–3, and 237 of that book). But the partial equilibrium nature of their theory and (as we shall see) its arm's-length relation to the economic and political sectors of society prevented them from coming to grips with how, systematically, their structure should be dynamized; for change arises substantially from the interplay of the economic, social, and political sectors of whole societies.

In assessing this limitation, I made the following comment which I would still hold to be relevant to the theory of action and analyses derived from it (pp. 539–41 and pp. 545–6 of my review).

Tracing the process of change in a society is an inordinately complex task . . .
. . . [It] always confronts the question of how the parts of society interact dynamically . . . Implicit in the whole approach of the authors is a non-Marxist interacting system. In their terms, action might change if the objects of orientation alter, if the content of roles were to alter, or if any of the modes of orientation were to alter. There is no assumption

here that change must be initiated from the side of the material objects of orientation: there is only a presumption that change, however initiated, will have consequences for all elements in the social–cultural system.

'. . . If, as is not unrealistic for most times and places over the past several centuries, we assume as the normal case that the environment – the 'objects of action' – of men and social structures is changing, what then becomes of the norm of integration? Is not a capability for adjustment to a changing field of action a quality different from integration? If, in short, the central problem for a theory of action is posed dynamically from the beginning, would its categories and even criteria for optimization not be different? Are not most problems of action, under dynamic circumstances, heavily concerned with understanding (and predicting) a changing set of objects and with choosing among conflicting value criteria alive in societies and men's minds at a given moment of time?

Few students or practitioners of the art of political development would, of course, disagree with this emphasis on the need for dynamic analysis. Indeed, by definition, political development is an inherently dynamic term. But a key problem remains; for modern social theory, due to its inherently partial equilibrium nature, denies itself a framework for weaving into the heart of its subject matter the forces arising from the economy; and even when social theory is applied to the social underpinnings of the political process, there is a sense that politics, in the ultimate sense, is left outside. To analyze the social sub-structure of politics (elite groups, parties, communication patterns, education, etc.) is a different matter than to analyze how actual political decisions are made and their content: or, to use the vocabulary of this book, how men, money, and obedience (or consent) are mobilized and allocated at particular times and places among the three abiding tasks of government. As we shall see, modern political scientists have sought to correct for this limitation; but it is worth noting how the economic system and the political system fell out of the General Theory of Action.

In 'A Note on the Place of Economic Theory and Political Theory in the General Theory of Action', the authors paid their respects to economic and political theory.

Economics was viewed as sub-theory of the general theory of action and separated from the other behavioral sciences on the basis of subject matter.

On this proposition I made an observation which foreshadows something of the approach used in this book (pp. 547-8):

Economic theory can be made relevant to the resource allocation process under a wide variety of institutional frameworks. The real difficulty arises from the fact that men do not necessarily so act as to maximize the economic possibilities open to them. Economic advance competes, in energy, time, and human resources, with other value objectives. This appears true in all societies, even the most acquisitive. The problem is how to indicate the extent to which the economic activity of men is either reinforced or diminished, in particular societies, by the attachment to values and the pursuit of goals other than economic advance. This is not done by bowing respectfully to the economist and getting on with a general theory of action ... A framework of the kind required would make economics not a discrete sub-area of action, but a part of the general action process.

(Mancur Olson Jr. writes perceptively on this problem in his 'The Relationship between Economics and the other Social Sciences: The Province of a "Social Report"', in *Politics and the Social Sciences*.)

With respect to politics, the authors of *Towards a General Theory of Action* made some observations which helped shape a good deal of the most fruitful work in political science of the next generation. They observed that traditional political theory has been more a 'philosophical and ethical explication' of the problems of government than an 'empirical analysis of its processes and determinants'. They noted (p. 29, quoted p. 549 of my review) that the role of government in societies varies widely and has

highly diffuse functions in social systems. It seems likely, therefore, that if the empirical focus of political science is to remain on the phenomena of government, it will not as a discipline be able to attain a sharpness of theoretical focus comparable to that of economics. It is more likely to draw from a much wider range of the components of the general theory of action and to find its distinctiveness in the way it combines these components in relation to its special empirical interests, rather than in the technical elaboration of a narrow and sharply focused segment of the theory of action, as is the case with economics.

On which I made this comment:

... in the analysis of societies the political process must be elevated, like the economic process, to somewhere near the center of a theory of action. Chapter 4, on 'The Social System', contains the following sentence (p. 202): 'The allocation of power in a society is the allocation of access to or control over the means of attaining goals, whatever they may be.' Power, in this general sense, can by no means be identified, in non-totalitarian societies, with political power. Nevertheless, in almost all modern societies, a substantial part of the control over the means of attaining goals lies with the state; and the manner in which that control is determined and the directions in which it is used is an integral aspect of a society's action...

In short, I have the same uneasy feeling with respect to politics, in this scheme, as with economics; namely, that a general theory of action cannot have it both ways: it cannot simultaneously claim to be general and, at the same time, maintain the arbitrary (but often convenient) specialist compartmentations into which the social sciences have come to be divided.

If my assessment is correct, then, political scientists have had to confront the following structural limitations of the General Theory of Action as they proceeded to apply its fruitful insights to the field of politics:
— the place of culture and national operating styles;
— the dismantling of the whole individual via role analysis;
— the partial, rather than general, equilibrium character of the general theory;
— the inherently static character of the theory which required change to be introduced from outside its structure;

— the putting aside of economic theory (and economic life) as a sub-system of the General Theory of Action (and society);

— the (in many ways correct) diversion of attention in politics to the empirical analysis of its social sub-structure, at the expense, however, of attention to the allocation decisions of government themselves and their interrelations with the society as a whole, including its international environment.

In the latter connection, I would add a further limitation not noted in my 1953 review: this framework of social theory tended inherently to focus analysis on national societies - or social sub-groups within them – and provided no clear linkage to the international environment, its threats and temptations. As the present book makes clear, this is a grave limitation in the inherently international field of political development, where intrusions of the more advanced on the less advanced – and the reactions of the latter to intrusion – are critical elements in the story.

In their own way, the many talented minds which have worked over the past generation on political development (and political science in the wider sense) have, explicitly or implicitly, struggled to overcome these limitations. In the passages that follow I shall try to suggest how some of them have sought to do so and how, out of that effort, the field of modern politics came to be fragmented.

Culture and politics

In a lucid and perceptive passage Almond and Powell (Chapter III, 'Political Structure and Culture', *Comparative Politics: A Developmental Approach*, pp. 42 ff.) return directly to the issues posed in *Towards a General Theory of Action* concerning the linkage of culture and the sociology of politics. They refer to a wide range of studies illustrating how that linkage can be brought about; for example, S. N. Eisenstadt, *The Political Systems of Empires*, Almond and Verba's *The Civic Culture*, Robert E. Scott's essay 'Mexico: The Established Revolution', in Pye and Verba (eds.), *Political Culture and Political Development*, Jean Grossholtz' *Politics in the Phillipines*, Lucian Pye's *Politics, Personality and Nation Building*, David E. Apter's *Ghana in Transition*, etc.

I would make two points.

First, the issue with which Almond and Powell are confronted – or anyone else seeking to elaborate a general theory of political development – is that the problem, to a significant degree, is insoluble. And it may be well to under-line this at the beginning. Nations are the product of unique histories. Over very long periods of time, patterns of culture emerge which suffuse their political life – and all other dimensions of their communal life. Certain consequences of those unique patterns for politics can be arrayed, measured, and compared. This, for example, is what Almond and Verba did in *The Civic Culture*. But, basically, there is no escape in political science from the study of history and from important elements of uniqueness in the cases. Put another way, when average behavior is measured, the spread about the averages is as important as the average itself. The field would be greatly strengthened if this fact were acknowledged and built into its vitals.

Second, I find the study of national character a slippery poetic field. I believe we can do better with what I call national style – which I once defined as follows:[1]

A national style – like the performance of a unique human personality – is likely to be the product of a variety of different elements. W. H. Auden once described T. S. Eliot not as a man but as a household: a high church archdeacon, a wise and passionate old peasant grandmother, and a young boy given to slightly malicious practical jokes, all living somehow together. The performance of nations is like that of individuals in that it combines discrete, fortuitous elements of heredity and environment, interacting, effectively coming to terms with problems (or failing to do so) in a recurrent fashion, building up over time relatively stable patterns of performance.

In dealing with nations, I am often driven back to this observation about individuals by James Cozzens:[2]

A man's temperament might, perhaps, be defined as the mode or modes of a man's feeling, the struck balance of his ruling desires, the worked-out sum of his habitual predispositions. In themselves, these elements were inscrutable. There were usually too many of them; they were often of irreducible complexity; you could observe only results ...The to-be-observed result was a total way of life. As far as the natural self-divisions in a human being would allow ... this way of life, conditioned all knowledge, all emotion, all action.

A national style is, then, the observed operating result of the complexities that yield a culture and national character.

Therefore, I have great sympathy with studies like Lucian Pye's *The Spirit of Chinese Politics*, an approach Nathan Leites and Ruth Benedict have also used creatively on different cultural materials.

It is in this direction, I believe, that Clyde Kluckhohn's debate with his colleagues in formulating *Towards a General Theory of Action* is to be reconciled. (Ronald Cohen's chapter in *Politics and the Social Sciences* should be noted on the difficulties and possibilities of linking anthropology and political science: 'Anthropology and Political Science: Courtship or Marriage?')

So far as this book is concerned, its heavily historical content flows, in part, from a willing recognition that the uniqueness of cultures determines that, as a science, politics must be substantially open-ended. Generalizations are not ruled out; but they are limited by the irreducible elements of uniqueness in the cases.

Economists are already far advanced in developing a balanced feel for what is general and what is unique in the finite number of cases of economic development within the human community. It ought not to be impossible, in time, to do the same in the more complex field of political development.

Role versus whole individuals

Whether assessing the political behavior of various individuals or groups of citizens in Athens during the fifth century B.C. or in contemporary America, this book seeks to deal with individuals in terms of a balancing process endlessly going on within them – a process which affects their actions, in different ways, in all the multiple roles they may perform in the society. How people earn their living does, of course, influence their political interests and attitudes. But the essential political calculus is between the multi-dimensional individual – in his setting – and his total environment as he perceives it. That interplay is obscured more than it is illuminated by the fragmentation of men into roles.

It is, in part, for that reason that I have not accepted as central to this book the suggestive but inconclusive definition of political modernization as embracing movement towards autonomy of sub-systems, structural differentiation, and cultural secularization of political systems (see, for example, Almond and Powell, *op. cit.*, pp. 306–10); for role analysis is closely linked to this formulation. It is, of course, true that a political system that applies more, rather than less, of modern technology and which seeks to administer a large, rather than a small, population will need more men who can manipulate modern technique. And, as Adam Smith pointed out, specialization of function is central to the efficient employment of modern technology. But I do not believe this economic, social, and political truism leads directly to the key elements which determine political behavior.

Moreover, when one can observe the emergence of specialized functions in government after the Zulu conquest of its neighbors; in the structure of the traditional empires when they were successful; in swiftly emerging Meiji Japan – I draw back from this excessively rigid sociological way of defining political modernization. In truth, a wide variety of social structures, suffused by quite different cultures, has exhibited a capacity to absorb modern science and technology – in some cases (e.g. Japan) while maintaining much of the old culture and, even, social relationships.

I take political systems to be progressively more modern to the extent that they can effectively govern societies which have absorbed progressively higher proportions of (then) existing modern technology. They will all expand their specialized bureaucracies along the way, spawn specialized interest groups in the society, and expand (irregularly) the proportion of GNP mobilized by the state, in response to the problems of each stage of growth and the enlarged inputs of resources available to the state, as the stages of growth unfold. I am not prepared to take these symptoms of the process as defining political modernization, because the range of possible social, political, and institutional patterns is too great.

Moreover, as noted earlier, there is a powerful static bias built into role analysis. In modern history men are not – and more than we often suppose, in pre-modern history men were not – engaged in situations of mutually harmonious role expectations. Equilibrium has not been the normal condition of man – but struggle to improve his net situation in an environment of change. And this was so even where change took the form of the rhythm of the harvests, war, or plague, against the background of relatively static structures of land tenure. In one Chinese village, for example, the records show 'no family. . . has been able to hold the same amount of land for as long as three or four generations' (Martin Yang, *A Chinese Village: Taitou, Shantung Province*, New York, 1946).

But if role analysis is set aside – or relegated to second order business – how does one portray the individual in society, seeking some kind of harmony or balance within himself and in relation to a changing environment, by maximizing satisfaction and minimizing deprivation?

Here I do not believe there is any real escape from a certain amount of artistry, combined, where possible, with the kind of sophisticated public opinion analysis which has developed so richly from the inspiration of Paul F. Lazarsfeld – and others. (Richard Jensen underlines the vast scale of this effort in the past generation in American political science in his 'American Election Analysis: A Case History of Methodological Innovation and Diffusion', *Politics and the Social Sciences*.)

Where modern polling techniques can be applied – or in-depth interviews – we can form a quite reasonable view of the shifting evaluations individuals make of their environment, the choices they perceive, and their preferences. We can observe individuals – in the state within them – seeking to do what governments do: array their priorities and act on them, within the realistic possibilities that are open, within the constitutional system under which they live.

Where we cannot have polls – and even where we can – I believe we need more imaginative efforts to evoke creatively how people actually feel and act in their special environments. Lucian Pye's studies on Malayan Communism and Burmese politics achieved much of this quality. So did Daniel Lerner's

The views of others in relation to the approach taken here

The Passing of Traditional Society and Raymond A. Bauer's *Nine Soviet Portraits*. Joyce Cary's *Mr Johnson* and D. K. Chisiza's *Africa – What Lies Ahead* tell us a great deal that formal social analysis would be hard pressed to catch. And so does Carlos Fuentes in his novelist's evocation of Mexico's evolution, *Where the Air is Clear*.

The best historians can recreate much of the human–societal equation from the past: Eileen Power's *Mediaeval People*, for example, Lewis Namier on the 'inevitable men' of the eighteenth-century British parliament; Sandburg on Lincoln. Kee Il Choi's account of Shibusawa, from his native village where he felt as a boy the impact of Perry's arrival to his retirement in 1905 from the boards of some hundred Japanese industrial firms, will, when published, add major human and social dimensions to the understanding of the emergence of modern Japan.

All that role analysis can contribute is in such efforts; but we are dealing – in the widest sense – with 'biography', not 'taxidermy'.

In the exercise in mapping which this book represents, I have had to deal with this dimension of politics rather more formally than I would have wished: in chapter 1 by linking the Platonic–Freudian view of man to the eternal tasks of politics; in evoking the struggle of the new and older men as the stages of growth moved on; in quotations from Cleaver, as well as Brimmer, in dealing with the Negro problem in America; and, at the close of chapter 8, on the conditions for peace. But I would hope that the rooting of this effort in Plato and Freud, rather than in Parsons and Shils, will stir some reflection and – hopefully – a creative response by others more gifted in capturing the whole individual in his political setting.

I wholly agree with Arnold A. Rogow's dictum: '. . .it is fair to say that the marriage of psychiatry and political science has never been properly consummated. . .' (in 'Psychiatry and Political Science: Some Reflections and Prospects', *Politics and the Social Sciences*). I have tried to make this book a contribution to, at least, encouraging the courtship.

Partial versus general equilibrium theory

One cannot tell – at least I cannot tell – the story of the movement of a whole society, in all its dimensions, all at once. This limitation – if shared – has its consequences for those who would accept the notion that societies are interacting dynamic organisms, with political, social, and economic levels, suffused with a unique culture. In my review of *Towards a General Theory of Action*, I noted (p. 541):

It is, perhaps, significant that those few studies in this area known to the reviewer which are concerned with dynamic problems are not focused on society as a whole, but on one clearly definable problem of change . . .

It is natural, therefore, that dynamic studies should be focused on problems in society where change is definable in conceptually quantitative terms.

I then cited, by way of example, three problem-oriented studies which sought to bring together the strands operating at different levels in American society around a lucid question: David Riesman's *The Lonely Crowd*, Samuel Lubell's *The Future of American Politics*, and Gunnar Myrdal's *An American Dilemma*.

In different ways the author's *The Dynamics of Soviet Society*, *The Prospects for Communist China*, *The United States in the World Arena*, and *The Stages of Economic Growth* are such efforts, as is the present book.

Here the question is: what political problems are seen to arise at each stage of growth and how are they resolved (or not resolved) in the course of modern history, if politics is viewed as the process of mobilizing men, money, and obedience (or consent) and allocating resources to security, welfare and growth, and the maintenance of a balance between justice and order in the constitutional system? On that problem I have sought to bring to bear what historical, social, economic – as well as political, diplomatic, and military – analysis might provide. The quantitative element built into this approach is the scale – absolute and relative – of the society's capacity to mobilize inputs for political purposes.

How does this approach differ from that of contemporary political scientists?

The answer is, of course, that they have perceived as well as I the gap between fine-grained studies of elements and institutions in the social sub-structure of politics and the political system viewed as a whole. They have reached out for a general political framework. There is, in fact, a consensus of a kind about what constitutes such a general framework. It is associated most directly with the work of David Easton and his 'systems approach' to politics, launched with his *The Political System* in 1953. Karl W. Deutsch produced in parallel a construct, more explicitly based on a cybernetics–communications model, in his *The Nerves of Government*. Others have elaborated this general systems approach; for example, Robert Chin, F. X. Sutton, and Neil J. Smelser in their essays on 'Societies as Systems', chapter 1 of Jason L. Finkle and Richard W. Gable's *Political Development and Social Change*.

The unsolved problems here are two.

First, the Easton type of model has remained, mainly, a suggestive empty box. The kind of sociological analysis of the sub-structure of politics, conducted by many modern practitioners, could not be linked in an orderly way to the flows of inputs and outputs which are the substance of government. I believe the introduction of the tripartite functions of government and the use of budgetary data to measure the shifting balances in outputs (as well as tax data, to measure the shifting incidence of the burden of certain inputs) give us a way of making a systems approach to government come alive. At its heart, government is budgeting and priorities. As indicated in chapter 1, there are limits to such a quantitative approach to government as an input–output system. But the work of Musgrave and Culbertson on the United States, Peacock and Wiseman on Great Britain, Andic and Veverka on Germany, Wilkie on Mexico, Shorter on Turkey, Oshima on Japan, suggests some of the possibilities.

And there is a large, promising literature which compares in cross-sectional terms the tax and allocation of policies of contemporary nations at different levels of GNP per capita, including the work of Joergen Lotz and Elliott Morss, H. T. Oshima, Richard Thorn, J. G. Williamson. (Richard Musgrave provides a useful bibliography of this literature in his *Fiscal Systems*, pp. 375 ff.) Its weakness, like all cross-sectional morphologies, is similar to that imputed to the Colin Clark–Kuznets, Adelman and Morris approaches, discussed below, pp. 351–4.

Specifically, it may prove profitable to link the analysis of public expenditures as a proportion of GNP – and, especially, the specific components of public expenditure – to 'stages of growth' analysis. This field of study begins with the proposition of Adolph Wagner, in the 1880s, that the economic and social outlays of the state expand with the passage of time and the progress of industrialization. It is evident, however, that this process is not continuous. As Musgrave notes (*Fiscal Systems*, p. 77):

In short, the ratio of public to total capital formation may be expected to be high at early stages and to decline at least temporarily after the "take-off" is reached. At the same time there may well be periods at later stages of development when the ratio of public to total capital formation rises. Much depends on the particular stage of income and its capital requirements, and there is little reason to expect a continuous trend to prevail.

The historical analysis contained in this book – covering, particularly, the U.K., Germany, U.S., Japan, Turkey, and Mexico – isolates certain linkages between movements in the security, social, and economic outlays of the state and stages of growth. The analysis here is not, of course, exhaustive; but the linkages noted are sufficiently suggestive, I believe, to justify further systematic study.

If one starts, then, from the individual as a tripartite unit in Platonic and/or Freudian terms, shifting his priorities in terms of his valuations of his environment in conformity to the law of diminishing relative marginal utility; moves to the notion of those with effective political power projecting their shifting valuations into government, under constraints and influences determined by the given constitutional system; and then examines the shifting

347

allocations of government among the three major outputs – one has the framework for a general political system of substance.

But here a second problem arises; and it flows directly from the partial equilibrium nature of modern social analysis. The budgetary data are a result, a reflection – a kind of score card – of how those with effective political power assess the pressures that weigh upon them and the priorities among the tasks they confront in carrying forward the three abiding tasks of government. A concentration of attention on the social (and cultural) sub-structure of politics does not generate the data which lead in an orderly way to an explanation of how problems within the economy generate demands for growth and welfare allocations. Nor does such an approach lead in an orderly way to an understanding of the calculus made, and the balances struck, by those who bear budgetary responsibility. (I believe this is ulti-mately the problem Giovanni Sartori is getting at from one direction in his 'From the Sociology of Politics to Political Sociology' in *Politics and the Social Sciences*; William C. Mitchell, from the other, in his 'The Shape of Political Theory to Come'.)

To be sure, decision-making has become a lively field of modern political science.[3] There are rational policy models, such as Hans Morgenthau, *Politics Among Nations*; Thomas Schelling, *The Strategy of Conflict*; Stanley Hoffmann, *Contemporary Theory in International Relations*; Anthony Downs, *An Economic Theory of Democracy*. There are organizational process models such as Richard Snyder (ed.), *Foreign Policy Decision Making*; Charles Lindblom's essays on 'The Science of Muddling Through'; Herbert Simon, *Administrative Behavior*; Richard Cyert and James March, *A Behavioral Theory of the Firm*; David Easton, *Systems Analysis*; Karl Deutsch, *The Nerves of Government*. There are bureaucratic politics models, applied to particular cases, such as Richard Neustadt, *Presidential Power*; Roger Hilsman, *To Move a Nation*. There are cognitive process models, probing the human roots of policy biases, such as John Steinbrunner's M.I.T. thesis, 'The MLF'; Erik Erikson's studies, *Young Man Luther* and *Gandhi's Truth*; Alexander and Juliette George's, *Woodrow Wilson and Colonel House*. There are external pressure or special interest models such as Robert Dahl, *Pluralist Democracy in the United States*; David Truman, *The Governmental Process*; Robert Paul Wolff, 'Beyond Tolerance' in *A Critique of Pure Tolerance*; C. Wright Mills, *The Power Elite*; Theodore Lowi, *The End of Liberalism*; William Appleman Williams, *The Tragedy of American Diplomacy*; Gabriel Kolko, *The Triumph of Conservatism*.

These studies do try – in one way or another – to get at the actual decisions of government rather than merely the social, cultural and institutional sub-structure of politics as a social system. And in some cases, real or believed

348

links are forged between forces working in the society, as a whole, (or in particular human minds) and the decisions of government.

But (excepting Erikson's work) this literature has been either mainly abstract or focused on the American scene or on particular American cases. The linkage between the forces at work in the political process and concrete decisions of government is not usually made in the literature of political development; although Samuel Huntington's *Political Order in Changing Societies* and Howard Wriggins' *The Ruler's Imperative* are beginning to forge the connection by going beyond the social and cultural sub-structure to some of the questions which arise in actually governing a nation. (I regard the opening sentence of Huntington's book as a wholesome way to begin: 'The most important political distinction among countries concerns not their form of government but their degree of government'; although chapter 7 above makes clear the values I attach to the creation of viable democracies.)

The framework used here for the analysis of decision-making would frame the issue in the inherently competitive setting of the three abiding tasks of government; and it would allow a place, potentially, for all the various elements which others would take into account. It would hold that governments, on the basis of the facts available to them – and their perception of the facts – array the choices open to them in a setting where the advantages of action in one direction must be weighed against its cost in others. How that calculus is made and the choice made within its framework cannot be deduced: it must be established by study – essentially historical study. We know that the perception of situations and of potential options, and the choices actually made, can depend on ideas and ideologies; on the nature of bureaucracies; on political pressures and how they are assessed within a given constitutional system; and – quite often the greatest variable of all – on the unique personality with the power to make a final choice within the framework of perceived possibilities.

Like culture, the role of the individual in history is real and powerful, within limits; and a serious theory of politics must leave play for both.

The static bias of modern social theory

We come now to the greatest limitation of modern social theory as a matrix for the study of political development: its static bias.

In *Towards a General Theory of Action* change is taken to arise from 'the sectors of unintegratedness – where expectations cannot be fulfilled in institutional roles or where need-dispositions are frustrated by institutionalized expectations or where the strain is not absorbed in safety-valve mechanisms . . .' (p. 26). In Easton, the capacity of his system to cope with externally generated 'disturbances' is the measure of its viability. Here is Almond's description of 'dysfunctional inputs' (from his essay on 'A Developmental Approach to Political Systems' in *World Politics*, January 1965, p. 207):

Suppose there is a depression and the unemployed in a political system demand jobs and food from the government, or a war breaks out and a neighboring power threatens its territory. Or suppose a new dynasty in a political system wants to engage in large-scale construction of temples, palaces, and tombs. Or suppose a political elite embarks on a radical departure in taxation; or requires a religious conformity of its entire population and suppresses other religions; or embarks on a large-scale program of welfare. Any one of these input flows may be innovative, dysfunctional – i.e., they may require significant changes in the magnitude and kind of performance of the political system. These dysfunctional input flows are what "cause" changes in the capabilities of political systems, in the conversion patterns and structures of the political system, and in the performance of the socialization and recruitment functions. What we need to know is how these dysfunctional flows affect political development, what kinds of dysfunctional flows affect what kinds of capability patterns.

This approach would treat as exogenous – that is, as an externally introduced new factor in politics – a circumstance forcing a change in inputs or outputs, or both, which would presumably lead the system to a new equilibrium. The nearest approximation to this kind of analysis would be what economists call the analysis of once-over change. And, indeed, there may be a virtue in conducting experiments in such analysis; for example, the political consequences of a once-over innovation such as the introduction of the potato into Ireland and China. But, in general, there are two basic limitations in seeking to apply the concept of 'dysfunctional inputs' to political analysis.

First, the dynamic interactions set in motion by a particular 'dysfunctional input' are so complex and likely to proceed over such a substantial period of time that their effects will be hard to disentangle from other dynamic forces playing on the political life of a nation. Political analyses of once-over change may be useful in only rare cases where the consequences of a particular 'dysfunctional input' can be tracked out with relative lucidity and isolation.

Second, one would hope that a good many of what Almond describes as 'dysfunctional inputs' – including some, at least, of the problems of security arising in the international arena of power – could be dealt with endogenously; that is, as forces inside the political process capable of being 'explained' rather than simply intruding arbitrarily on the political process.

There is nothing in the formal models of social or political systems, as a whole, which make change an inherent characteristic of the system. That is, essentially, why I believe something like the stages of growth must be married to a political model if we are to have a system for political development dynamic of its nature.

Again, modern political analysts have not been insensitive to the problem. They have sought to dynamize their analyses in various ways.

Those with an historical bias (like Cyril Black) have introduced, for example, the notion of 'defensive modernization' which bears a close relation to the role in this book of reactive nationalism in response to real or threatened external intrusion.

Others have developed, out of a generalization of history, a grand sequence of typical political problems to which their essentially sociological or cultural analyses can be linked: for example, problems of achieving statehood, generating a sense of nationhood, responding to rising pressures for political participation, and, then, to rising pressures for an increasingly equitable sharing of welfare.

This *ad hoc* sequence is suggestive and, often, useful. But, it is not universal; and, it is more discrete than life and history. Some nations at low levels of development have long enjoyed a sense of nationhood as well as formal statehood; for example, Ethiopia, Liberia, Thailand. China, from 1842 to 1949, for example, may be said to have had a deeply engrained sense of nationhood, although its statehood was badly corrupted. Moreover, in the nineteenth century, as well as in the twentieth, the demands for political participation and welfare did not unfold in a neat sequence. As chapter 4 makes clear, certain kinds of demands for both participation and welfare characterize early stages of industrialization while other types of both demands are likely to come later. Finally, the constitutional pressures for enlarged participation and the pressures for enlarged welfare, of different kinds, relate regularly to the claims of security, which have no place in the scheme.

In short, I would suggest that the approach used here – of examining the kinds of problems thrown up by each stage of growth for political resolution under each of the abiding tasks of government – is a more systematic way to solve the problem of dynamism; it is more flexible, and capable of greater refinement.

There is a quite different approach to the dynamics of modernization; that is, the attempt to link degrees of political, social, and economic modernization by statistical means. To identify all who have contributed to these exercises would require a substantial special bibliographical appendix.[4]

From such early efforts as that of Coleman and his predecessors to the complex factor-analysis calculations of Adelman and Morris,[5] two broad conclusions emerge: first, there is a systematic average correlation between the degree of political and social modernization, somehow defined, and the degree of economic modernization; second, there is a long-run, but not a short-run, correlation between the degree of democracy which societies

351

appear capable of sustaining and their degree of modernization; but there are important exceptions (see chapter 7, pp. 289–95).

There is no doubt that such statistical analyses give a useful feel for what societies at different overall levels of modernization look like in terms of a number of important economic, social, and political reflectors. This kind of work belongs in the same family of analysis as the economic studies initiated by Colin Clark and carried forward with such industry and fruitfulness by Simon Kuznets and those he has inspired. (By way of example, one of the most useful economic–social arrays is that of Hollis Chenery, reflected in the accompanying table.[6]) Like Clark–Kuznets' statistical analyses of the morphology of economic growth, however, they suffer an important weakness, especially in the context of the present analysis; that is, they describe the average contours of societies at different levels of political, social, and economic development but do not illuminate sharply either individual cases or the process by which the individual nation (or the abstract average case) moves from one level to another. In this sense, they recall the studies of children at different ages, conducted by Dr Arnold Gesell.[7] On the basis of meticulously observed behavior, Gesell tells us much about the average behavior of a child from birth to five years; but we learn less than we might from him about the problems a particular child (or the 'average' child) must solve and how he solves them in getting from one age to another.

As indicated elsewhere in this book (p. 179 n.), the stages of growth cannot automatically be measured in terms of levels of GNP per capita. (The author's task would have been much easier if it could be done in good conscience.) Those (like Kuznets) who accept an aggregative analysis of growth and those (like myself) who suggest the need for its linkage to detailed sectoral and sub-sectoral data start from the same point which Kuznets has stated very well: 'Behind all this is the increasing stock of useful knowledge derived from modern science, and the capacity of a society, under the spur of modern ideology, to evolve institutions that permit a greater exploitation of the growth potential provided by that increasing stock of knowledge' (p. xxiii, *Economics of Take-off into Sustained Growth*, W. W. Rostow, editor).

If this view is accepted, the measure of economic modernization is the degree to which modern technology has been effectively absorbed in the economy. This is a quite different matter than the level of GNP per capita, which can depend on the population/resource balance, foreign aid, etc. – as well as the degree of absorption of modern technology.

For this reason, the stages of growth are based on a sectoral analysis of production, where the absorption of successive technologies can be tracked out. They cannot be sensitively tracked in GNP data, or even in such ambiguous, omnibus sectors as manufacturing or services – or even chemicals or

TABLE 43. *Normal variations in economic structure with level of development (level of GNP per capita (1964))*

	50	100	200	300	400	600	800	1000	2000
I. ACCUMULATION									
1. Gross national savings, as % of GNP	9.4	12.0	14.8	16.4	17.6	19.3	20.5	21.5	24.6
2. Gross domestic investment, as % of GDP	11.7	15.1	18.2	19.7	20.8	22.2	23.0	23.7	25.4
3. Tax revenue, as % of national income	9.8	12.7	16.7	19.5	21.8	25.3	28.0	30.3	28.0
4. School enrollment ratio	17.5	36.2	52.6	61.2	66.9	74.2	78.9	82.3	91.4
5. Adult literacy rate	15.3	36.5	55.2	65.0	71.5	80.0	85.4	89.4	93.0
II. OUTPUT COMPOSITION									
6. Primary share of GDP	58.1	46.4	36.0	30.4	26.7	21.8	18.6	16.3	9.8
7. Industry share of GDP	7.3	13.5	19.6	23.1	25.5	29.0	31.4	33.2	38.9
8. Services share of GDP	29.9	34.6	37.9	39.2	39.9	40.5	40.5	40.4	39.3
9. Utilities share of GDP	4.6	5.7	7.0	7.7	8.3	9.1	9.7	10.2	11.7
III. LABOR FORCE									
10. Primary labor, as % of total labor force	75.3	68.1	58.7	49.9	43.6	34.8	28.6	23.7	8.3
11. Industrial labor, as % of total labor force	4.1	6.9	16.6	20.5	23.4	27.6	30.7	33.2	40.1
12. Services labor, as % of total labor force	20.6	22.3	26.7	29.3	31.7	35.8	39.2	42.2	51.6
13. Urban population, as % of total population	4.1	20.0	33.8	40.9	45.5	51.5	55.3	58.0	65.1
IV. TRADE									
14. Exports of Goods & Services as % of GDP	9.9	13.2	16.3	18.0	19.1	20.7	21.8	22.5	24.8
15. Imports of Goods & Services as % of GDP	16.6	18.7	20.6	21.6	22.3	23.2	23.8	24.3	25.5

Levels for 50, 100, and 1000 have been adjusted proportionately to total 100%.

All values are computed from multiple regressions for a sample of about 100 countries over the period 1950–65. The values shown apply to a country of 10 million population in the year 1960. Underlying data are taken from the IBRD, *World Tables*, December 1968. Further details are given in Chenery, Elkington, and Sims, 'A Uniform Analysis of Development Patterns', January 1970.

metal-working which are, in fact, collections of sectors with quite different technological histories. (Although still not sufficiently disaggregated, in my view, one can observe clearly what disaggregation can illuminate in the latter sections of Hollis B. Chenery and Lance Taylor's 'Development Patterns: Among Countries and Over Time', *The Review of Economics and Statistics*, November 1968, pp. 405-12. As the industrial structure is decomposed 'early', 'middle', and 'late' industries emerge, not unlike my leading-sector complexes.)

So far as analyses of the type conducted by Morris and Adelman are concerned, I would simply say that they could contribute more to the whole body of political science if they were conducted not merely in terms of GNP and other aggregative indexes but in terms of stages of growth. Morris and Adelman do, indeed, use a concept of 'low', 'intermediate', and 'high' stages of development which bear a family relation to preconditions, take-off, and (early stage of) drive to technological maturity. But because these stages are statistically rather than analytically defined, they are difficult to link with other types of economic, social, and political analysis. But, like Chenery's work, I regard the Morris and Adelman study as moving us closer together.

Domestic political development and the external environment

It cannot be argued that modern political science has ignored international affairs. An elaborate conceptual literature has grown up, linked in some cases with revisionist interpretations of the Cold War and U.S. foreign policy since 1945. On these substantive matters, the present book speaks for itself, notably, but not exclusively, chapter 8. But, just as the specialist literature on decision-making is generally separated from the main body of work on political development, so is the question of war and foreign policy.

The case against the abstraction of domestic political analysis from issues of foreign and military policy runs from one end of this book to the other. The intrusion of the strong on the weak – and its consequences – is a central theme, given the author's view of the international dynamics of modernization. And if there is anything I have to contribute from experience as a public servant, it is that such abstraction is unreal. Almost every chief of government I have heard speak in private related instinctively and directly his foreign policy and military dispositions to his domestic political situation and problems.

Moreover, history and contemporary political life underline the tragic truth of Radcliffe-Brown's dictum: '. . . at least a good half of the history of political development is in one way or another a history of wars.'

I would hope that the treatment in this book of politics in terms of the three abiding, competing, interrelated tasks of government – including security policy – and the inherent links of the stages of growth to the framework of international power and the temptation to war, will help bring the security factor into the center of political development analyses – rather than leave it for introduction as a 'dysfunctional input'.

Conclusion

The argument comes to this. The application of the General Theory of Action has yielded a solid and important body of analysis of the social, cultural and institutional sub-structure of politics, permitting significant cross-comparisons of historical and contemporary experience. This part of modern political science is on its way to being a useful sector of what one might call a biological science of politics.

In seeking to deal with its limitations, however, modern political science has fragmented into a variety of specialist fields:
— political cultures and national styles;
— efforts to assemble the whole individual, dismantled by role analysis;
— abstract general systems analyses;
— divers unrelated efforts to introduce dynamism into an inherently static structure;
— decision-making analyses;
— international political systems analysis.

This has happened because politics is not a special academic discipline: it is a special set of problems. And these problems cannot be fully understood unless all that psychology and anthropology, sociology and economics and history can offer – as well as politics in the narrow sense – is brought to bear. This is the underlying perception which has caused both the sociological revolution of the last generation in the study of politics and the present state of fragmentation of political science.

The structure that informs this book may help move political science back towards unity. It offers a more general and dynamic framework – through the linkage of the three abiding tasks of government to the stages of growth. This may permit the authentic insights and legitimate methods applied in these specialist branches to be brought into closer and more explicit relation to each other.

Specifically, this book's insistence on the inescapable uniqueness of culture – and, therefore, its unabashed, theoretical open-endedness – may encourage more work on culture, spirit, or national style, more work in history, and

355

persuade conventional social analysts to weave the findings of such efforts into their exercises in the comparative analysis of institutions and political behavior.

Its revival of the Platonic–Freudian state within us – and its linkage to the three abiding tasks of government – may free us a bit from role analysis and, perhaps, suggest new frameworks for polling, as well as more creative, even if free-hand, efforts to picture the whole individual in relation to his political environment.

Certainly, the three tasks of government – with its potential for filling the empty boxes with fiscal data, and its built-in competitive tension, governed by the law of diminishing relative marginal utility – should provide scope for making vital a systems approach to politics. Moreover, it should provide a focus around which institutional and social analyses of the political process can be linked to the facts and pressures of economic growth and welfare and to the mechanisms of the decision-making process, from both of which they are often substantially divorced.

The stages of growth, with dynamism built into it, may provide a more sensitive framework for posing the sequence of tasks confronted in political development; and it offers the experts in correlation a framework which suggests how societies get from one statistical level to another and the problems encountered en route.

Finally, the place of security factors among the three tasks of government, combined with the insights on international conflict built into the stages of growth, should force the study of political development to take this factor systematically into account.

Those are my hopes. It is for others to decide.

A note on the political theories of the New Left

Although this book is not exactly a New Left tract, two aspects of formal New Left theories are consonant with its structure: first, the insistence that man should be viewed as a whole, in his relations to society, not as an assembly of roles; second, the inherently dynamic view of politics, and its relation to what I would call stages of growth.

As chapter 6 makes clear, I do not agree with many of the propositions drawn from these formal characteristics of New Left theories. And it may, therefore, be worth trying to identify formally the locus of the differences in this Appendix.

I shall take Herbert Marcuse's 1966 edition of *Eros and Civilization* as a text, because, with its new preface, it seems fairly to represent New Left theory as a whole. Marcuse's neo-Freudian view of man and his view of politics, including its security dimension, are explicitly linked. The linkage can be paraphrased in the vocabulary of this book.

In terms of the tripartite functions of government, Marcuse appears to hold to these propositions: the security problem of the United States is manufactured by the forces at work within its high mass-consumption society: there is, therefore, no legitimate security problem for the United States. The growth problems of the United States are equally the product of the inner imperatives of the high mass-consumption society: the time of scarcity and of the need for toil has, in fact, passed. Since the disciplines of patriotism and scarcity are the basis for the restraints on the individual's full and natural pursuit of personal happiness, and these disciplines are now wholly artificial, men should turn to destroy the system which artificially constrains them. He bypasses the imperatives of law and order that might still operate in the more relaxed utopian setting of a world where security and scarcity problems have been solved.

This, as I see it, is how his argument unfolds:

— Man has over the centuries suppressed his instincts (or deflected them for social and cultural purposes) because of the common requirement to struggle against scarcity, to defend the community against others, and to maintain order as well as freedom in the common life.

— Thus, Plato's 'reason' and Freud's super-ego have channelled the 'spirited' side of man and the id into constrained and distorted expressions of the ego.

— These constraints and channellings have been essential to the building of modern industrialized nations; but the result of high mass-consumption has been still further distortion of human instincts. Therefore, the chains that bind men in an affluent society must be broken by reversing its upward course: '. . . Liberation of the instinctual needs for peace and quiet, of the 'asocial' autonomous Eros presupposes liberation from repressive affluence: a reversal in the direction of progress.'

— On the international scene, Marcuse's proposition is that a high mass-consumption society requires for its economic and psychological survival war and the exploitation of societies at earlier stages of growth. Thus, his phrase: 'Welfare Through–Warfare State'. And thus, also, he links what I would call the romantic revolutionaries of the developing world to the affluent white dissident:

'Revolt against the false fathers, teachers, and heroes – solidarity with the wretched of the earth: is there any 'organic' connection between the two facets of the protest? There seems to be an all but instinctual solidarity. . . The body against the machine: men, women, and children fighting, with the most primitive tools, the most brutal and destructive machine of all times and keeping it in check – does guerrilla warfare define the revolution of our time?'

— Finally, he commends sabotage of existing institutions of advanced societies as the appropriate response to both the constraints of affluence and its alleged expansionist course on the world scene:

'... the general presumption is that aggressiveness in defense of life is less detrimental to the Life Instincts than aggressiveness in aggression ...

'... The system has its weakest point where it shows its most brutal strength: in the escalation of its military potential (which seems to press for periodic actualization with ever shorter interruptions of peace and preparedness). This tendency seems reversible only under strongest pressure, and its reversal would open the danger spots in the social structure: its conversion into a "normal" capitalist system is hardly imaginable without a serious crisis and sweeping economic and political changes ...

'... Today, the organized refusal to cooperate of the scientists, mathematicians, technicians, industrial psychologists and public opinion pollsters may well accomplish what a strike, even a large-scale strike, can no longer accomplish but once accomplished, namely, the beginning of the reversal, the preparation of the ground for political action ... The intellectual refusal may find support in another catalyst, the instinctual refusal among the youth in protest ... in the administered society, the biological necessity does not immediately issue in action; organization demands counter-organization. Today the fight for life, the fight for Eros, is the *political* fight.'

I would question the moral and economic assumptions underlying these propositions as well as the view taken of the forces at work on the world scene.

First, the issue of ends and means. Recall Marcuse's image of man, freed from problems of security and scarcity: '... man intelligent enough and healthy enough to dispense with all heroes and heroic virtues, man without the impulse to live dangerously, to meet the challenge: man with the good conscience to make life an end-in-itself, to live in joy a life without fear'. This romantic evocation is quite incompatible with the life of the revolutionary and saboteur he now commends to the young. The choice between withdrawal from society to private retreat and professional revolutionary activity is real enough. Whatever the linking slogans – for example, make love not war – the psychological cast of the revolutionary is shot through with hatred, violence, ugliness, danger, and heroics – not living in joy a life without fear as an end-in-itself. What Marcuse asserts, in effect, is that the correct route to the life and values of his 1955 edition is through the violence he commends in 1966. There is nothing in history or contemporary experience that suggests the viability of such a separation of ends and means in politics:

'peace and quiet' have not been the fruits of violent revolution or attempted violent revolution.

Second, if I understand Marcuse, he would abandon current efforts to improve the quality of life by conventional means, and commend a concentration of effort on bringing down the institutions of an affluent society until the society as a whole can be reconstructed on lines he does not define except in terms of 'sweeping economic and political changes'. Other New Left writing is not quite so apocalyptic. It would recognize that those who can take for granted the benefits of affluence are, even in the United States, a small minority. The gap between the margin and the average – the minority and the majority – is covered in alternative ways: by inaccurate projections of what science and technology could rapidly achieve if properly managed; or by commending to the poor or striving that they forego the dubious blessings of high mass-consumption already enjoyed – but rejected – by the affluent minority. There is, indeed, a strand of the former view in Marcuse, with his assertion that 'the rationale for the continued acceptance of domination no longer prevailed, that scarcity and the need for toil were only "artificially" perpetuated. . .'

If Marcuse's 'reversal in the direction of progress' means what I believe it means, I disagree. I know no rational case for believing that net good would come for the poor of the world or for the affluent seeking greater personal fulfillment if, say, the American economy is wrecked; and the notion that the United States – let alone the rest of the world – has moved beyond the disciplines of scarce resources with alternative uses is, simply, bad economics.

The point made in chapter 6 about Kenneth Keniston's casual rejection of 'unfinished business' (pp. 253–4) applies; that is, if a society of quality has any meaning, in some of its dimensions it is going to be costly to achieve and require sustained constructive effort.

Third, it is simply not true that the growth and prosperity of the more advanced societies require war and the exploitation of less developed areas.

Any competent modern economist could design, for example, a post-Vietnam war program to maintain reasonably full employment in the United States. The real problem – technical and political – would be the proportioning of resources saved as between the private sector (via a possible tax decrease) and enlarged public outlays for civil purposes.

Fourth, I believe, as chapter 7 (pp. 280–2) suggests, that the romantic revolutionaries of the developing world are not the wave of the future and that guerrilla war does not 'define the revolution of our time'. For the developing world, the revolution of our time is the effort to produce independent, modern societies, true to their own cultures, traditions, and ambitions, societies that can live with dignity and at peace with their neighbors in a modern world and, perhaps, as they move forward, create more graceful versions of high mass-consumption, at less social cost.

Fifth, I do not believe peace in the world will be brought nearer by the unilateral weakening of American power and influence on the world scene, through the exacerbation of already sufficiently difficult domestic problems. I believe the right path for American foreign policy is a progressive shifting of responsibilities to others as they acquire the capacity to carry them, to a point where the United States does not return to isolation but carries, in some meaningful sense, its fair share of the burdens of international responsibility as we all strive for stable peace. But convulsive United States withdrawal would, in my view of the shape and dynamics of the world arena, increase the risks of conflict in the world, not bring us towards stable peace.

Taken as a whole, the extreme New Left – in theory and practice – holds up an attractive image of a human situation where the security of nations and their affluence are, somehow, automatically assured; and the disciplines of order in national societies can be relaxed in favor of justice and enlarged freedom for the individual. In terms of the three abiding tasks of government, this doctrine would assert that security, growth and welfare are already anachronistic problems; and, therefore, in the constitutional balance, liberty, as the individual defines it, can be fully unleashed, since the need for order derives solely from the imperatives of external security and scarcity. It holds that all that stands in the way is the mechanics of the presently structured advanced societies – notably, the United States.

The creation of a setting of assured affluence and security for men and nations – and seeing what man will make of it – is the object of much striving by many hands for economic and social progress and for stable peace. But if the analysis of this book is roughly correct, the human community still has a long, hard road ahead on which all it can summon in human dedication and endurance, talent and idealism – and resources – will be required for ultimate success.

To hold up such a vision – as if it were just within grasp for all – and draw from the inevitable frustration of its instant achievement prescriptions for violence at home and abroad – is a cruel deceit.

NOTES

CHAPTER 1

1. *Civilization and Its Discontents*, James Strachey (tr. and ed.), New York, 1961, p. 30. Freud starts with the proposition that man strikes a balance between seeking pleasure and avoiding pain. He then arrays the paths by which these balances are struck: the (inherently transitory) satisfaction 'of needs which have been dammed up to a high degree'; 'voluntary isolation'; 'becoming a member of the human community, and ... going over to the attack against nature'; 'intoxication'; 'master the internal sources' of needs via yogi practices, etc.; the creative pursuit of intellectual or artistic excellence; the enjoyment of art; madness; work; and love. On the basis of this illustrative array, Freud posits each individual as unique and concludes: 'The programme of becoming happy, which the pleasure principle imposes on us, cannot be fulfilled; yet we must not – indeed, we cannot – give up our efforts to bring it nearer to fulfilment by some means or other. Very different paths may be taken in that direction, and we may give priority either to the positive aspect of the aim, that of gaining pleasure, or to its negative one, that of avoiding unpleasure. By none of these paths can we attain all that we desire. Happiness, in the reduced sense in which we recognize it as possible, is a problem of the economics of the individual's libido. There is no golden rule which applies to everyone: every man must find out for himself in what particular fashion he can be saved.' (pp. 23–30.)

2. J. M. Keynes, *The General Theory of Employment, Interest and Money*, New York, 1936, p. 150.

3. Harold D. Lasswell, *Psychopathology and Politics*, reprinted in *The Political Writings of Harold D. Lasswell*, Glencoe, 1951, p. 1.

4. Harold Lasswell called attention to the linkage of Plato and Freud in these terms: '... it is not exaggerating to say that no one went beyond Plato's insight into the dynamics of the human soul until Freud penetrated once again into the lurid depths of the unconscious, and brought to the surface once more "the state within us", and revealed again the niagara of love and destruction within every living person.' (*Democratic Character*, reprinted in *The Political Writings of Harold D. Lasswell, op. cit.*, pp. 468–9.) Werner Jaeger's *Paideia: The Ideals of Greek Culture*, New York, 1943, explored this dimension of Plato at some length. Lasswell and his successors, in bringing Platonic and Freudian insights to bear on politics, have, however, taken a somewhat different tack from that taken here. They have picked up the notion of ideal personality types as they relate to democracy and totalitarianism; and they have applied Freudian insights to major political figures – some, like Erik Erikson, with great distinction. In this book the Platonic–Freudian elements of the human personality are seen more generally struggling towards livable balance in the changing environment they confront, projecting that private, inner struggle into politics. Freud, of course, is not primarily interested in the political projection of his system; although he deals occasionally with the linkage in general terms, notably in *Civilization and its Discontents*.

This is not the occasion to rehearse the dynamic process by which, in Freud's view, the id, ego, and super-ego evolve: for these purposes, the rough analogy between Plato's and Freud's tripartite view of the human personality suffices. I should note, however, that

Thomas Gould (and perhaps other Platonists and Freudians) would challenge the linking of Plato's spirited side of man to Freud's id. He would hold that a part, at least, of Plato's 'spirit' belongs with Freud's super-ego. This is a question that does not require resolution for the purposes of this book. I am prepared to leave it to the experts, and hope this book encourages them to go at it.

What I am asserting here is that there is a linkage between the contending elements in the human personality and the abiding tasks of government which emerge as man organizes himself as a social animal. The linkage is complex, not one-to-one. Men may bring elements of 'appetite' and 'ego' to issues of war and peace as well as 'spirit' or 'id'. In pursuit of wealth, men may bring elements of aggressive 'spirit' or 'id' as well as 'ego' and 'appetite'. I am simply noting that the two greatest scientist-poets of the human personality (Plato and Freud) came to a similar – not necessarily identical – tripartite identification of human complexity under headings which can be roughly related, in complex ways, to the political tasks of security, welfare, and the balancing of justice and order.

I am also asserting that to understand man in politics one must draw back from role analysis and view him, in all his societal relations, including politics, as a whole unit endlessly balancing within himself his multiple, usually divergent, impulses. The subject matter of this book does not, however, depend on a definitive solution to the problem of isolating precisely the elements which enter the balancing process. I am prepared to accept the drastic and imaginative tripartite simplifications of Plato and Freud as the best we have, without believing they are ultimate truth or require total reconciliation before use in this context.

There remains, however, the intriguing question of Plato's influence on Freud, and the broad similarities and differences in their views.

References to Plato in Freud's work and life are sparse, but relate to important issues or moments. See, for example, 'Beyond the Pleasure Principle', in *The Major Works of Sigmund Freud*, Chicago, 1952, p. 661; *General Introduction to Psycho-Analysis*, New York, 1924, p. 153; *Autobiography* (tr. James Strachey), New York, 1935, pp. 42–3; Ernest Jones, *The Life and Work of Sigmund Freud*, New York, 1953, Vol. 1, p. 56 and Vol. 3, p. 275 (including relevant footnotes).

The most extensive exploration of the relation between Plato and Freud is in Thomas Gould's brilliant *Platonic Love*, New York, 1963. He summarizes, at one point (pp. 14–17), as follows:

'. . . Freud deserves special consideration as a philosopher, and it is not grotesque to put up his theory of love as a rival to Plato's. That they are talking about the same thing, for all their differences, it is surely impossible to deny. Freud even borrows the word *eros* from Plato, and took great pleasure in an article published in his lifetime demonstrating the resemblance between Plato's theory and his own. To all the enemies of his new ideas Freud said: "As for the 'stretching' of the concept of sexuality . . . anyone who looks down with contempt upon psychoanalysis from a superior vantage point should remember how closely the enlarged sexuality of psychoanalysis coincides with the Eros of the divine Plato (*wie nahe die erweiterte Sexualität der Psychoanalyse mit dem Eros des göttlichen Plato zusammentrifft*)."

'Let us see just how closely they do coincide. Both begin with a concern for human unhappiness and both diagnose this as a civil war within the *psyche*. One of the antagonists, the lifegiving one, is in both cases desire, an upward desire for union, happiness, and fulfillment. As to the exact nature of its opponent, neither Plato nor Freud gives the same answer through his life. Both, however, recognize the play of a longing for release from life, the death wish, or μελέτη θανάτου. Both assert that self-knowledge is the only hope for happiness, and that this, in turn, consists of two things: an appreciation of that part of the self which is revealed only in dreams, and rationality – that is, an understanding of reality. Maturity is identical with scientific knowledge. In both cases the cure is effected by conversation. *Logos*, Freud says, is his god. The aim is to establish a harmony within the *psyche*, the ideal being "the man who dreamed in a way no different from that in which he thought while awake". The result would be a recapturing of a happiness lost at birth: every discovery is a rediscovery. Both men admit their profound debts to the poets, but both came finally to distrust the arts as antirational. On the other hand, art, like all great achievements and brave deeds, can be traced to love. Love in both philosophies is the great narcissistic pleasure principle to which all life-giving energy can be traced, including altruism, generosity and self-sacrifice. There is even an elaborate comparison by Freud between the power structure within the *psyches* and the situation within various happy and unhappy cities, remarkably like that which Plato worked out in the *Republic*. Although Freud, as a doctor, had regularly to accept society as a "given" in his attempts to help his patients to happiness, he was, like Plato, very well aware that neurosis was a social as well as a personal matter, and that whole societies, though creations of the *psyches* within them, might be so constructed that the love inspiring these individual *psyches* might not have a Chinaman's chance of fulfillment. Finally, both Freudian and Platonic theories, in contrast to Christian and some forms of the Romantic idea, happily accept the powerful and ubiquitous occurrence of the desire for sexual release as an absolutely integral and natural manifestation of the love which is the key to everything.

'No sooner do we say this, however, than the feeling comes flooding in on us that there are profound differences between Plato and Freud. One: the nature of the opposition between love and the other principle was understood very differently by the two thinkers. Freud supposed that love was a pleasure principle in a fairly simple sense, and that rationality discovered a reality which must unhappily limit this at every turn. Plato believed that the world as understood by the lover *was* reality, and that that which limited this insight was by definition irrational and therefore neither comprehensible nor ultimately very important compared to the other. Two: the coincidence of a drive in man and in the other animals signified very different things for the two men. For Freud the lower the drive the more it is to be honored – not only as being ineradicable but also as a key to what we really want and therefore what we must pursue if we are not to drift inevitably farther and farther away from fulfillment. For Plato, on the other hand, to say that the lowest common denominator was the important thing was to be unforgivably blind to the necessity of civilization and intelligence and to court bestiality, the most unhappy of states for any man. Three: the search for happiness as an attempt to recover a lost vision was understood in very different senses by the two. Freud could only conclude that we are forever hoping vainly to recapture a sexual bliss lost in infancy. Plato thought we longed for a true vision of the world as it really is – incomparably more beautiful than the young, the simple, and the ignorant suppose it to be. Finally, the two men came to opposite decisions as to the relation between sexuality and the other activities which can be traced to the same source of energy. Freud supposed that sublimated love, desexualized or partially desexualized attachments to people and things, though the source of great and necessary achievements, could never arise if we did not need a substitute for frustrated sexual longings. It never occurred to Plato, on the other hand, that it would make any sense to say that the more beautiful, necessary, and admirable expression was less natural or direct. From Plato's vantage point, Freud is the product of one side of the 'Romantic' movement, carried to its wildest limit.'

Gould notes (p. 188, note 24) the following literature on the relation between Plato and Freud: 'S. Nachmansohn, "Freuds Libidotheorie verglichen mit der Eroslehre Platos", *Internazionale Zeitschrift für ärtzliche Psychoanalyse* III (1915), 65–83. There have been other comparisons of this sort also, none very good, e.g., O. Pfister, "Plato, a Forerunner of Psychoanalysis", *International Journal of Psychoanalysis* III (1922), 169–74, H. Kelsen, "Platonic Love", *The American Imago* III (1942), 3–110, and Garfield Tourney, "Empedocles and Freud, Heraclitus and Jung", *Bulletin of the History of Medicine* XXX (1956), 109–23, esp. 114–16; and many people, e.g., Cornford and Dodds, are fond of making the comparison just in passing.'

5. Freud also recognizes the instability inherent in the obsessive pursuit of any one human objective: 'When any situation that is desired by the pleasure principle is prolonged, it only produces a feeling of mild contentment. We are so made that we can derive intense enjoyment only from contrast and very little from a state of things ... Any choice that is pushed to an extreme will be penalized by exposing the individual to the dangers which arise if a technique of living that has been chosen as an exclusive one should prove inadequate.' (*Civilization and Its Discontents*, pp. 23 and 31.)

6. See, for example, *Statesman*, especially p. 608, in *The Dialogues of Plato* (tr. B. Jowett), Encyclopedia Britannica edition, Chicago, 1952.

7. C. Northcote Parkinson, *The Evolution of Political Thought*, New York, 1958, pp. 17–18. For a vivid evocation of how the initial sense of ego identity is linked to maternal care – to the infant's problems that outside forces can and cannot solve – see Erik H. Erikson, *Childhood and Society*, New York, 1950, especially pp. 219–22.

8. Freud develops with some care, in his own terms, how this surrender to sovereignty – or 'civilization' and 'culture' – comes about. See *Civilization and Its Discontents*, pp. 42–5.

9. M. Fortes and E. E. Evans-Pritchard (eds.), *African Political Systems*, Oxford, 1940, p. xix.

10. Quoted *Time* magazine, 11 April 1969, p. 108. Mr Vonnegut confirms the accuracy of this quotation which was made initially in the course of an interview but never used by him in written context.

11. Confucius also accepts security, growth, welfare, and constitutional functions for the state, allocating a peculiar importance to the latter in the following passage: 'Tsekung asked about government, and Confucius replied: "People must have sufficient to eat; there must be a sufficient army; and there must be confidence of the people in the ruler." "If you are forced to give up one of these three objectives, what would you go without first"? asked Tsekung. Confucius said, "I would go without the army first." "And if you were forced to go without one of the two remaining factors, what would you rather go without"? asked Tsekung again. "I would rather go without sufficient food for the people. There have always been deaths in every generation since man lived, but a nation cannot exist without confidence in its ruler."' Charles P. Curtis, Jr. (ed.), *The Practical Cogitator*, Boston, 1950 revised edition, p. 87.

12. *The Spirit of Laws*, Encyclopedia Britannica edition, Chicago, 1952, p. 70.

13. *Loc. cit.*, p. 780.

14. I would underline that this tripartite view of the functions of government and the terrain of politics is not new. Adam Smith stated it, for example, with clarity: 'According to the system of natural liberty, the sovereign has only three duties to attend to; three duties of great importance, indeed, but plain and intelligible to common understandings: I. the duty of protecting the society from the violence and invasion of other independent societies; II. the duty of protecting, as far as possible, every member of the society from the injustice or oppression of every other member of it, or the duty of establishing an exact administration of justice; and III. the duty of erecting and maintaining certain public works and certain public institutions, which it can never be for the interest of any individual, or small number of individuals, to erect and maintain, because the profit could never repay the expense to any individual or small number of individuals, though it may frequently do much more than repay it to a great society.' *Wealth of Nations,* prefatory observations to Book V, 'Revenue of the Sovereign or Commonwealth', London (Rout-

ledge edition), 1890, p. 540. Smith goes on to foreshadow the input–output approach to government with this sentence: 'The proper performance of those several duties of the sovereign necessarily supposes a certain expense; and this expense again necessarily requires a certain revenue to support it'.

15. *An Essay on The Nature and Significance of Economic Science*, London, 1945 edition, p. 16.

16. Plato defines in Book 9 of *The Republic* the middle ground between the wise philosopher and those so governed by passion that only the law can constrain them (F. M. Cornford translation, p. 318): 'It is better for everyone, we believe, to be subject to a power of godlike wisdom residing within himself, or, failing that, imposed from without, in order that all of us, being under one guidance, may be so far as possible equal and united. This, moreover, is plainly the intention of the law in lending its support to every member of the community, and also of the government of children; for we allow them to go free only when we have established in each one of them as it were a constitutional ruler, whom we have trained to take over the guardianship from the same principle in ourselves.'

Plato clearly implies that some, incapable of ultimate philosophic wisdom, can absorb within themselves elements of balance and control that harmonize with the interests of their society; and this he takes to be a function of education.

It is to these internalized elements of the constitution that political leadership at its highest often seeks to appeal – not always with success; e.g. Lincoln's First Inaugural Address.

17. Frederic C. Shorter, 'Military Expenditures and the Allocation of Resources', *Four Studies on the Economic Development of Turkey*, (F. C. Shorter *et al.*), London, 1967, p. 55.

18. 'Patterns of Public Revenue and Expenditure'. On the American scene, this kind of analysis was earlier pioneered by Solomon Fabricant, *The Trend of Government Activity in the United States Since 1900*, New York, 1952; and Richard A. Musgrave and J. M. Culbertson, 'The Growth of Public Expenditures in the United States, 1890–1948', *National Tax Journal*, June 1953.

19. Richard A. Musgrave, *Fiscal Systems*, New Haven and London, 1969, table 4-1, pp. 94–5, where sources are indicated. Outlays to support the public debt are transfer payments within the society, usually strongly influenced by past military outlays.

20. This view is set out in the author's *British Economy of the Nineteenth Century*, chapter 6, Oxford, 1948. This chapter also contains the following passage on the role of the individual in history, which I would still regard as germane:

'The area for freedom of action afforded to the individual in politics is certainly not infinite; but it is real. Referring to an incident that involved F. E. Smith, Mr. Churchill once wrote: "This probably turned the scale in favor of Mr. Bonar Law's leadership, and may traceably have altered the course of history. However, it is always being altered by something or other."

'Within economic life, as well, technical conditions and the economic environment are given, but progress is achieved by the efforts of men stretched to the limit of their energy, imagination, and competence, as the history of any great firm will attest. There is, in short, a considerable place for the individual within each level of this structure. On occasion it may be proper to regard the course of history as inevitable, *ex post;* but not *ex ante*.

'Secondly, there is the question of motives. Is man in society basically economic man? Here only a very limited observation will be hazarded. It appears necessary to distinguish the behavior and motives of individuals from those of economic, social, and political groups. In devoting his efforts to the repeal of the Corn Laws John Bright was no doubt helping to effect a shift in relative economic advantage among the economic and social classes of Britain. One can scarcely imagine an issue more purely economic in its character or intent; and without its economic substance there would have been no such well-financed agitation. Yet Bright, the Quaker, threw himself into the great crusade out of the broadest of motives, as a whole man; and as his later positions on the Crimean War, the American Civil War, and the Second Reform Bill indicate, he regarded the repeal of the Corn Laws as part of a larger political conception for Britain and the world. There is little doubt that many of his followers shared the Free Trade vision, with its full penumbra of hopes for peace, democracy, and universal prosperity.

'. . . Men may seek in politics the opportunity to exercise powers of leadership or of oratory; they may enter politics from a sense of service or out of family or social tradition like Namier's "Inevitable Parliament Men" of the eighteenth century. The interplay of personal motives and impersonal political forces is, surely, a relevant and interesting aspect of the study of society. It appears necessary, however, to avoid treating them as identical.

'At every stage, then, the individual appears to work out his destiny within limits which, while narrow from the perspective of the whole evolution of society, provide, more or less adequately, for the expression of his full energies and aspirations. History seems to be tolerant of the individual if he avoids the larger illusions of grandeur.' (pp. 143–4.)

21. For an elaboration of this view in general, see W. W. Rostow (ed.), *The Economics of Take-off into Sustained Growth*, New York, 1963, chapter 1. For an application to the contemporary world, see 'The Past Quarter-Century as Economic History and the Tasks of International Economic Organization', *The Journal of Economic History*, Vol. xxx, March 1970, pp. 150–87.

22. *The Stages of Economic Growth*, Cambridge, Mass., 1960, p. 14.

23. Arthur M. Schlesinger, Sr., *Paths to the Present*, New York, 1949, chapter 4, 'The Tides of National Politics'.

24. See, for example, the author's *Process of Economic Growth*, second edition, Oxford, 1960, chapter 5, 'Growth and Business Cycles'.

25. L. B. Namier, *Avenues of History*, London, 1952, p. 5.

26. Aleksandr I. Solzhenitsyn, *The First Circle* (tr. Thomas P. Whitney), New York, 1968, p. 114.

CHAPTER 2

1. The conditions for this transformation are discussed more fully in chapter 3, pp. 56–60.

2. For a formal analysis of traditional economies under three different assumptions concerning their technological limits (no technical progress; neutral technical progress; intermittent technical progress), see S. C. Tsiang, 'A Model of Economic Growth in Rostovian Stages', *Econometrica*, October 1964, pp. 627–37.

3. E. F. Heckscher, 'Swedish Population Trends before the Industrial Revolution', *Economic History Review*, Second Series, Vol. II, No. 3, 1950, pp. 266–77. The surges in death rates in Sweden of the 1740s, 1770s, and towards the close of the first decade of the nineteenth century suggest the Chinese proverb that 'in every thirty years there is a small upheaval . . .' Ssu-yü Teng, *New Light on the History of the Taiping Rebellion*, Cambridge, Mass., 1950, p. 38.

4. For some fragmentary but suggestive data on income and its fluctuations in traditional empires, see Colin Clark, *The Conditions of Economic Progress*, Second edition, London, 1951, 'Excursus. Economic Comparisons with the Ancient World', pp. 542–67.

5. The dynamics of cycles similar to those described here have been formalized in the study of certain natural phenomena; e.g. fluctuations in the populations of two species of

fish, one of which feeds off the other, and in the cyclical interplay between plants and their parasites. See, notably, V. Volterra, *Leçons sur la Théorie Mathématique de la Lutte pour la Vie*, Paris, 1931; and A. J. Lotka, *Elements of Physical Biology*, Baltimore, 1925.

6. M. M. Postan, 'Some Economic Evidence of Declining Population in the Later Middle Ages', *Economic History Review*, Second Series, Vol. II, No. 3, 1950, p. 246.

7. *Idem.*

8. M. Fortes and E. E. Evans-Pritchard (eds.), *African Political Systems*, Oxford, 1940, pp. 197 ff., 239 ff., and 272 ff., respectively.

9. A formal theory should, if possible, identify a marginal case where its failure to apply illuminates the nature of the theory itself. The three African tribes considered briefly here are such a marginal case. The simplicity of their technology and level of life combined with the limits set on violence *vis-à-vis* their neighbors permitted organized life without the central mobilization of resources for the three tasks of government. They thus underline the role of war, the absorption of higher technologies, and the expansion of welfare in the creation of recognizable government.

10. *Ibid.*, p. 227.

11. *Ibid.*, pp. 227–8.

12. *Ibid.*, p. 225.

13. *Ibid.*, pp. 25 ff. and 121 ff., respectively.

14. M. G. Smith, *Government in Zazzau, 1800–1950*, London, 1960. More than the rather cross-sectional essays in Fortes and Evans-Pritchard, Smith focuses on the process of constitutional and governmental change in the life of the Zazzau, covering, in effect, a century and a half of political history. For the impact on African economic and political organization of large international trade (mainly in gold) see S. H. Hymer, 'Economic Forms in Pre-Colonial Ghana', *Journal of Economic History*, March 1970, pp. 33 ff. Trade (and its protection) as well as war is seen as a task forcing the elaboration of governmental functions.

15. M. Fortes and E. E. Evans-Pritchard, *op. cit.*, p. 122.

16. *Ibid.*, p. 128.

17. M. G. Smith, *op. cit.*, p. 5.

18. On slavery in Greece from the Persian Wars to Alexander, see William L. Westermann, *The Slave Systems of Greek and Roman Antiquity*, Philadelphia, 1955, pp. 5–27. Westermann notes an increased demand for slave labor in the fifth century due to 'constant wars and the steady demand for war materials, and the withdrawal of citizen workers from the labor market both by recruitment of service in the field of war and through the increased political demands upon their time arising from the steady course of democratization' (p. 7).

19. *The Cambridge Ancient History*, Vol. 5, Cambridge, 1927, p. 16.

20. *Ibid.*, p. 31.

21. A. J. Toynbee, *Hellenism*, New York and London, 1959, p. 107.

22. M. Rostovtzeff, *History of the Ancient World*, Vol. 1, Oxford, 1926, p. 275.

23. Thucydides, *History of the Peloponnesian War* (tr. Rex Warner, Penguin edition), 1954, p. 62.

24. *The Cambridge Ancient History*, Vol. 5, Cambridge, 1927, p. 92.

25. Thucydides, *op. cit.*, p. 184.

26. *Ibid.*, pp. 187, 188, 189.

27. *The Cambridge Ancient History*, Vol. 5, Cambridge, 1927, p. 102.

28. *Ibid.*, p. 168.

29. *Ibid.*, pp. 322–3.

30. *The New Cambridge Modern History*, Vol. 7, Cambridge, 1957, p. 45.

31. M. Rostovtzeff, *The Social and Economic History of the Roman Empire*, second edition, Oxford, 1957, Vol. 1, p. 2.

32. *The Cambridge Ancient History*, Vol. 5, Cambridge, 1927, p. 359.

33. Thucydides, *op. cit.*, p. 55.

34. A. J. Toynbee, *op. cit.*, pp. 176–7.

35. A. H. M. Jones places a special emphasis on this interacting process in the burden of taxation as it came to rest on tenant farmers. See 'The Decline and Fall of the Roman Empire', *History*, October 1955, especially pp. 217–8. Arthur E. R. Boak argues that the tax burden, combined with other factors which inhibited a rise of agricultural and industrial productivity, consumed the capital resources of the taxpayers, gutted the fabric of the economy, and yielded a decline of the population as a decisive end result (*Manpower Shortage and the Fall of the Roman Empire in the West*, Ann Arbor and London, 1955). A. H. M. Jones supports a place for population decline in the dynamics of the Empire's decline in his summation at the close of *The Later Roman Empire*, Oxford, 1964, Vol. 2, pp. 1040–5. His final dictum is (p. 1045): 'The basic economic weakness of the empire was that too few producers supported too many idle mouths.'

36. *Op. cit.*, p. 217.

37. *Loc. cit.*, p. 533.

38. *History*, October 1955, p. 226.

39. *Loc. cit.*, p. 538.

40. *Op. cit.*, p. 216.

41. M. Rostovtzeff, *A History of the Ancient World*, Vol. 2, Oxford, 1927, pp. 94–7, for the process by which these groups emerged from the Punic Wars.

42. A footnote, at least, should note the survival of the Byzantine empire for a further eleven hundred years. The reasons for its capacity to persist in an environment of endemic military struggle to the west and north and east is somewhat less well-ploughed ground than the reasons for the decline of Rome. Was it the fresh impetus of building a new, great city as the Roman center declined and creating the administration to carry forward the imperial inheritance? The genius of Constantine's conversion and tolerance of the pagans? The sounder economic base of Constantinople, at the center of vital trade routes and with a larger population on which to draw, with a consequent capacity to amass and renew its gold reserve after military campaigns? The invulnerability, for so long, of Constantinople, protected by the sea, by walls, and by a military skilled in defensive doctrines and tactics? A diplomacy of divide and rule among the outer barbarians? The technology of Greek fire, which intervened at critical moments to tip the balance, notably against the Arabs, in the seventh century and against the Russians in the tenth and eleventh centuries?

43. Ping-ti Ho, 'Salient Aspects of China's Heritage', in *China in Crisis*, Vol. 1, Book 1, Chicago, 1968, pp. 15–16 (eds. Ping-ti Ho and Tang Tsou). For some reservations on Ho's dictum, in times of dynastic stability, by Herbert Franke, see p. 46.

44. The Japanese scholar Naitō Torajirō (1886–1934) was a pathfinder in developing the latter view. See notably, Hisayuki Miyakawa, 'An Outline of the Naitō Hypothesis and its Effects on Japanese Studies of China', *Far Eastern Quarterly*, August 1955, pp. 533–52. Naitō emphasizes progressive stages in Chinese political development accompanied by waves in the outward extension of Chinese culture followed by periods of external pressure on China from the outer barbarians (pp. 541–2). It should be noted that such a theory need not be inconsistent with a Malthusian cycle having its impact on the political life of China. There is nothing in the view developed here which requires cycles about static political or economic levels.

45. Mary Clabaugh Wright, *The Last Stand of Chinese Conservatism*, Stanford, 1957, pp. 43–4.

46. K. S. Latourette, *The Development of China*, Boston, 1917, pp. 16–17.

47. Ping-ti Ho, *Studies on the Population of China, 1368–1953*, Cambridge, Mass., 1959.

48. *Ibid.*, pp. 271–2. Hung preceded Malthus in publishing his theory by five years.

His eight points are summarized by a modern Chinese scholar. The passage beginning with the question is from Hung's text. Ho points out that Hung failed to grasp the existence of diminishing returns in his estimate of the possibilities of expanding production; and, of course, he did not allow for 'the effect of technological inventions and scientific discoveries on agricultural and industrial production'. For seventeenth-century linkages of population movements to the dynastic cycle, see pp. 261–2.

49. *Op cit.*, pp. 277–8.

50. C. C. Chang, *An Estimate of China's Farms and Crops*, 1932, pp. 11–14, quoted in A. K. Chiu, 'Agriculture', *China*, H. F. MacNair, ed., Berkeley, 1946, chapter 32, p. 469.

51. E. O. Reischauer and J. K. Fairbank, *East Asia, The Great Tradition*, Boston, 1960, p. 244; chapter 7, 'China and the "Barbarians": The Mongol Empire', pp. 243 ff., elaborates this view. See, also, Wolfram Eberhard, *Conquerors and Rulers* (2nd edition), Leiden, 1965.

52. On the role of the horse in the interplay between the Chinese and the Mongols, see, for example, H. G. Creel, 'The Role of the Horse in Chinese History', *American Historical Review*, April 1965, pp. 647–72; and S. Jagchid and C. R. Bawden, 'Some Notes on the Horse-Policy of the Yüan Dynasty', *Central Asiatic Journal*, Dec. 1965, pp. 246–68. Also C. Northcote Parkinson's general observations, *The Evolution of Political Thought*, New York, pp. 45–9.

53. S. N. Eisenstadt, *The Political Systems of Empires*, New York, 1963, p. 349.

54. See statistical table 3, p. 183 (from J. Marshall, *Digest of All the Accounts*), in T. S. Ashton, *Economic Fluctuations in England, 1700–1800*, Oxford, 1959.

55. T. S. Ashton, *The Industrial Revolution, 1760–1830*, London, 1948, p. 161

CHAPTER 3

1. To illustrate the arbitrariness of dating the start of the preconditioning process, it should be noted that Robert T. Holt and John E. Turner, *The Political Basis of Economic Development*, Princeton, 1966, in an effort that bears a family resemblance to this chapter, chose the following dates for certain of the countries cited here: France, 1600; China, 1644; Japan, 1603; England, 1558. I have no quarrel with these earlier dates. And the reader will find occasional reference in this chapter to events which precede the initial dates given here. The point to be noted is simply, that the choice is inherently arbitrary. As Henry Rosovsky has said: '. . . the search for preliminary stirrings is likely to be endless'. 'Japan's Transition to Economic Growth 1865–1885', in *Industrialization in Two Systems: Essays in Honor of Alexander Gerschenkron* (ed. H. Rosovsky), New York, 1966, p. 96.

2. For the author's definition of the concept of an operational national style (as opposed to national character or culture), see 'The National Style' in E. E. Morison (ed.), *The American Style*, New York, 1958, pp. 246 ff., especially pp. 246–9.

3. The intrusion of militarily more advanced on less advanced societies is a feature of ancient as well as of modern history as C. N. Parkinson so clearly perceived (*East and West*, London, 1963). And as, he notes, the reaction to intrusion was a national impulse to resist and respond in kind, yielding his central dictum about the piston-like movement of ancient history (p. 7): '. . . ascendancy creates resistance and resistance turns into a new ascendancy'. In chapter 2, for example, Athens and Rome were seen to enter on the path to empire after surviving dangerous external assaults (see above, pp. 20 and 42–3); and at least one theory of the Chinese dynastic cycle is rooted in the purging and stimulating effects of barbarian intrusion when the old dynasty had grown slack (see above, p. 59).

4. Although physical intrusion (including colonialism) and fear of military or economic domination have been the primary instruments for the diffusion of modernization,

profit possibilities, of course, played a role, occasionally with little or no element of intrusion or fear; for example, in the Swedish take-off in the last third of the nineteenth century.

5. There is nothing in pure theory which would prevent nations from wholly abandoning the modernization effort, as some American Indians have abandoned modern life and returned to the reservation. There has been a phase of something like this reaction in contemporary Burma. But it has not yet happened to a nation over a sustained period. And it is unlikely, given the intrusiveness of modern power and communications, and the fact that the universal acceptability of that form of modernization represented by public health is likely to set in motion a rapid rise in population which requires modernization elsewhere to balance it, if a degeneration of economic and social life is not to occur. The prospects for national withdrawal from the modern world for nation states is, therefore, not promising.

6. These external expressions of reaction from the past, combined with a new sense of capacity and external mission, can occur, as indicated in chapter 4, during the take-off period rather than in the preconditions; e.g., Germany in the 1860s and Japan in the 1890s. Chapter 5 suggests that in its Canadian venture during the War of 1812 and manifest destiny of the 1840s the United States was not immune from such temptation during both the preconditions and take-off periods.

7. *The Stages of Economic Growth*, pp. 34–5.

8. The price for 1688 was high. Of a population of 5 million, at least 100,000 Englishmen were killed in the Civil War. Ireland lost over 40 per cent of its population. And Scotland, too, was scourged. See, for example, H. N. Brailsford, *The Levellers and the English Revolution* (ed. Christopher Hill), Stanford, 1961, p. 1. The role of such domestic strife in creating subsequent conditions for mutual accommodation (as, for example, in the United States, Mexico, and Colombia) is considered in chapter 7.

9. F. Crouzet, 'England and France in the Eighteenth Century: A Comparative Analysis of Two Economic Growths', chapter 7 of R. M. Hartwell, *The Causes of the Industrial Revolution in England*, London, 1967, p. 156.

10. It is a considerable irony that the disaster of Britain's war with the American colonies, which gave France some considerable satisfaction for earlier losses elsewhere, was so costly to the weak French financial structure as to set the stage for the crisis of 1788–9 – just as Britain's triumph over the French in North America in 1763 set up the financial pressures which ultimately triggered the American Revolution.

11. Paul Mantoux observes of the British: 'Whilst the nobility was trying to get rich by trade, the merchant aristocracy was dreaming of that power and ascendancy which, in a country where the land system had long remained so traditional, is only acquired by the ownership of land.' *The Industrial Revolution in the Eighteenth Century*, revised edition, London and New York, 1961, p. 135. For a more full comment on interactions within the relatively flexible British social structure of this period, see David S. Landes, *The Unbound Prometheus*, Cambridge, 1969, pp. 69–74.

12. For the role of Indian cotton imports in the development of the British cotton industry, see Mantoux, *op. cit.*, pp. 199–201. As Mantoux points out (pp. 133–4), this subtle potentiality of the Indian trade was perceived, in general terms, by an unknown author as early as 1701: 'The *East-India* Trade procures things with less and cheaper labour than would be necessary to make the like in *England*; it is therefore very likely to be the cause of the invention of Arts, and Mills, and Engines, to save the labour of Hands in other Manufactures.' The title of the essay from which the quotation derives is 'Considerations upon the East-India Trade'.

13. J. U. Nef, *War and Human Progress*, Cambridge, Mass., 1950, especially chapter Nine, 'Less Blood and More Money', pp. 155–66. In the two critical battles for India

(Plassey and Wandewash) the British lost only 214 Europeans. The cost of the conquest of Canada was officially stated to be less than 1500 men (H. A. L. Fisher, *A History of Europe*, London, 1936, p. 766).

14. For a brief casting up of the various effects of the wars on the French economy, see, especially, D. S. Landes, *op. cit.*, pp. 142–7. See also F. Crouzet, *op. cit.*, pp. 173–4.

15. This story is sensitively told by D. S. Landes, *op. cit.*, chapters 3 and 4.

16. *Ibid.*, p. 139.

17. Hajo Holborn, *A History of Modern Germany, 1840–1945*, New York, 1969, p. 20.

18. Quoted, H. A. L. Fisher, *op. cit.*, p. 746.

19. *Ibid.*, p. 766.

20. For a concise account of the pre-1806 background to the Stein-Hardenberg reforms see David S. Landes, 'Japan and Europe: Contrasts in Industrialization', in W. W. Lockwood, *The State and Economic Enterprise in Japan*, Princeton, 1965, pp. 119–35.

21. H. Holborn, *op. cit.*, pp. 18–20.

22. The power and persistence of these memories is suggested by the recent lines of Y. Yevtushenko, evoking the first Russian victory over the Mongols at Kulikovo in 1380, in the context of a clash on the Sino–Soviet border: 'Vladimir and Kiev, you can see in the murky twilight that the new Mongol khans have bombs in their quivers. But if they come the warning bells will peal out and there will be enough warrior knights for many more Kulikovos.' Quoted, *Atlas*, May 1969, p. 15.

23. For a recent analysis of how the wars starting in the second half of the fifteenth century led to the institution of serfdom in Russia, see Evsey Domar, 'The Causes of Slavery or Serfdom: A Hypothesis', *Journal of Economic History*, March 1970, pp. 18 ff. Domar's chain of logic, which bears on the dynamics of pre-Newtonian empires considered in chapter 2, is roughly as follows: the wars of this period required tax revenues beyond the capacity of the state to mobilize; the state assigned land to those capable and willing to join in the struggle ('servitors'); but labor was the scarce factor in Russian agriculture, not land, and it became relatively more so with successful conquests; therefore the state moved towards serfdom to assure adequate support from its 'servitors'.

24. For an interesting interpretation of Peter the Great's policy as a Russian variant of mercantilism, see A. Gerschenkron, *Europe in the Russian Mirror*, Cambridge, 1970, chapter 3. With respect to serfdom, Gerschenkron notes (p. 91): '... when finally the Industrial Revolution in England ushered in a new era in industrial history, then it was precisely the institution of serfdom, so greatly reinforced by Peter and one of the carrying pillars of his edifice of economic development, that became the major block in the path of Russia's participation in the new industrial progress.'

25. 'No one studying the course of economic change in Russia during the period under review can fail to be impressed with the extent and intensity of the government's intervention. Military pressures, grand designs in the field of foreign policy, old fears and new resentments visibly hovered over Russian policies of industrialization. After the defeat in the Crimean War it was believed that the abolition of serfdom, construction of railroads with imported materials and equipment, and comprehensive judicial and administrative reforms would suffice to change Russia's military position in the world. The ease with which Disraeli deprived Russia of many of the fruits of her victory over the Turks and Prince Gorchakov's helplessness at the Congress of Berlin (1878) demonstrated to Russian statesmen that further and more positive action in the economic field was called for, if the balance of power was to be redressed. True, the diplomatic defeat at Berlin was not immediately followed by rapid industrialization. It took several years to draw the inferences and to overcome the traditional aversion from industrialization. But the connexion between the two phenomena is undeniable. Nor can it be gainsaid that the government's interest in railroad building and in industries serving railroad construction

was clearly co-determined by considerations of military strategy and the desire to assure for the army and the navy more efficient and more plentiful supplies of products of domestic industries.' A Gerschenkron, 'The Early Phases of Industrialization in Russia: Afterthoughts and Counterthoughts', *The Economics of Take-off into Sustained Growth* (ed. W. W. Rostow), pp. 158–9.

26. W. W. Lockwood, *The Economic Development of Japan*, Princeton, 1954, p. 4.

27. D. S. Landes, *loc. cit.*, p. 111.

28. Mary Clabaugh Wright, *The Last Stand of Chinese Conservatism*, Stanford, 1957.

29. I refer to Robert E. Ward and Dankwart A. Rustow (eds.), *Political Modernization in Japan and Turkey*, Princeton, 1964, especially chapters 3B (pp. 91 ff.); 4B (pp. 146 ff.); and 8B (pp. 352 ff.).

30. 'What was new and anti-traditional in his measures was the introduction not only of European weapons but also of the sciences, training procedures and uniforms of Europe. For Western scientific thought challenged traditional Muslim thought, and the European uniforms challenged traditional symbols.' *Ibid.*, p. 49.

31. *Ibid.*, pp. 447–8.

32. *Mexico and the Americans*, New York, 1963, p. 17. Cuba, Haiti, the Dominican Republic, as well as certain Central American nations, did, of course, feel the weight of direct U.S. intrusion at various times, as well as Mexico.

33. *Ibid.*, p. 33.

34. As Leonard Gordon points out, there is no firm evidence that Lincoln and Juárez ever directly communicated, 'Lincoln and Juárez – A Brief Reassessment of Their Relationship', *The Hispanic American Historical Review*, February 1968, pp. 75 ff.

35. Lewis Namier, *Personalities and Powers*, London, 1955, pp. 57–8.

36. In R. E. Ward and D. A. Rustow, *op. cit.*, pp. 80–1.

37. Roderic H. Davison's *Reform in the Ottoman Empire, 1856–1876*, Princeton, 1963, provides a detailed analysis of this critical transitional period.

38. In R. E. Ward and D. A. Rustow, *op. cit.*, p. 102.

39. T. S. Ashton (*The Industrial Revolution, 1760–1830*, London, 1948, pp. 11–12) makes this point as follows: 'The sentiments and attitudes of mind of the period were propitious. The religious and political differences that had torn society apart in the two preceding centuries had been composed; and if the eighteenth century was not markedly an age of faith, at least it practised the Christian virtue of tolerance. The regulation of industry by guilds, municipalities, and the central government had broken down or had been allowed to sleep, and the field was open for the exercise of initiative and enterprise. It was perhaps no accident that it was in Lancashire and the West Riding, which had been exempted from some of the more restrictive provisions of the Elizabethan code of industrial legislation, that the development was most marked. It was certainly no accident that it was the villages and unincorporated towns – places like Manchester and Birmingham – that grew most rapidly, for industry and trade had long been moving away from the areas where some remnants of public control were still in operation.

'During the seventeenth century the attitude of the Law had changed: from the time of Coke judgments in the courts of Common Law had become tender indeed to the rights of property, but hostile to privilege. In 1624 the Statute of Monopolies had swept away many vested interests, and a century and a half later Adam Smith was able to say of English men that they were "to their great honour of all peoples, the least subject to the wretched spirit of monopoly".'

40. The role of extra-European trade in the late eighteenth century is suggested by the accompanying figures for 1792, at the peak of the prewar boom, in official values (volume index), for total exports (in £millions):

U.S.A.	4.1
British West Indies	2.4
Asia	2.4
Germany	2.1
Holland	1.3
France	1.2

(A. D. Gayer, W. W. Rostow, Anna Jacobson Schwartz, *British Economy, 1790–1850*, Oxford, 1953, Vol. 1, p. 13.)

41. For recent emphasis on this point see R. T. Holt and J. E. Turner, *op. cit.*, pp. 249–55. See, also, T. S. Ashton, *An Economic History of England: The 18th Century*, London, 1955, pp. 72–6.

42. See, especially, T. S. Ashton, *loc. cit.*, pp. 104–8.

43. Despite Marczewski's criticism of my dating of the French take-off between 1830 and 1860, I am inclined, without dogmatism, to keep that interval as the benchmark period. By 1860 the multiple impact of the railroads was self-evident. The key question is: should the 1830s be included, although railways are, themselves, only a modest element in the French economy of the decade. I would regard the 1830s as a critical part of the emergence of heavy industry as a leading sector because of significant progress in coal, metals, and machinery, as well as the early beginnings of railroadization itself. Note, for example, the radically different composition of industries whose rate of growth exceeded the average by at least 20 per cent for the period 1825–34 to 1835–44 as compared to the period 1803–12 to 1825–34 in Marczewski's Table 4, p. 124. 'The Take-off Hypothesis and French Experience', *The Economics of Take-off into Sustained Growth*. Marczewski himself notes (p. 128): 'All in all, the first forty years of the nineteenth century constitute a fairly homogeneous period of fast growth (3 to 3.6 per cent annually), largely dominated by the cotton and silk industries. Engineering, the iron and steel industry, and coal assume importance only towards the end of the period.' For illustrative specific confirmatory data on the emergence of heavy industry in this period, see also David S. Landes, *The Unbound Prometheus*, Cambridge, 1969, pp. 175, 176, 180, 181, 182, n. 1. In terms of larger aggregates, as well, I find Marczewski's data confirmatory for the importance of the 1830s; for example, Table 1, p. 120; Tables 2 and 3, p. 121; Table 10, p. 135, including his observations on periods of maximum growth. I believe the real difference between Marczewski's view and mine rests in my judgment that textiles in France, without the possibility of great export markets, was an insufficient initial basis for a sustained industrial process. A heavy industry base and the multiple effects of the railway were required for take-off.

44. See, notably, F. Crouzet's excellent summary of evidence on French progress in the eighteenth century, in 'England and France in the Eighteenth Century: A Comparative Analysis of Two Economic Growths', chapter 7 of R. M. Hartwell, *The Causes of the Industrial Revolution in England*, London, 1967.

45. *Op. cit.*, p. 155.

46. J. H. Clapham, *The Economic Development of France and Germany, 1815–1914*, Cambridge, 1928 (3rd edition), p. 54.

47. See, for example, *ibid.*, pp. 71–5. C. P. Kindleberger emphasizes the efforts under the July Monarchy of 1830 to press forward the planning of canals as well as railroads (*Economic Growth in France and Britain, 1851–1950*, Cambridge, Mass., 1964, p. 185).

48. *The Economics of Take-off into Sustained Growth*, chapter 5, p. 84.

49. *Ibid.*, p. 113.

50. Walther Hoffmann's evidence on the increase of producer goods (as well as railway construction) in the 1840s constitutes a strong case for the judgment that the period of

German take-off should include that decade (*ibid.*, pp. 96, 104–7, and 114). Formally, Hoffmann defines the preconditions period from 1800 to 1830–5; the take-off from 1830–5 to 1855–60.

51. Quoted, J. H. Clapham, *op. cit.*, p. 150, from *Deutsche Geschichte*, Vol. IV.

52. See above, pp. 371–2, note 25. P. I. Lyashchenko strongly emphasizes the relation of the early railways to enlarging the flow of agricultural supplies from the countryside (*History of the National Economy of Russia*, New York, 1949, pp. 511–12).

53. P. I. Lyashchenko, *op. cit.*, pp. 491–2.

54. *Ibid.*, p. 543.

55. *Ibid.*, p. 536.

56. *Ibid.*, p. 553.

57. This period has been well charted and analyzed in: W. W. Lockwood, *op. cit.*; R. E. Ward and D. A. Rustow, *op. cit.*, especially chapters 4A and 5A; and R. T. Holt and J. E. Turner, *op. cit.*, especially chapters 4, 5, and 6. Henry Rosovsky has written a masterly summation of precisely these years in 'Japan's Transition to Modern Economic Growth, 1868–1885', in *Industrialization in Two Systems: Essays in Honor of Alexander Gerschenkron* (ed. H. Rosovsky), New York, 1966. On these pre-take-off years see, also, K. Ohkawa and Henry Rosovsky, 'A Century of Japanese Economic Growth' in W. W. Lockwood (ed.), *The State of Economic Enterprise in Japan*, Princeton, 1965, pp. 53–66. Although the major policies of the preconditions were launched only after 1868, it should be noted that the first Japanese reverberatory furnace was constructed in 1852; a lathe machine imported in 1856; the ports opened to external trade in 1859; and a shipyard was constructed for steam-run warships in 1863.

58. S. Tsuru, 'The Take-off in Japan, 1868–1900', chapter 8 in *The Economics of Take-off into Sustained Growth*, p. 144.

59. H. Rosovsky, *Capital Formation in Japan, 1868–1904*, Glencoe, 1961, especially pp. 164, 204, 207, 321.

60. K. Ohkawa *et al.*, *The Growth Rate of the Japanese Economy Since 1878*, Tokyo, 1957, pp. 16–34.

61. R. E. Ward and D. A. Rustow, *op. cit.*, p. 188. H. Rosovsky, *op. cit.*, pp. 105–7, summarizes the evidence for a relatively high educational base in Tokugawa Japan.

62. See the author's *The Prospects for Communist China*, Cambridge, Mass., 1954, p. 224. The data in this section are derived mainly from Part 5 of that work, which owes a great deal to the scholarship of Professor Alexander Eckstein. But see, also, John K. Fairbank, Alexander Eckstein, and L. S. Yang, 'Economic Change in Early Modern China: An Analytic Framework', *Economic Development and Cultural Change*, October 1960, Part 1.

63. *The Prospects for Communist China*, p. 229, where sources are indicated.

64. *Ibid.*, p. 239.

65. Taken all in all, there were remarkable similarities between the positions of China and India as of, say, 1952, as they emerged, respectively, from a quasi-colonial and colonial past to make their first independent dispositions with respect to industrialization – a parallelism suggested in the accompanying table (*ibid.*, p. 259). Aside from the political framework of the two nations in 1952, the major differences are three: the larger Chinese population; the greater productivity per acre of Chinese agriculture, where irrigation and double cropping had been systematically applied; the relatively greater scale of the Indian cotton textile industry.

66. Z. Y. Hershlag, *Turkey, The Challenge of Growth*, Leiden, 1968, Table XVI, p. 121.

67. *Ibid.*, pp. 83–4.

68. Daniel James, *op. cit.*, p. 123. See also Raymond Vernon, *The Dilemma of Mexico's Development*, Cambridge, Mass., 1963, pp. 78–86.

Indicators of comparative levels of development in mainland China and India[a]

		India		China	
	Units	Amount	Year	Amount	Year
GNP	billions of 1952 U.S. dollars	$22.00	1950	$30.00	1952
GNP per head	1952 U.S. dollars	$60.00	1950	$60.00	1952
Population	millions	358.00	1950	582.00	1953
Crude birth rate	per 1,000	38.00	1949	40.00	1930–5
Crude death rate	per 1,000	24.00	1949	34.00	1930–5
Proportion in agriculture and fishing		68.00	1931	80.00	1952
Agriculture					
Number of persons dependent on agriculture per acre of cultivated land	persons per acre	0.60	1931	1.90	1953
Paddy rice yield	metric quintals per hectare	13.30	1934–8	25.30	1931–7
Wheat yield	metric quintals per hectare	6.80	1937–9	10.80	1931–7
Industry					
Coal	total in million metric tons	34.90	1951	53.00	1952
	kilograms per capita	97.00	1951	91.00	1952
Pig iron	total in million metric tons	1.90	1951	1.60	1952
	kilograms per capita	5.00	1951	2.75	1952
Crude steel	total in million metric tons	1.50	1951	1.20	1952
	kilograms per capita	4.00	1951	2.00	1952
Finished steel	total in million metric tons			0.70	1952
	kilograms per capita			1.20	1952
Generating capacity of electric power	total in thousand kilowatts	2,409.00	1951	2,850.00	1952
	kilowatts per capita	0.01	1951	0.005	1952
Cotton spindleage in industry	total in thousands	10,144.00	1952	5,000.00	1952
	units per capita	0.03	1952	0.01	1952
Cement	total in million metric tons	3.20	1951	2.30	1952
	kilograms per capita	9.00	1951	4.00	1952

[a] From the author's *The Prospects for Communist China*, Cambridge, Mass., 1954, Table 6, pp. 258–9.

69. The concessions to foreign capital were not direct. As M. S. Wionczek points out: 'Of some two hundred concessions granted or confirmed by the central government between 1895 and 1910, the overwhelming majority were given to nationals, who speedily sold them to interested foreign parties', R. Vernon (ed.) *Public Policy and Private Enterprise in Mexico*, Cambridge, Mass., 1964, p. 25.

70. For reference to pre-1910 industrialization, see, for example, W. P. Glade Jr. and Charles W. Anderson, *The Political Economy of Mexico*, Madison, 1963, p. 81.

71. Ernesto Galarza, *La industria eléctrica en México*, Mexico, D.F., 1942, p. 74, quoted by M. S. Wionczek, *op. cit.*, p. 25.

72. M. S. Wionczek, *op. cit.*, p. 37. But Mexican gross national product was less than 10 per cent above the 1910 figure in 1930, reflecting a net decline in agriculture. See historical estimates of Enrique Perez Lopez, 'The National Product of Mexico: 1895 to 1964' in Tom E. Davis (ed.), *Mexico's Recent Economic Growth, The Mexican View*, Austin and London, 1967.

CHAPTER 4

1. The take-off and drive to technological maturity are fully defined in chapters 4 and 5 of the author's *The Stages of Economic Growth*, Cambridge, 1960.

2. See, for example, Walther Hoffmann, *British Industry, 1700–1950*, Oxford, 1955, pp. 228–31.

3. For considerations bearing on this choice, see *The Stages of Economic Growth*, 68–70.

4. S. Kuznets, 'Quantitative Aspects of the Economic Growth of Nations: I. Levels and Variability of Rates of Growth', *Economic Development and Cultural Change*, Chicago, Vol. 5, No. 1, October 1956, p. 13.

5. For a detailed analysis of these interconnections, see the author's *British Economy of the Nineteenth Century*, chapters 5 and 6.

6. For industrial production and population growth rates, *ibid.*, p. 8; for national income growth rates, P. Deane and W. A. Cole, *British Economic Growth, 1688–1959*, Cambridge, 1962. Deane and Cole's calculations for the rate of growth of manufactures, mining, and building for the years 1801–1901 average 3.3 per cent.

7. J. H. Clapham, *An Economic History of Modern Britain, The Early Railway Age, 1820–1850*, Cambridge, 1930, pp. 66–7.

8. It was not until the Reform Act of 1918 that voter registration was effectively simplified and universal suffrage, including women, in fact, installed.

9. These figures are derived from J. Marczewski, *op. cit.*, pp. 135–6.

10. As H. A. L. Fisher (*A History of Europe*, London, 1936, pp. 909–10) remarks of the Revolution of 1848: 'The new Assembly was to be elected by universal suffrage. A truth was then discovered which, had it been divined by Louis Philippe and his ministers, might have saved the monarchy. In a land of peasant proprietors universal suffrage may well yield not a radical but a conservative result. An electorate of two hundred thousand well-to-do bourgeois guaranteed neither loyalty in the Chamber nor confidence in the country, encouraged corruption, aroused jealousies, deadened enthusiasm. But universal suffrage would have been for the monarchy a gilt-edged investment. On its first application after the revolution of February, the poll being the heaviest on record, it returned a Chamber of bourgeois, in which the republicans were only as one to eight.' The point is echoed by a more recent commentator, Antony Jay, in *Management and Machiavelli*, New York, 1967, p. 223: 'Bismarck and Disraeli both saw that to keep themselves securely in power the best way was to widen the franchise. A narrow franchise favored the well-informed

liberals, who could force them out; a wide one enabled them to play on the simple, elemental hopes and fears of the ill-informed masses.'

11. 'The June insurrection, in which not a single radical leader participated and which was therefore an unplanned, disorganized outbreak, never had much chance of success . . . On June 24 and 25 thousands of provincials, eager "to defend society against the threat of anarchic doctrines and to put an end to the intolerable dictation of the chronically insurgent Parisian workers" arrived in the capital. For the most part they were too late to share in the fighting, but they were used for guard duty and in general exercised a significant moral influence.

'. . . In four days of desperate fighting the insurgents had lost 400–500 men, while the attacking forces had something like twice that number of dead. In terms of human life, the worst, however, was still to come. The insurgents were hunted through houses and alleys and some 3,000 were cut down in cold blood. Alexander Herzen, watching the slaughter, noted that Russian Cossacks and Austrian Croat troops were meek as lambs compared to the ferocious French guards. In addition to the slain, about 12,000 persons were arrested, some of whom were released after four to six months, while most were summarily deported to Algerian labor camps.

'. . . The end result, however, was to deepen class antagonisms and strengthen suspicions and fears, making even gradual social reform ever more difficult. The fruits of the June Days took the form not of democracy but of reaction.' W. L. Langer, *Political and Social Upheaval, 1832–1852*, New York, 1969, pp. 349–50.

12. 'A second, and more powerful reason, lay in the revolutionary memories of France. Again and again resolute minorities had overthrown governments. Why should not a resolute minority bring down a whole social system, by one well directed blow, instead of laboriously accumulating fighting funds, or bargaining and compromising with politicians? The thing seemed at least worth trying. It was open to the socialistic workman to use both methods and he very often did. As a politician he would support the United Socialists, or some other socialist group. As a member of his little syndicate he could vote for affiliation to the C.G.T. and perhaps take part in a strike with a wider, vaguer, more soul-satisfying aim than that of the local strike for the local grievance. His parliamentary representative and his ultimate leader in the governing councils of the C.G.T. were always warning him against the dangers of that concentration of industrial power into fewer hands, which had been making steady progress since about 1895. If the progress was slight in relation to the whole economic life of France, it was still definite enough to give support to Marxian dogma and to strengthen his instinctive dislike of a system which, as his leaders told him and he was disposed to believe, imperilled liberty, made nonsense of equality, and bred hatred in place of fraternity.' J. H. Clapham, *The Economic Development of France and Germany, 1815–1914*, Cambridge, England, 1928, pp. 276–7. See, also, Val R. Lorwin, *The French Labor Movement*, Cambridge, Mass., 1954, chapter 3, 'The Force of Syndicalism'.

13. For an account of Prussian politics, from Bismarck's becoming Prime Minister to the proclamation of the German Empire, see Hajo Holborn, *A History of Modern Germany, 1840–1945*, New York, 1969, pp. 157–229.

14. For an analysis of the party structure of German politics in this period, see Donald J. Ziegler, *Prelude to Democracy, A Study of Proportional Representation and the Heritage of Weimar Germany, 1871–1920*, University of Nebraska Studies, New Series No. 20, Lincoln, Nebraska, October 1958. On the revival of the suffrage issue in the German states in the years before 1914, see H. Holborn, *op. cit.*, pp. 364–5.

15. H. Holborn, *op. cit.*, p. 366.

16. J. H. Clapham, *op. cit.*, p. 324.

17. This sequence is traced out in somewhat more detail in chapter 8.

18. *History of the National Economy of Russia to the 1917 Revolution*, New York, 1949, pp. 563–4.

19. 17 January 1895, Nicholas speaking to the representatives of the nobility, the zemstvos, and the city councils, quoted in Sergei Pushkarev, *The Emergence of Modern Russia, 1801–1917*, New York, 1963, p. 231.

20. These are almost precisely the elements perceived as potentially explosive in the contemporary Soviet Union by Andrei Amalrik, *Will the Soviet Union Survive Until 1984?*, New York, 1970. On analogy with 1905 he evokes a frustrating war in Asia – this time against China rather than Japan – as the triggering mechanism.

21. The official casualty figures were 130 dead, 299 wounded and recovered. But contemporary journalists presented to the Ministry of Interior a list of 4600 names claimed to represent dead and wounded. (S. Harcave, *The Russian Revolution of 1905*, London, 1970 edition, p. 93. Harcave's is an excellent account of the background, dynamics, and outcome of the 1905 Revolution.)

22. R. W. Goldsmith, 'The Economic Growth of Tsarist Russia 1860–1913', *Economic Development and Cultural Change*, April 1961, p. 450.

23. *Ibid.*, p. 463.

24. S. Pushkarev, *op. cit.*, pp. 281, 290–1. The census of 1897 indicated only 21 per cent of the Russian population was literate; by 1914 approximately 44 per cent was estimated as literate (p. 292).

25. G. W. Nutter, *Growth of Industrial Production in the Soviet Union*, Princeton, 1962, Table 37, p. 165. The high rate of growth of consumers durables in this period reflects the low initial figure for 1928 rather than a substantial role in Soviet growth before 1940.

26. On the emergence of a new Soviet elite from the purges of the 1930s, see S. Bialer (ed.), *Stalin and His Generals*, New York, 1969, especially pp. 89 ff. For estimates of the numbers killed, see Z. Brzezinski, 'The Soviet Past and Future', *Encounter*, March 1970, p. 4n. Brzezinski states: 'Stalin's terror consumed at least six and a half million lives during the crucial years, 1930–1940.'

27. See, for example, *Survey of Europe in 1957*, United Nations, Geneva, 1958, chapter I, p. 38. Also, the author's *The Stages of Economic Growth*, pp. 102–3.

28. *Op. cit.*, p. 32. For a less apocalyptic but still somber view of the Soviet future, see Z. Brzezinski, *op. cit.*

29. G. A. Almond and Sidney Verba, *The Civic Culture*, Princeton, 1963.

30. *The Republic*, Book 8, tr. F. M. Cornford, p. 268.

31. In 'A Century of Japanese Economic Growth' (W. W. Lockwood (ed.), *loc. cit.*, pp. 52–3), Kazushi Ohkawa and Henry Rosovsky have broken down Japanese economic history into five phases which bear a family relation to the stages of growth as I have defined them. They can be set out as follows:

OHKAWA–ROSOVSKY	STAGES OF GROWTH
A. *The First Modern Phase of Modern Economic Growth, 1868–1905*	
I. Transition, 1868, 1885	Preconditions for take-off (late period)
II. Initial Modern Economic Growth, 1886–1905	Take-off
B. *The Second Phase of Modern Economic Growth, 1906–52*	
III. Differential Structure: Creation, 1906–30	Drive to technological maturity (choice of military option; postwar recovery; completion technological maturity on civil basis)

378

IV. Differential Structure: Economic
and Political Consequences, 1931–
52

C. *The Third Phase of Modern Economic Growth, 1953–present*   High mass-consumption

The aggregative data array as in the accompanying table, according to the Ohkawa–Rosovsky phases (pp. 91–2).

Selected phase indicators

Phases		Rate of increase total population per annum	Rate of increase GNP per annum	Rate of increase GNP per head per annum	Gross domestic capital formation (% of GNP)	% of non-agricultural labor force in the total	Agricultural output (% of NNP)	Output of factory manufactures (% of NNP)
		(%)	(%)	(%)				
I	1879				n.a.	17.1	64.4	3.2
	1885	0.8	1.2	0.3	n.a.	20.8	55.7	4.1
II	1886				11.1	21.5	53.0	5.2
	1905	1.1	2.4	1.3	13.9	33.4	39.0	9.1
III	1906				13.8	34.2	41.0	8.9
	1930	1.3	3.8	2.5	18.8	50.3	18.6	17.3
IV	1931				11.3	49.0	17.4	18.1
	1952	1.3	1.8	0.5	22.5	54.7	23.9	25.5
IV	1931				11.3	49.0	17.4	18.1
	1944	1.0	2.9	1.8	29.5	57.3	17.8	13.2
V	1953				26.3	55.1	22.0	29.5
	1960	1.0	9.2	8.1	40.1	65.3	15.1	33.5

Ohkawa and Rosovksy, for reasons of space, do not present the analysis of the changing industrial structure on which, I would assume, the distinction is made among their phases.

In stages of growth analysis, the leading sectors are seen to shift from textiles and other light industries during take-off; to the heavy industry and fabricating complex during the drive to technological maturity (coal, pig iron, steel, machine tools, fertilizers, pulp and paper, etc.); to the automobile and related sectors (including durable consumers goods) during high mass-consumption. (For references to Japan in these terms, see the author's 'The Past Quarter-Century as Economic History and the Tasks of International Economic Organization', *The Journal of Economic History*, March 1970, especially pp. 154–6, 158–61.)

Yuichi Shionoya ('Patterns of Industrial Development', chapter 3 in Laurence Klein and Kazushi Ohkawa (eds.), *Economic Growth, The Japanese Experience since the Meiji Era*, Homewood, Ill., 1968) disaggregates Japanese industrial production by sectors in an analysis broadly consistent with the leading sector sequence underlying the stages of growth.

In short, with respect to Japan, we are close to a reconciliation of aggregative and sectoral perspectives on growth analysis.

32. The politics of this period is well traced in the Introduction to R. H. P. Mason, *Japan's First General Election, 1890*, Cambridge, 1969. The process is complex because of the interweaving of old links to the pre-1868 fiefdoms and more modern alignments,

based on differing interests and outlooks of the bureaucrats, industrialists, farmers, intellectuals, etc. See, also, the fundamental study of R. Scalapino, *Democracy and the Party Movement in Prewar Japan: The Failure of the First Attempt*, Berkeley, 1953.

33. R. H. P. Mason, *op. cit.*, p. 197.

34. *Ibid.*, pp. 199–200.

35. Nobutaka Ike's observation on the parties and universal suffrage should be noted (Robert E. Ward and Dankwart A. Rustow (eds.), *Political Modernization in Japan and Turkey*, Princeton, 1964, p. 406): 'When noting the expansion of the electorate, however, one should be aware that the parties have not always sought to bring more people into the electoral process. After the end of the First World War there was agitation by intellectuals, students, journalists, and others for abolishing the tax qualification for voting, but most party leaders were less than enthusiastic supporters of that proposal. Some even argued that universal manhood suffrage would break down the system of social classes and lead to instability. Even the socialists who would presumably have benefitted from the extension of the vote to the propertyless had their misgivings. At the turn of the century, Japanese Socialists had placed great faith in the parliamentary system, arguing that, if the poor could send their own representatives to the Diet, all Socialist aims could be attained through legislation. But before long they became disillusioned with parliamentary process. By the 1920s many leaders of the left had become convinced that a grand extension of the vote would only blunt the revolutionary edge of their movement, and were favoring instead such techniques of "direct action" as the general strike. When, despite the misgivings of both right and left, universal manhood suffrage was enacted in 1925, a number of so-called proletarian parties did make their appearance, but won under five per cent of the popular vote in the general election of 1928.'

36. *Ibid.*

37. For a parallel formulation, see W. W. Lockwood, *ibid.*, pp. 140–1.

38. For an authoritative account of this period, see W. F. Weiker, *The Turkish Revolution 1960–1961*, Washington, D.C. 1963. For an interpretation of the return to civilian rule as a decisive step towards the emergence of civilian political leadership in modern Turkey, see Kemal H. Karpat, 'The Military and Politics in Turkey, 1960–64: A Socio–Cultural Analysis of a Revolution', *The American Historical Review*, October 1970, pp. 1654 ff.

39. J. W. Wilkie, *The Mexican Revolution: Federal Expenditure and Social Change Since 1910*, Berkeley and Los Angeles, 1967, p. 279. For a debate on Wilkie's method and conclusions, see T. E. Skidmore and P. H. Smith, 'Notes on Quantitative History: Federal Expenditure and Social Change in Mexico Since 1910', and Wilkie's reply in *Latin American Research Review*, Spring 1970, pp. 71 ff.

40. 'Why have Mexicans condoned the manner in which their Revolution has developed over the past two decades? The privileged, forming the top 20 per cent, naturally accept the present direction. Most of the rest probably do not accept it, but they are led by men from the privileged class . . . Meanwhile, what can the masses do about their plight? They may be conscious of long-range benefits brought by the Revolution – political stability; relative freedom of speech, press, religion, and assembly; education; roads; the promise of electrification; irrigation; sanitation – all of which tends to soothe day-by-day poverty. They may even think that they are contributing to the building of a greater Mexico, to national integration, and to other planks in the Revolutionary Creed. But if they chose to force the issue of real-wage increases now, of easier access to credit, and of a bigger share in national income, how would they proceed? Would the central government order the army, navy, and air force to repress an armed rebellion of the peasantry and proletariat? Would they choose to shoot down the very elements that the Revolution purportedly represents? So far the government has snuffed out armed factions founded on basic discontents before they could grow into serious threats.

'. . . All in all, the success of liberal authoritarianism in six-year doses owes much to the security apparatus of the Revolutionary elite heading Mexico.

'Little by little, the gap between the President of Mexico and the people of Mexico is closing. Presidents have become less fearful of the people and the people less afraid of their presidents. This encouraging state of affairs improves tolerance and extends freedom. Violence is rarely employed by a president to sustain himself in power – although, on the other hand, opposition elements have never been permitted to acquire enough power to be in a position to challenge the Revolutionary elite . . . When questioned on abuses of the ruling elite, the Mexican usually replies with a stock answer: Politics is that way; anyway, we have more freedom today, and we do not like the thought of returning to the cruelty and destruction of the first decade of the Revolution. Besides, Mexicans today have the good fortune of a turnover in dictators every six years.

'. . . Fifty years of Revolution suggest that the appearance of effective interest groups and political parties unimpeded by constant governmental intervention is wishful thinking. In working toward the fulfillment of ideals in the Revolutionary Creed, the Revolutionary Family has brought a fair measure of political liberalism into Mexican life. It has also shown itself sensitive and responsive to many popular needs. But the future, like the past five decades, holds little promise of improving democratic goals beyond the expectation of placing in the presidential office a tolerant, powerful chief executive – of retaining the "liberal Machiavellian".' Frank Brandenburg, *The Making of Modern Mexico*, Englewood Cliffs, 1964, pp. 162–5.

41. *Op. cit.*, pp. 177 and 186.

42. *Ibid.*, p. 503.

43. This sequence is traced out in the author's *British Economy of the Nineteenth Century*, pp. 109–14.

44. Richard A. Musgrave, *Fiscal Systems*, New Haven and London, 1969, p. 94. See, also, the discussions in G. D. H. Cole and R. Postgate, *The Common People, 1746–1946*, London, 1946 edition, pp. 501–3.

45. P. Deane and W. A. Cole, *British Economic Growth, 1688–1959*, Cambridge, 1962, p. 247, where sources are indicated.

46. See, especially, Wallace C. Peterson, *The Welfare State in France*, University of Nebraska Studies: New Series No. 21, Lincoln, Nebraska, February 1960.

47. Val R. Lorwin, *op. cit.*, pp. 27–8.

48. *Op. cit.*, p. 322.

49. S. Andic and J. Veverka, 'The Growth of Government Expenditure in Germany Since the Unification', *Finanzarchiv*, January 1964, p. 189.

50. *Ibid.*, p. 189.

51. *Ibid.*, p. 199.

52. *Op. cit.*, p. 95.

53. S. Andic and J. Veverka, *op. cit.*, p. 247.

54. P. I. Lyashchenko, *History of the National Economy of Russia*, New York, 1949, p. 558.

55. *Ibid.*, p. 713.

56. For an excellent summary, see Janet G. Chapman, 'Consumption', in A. Bergson and S. Kuznets, *op. cit.*, pp. 235 ff.

57. R. Musgrave, *op. cit.*, p. 41. These comparisons do not reflect, of course, the relatively low level of housing standards in the U.S.S.R., an area engaging public policy and resources on a large scale in advanced Western societies.

58. W. W. Lockwood, *The Economic Development of Japan, 1868–1938*, Princeton, 1954, pp. 557–60.

59. *Ibid.*, p. 560.

60. 'Meiji Fiscal Policy and Economic Progress' in W. W. Lockwood (ed.), *The State and Economic Enterprise in Japan*, Princeton, 1965, chapter 8. Oshima promises (p. 383) a forthcoming volume on the revenue and expenditures of Japanese governments, 1868–1960.

61. Frederic C. Shorter *et al.*, *op. cit.*, p. 43.

62. R. Musgrave, *op. cit.*, p. 366.

63. Shorter (*op. cit.*, p. 42) states: 'Health and education budgets totalled two per cent of GNP at the beginning of the period [1948] and three per cent at the end' [1962]. The 1965–6 Turkish budget for education, health, and welfare was about 4.5 per cent of 1965 GNP (Hershlag, *op. cit.*, pp. 337 and 341).

64. Tom E. Davis (ed.), *Mexico's Recent Economic Growth, The Mexican View*, Austin and London, 1967, from Enrique Perez Lopez, 'The National Product of Mexico, 1895 to 1964', p. 32, Table 5. The Mexican proportion of GNP invested (and its marginal capital–output ratio) is abnormally low, for the rate of growth sustained in recent years. In a personal communication, P. N. Rosenstein-Rodan has observed that this may be the result of steady access to the American capital market for working capital on terms which make such resources tantamount to long-term investment. The extremely low capital–output ratios of the period 1941–5 reflect the existence of idle capacity in the 1930s brought to full utilization during the war years, against the background of considerable build-up of social overhead capital in the previous decade.

65. *Ibid.*, p. 111, from Alfredo Navarrete, 'The Financing of Economic Development'.

66. *Ibid.*, p. 110.

67. R. Vernon, *The Dilemma of Mexico's Development*, Cambridge Mass., 1963, p. 188.

68. T. E. Davis (ed.), *op. cit.*, p. 186, Victor L. Urquidi, 'Fundamental Problems of the Mexican Economy'. The 1967 figures have been added from United Nations sources. Note Urquidi's discussion of this sectoral transition and its problems, pp. 186–90.

69. *Op. cit.*, pp. 13 and 100–6, Wilkie includes Mexico's relatively declining military outlays in administrative expenditures.

70. *Ibid.*, p. 38; tables, pp. 32 and 36.

71. *Ibid.*, p. 7.

72. *Ibid.*, p. 234.

73. E. Heckscher, *The Continental System*, Oxford, 1922, p. 253.

74. For an excellent short account of the problems and policy of the Austro-Hungarian Empire in this period, see G. A. Craig, *Europe Since 1815*, New York, 1961, pp. 395–408 and 447–80. For a full-length account, see, especially, Arthur J. May, *The Hapsburg Monarchy, 1867–1914*, Cambridge, Mass., 1965. For an effort explicitly to link domestic problems of economic and social modernization to the nationality question and foreign policy, see *Austrian History Yearbook*, Vol. III, Part 3, 1967 (Rice University, Houston), Solomon Wank, 'Foreign Policy and the Nationality Problem in Austria–Hungary, 1867–1914', and the 'Comments' of Stephen D. Kertesz, who observes (p. 59): 'Some of the problems of the Danubian empire foreshadowed the present-day convulsions connected with awakened nationalism in Africa and Asia and the relations between underdeveloped and industrialized regions of the world.'

75. These cross-cutting efforts are vividly evoked in Barbara Tuchman's *The Guns of August*, New York, 1962, chapter 1.

76. H. Holborn, *op. cit.*, p. 348.

77. W. Averell Harriman is the source for this conversation, in a verbal communication with the author.

78. For an account of the process by which the takeover of Eastern Europe occurred, see, for example, the author's *The United States in the World Arena*, New York, 1960, pp. 89–118 and 177–95.

382

79. See, especially, William E. Griffith, *The Sino–Soviet Rift*, Cambridge, Mass., 1964, p. 29. Griffith regards the cancellation of Soviet atomic aid to Communist China in June 1959 as a critical date, reflecting an assessment in Moscow that the rift was already 'irreparable'. That act obviously helped make it so.

80. J. W. Wilkie, *op. cit.*, pp. 17–21.

CHAPTER 5

1. The dynamics of this germination from transplanted British seeds in a 'lengthy and complicated process' is well evoked in J. R. Pole, *Political Representation in England and the Origins of the American Republic*, London and New York, 1966.

2. P. Bradley (ed.), *Democracy in America*, New York, 1954, Vol. II, p. 78.

3. *An American Dilemma*, New York, 1944, Vol. 1, p. 21.

4. Jean-Paul Sartre, 'Americans and Their Myths', *The Nation*, Vol. 165 (October 18, 1947), p. 403.

5. *The Irony of American History*, New York, 1952, p. 24.

6. This dating gains some support from Richard L. Merritt's original essay on 'The Emergence of American Nationalism. A Quantitative Approach', in Seymour M. Lipset and Richard Hofstadter (eds.), *Sociology and History: Methods*, New York and London, 1968, pp. 138 ff. (reprinted from *The American Quarterly* (1965), pp. 319 ff.). Merritt notes (p. 154): 'It was not until the years after 1764 that the distinction between "His Majesty's Subjects" or "British Colonists" and "Americans" became a real one in the Colonial press.'

7. For a discussion of this point see S. P. Huntington, *Political Order in Changing Societies*, New Haven and London, 1968, pp. 134–5. Also, D. Boorstin, *The Genius of American Politics*, Chicago, 1953, especially chapter III.

8. See, for example, J. R. Pole, *op. cit.*, pp. 173–4. Also, for the latest phase of the debate on the dynamics of colonial politics centered on the legislatures, see J. P. Greene, 'Political Mimesis: A Consideration of the Historical and Cultural Roots of Legislative Behavior in the British Colonies in the Eighteenth Century'; 'A Comment' by Bernard Bailyn; 'Reply' by J. P. Greene – in *The American Historical Review*, December 1969.

9. J. R. Pole, *op. cit.*, p. 341.

10. Robert E. Brown, *Charles Beard and the Constitution*, New York, 1956 edition, especially chapters IV and VI. On Massachusetts, for example, see J. R. Pole's conclusion, *op. cit.*, p. 245: 'The property qualifications placed little material restriction on the extent of the suffrage. The haphazard kind of enforcement which had been observed before the Revolution continued to prevail; so that although a proportion of the people were excluded by legal definition, they do not appear to have constituted that kind of aggrieved group or class whose demands make themselves felt in pressure on the legislature. The best evidence of this point is that of their silence. During the years of depression and strife after the end of the War, huge numbers of petitions were despatched to the General Court, giving a vivid and detailed account of the grievances of the inhabitants of different towns and sections; and the absence of demands for suffrage extension can best be interpreted to mean that suffrage restrictions were not felt to be a grievance.'

11. Richard P. McCormick, 'New Perspectives on Jacksonian Politics', *The American Historical Review*, January 1960, p. 297. McCormick argues persuasively that the rise of voters' participation in presidential elections is not the result of either marked widening of the franchise or the charismatic personality of Jackson, since the benchmark is 1840 rather than 1828, 1832, or 1836. He attributes the surge to 78 per cent participation in the election of 1840 to the palpable closeness of the race, which diminished apathy evident on

earlier occasions, and the emergence of the two-party system on a more solid base than with its debut in 1800.

12. P. L. Ford (ed.), *The Works of Thomas Jefferson*, New York, 1905, Federal edition, Vol. XI, p. 504.

13. Some of the major contributions to the debate are those of A. Fishlow, *American Railroads and the Transformation of the Ante-Bellum Economy*, Cambridge, Mass., 1965; R. W. Fogel, *Railroads and American Economic Growth: Essays in Econometric History*, Baltimore, 1964; C. H. Hession and H. Sardy, *Ascent to Affluence*, Boston, 1969, especially chapters 11, 12 and 13; D. C. North, 'A Note on Professor Rostow's "Take-off" into Self-sustained Economic Growth', *The Manchester School*, January 1958.

14. See, notably, *Output, Employment, and Productivity in the United States after 1800, Studies in Income and Wealth*, Vol. 30, New York and London, 1966: R. E. Gallman, 'Gross National Product in the United States, 1834–1909', especially pp. 20–4; S. Lebergott, 'Labor Force and Employment, 1800–1960', especially pp. 117–21; V. F. Eliasberg, 'Some Aspects of Development in the Coal Mining Industry, 1839–1918', especially pp. 410–13, 417–18, and 428–34.

15. See, especially, Eugene V. Rostow, 'The Supreme Court as a Legal Institution', in Ralph Freedman *et al.*, *Perspectives on the Court*, Evanston, 1967.

16. Henry Steele Commager (ed.), *Documents of American History*, New York, 1963, 7th edition, Vol. 1, p. 298.

17. Quoted in A. D. Chandler, Jr., *Strategy and Structure*, Cambridge, Mass., 1962, pp. 21–2.

18. *Law and the Conditions of Freedom in the Nineteenth Century United States*, Madison, 1956.

19. H. S. Commager, *op. cit.*, Vol. 1, p. 543.

20. *The Triumph of Conservatism*, Glencoe, 1963, especially pp. 279–305. I would not accept the implications of the title of Kolko's final chapter, 'The Lost Democracy'. The allocation of power and resources in, say, America of the 1960s more nearly approximates the democratic norms set out in chapter 7 than in America of, say, 1914 or 1940.

21. For a sophisticated refinement of the classic debate on the relation of tariff changes to the course of pig iron production in the period 1840–60, when the shift from charcoal to coal fuel was under way, see R. W. Fogel and S. L. Engerman, 'A Model for the Explanation of Industrial Expansion during the Nineteenth Century: With an Application to the American Iron Industry', *Journal of Political Economy*, May/June 1969.

22. E. E. Schattschneider, *Politics, Pressures and the Tariff*, New York, 1935, p. 283. A definitive economic evaluation of the American tariff from, say, 1816 to 1933 remains still to be done. Clearly, it did not determine fundamentally the contours of American economic growth; but it is too massive a phenomenon to be dismissed simply with that judgment. From a 20 per cent tax on dutiable imports (16 per cent on total imports) in 1860, the figures rose to 48 per cent by the end of the Civil War (38 per cent on total imports) and remained in the range of 40–50 per cent to the eve of the First World War (20–30 per cent on total imports). For the quite different environment of post-World War II tariff politics see, especially, R. A. Bauer, Ithiel Pool, and L. A. Dexter, *American Business and Public Policy*, New York, 1963, especially pp. 396–6.

23. John R. Commons *et al.*, *History of Labour in the United States*, New York, 1918 (reprinted 1936), Vol. 1, p. 185.

24. Leo Wolman, *Ebb and Flow in Trade Unionism*, New York, 1936, p. 16.

25. A. H. Hansen, 'Factors Affecting the Trend of Real Wages', *The American Economic Review*, Vol. XV, 1925, p. 32.

26. From P. B. Kenen, 'A Statistical Survey of Basic Trends', in S. Harris (ed.), *American Economic History*, New York, 1961, p. 78.

27. Richard A. Musgrave, *Fiscal Systems*, New Haven and London, 1969, p. 94.

28. H. Wayne Morgan makes a strong case for the inevitability of the decision to go to war, whoever held the presidency (*America's Road to Empire*, New York, 1965, pp. 60–63).

29. R. A. Musgrave and J. M. Culbertson note: 'Development expenditures throughout this period were dominated by outlays for transportation, largely for highway facilities, which accounted for over 80 per cent of the expenditures in this category for the years through 1929. Thus, the growth of the highway system, related to the development of the automobile, explains the drastic expansion in the relative importance of outlays for economic development during the twenties and provides a striking illustration of the impact of technological change on the public budget.' ('The Growth of Public Expenditures in the United States, 1890–1948', *National Tax Journal*, June 1953, pp. 102–3.)

The absolute and relative outlays for economic development moved as in the accompanying table.

	Expenditures (in millions of dollars)	Expenditures as percentage of total public expenditures for civilian purposes)	Expenditures (as percentage of GNP)[a]
1902	163	14	2.1
1913	441	20	2.6
1923	1,536	27	3.6 (1922)
1929	2,314	26	3.6 (1927)

[a] From R. A. Musgrave, *Fiscal Systems*, p. 94.

30. A. H. Hawley, *The Changing Shape of Metropolitan America*, Glencoe, 1956, p. 2.

Table showing per cent change of population in the United States, in metropolitan areas, and in area outside of metropolitan areas, 1900–50

Type of place	1940–50[a]	1930–40[b]	1920–30[b]	1910–20[b]	1900–10[b]
Total United States population	14.5	7.2	16.1	14.9	21.0
All metropolitan areas reported	22.0	8.1	28.3	26.9	34.6
Central cities	13.9	5.1	22.3	25.2	33.6
Satellite areas	35.6	15.1	44.0	32.0	38.2
Area outside metropolitan areas	6.1	6.5	7.9	9.6	16.4
Number of metropolitan areas	168	140	97	58	44

[a] Seventeenth Census of the United States.
[b] W. S. Thompson, *The Growth of Metropolitan Districts in the United States: 1900–40*, Washington, D.C., U.S. Government Printing Office, 1947.

31. R. A. Musgrave, *op. cit.*, p. 94.

32. See, for example, H. G. Vatter, *The U.S. Economy in the 1950s*, New York, 1963, especially pp. 158–63.

33. William Brink and Louis Harris, *The Negro Revolution in America*, New York, 1963, p. 39.

34. The author's views on the evolution of U.S. military and foreign policy down to 1958 are set out in *The United States in the World Arena*, New York, 1960. Observations on American foreign policy are also to be found in chapters 6 and 8.

35. A. Maddison, *Economic Growth in the West*, New York, 1964. S. S. Kuznets, *Modern Economic Growth*, New Haven, 1966. E. F. Denison, *Why Growth Rates Differ*, Washington, D.C., 1967. C. P. Kindleberger, *Europe's Postwar Growth*, Cambridge, Mass., 1967. M. M. Postan, *An Economic History of Western Europe, 1945–1964*, London, 1967.

36. I. Svennilson, *Growth and Stagnation in the European Economy*, Geneva, 1954, pp. 46–7.

37. *Op. cit.*, pp. 236–7.

CHAPTER 6

1. *The Stages of Economic Growth*, p. 91.
2. New York, 1968, p. 1.
3. *Ibid.*, pp. 75–6.
4. *Ibid.*, pp. 84–5.
5. H. S. Houthakker and L. D. Taylor, *Consumer Demand in the United States, 1929–1970*, Cambridge, Mass., 1966, chapters 4 and 5. See, especially, summary pages 154 ff.
6. From data in *Economic Report of the President*, January 1969, pp. 227, 234, and 301.
7. 'The Budget Message of the President', January 15, 1969. p. 27, in *The Budget of the United States Government*, Fiscal Year 1970.
8. These groupings were calculated as follows from U.S. Department of Commerce, *Survey of Current Business*, Vols. 44, 48, and 49.

SECURITY

National Defense : military services and foreign military assistance; atomic energy development; space research and technology; other.

International Affairs and Finance : conduct of foreign affairs and informational activities; foreign economic assistance and other transfers.

Veterans Disability Compensation and Pension Allowances.

INTEREST

Net Interest Paid.

LAW, ORDER AND ADMINISTRATION

General Government : general administration; general property and records management central personel management and employment costs; other.
Police.
Prisons and Correction.

ECONOMIC AND ENVIRONMENT

Fire.
Labor and Manpower.
Other (HEW).
Regulations of Commerce and Finance.

Transportation : highways; water; air.
Public Utilities : transit; electricity; water and gas.
Postal Services.
Other (Commerce and Housing).
Agriculture and Agricultural Resources : stabilization of farm prices and income; financing farm ownership and utilities; conservation of agricultural resources; other services.
Conservation and Development of Resources.
Other (Natural Resources).

SOCIAL WELFARE
Public Health and Sanitation.
Education : elementary and secondary; higher; other.
Social Security and Special Welfare Services : public assistance and relief; unemployment benefits; old age and retirement benefits; other.
Veterans Educational, Training, and Other Benefits.
Veterans Insurance.
Veterans Hospitals and Medical Care.
Veterans Administration and Other Services.
Housing and Community Redevelopment (including urban renewal and public housing).
Recreational Use of Natural Resources.

9. Nestor E. Terleckyj and Harriet J. Halper, 'Research and Development: Its Growth and Composition', National Industrial Conference Board, Inc., New York, 1963, p. 53.

10. For example, P. N. Rosenstein-Rodan estimates a deceleration in the U.S. rate of growth in the period 1970–2000, on this account. See 'The Have's and the Have-not's around the year 2000', a report presented at the World Law Fund Conference, June 1969 (mimeograph).

11. The author's basic case for the need to supplement conventional fiscal and monetary policy with a kind of social contract among labor, business, and government is made in *The Process of Economic Growth*, New York, 1952 edition, pp. 225–35; Oxford, 1960 edition, pp. 227–37. See, also, 'The Chapter Keynes Never Wrote', Department of State *Bulletin*, 29 March 1965, pp. 454–9. For a decorous debate on the subject, see Arthur F. Burns and Paul A. Samuelson, *Full Employment, Guideposts and Economic Stability*, Rational Debate Seminars, Washington, D.C., 1967.

12. Paul Rosenstein-Rodan makes the case well in 'The Role of Income Distribution in Development Programs', *Essays in Honor of Marco Fanno*, Padova, 1966, p. 570: 'In contrast to the nineteenth century the automatism of supply and demand does not determine "optimum" wages in our present economic system. The wage level today is "indeterminate". In the atomistic structure of the nineteenth century any wage adjustment occurred in one enterprise out of thousands and affected fifty or one hundred workers while wages of the other several million workers remained unchanged. Under such circumstances only the substitution effects (costs) were affected by the wage revision while income effects were infinitesimal and negligible. The synhcronized collective bargaining in the modern economies brings about wage revisions which at the same unit of time affect a high proportion of the total working class and, therefore, a high proportion of total effective demand. It releases not only substitution but also income effects; while costs are raised, effective demand is raised too, and an unequivocal and unique determination of wages does not result any more from the market mechanism. The pre-1914 economic system was thought to be regulated by monetary policy. The lesson of the inter-war period was to recognize that monetary policy must be supplemented by fiscal policy. The lesson of our generation is that monetary, plus fiscal policy are insufficient and must be supplemented by an income policy. This involves a social agreement on a new type of "Contrat Social",

agreeing on the distribution of the burden of sacrifices for development among different classes. The higher income classes have to accept an effective increase of the tax burden (in order to secure sufficient national investment) while the working classes may accept certain guidelines about wage policy conducive to high growth. The forms and the institutions which will carry out this new "Contrat Social" have not been worked anywhere yet. We are groping in the dark, or semi-obscurity, to work out the solution of this problem, which will necessarily involve a complete participation of all the classes implicated in the process of production and a high degree of social cohesion, confidence and responsibility. That is, however, the task of our generation, and those of us who have confidence in human reason as a basis for social progress, can view with optimism the general trend even if we cannot trace the path in all its details.'

13. For an interesting theoretical formulation of the implications of these problems for welfare economics, see A. V. Kneese and R. C. d'Arge, 'Pervasive External Costs and the Response of Society', printed in *The Analysis and Evaluation of Public Expenditures: The PPB System*, Joint Economic Committee, Volume I, pp. 87 ff., Washington, D.C., 1969.

14. For a pioneering effort to measure the cost of reaching some sixteen quality goals in American society by 1975, see L. A. Lecht, *Goals, Priorities, and Dollars*, New York, 1966. These include space and international aid, as well as education, health, urban reconstruction, etc.

15. *Examination into the Effectiveness of the Construction Grant Program for Abating, Controlling and Preventing Water Pollution*, Report to the Congress by the Comptroller General of the United States, Washington, D.C., 1969.

16. 'Moving Toward Realistic Housing Goals' in Kermit Gordon (ed.), *Agenda for the Nation*, Washington, D.C., 1968, pp. 141 ff.

17. *The Negro Revolt*, New York, 1962, p. 223.

18. 'The Black Revolution and The Economic Future of Negroes in The United States', *The American Scholar*, Autumn 1969, pp. 637–8. For a debate on statistics of Negro relative progress and their social and psychological meaning see Richard Young and Nathan Glazer in *Encounter*, December 1969, pp. 80–7.

19. For psychiatric evidence on this point see, for example, Herbert Hendin, 'Black Suicide', *Columbia Forum*, Vol. XII, No. 3, Fall 1969, pp. 13–17.

20. Malcolm X, with the assistance of Alex Haley, *The Autobiography of Malcom X*, New York, 1964, p. 386.

21. *Soul on Ice*, New York, 1968, pp. 61, 17, and 210.

22. *Beyond Racism*, New York, 1969, p. 46.

23. Whitney Young, Jr., *op. cit.*, p. 13.

24. A very small minority of Negroes have associated their problems with the nature of capitalism and call for its overthrow as a prerequisite for social and economic equality. It is the prime objective of traditional Communist policy in the United States to link racial and white economic and social discontents. But this is a relatively minor theme thus far; and, at Negro insistence, black and white radical movements are quite sharply segregated.

25. *The Republic* (F. M. Cornford, trs.), New York and London, 1952 ed., pp. 288–9 and 285–6. See, also, Werner Jaeger, *Paideia: the Ideals of Greek Culture*, translated from the German manuscript by Gilbert Highet, Vol. II, New York, 1943, pp. 337–8, 340–1; and the commentary on this theme by Harold Lasswell in *Democratic Character*, reprinted in *The Political Writings of Harold Lasswell*, Glencoe, 1951, pp. 465 ff.

26. *Prospect for America*, New York, 1961.

27. *Goals for Americans*, New York, 1960.

28. *The Stages of Economic Growth*, p. 16.

29. I agree that the war in Vietnam is anachronistic; but the anachronism lies in the

old-fashioned dream of Ho and his successors, rooted in memories and experiences that go back to the Second World War (and, even, to the 1920s) that they have the right and duty to succeed to the French colonial empire in Asia. In pursuit of this obsessive vision they have sacrificed hundreds of thousands of lives and the economic and social development of North Vietnam, backed by Peking and Moscow, each for its own reasons. The pattern of thought underlying Hanoi's policy – and that of other revolutionary romantics – is considered in chapter 7.

30. This point is lucidly made by Francois Crouzet in 'A University Besieged: Nanterre, 1967–69', *Political Science Quarterly*, June 1969, pp. 349–50.

31. The findings are well summarized in S. M. Lipset, 'The Politics of Academia', paper prepared for American Council on Education, Commission of Higher Education.

32. Quoted, *ibid.*, p. 44.

33. *The Uncommitted*, New York, 1965, pp. 425–47.

34. S. M. Lipset, *op. cit.*, p. 21, quotes the following array of 'Liberalism' by academic discipline:

Political behavior and attitudes of selected academic professions (per cent)

Disciplines	Liberal on 14-item domestic issues Attitude scale
Philosophers	91
Sociologists	88
Political scientists	90
Historians	83
Psychologists	74
Botanists	49
Geologists	39
Mathematicians	46
Engineers	34

SOURCE: Charles B. Spaulding and Henry A. Turner, 'Political Orientation and Field of Specialization Among College Professors', *Sociology of Education* (1968), p. 253.

35. *The New York Times Book Review*, 22 February 1970, p. 42.

36. Quoted, E. V. Rostow, 'The Consent of the Governed', *The Virginia Quarterly Review*, Autumn 1968, p. 530. This essay explores the problem of civil disobedience in democracy, employing a counterpoint between Socrates and Thoreau.

37. *Ibid.*

38. *Social Origins of Dictatorship and Democracy*, Boston, 1966.

39. *Ibid.*, p. 506.

40. *The American Science of Politics*, Berkeley and Los Angeles, 1959, p. 245.

41. *Weekly Compilation of Presidential Documents*, 16 September 1968, Vol. 4, No. 37, pp. 1335–6.

42. Philip Geyelin, *Austin American-Statesman*, 30 November 1969, p. 6.

43. See, for example, Royal Commission on Canada's Economic Prospects, 'The Service Industries' by the Bank of Montreal, March 1956; Milton Gilbert *et al.*, 'Com-

parative National Products and Price Levels', (O.E.E.C., Paris, 1958). For more recent estimates, see Maurice Lengelle, *The Growing Importance of the Service Sector in Member Countries* (O.E.C.D., Paris, 1966); H. S. Houthakker and L. D. Taylor, *op. cit.*, for a comparison of their findings with those of J. Sandee (ed.), *Europe's Future Consumption*, Amsterdam, 1964; and the discussion of comparative patterns of service outlays in V. R. Fuchs, *op. cit.*, pp. 24–31.

44. Ottawa, 1 February 1965, pp. 80 and 114–18.

45. 'Student Rebellion: Vision of the Future or Echo from the Past?' *Political Science Quarterly*, June 1969, pp. 308–10.

46. *The Common Problem*, London, 1969, quoted in *The Sunday Times*, London, 20 July 1969.

47. Alan Bennett, London. Quoted with permission of the author.

CHAPTER 7

1. *The Civic Culture*, Princeton, 1963.

2. David E. Apter, *The Politics of Modernization*, Chicago and London, 1965, p. 452.

3. F. R. von der Mehden, *Politics of Developing Nations*, Englewood Cliffs, 1964, pp. 117–40, arrays some of these variant formulations and rationalizations.

4. *Partners in Development*, Report of the Commission on International Development, Chairman: Lester B. Pearson, New York, 1969, Table 17, p. 378. Debt service payments for developing countries rose from $2.3 billion in 1961 to $4.0 billion in 1968 (*ibid.*, p. 372).

5. *Ibid.*, p. 28. P. N. Rosenstein-Rodan notes that 'more than five-sixths of the population of the underdeveloped world had a rate of growth of 4–4.5 per cent' in the 1960s ('The Have's and the Have-not's Around the Year 2000', report presented at the World Law Fund Conference, June 1969). His calculation eliminates Yugoslavia, Spain, Greece, Israel, and some East Asian countries with high growth rates.

6. *Ibid.*, p. 27. Although projections of the kind done by Herman Kahn and A. J. Wiener (*The Year 2000*, New York, 1967) and P. N. Rosenstein-Rodan (*loc. cit.*) are helpful in many ways, I believe the emphasis often given to the gap between rich and poor nations in GNP per capita is misleading, whatever virtues it may have as propaganda for external development assistance. First, comparisons of income levels at widely differing stages of growth are technically – even philosophically – ambiguous. Second, what matters within a society is the rate and steadiness of its growth; and the movement within it towards equality of opportunity and other forms of equity in sharing the benefits of modernization. The gap between rich and poor within a developing nation may be politically and psychologically significant. But what worries a peasant or urban worker in a developing nation is not how Americans live but whether he and his children can be confident of improvement from where they are, in the span of their lives. I am, therefore, much less concerned that in the year 2000 GNP per capita may have attained only, say $300–700 per capita in the present developing world versus, say, $4000–9000 per capita in the developed world, than I am about the developing world getting to the $300–700 per capita range in reasonable order and continuity, dealing along the way with the problem of bringing birth rates down. That would mean by the year 2000 that the presently developing world would either be completing the drive to technological maturity or in an early phase of high mass-consumption. As post-1945 experience in Western Europe and Japan indicates, it is not much of a trick to roll on from there. And, as chapter 6 indicates, there is ample reason for concern about how the developed nations will manage their affairs as they move from high mass-consumption through the challenges and vicissitudes of the search for quality. In short, each stage of growth has its distinctive problems and opportunities which differ in their

contours, in each national case; and it is to these that men mainly address themselves within national societies, at particular periods of time. We should not be taken in by magic of our own creation, in the form of GNP per capita measurements.

7. In his paper on 'Growth and Structural Change in the Middle East' (prepared for the Columbia University Conference on International Economic Develompent, 15–21 February 1970), Charles Issawi indicates the further rise in the late 1960s of military expenditures in the area: 'As a percentage of GNP, between 1965 and 1969 they rose as follows: Iran, 4.4 to 5.9 per cent, Iraq 10.2 to 12.4, Israel 11.7 to 21.3, Jordan 12.9 to 25.2, Saudi Arabi 8.6 to 12.7, Syria 8.4 to 17.8 and UAR 8.6 to 14.6, while Turkey remained unchanged at 4.3' (p. 22, mimeograph). In a footnote Issawi quotes evidence that the UAR figures may have reached 20 per cent of GNP in the Noveber 1969 budget.

8. *Op. cit.*, p. 65.

9. *Op. cit.*

10. *Ibid.*, p. 276. My own earlier observations on this theme are contained in 'The Challenge of Democracy in Developing Nations', chapter VIII in *View From the Seventh Floor*, New York, 1964, pp. 98–9.

11. Quoted from Hsia Yen, former vice-minister of culture, in C. K. Yang, 'Cultural Revolution and Revisionism', *China in Crisis*, Ping-ti Ho and Tang Tsou (eds.), Vol. 1, Book Two, Chicago, 1968, p. 516.

12. Quoted, E. F. Heckscher, *The Continental System*, Oxford, 1922, p. 253.

13. I remember a conversation in 1961 between President Keita of Mali and President Kennedy in which Keita explained how his first need after independence was for a few DC-3 aircraft and a few armored jeeps for his police. He said he found himself responsible for a piece of territory that called itself a nation. The people had to feel that the government could make its presence felt in every part of the country, and that it had instruments to effect its authority.

14. I. L. Markovitz (ed.), *African Politics and Society*, New York, 1970, pp. 1–12. Markovitz uses the French term *encadrement* for the process of engaging the people systematically in development activities.

15. Immanuel Wallerstein, chapter 7, in J. LaPalombara and M. Weiner (eds.), *Political Parties and Political Development*, Princeton, 1966.

16. *Economic Survey of Africa Since 1950*, United Nations Department of Economic and Social Affairs, New York, 1959, p. 135.

17. *Ibid.*, p. 187.

18. Philip Ndegwa, 'Requirements of More Rapid Growth in "Black Africa" During the Next Decade', paper prepared for Columbia University Conference on International Economic Development, 15–21 February 1970, p. 13 (mimeograph). The latest estimate for the expansion of manufacturing in Africa (*Economic Conditions in Africa in Recent Years*, Economic Commission for Africa, Secretariat paper prepared for Commission meeting, 3–14 February 1969, dated 31 December 1968, p. 104) concludes that the industrial growth rate in the period 1960–6 was 5.5 per cent as opposed to 3.7 per cent for total GDP. The development plans of African countries call for rapid increases in manufacturing output (*ibid.*, p. 101); but, excepting certain North African countries, South Africa, and Rhodesia, they start from a low base (*ibid.*, p. 103).

19. See discussion in *The Stages of Economic Growth*, especially pp. 41–2, 62–3. Also, the author's observations in *Pan-Africanism Reconsidered*, edited by the American Society of African Culture, Berkeley and Los Angeles, 1962, pp. 161–3.

20. In a perceptive essay, reprinted in I. L. Markovitz, *op. cit.*, pp. 226–41, David Apter discusses the emergence of political oppositions in Africa and the dilemmas they create ('Some Reflections on the Roles of a Political Opposition in New Nations').

21. J. LaPalombara and M. Weiner, *op. cit.*, p. 396.

22. Washington's Farewell Address, 17 September 1796.

23. David Apter, *loc. cit.*, p. 228.

24. *Thailand: The Modernization of the Bureaucratic Polity*, Honolulu, 1966.

25. L. Pearson, *op. cit.*, pp. 249 and 255. The chart is from Daniel M. Schydlowsky, 'Latin American Trade Policies in the 1970s: A Prospective Appraisal', Columbia University Conference on International Economic Development, 15–21 February 1970. For a parallel discussion of the relation between economic development and political instability, see S. P. Huntington, *Political Order in Changing Societies*, New Haven, 1968, pp. 49–59.

26. For a recent statement in the spirit of J. Q. Adams on the lack of a democratic tradition in Latin America, see Glen Dealy, 'Prolegomena on the Spanish American Political Tradition', *The Hispanic American Historical Review*, February 1968, pp. 37 ff.

27. Adrienne Koch and William Peden (eds.), *The Selected Writings of John and John Quincy Adams*, New York, 1946, p. 319.

28. Bolivar is quoted in S. Huntingdon, *op. cit.*, p. 29: 'There is no good faith in America, either among men or among nations. Treaties are paper, constitutions books, elections battles, liberty anarchy, and life a torment. The only thing one can do in America is emigrate.'

29. For data on some heavy industry and fabricating sectors in key Latin American countries during the 1960s, see *United Nations Monthly Bulletin of Statistics*, New York, December 1968, pp. 52–4 (fibres), 56 (newsprint), 60–4 (chemicals), 68–71 (pig iron, ferroalloys, and steel). Progress will be seen as generally irregular, excepting the case of Mexico. With respect to Mexico, see Alan S. Manne 'Key Sectors of the Mexican Economy, 1962–72', chapter 10 in Irma Adelman and Erik Thorbecke (eds.), *The Theory and Design of Economic Development*, Baltimore, 1966. Working with the Nacional Financiera, S.A., Manne analyzes prospects for the following key sectors, most of which are typical of the drive to technological maturity: paper, heavy chemicals, petro-chemicals, petroleum, cement, steel, copper, aluminium, foundries, machinery production, electricity and railroad services.

30. For a more extended statement of this argument, see the author's 'The Past Quarter-century as Economic History and the Tasks of International Economic Organization', *The Journal of Economic History*, March 1970, pp. 150–87.

31. Joseph LaPalombara and Myron Weiner, *op. cit.*, pp. 397–8.

32. For a parallel effort to draw lessons for the prospects of democracy, see, especially, Reinhold Niebuhr and Paul E. Sigmund, *The Democratic Experience*, New York, 1969. Their chapter 10 reviews recent literature on the subject. See, also, Edward Shils, *Political Development in the New States*, The Hague, 1965, for a distinguished reflective essay, more analytic than prescriptive.

33. The context of Dr Busia's statement is as follows: 'You have handed to me, as a symbol of the transfer of power from you to a democratically-elected civilian government, our new Constitution. It is a Constitution which seeks to place the exercise of power under restraint. It is the fruit of our recent experience. It bears the marks of our scars, our fears and our aspirations. Its underlying philosophy is that no man, or group of men, is virtuous enough to hold power without checks.' From speech by Dr K. A. Busia, Prime Minister, at the Inauguration of the Second Republic at Black Star Square in Accra, 1 October 1969, Ghana Publishing Corporation, Accra–Tema, Ghana.

CHAPTER 8

1. The author has traced out this sequence in greater detail (down to mid-1958) in *The United States in the World Arena*, New York, 1960; in 'The Third Round', *Foreign Affairs*, October 1963; and in *The Great Transition*, Leeds, 1967.

2. This debate is well documented by D. S. Zagoria in *The Sino–Soviet Conflict, 1956–*

61, Princeton, 1962, especially chapter 10, pp. 245–76. For the later interweaving of the debate on 'wars of national liberation' with the debate on nuclear weapons see William E. Griffith, *The Sino–Soviet Rift*, Cambridge, Mass., pp. 20, 21, 110, 146, 228.

3. Quoted from *Studies on Viet Nam*, Department of External Affairs, Canberra, Australia, August 1965, p. 23. Minister of Defense Giap made the statement on the tenth anniversary of the Geneva Agreement of 1954 (19 July 1964, in *Nhan Dan*).

4. See above Table 40, chapter 7, p. 244.

5. See, for example, the *New York Times* assessment, March 7, 1966.

6. Lester Pearson, *Partners in Development*, New York, 1969.

7. *Development Assistance, 1968 Review*, Report by Edwin M. Martin, O.E.C.D., Paris, December 1968, Table 1, p. 255.

8. Thucydides, *History of the Peloponnesian War*, Rex Warner, tr., Baltimore, 1954, p. 55.

9. Konrad Lorenz, *On Aggression*, New York, 1966, pp. 268–74.

10. Robert Ardrey, *The Territorial Imperative*, New York, 1966, p. 351.

11. *Ibid.*, p. 351.

12. C. Curtis, *A Commonplace Book*, New York, 1957, pp. 112–13.

13. *Op. cit.*, p. 276.

14. *The Horse's Mouth*, New York, 1944, p. 311.

APPENDIX

1. 'The National Style', in E. E. Morison (ed.), *The American Style*, New York, 1958, pp. 248–9.

2. James Gould Cozzens, *By Love Possessed*.

3. I am indebted to Doris Kearns for this array of categories of decision-making analyses.

4. G. A. Almond and J. S. Coleman (eds.), *The Politics of the Developing Areas* (Princeton, 1960), already reflected in their 'Conclusion' (pp. 532 ff.) quite elaborate prior analyses of the relation between economic and social progress and forms of political systems. Behind their work lay the following, at least:

K. Davis and H. H. Golden, 'Urbanization and the Development of Pre-Industrial Areas', *Economic Development and Cultural Change*, Vol. III, No. 1, October 1954.

H. H. Golden, 'Literacy and Social Change in Underdeveloped Countries', *Rural Sociology*, Vol. 20, No. 1, March 1955.

D. Lerner, 'Communications Systems and Social Systems. Statistical Exploration in History and Policy', *Behavioral Science*, Vol. 2, No. 4, October 1957.

D. Lerner, with L. W. Pevsner, *The Passing of Traditional Society*, Glencoe, Ill., 1958.

L. W. Shannon, *Underdeveloped Areas*, New York, 1957.

L. W. Shannon, 'Is Level of Development Related to Capacity for Self-Government?' *American Journal of Economics and Sociology*, Vol. 17, July 1958.

L. W. Shannon, 'Socio–Economic Development and Political Status', *Social Problems*, Vol. VII, No. 2, Fall 1959.

S. M. Lipset, 'Some Social Requisites of Democracy: Economic Development and Political Legitimacy', *The American Political Science Review*, Vol. LIII, No. 1, March 1959.

5. Irma Adelman and Cynthia Taft Morris, *Society, Politics & Economic Development*, Baltimore, 1967.

6. From Hollis Chenery, 'Targets for Development' (following p. 5), Economic Development Report No. 153, March 1970, Project for Quantitative Research on Economic Development, Cambridge, Mass.

7. For example, A. Gesell and F. Ilg, *Infant and Child in the Culture of Today*, New York, 1943.

INDEX

Action, General Theory of, 335
  criticisms of, 336–54
Adowa, battle of (1896), 164, 218
Aehrenthal, A., 163, 169
Afghanistan, 282–3
Africa
  British and French holdings in, 161, 164, 165, 166
  new nations of: capital needed by, 329; China and, 306; government expenditure by functions in, 277; growth rate in, 275, 276; and Negroes in USA, 242; population growth in, 274; regional institutions of, 309, 311
  primitive government in, 32–5, 367
  see also individual countries
agricultural production
  as percentage of GNP, 105, 108, 113, 379; USA, 197
  prices for, 145, 207
  rate of growth of, 105, 108, 113, 120, 121
agricultural productivity
  breakthrough in, 298, 317
  in China and India, 374, 375
  in USA, 185, 234
agriculture
  Communism and, 289, 298; in China, 132–5 *passim*; in Russia, 122, 123, 125, 126, 289
  in developing countries, 274, 317; Latin America, 292
  in drive to maturity, 101, 177
  New Deal and (USA), 221
  in take-off, 54, 56–7, 99
  tariffs to protect, 141, 142, 143, 144, 149–50
  in traditional societies, 27, 28, 35, 52; Roman Empire, 44, 56
  in transition to take-off, 84, 93, 95
aircraft industry, 234
  research component in, 235, 236
Albany Plan (1759), 187
Alcock Convention, on China, 72
Alexander II of Russia, 70, 169, 181
Algeciras Conference (1906), 162, 164

Algeria, 165, 280, 281, 309
Alliance for Progress, 175, 259, 305, 316
Alsace-Lorraine, 167
American Federation of Labor, 201
American Indians, 185–6
Americanism, 184
anarchism, basic tenets of, 256, 257
Angola, 322
anthropology, and political science, 342
'anti-imperialism,' developing countries with politics based on, 279
Anti-Trust Act (USA, 1890), 204
ANZUS, 310
Arabs, schisms between, 311
Argentina, 164
  GNP per capita in, 279
  inflation in, 290, 291, 294
  military dictatorship in, 279, 289, 293
Aristides, 38
Aristotle, on pastoral peoples, 32
arms control, work towards, 260, 326
Articles of Confederation, USA, 188, 189, 192
ASEAN (Association of South-East Asian Nations), 311
Asia
  elections in, 301
  government expenditure by functions in, 277
  regional spirit in, 310–11
  see also individual countries
Asia, Eastern and Southern
  growth rates in, 275
  population growth in, 274
Asian Development Bank, 311
ASPAC (Asian and Pacific Council), 310–11
Atatürk, Kemal, 5, 14, 81, 92, 93, 137
Athens (5th century B.C.), 35–42, 280, 326
Atmospheric Test Ban Treaty (1963), 305, 313
Augustus, Roman Emperor, 43–6
Austria, defeat of (1866), 165–6
Austro-Hungarian Empire, 162–3, 167, 382
  lag in take-off in, 219
automobile industry
  in Latin America, 292

395

capital
 consumption of, in pollution, 226, 239, 262
 for developing countries, 276, 293, 329
 foreign: in Mexico, 94; in Russia, 87, 148
 formation of: as percentage of GNP (Japan),
  379; ratio of public to private, at different
  stages of growth, 347
 New Deal and markets for (USA), 221
 in preconditions for take-off, 22, 56
 see also social overhead capital
capital intensive industries, in Latin America,
 292, 293
Capitulations, to foreigners in Turkey (from
 1740), 92
Carthage, and Rome, 43
Castro, Fidel, 267, 279, 280, 281, 305
 China and, 306
 Mexico and, 175
cement industry, in China and India, 375
CENTO (Central Treaty Organization), 175
Central American Common Market, 285, 288,
 316
Charles X of France, 78
chemical industry
 in drive to maturity, 101, 123, 132, 149, 157
 research component in (USA), 235, 236
Chiang Kai-shek, 73
Chile, 316
 growth rate in, 290
 inflation in, 290, 291
 political instability in, 289, 294, 296
China
 constitutional change in, 132–5
 democratic aspirations of Republic of, 267,
  271
 Communists come to power in, 73–4, 80,
  133–5, 171, 304, 322
 external intrusion on, 72–4
 India and, 328
 Japan and, 169, 172
 levels of development in India and, 374, 375
 modernization in, 282
 opened to trade (1840s), 161
 outlook for: domestic policy, 261, 313–14,
  327, 328; foreign policy, 260, 326
 Pakistan and, 310, 323
 preconditions for take-off in, 61; public
  policy in, 89–92
 relations of Russia and, 117, 127, 174, 305,
  307, 312, 328, 383
 security policy in, 173–4
 sense of nationhood in, 351
 take-off in, abortive, 55, 217
 traditional society in, 47–50, 360, 369
 USA and, 212
 welfare policy in, 153
choice, pattern variables in, 337–8

Christianity, in Roman Empire, 44, 45, 47
Churchill, Winston, 173, 365
civil rights, of Negroes in USA, 198, 199–200,
 225, 242, 254
Civil Rights Act (USA, 1957), 225
civil war
 in Britain, 297, 370
 creates conditions for mutual accommodation,
  370
 in USA, 165, 193, 198, 199, 297
Clay, Henry, 193, 210–11
Clayton Act (USA, 1914), 198, 202, 204
Clemenceau, G., 112
Cleveland, President, 206, 213
coal production, 119
 in Britain, 103
 in China and India, 375
Cobden Treaty (between Britain and France,
 1860), 143
Colbert, J. B., 55, 66, 84
Cold War, 117, 175, 251, 263
 consequences of, 273
 heightens constitutional issues, 323
 rules for conduct of, 307–8, 314
Colombia, 295, 296, 297, 316
 inflation in, 290, 291
colonialism, form of intrusion of advanced on
 backward societies, 101, 326–7
colonies, 65, 84
 goal of independence in, 59–60
Combination Acts (Britain), 107
commerce, in transition to take-off, 96
communications, 54, 101
 pressure of modern, 282
communism
 basic tenets of, 257
 modernization by methods of, 273
 political future of nations under, 5–6
 waves of external effort by (from 1946), 303–7
 see also under agriculture
confidence, important component for development, 317
Confucius, 333, 364
Congo, 285, 305
 crises over, 309, 320
constitutional changes, 22, 23, 25
 in preconditions for take-off, 63, 66, 77–83;
  USA, 186, 190–3
 in take-off and drive to maturity, 102–41, 177
constitutional order
 objectives of, in UN Charter, 303, 321–6
 reconciliation of, with stages of growth, as
  one task of government, 2, 4, 11–12
constitutions
 of developing countries, democracy in, 272
 France, 109, 110
 Germany, 79, 112, 114, 128

Index

Index

foreign capital
  in Mexico, 94
  needed in developing countries, 276, 293, 329
  in Russia, 87, 148
foreign exchange earnings, in take-off, 21–2, 56, 57
foreign intrusion in preconditions for take-off, 63–77, 369
  modernization as response to, 3, 95, 332
  nationalist reaction to, 59–60, 61, 62–3, 95
  in USA, 186, 187–9
Formosa, see Taiwan
France
  constitutional change in, 78, 107–12, 271, 376
  in Far East, 211
  growth rate in, 275
  Napoleonic external adventure of, 64, 65–7, 160, 280, 327
  preconditions for take-off in, 61; public policy and, 84–5
  reaction to student revolt in, 264
  revolutions in, 66, 109, 111, 377
  security policy in, 165–6
  take-off in: dating of, 55, 373; population growth at, 274
  USA and, 259, 315
  welfare policy in, 143–4
franchise, see electorate, suffrage
Francis Ferdinand of Austria, assassinated, 167
Franco-Prussian War, 110, 115, 120, 166
Frankfurt Parliament, 78–9, 112
Franklin, Benjamin, 187, 297
Frederick II (the Great) of Prussia, 68
Frederick William I of Prussia, 55, 68
Frederick William III of Prussia, 68
Frederick William IV of Prussia, 78, 112
Free Trade, vision of, 366
Freeport Doctrine on slavery (USA), 199, 200
Frei Montalva, E., 294, 296
Freud, S., 1, 7, 332, 345
  and tripartite nature of man, 8, 11–12, 331, 357, 361–4
frontiers, violence across, 321–2
Fulani kingdom, primitive government in, 34

Gallatin, A., 195
General Motors' pattern of organization, 204
Geneva Accords (1954), 322
George III, 77, 187
Germany
  constitutional change in, 78–9, 112–17, 271
  'democratic analysis' for, 140
  enterprises of external expansion by, 67–9, 102, 327

government expenditure by functions in, 15, 277
  gropings towards solution of problem of, 312
  growth rate in, 276
  industrial maturity in, 217
  preconditions for take-off in, 61; public policy and, 85–7
  security policy in, 166–8
  take-off in: dating of, 55; population growth at, 274
  wage–price discipline in, 320
  welfare policy in, 145–9
Ghana, 279, 280, 285, 392
GNP (gross national product), see product, national
Gompers, S., 201–2
government
  as budgeting and priorities, 347
  Confucius on, 364
  consent and dissent to, 269–70
  in developing countries, 276–8
  and industrialization, 177; China, 91; Germany, 85–6; Japan, 88; Mexico, 186; Russia, 87–8, 147, 371
  input–output approach to, 12–14, 16, 56, 346–7, 375
  irregular changes of, 5
  persuasion an instrument of, 13–14
  politics as the exercise of power through, 2, 7
  in preconditions for take-off, 57, 62, 63, 83–95, 186, 193–6
  and private enterprise, in search for quality, 234
  three tasks of, 2, 11–12, 346, 348, 355; Adam Smith on, 364; in UN Charter, 302
  trade forces elaboration of functions of, 367
  in traditional societies: African tribes, 32–5; Athens, 36
government expenditure
  a critical variable, 238
  by functions, 14–16, 149; in developing and industrialized countries, 277; Germany, 145; Japan, 152; Mexico, 158; USA, 209, 223, 224, 232, 233
  as percentage of GNP, 3, 347, 348; Britain, 105; France, 108; Germany, 113, 146; Japan, 129; Mexico, 139, 158; USA, 197
governments of states in USA, 184, 191
  and federal government 198, 224–5
  and social legislation, 200, 207
Gracchi, 43
gradualism, violence v., 256–7
growth, see economic growth
Guadalupe Hidalgo, Treaty of (1848), 76, 210
Guinea, 284

Index

Inonu, Ismet, 137
input–output approach to government, 12–14, 16, 56, 346–7
    Adam Smith and, 365
insurance, social, 106, 142, 145–7, 150, 154
interest, rate of, and housing construction (USA), 240
international economy, take-off brings societies into, 99, 104
International Monetary Fund, 315, 317, 319
Interstate Commerce Act (USA, 1887), 204
investment
    by government: by functions (Mexico), 157; as percentage of GNP, 277
    as percentage of GNP: at different levels of GNP per capita, 353; Japan, 89, 151, 152, 379; Mexico, 155, 382; Russia, 123; Turkey, 155
Iran, 175, 287, 391
    growth rate in, 276, 316
    Russia and, 174, 304, 308
Ireland, 52
    Northern, 262
iron production, 103, 119
    amount of: in China, 90, 91, 375; in India, 375; in Russia, 123
Israel, 282, 307, 391
Italy, 162, 165, 217, 263
    'democratic analysis' for, 140
Ivory Coast, 284, 285
Izvolsky, A., 163, 169

Jackson, President, 190, 193, 195
Japan
    constitutional change in, 79–80, 128–32, 267, 271, 396
    enterprises of external expansion by, 73, 169, 172, 312, 327
    government expenditure by functions in, 277
    high mass-consumption stage in, 5, 128, 152, 262, 327, 328
    preconditions for take-off in, 54, 374; public policy and, 88–9
    reaction to student revolt in, 264
    retention of old culture in, 343
    security policy in, 172–3
    stages from transition to high mass-consumption in, 378–9
    take-off in: dating of, 55, 217; population growth at, 274
    welfare policy in, 149–52
Jefferson, President, 189, 192, 193, 195
    on majority vote, 255
Joffe, Adolph, 80
John XXIII, Pope, 299
Johnson, President, 259, 312, 315, 324

Jordan, 391
Juárez, B. P., 76, 82
Junkers, 115
justice and order
    balance between, 238, 346
    emergence of new issues of, with industrialization, 22
    maintenance of, as one task of government, 11, 12
    in stage beyond high mass-consumption (USA), 240–58

Kansas, constitution of, 198
Kennedy, President, 305, 312, 315, 316, 323
Kenya, 285
Kerensky, A., 121
Khrushchev, N., 117, 125, 304–5
Kim Il Sung, 279, 281
king, in African tribes, 32, 33–4
Knights of Labor, 201
Korea, 5, 169, 172
    North, industrial growth in, 280
    South: growth rate in, 276, 280, 288, 316, 328; USA and, 310
Korean War, 171, 173, 242, 281, 304, 308
Kruger, P., Kaiser's telegram to, 213
Kuomintang, 73, 80

labor force
    percentage of: in farming and manufacturing (USA), 197; non-agricultural (Japan), 379; in primary production, industry, and services, at different levels of GNP per capita, 353; in services (USA), 231
    trained, and take-off, 56
labor legislation, see social and labor legislation
laissez-faire, policy of, in Britain (18th cent.), 83
land
    abundance of, in USA, 185, 200
    tenure of: in Communist China, 134; in preconditions for take-off, 79, 88, 96
    in traditional societies, 28, 29, 30, 52; Greece 41; Roman Empire, 43, 44
land grant colleges (USA), 205
Land Tax (Britain), 142
landowners
    sale of land by, in Tsarist Russia, 118
    shift of power from, in Latin America, 292
Laos, 166, 306, 310, 322
Latin America, 161, 162
    at Bretton Woods, 319
    committed to democracy, 267, 301
    failures of democracy in, 5, 289–95
    government expenditure by functions in, 277
    growth rate in, 275, 276
    heavy industry in, 293, 392

Index

product, national
  distribution of, to labor, profits, and rent (USA), 208, 209
  primary and industry shares of, 178, 197
  rate of growth of: Britain, 104, 105; developing and industrialized countries, 275–6; France, 107, 108; Germany, 113; Japan, 129, 379; Mexico, 94, 139, 156; Russia, 118; Turkey, 93, 136, 155; USA, 185, 197, 232
  government expenditure as percentage of, *see under* government expenditure
  percentage invested, *see under* investment
product, national, per capita
  changes in, 104; Britain, 105; developing countries, 276; France, 108; Japan, 379; Turkey, 93, 136
  level of: less important than progress from lower values, 390; not associated with degree of democracy, 279; required to release stage of high mass consumption, 179, 227
  rise in, required for recovery from depression, 220
  stages of growth not automatically measured by, 352
  variations in economic structure with level of, 353
production, *see* agricultural, industrial, *and* primary production
productivity
  agricultural, 317; in China and India, 374, 375; in USA, 185, 234
  education and, 207
  linking of wage rates to, 320
  relative increase in (USA), 233, 235, 258
  in service sector, 231
professions, in preconditions for take-off, 57
profits
  effort to maximize, 7
  plough-back of, in preconditions, 56
  percentage of GNP going to, 237
Progressive Movement, USA, 203, 208, 209, 217, 218
Prussia, 68, 79, 112
public debt, government expenditure on (Britain, Germany, USA), 15
public health
  improvement of, as future aim, 254
  technology of, effective, cheap, and popular, 273–4, 370
  USA expenditure on, 232
public opinion, analysis of, 344
Pullman strike, 201
Punta del Este, meeting of American Presidents at, 324
purge in Russia (1930s), 123, 378
Puritanism, American tradition of, 185

quality, search for (stage beyond high mass-consumption), 22, 330
  options in, 258, 265
  politics of: USA, 230–61; elsewhere, 261–4
  will it succeed? 264–6, 390
Quemoy and Matsu, Taiwan Straits, 173, 305

radicals
  among Negroes, 243, 244–6
  among white youth, 248–53, 263
  black and white, segregation of, 388
  conservative reaction against, 247, 248, 252, 255–6, 264
railroads
  in Britain, 103
  in France, 84, 85, 373
  in Germany, 86, 166
  heavy industry and, 88, 99
  in Mexico, 94
  in Russia, 87, 88, 119, 121, 371, 374
  in Turkey, 92
  in USA, 186, 199, 202, 203
raw materials, processing of, in developing countries, 93, 285, 286
rayon, in Japan, 149
reconciliation, task of, 254, 296, 325, 326
Reform Bills (Britain), 103, 106, 107
regional cooperation, 259, 324, 326
  in security arrangements, 308–12, 314, 315
Reichstag, Germany, 114, 115
religious institutions, in transitional stage, 96
representation, compromise with pure democratic conception involved in, 270
research component in industry (USA), 235, 236
revolutionary romantics of developing nations, politics of, 279–82, 327, 329, 357, 359, 389
revolutions, causes of, 23, 25, 96, 191
Rhodesia, 309, 322, 323
rice, yield of, in China and India, 375
Rio Treaty system, 308
roads, automobiles and (USA), 219, 224, 385
role analysis, 8, 337, 343–5, 356
  dismantling of whole individual by, 338, 340, 362
Roman Empire, 43–7
Roosevelt, President Franklin, 170, 172, 173, 227, 261
  and Negroes, 225
  and New Deal, 220–1, 222
Roosevelt, President Theodore, 168, 181, 209, 212
Russia
  constitutional change in, 117–28, 271
  enterprises of external expansion by, 102, 117, 327
  external intrusion on, 69–70
  growth rate in, 276

Index

Standard Oil Trust, 203
steel industry, in drive to maturity, 101, 149
steel production: in China, 132, 375; in India, 375; in Mexico, 157; in Russia, 124
Stolypin, P. A., 120
suburbanization, in USA, 219, 223, 224
Suez Canal, France and, 164, 165, 166
Suez Crisis (1956), 304
suffrage, adult male
demand for, with industrialization, 22, 106
effects of, 380, 396
extension of, to women, 132, 300
see also electorate
Sukarno, A., 279, 280, 281, 286
Sun Yat-sen, 73, 80
Supreme Court, USA, 189
Sweden, 274, 285, 366, 370
Syria, 165, 391

Taff Vale case, 107, 202
Taft, President, 76
Taiping rebellion (China, 1848), 72
Taiwan, 74, 288, 328
growth rate in, 276, 316
USA and, 310
take-off, 98–100
dating of, 55
politics of drive to maturity and, 102–83, 288
population growth at, 274
possibilities for democracy increase with, 279
preconditions for, see preconditions
Tanzania, 284
Tanzimat reforms, Turkey, 81
tariffs, 177
Austria, 145
Britain, 141, 142, 365–6
France, 85, 143, 144, 145
Germany, 145
Italy, 145
Japan, 149
Latin America, 292, 293
Mexico, 95
Russia, 87, 145, 147
Turkey, 92, 153
USA, 145, 188, 193, 194, 195, 205–7, 319, 384
taxes
British, on American colonies, 187, 188, 191
in developing countries, 317
at different levels of GNP per capita, 347
in Latin America, 292
revenue from: for national investment, 388; as percentage of GNP at different levels of GNP per capita, 353
in traditional societies, 28, 29, 30; Athens, 36; Roman Empire, 44, 46, 468
and welfare outlays (USA), 238, 240

technology, absorption of, 100, 354
measurement of modernization by extent of, 352
political development to deal with, 3
in preconditions for take-off, 26, 54, 85
in service sub-sectors, 233
social and political implications of, 176
by a variety of social structures, 343
television, 242, 274
Teller Amendment, on Cuba, 212
Tennessee Valley Authority, 221
Texas, 're-annexation' of, 210
Thailand, 287, 288, 306, 316, 351
Thiers, L. A., 165
Thucydides, 38
Tibet, China and, 173
Tokugawa dynasty, Japan, 71, 79
totalitarian rule, 13
trade
of Britain, extra-European (1792), 84, 372–3
forces elaboration of government functions, 367
international, 276, 318
in traditional societies, 28, 36, 41, 44, 52
trade cycles, 99, 104, 120
and political disequilibrium, 180
and trade unions (USA), 200, 201
trade depression
of 1870s, 143, 145
of 1930s: in Japan, 131, 150, 172; in Latin America, 292; in USA, 207, 220–3
trade unions
balance of power among, 237
in Britain, 106–7, 142
in France, 111–12, 144, 377
in Germany, 115–17
in Japan, 132
in Latin America, 292
in Russia, 125
in Turkey, 138, 153–4
in USA, 200–2, 203, 207, 208
traditional societies (pre-Newtonian), 23–9, 58
economics of, 366
fatalism of, 177
politics in, 26–53
Trafalgar, battle of (1805), 160
transport
government expenditure on, Mexico, 157
infrastructure of, for take-off, 21, 54, 57, 88, 96, 97, 274
in modern cities, 234
in USA, 185, 194, 195
Trans-Siberian Railway, 169, 172
travel, increased expenditure on, 231, 232, 234
tribalism, 35, 309
Truman, President, 171, 174, 223, 225, 316
and regionalism, 259, 315, 324